PITTSBURGH

DAN ELDRIDGE

DISCOVER PITTSBURGH

Although the Steel City is still famous for its industrial past, almost no vestiges of that era remain. Instead, at the beginning of the 21st century, Pittsburgh is nothing less than a remarkable model of what might be called Rustbelt Renewal. Formerly known as the Smoky City because of the pollution produced by its steel and coal mills, visitors today are often astonished to discover not only acres of green parkland and miles of biking and jogging trails, but also perfectly breathable air.

But the renewed and revitalized Pittsburgh is about much more than just greener flora and healthier fauna. During your exploration of the city's 91 distinct neighborhoods, you can expect to encounter contemporary art galleries, high-end eateries, and million-dollar sports stadiums. You'll experience all the same things you'd expect to in any middle-size American metropolis.

Pittsburghers are once again holding their heads high with an obvious sense of civic dignity. After all, in the early 20th century,

Pittsburgh after dark

thanks to its wildly successful steel-producing and banking indus-tries, this relatively small region of the United States was among the nation's most wealthy. It wasn't until the late 1970s, when America's steel industry began its eventual shift toward cheaper production in Asia, that the terminally depressed and unemployed Pittsburgh of modern popular lore was born. And although decades have since passed, and Pittsburgh in the interim has managed to grow suc-cessful new industries, that hopelessly outdated image of the city somehow continues to thrive. It's unfortunate that this newly revital-ized modern city, with its world-class institutions of higher learning, a thriving arts scene, and its astonishingly affordable real estate, continues to be judged by a reputation that hasn't been accurate for two decades.

But it simply wouldn't be correct to claim that no one outside the reach of the Golden Triangle has taken notice of the unique-ness of Pittsburgh. Some of the most storied and respected news

the University of Pittsburgh's mascot guarding the Panther Hollow Bridge in Oakland

organizations in the United States have been attempting to give up Pittsburgh's secret for years. In the *New Yorker* in 1989, the late Brendan Gill claimed that, "If Pittsburgh were situated somewhere in the heart of Europe, tourists would eagerly journey hundreds of miles out of their way to visit it. Its setting is spectacular, between high bluffs where the Monongahela River and the Allegheny River meet the Ohio."

But perhaps even more impressive are the ways in which Pittsburgh is making itself known today. The newly redesigned David L. Lawrence Convention Center has won wide acclaim as the world's largest LEED-certified green building; its location is the northeastern border of Downtown, practically a stone's throw from the site of former mills that once pumped pollution into the air at all hours. Pittsburgh is also now home to the Senator John Heinz Pittsburgh Regional History Center, which proudly proclaims its affiliation with Washington D.C.'s Smithsonian Institution. On the North Side of the city sits the Andy Warhol Museum, a fascinating tribute to one of

the outdoor pond at Phipps Conservatory and Botanical Gardens in Schenley Park

the city's most famous sons and the largest single-artist museum in the United States.

And if you've come to Pittsburgh with the intention of digging deep into the city's past, that too can be accomplished in neighborhoods such as the Strip District, an area that has played host to wholesale produce merchants since the late 19th century. While the majority of Pittsburgh's legendary funiculars have long since disappeared, two of them remain – the Monongahela Incline and the Duquesne Incline. Both continue to shuttle tourists and local commuters up and down the South Side's Mount Washington on a daily basis.

Even the most dedicated and loyal Pittsburgher, though, will admit that the city has made its fair share of mistakes along the road to reinvention. In 2004, Pittsburgh found itself in such poor economic shape that its civic leaders were forced to declare bankruptcy. Yet it's also true that because of the city's extraordinarily low cost of living, Pittsburgh is now gradually becoming known as an

the West End Bridge and Downtown skyline

ideal place in which to reinvent a career or to launch a lifestyle that would be prohibitively more expensive in a trendier locale.

Whether it's ancient history you've come to uncover or post-modern culture and technology you've come to explore, in today's Pittsburgh, you're likely to find what you're looking for. But no matter how impressive its story of rebirth and renewal, Pittsburgh hasn't exactly managed to conquer the world just yet. And maybe that's why the city today is such a fascinating place. It's a region that clearly doesn't care to let go of the reins of its blue-collar history, and yet continues to be one of America's most tenacious and unusual urban landscapes.

Times building, Downtown

Contents

The Neighborhoods. 12
Planning Your Trip. 16
Explore Pittsburgh 18
The Two-Day Best of Pittsburgh. 18
Fun and Cheap: Pittsburgh on a Budget 20
A Rainy Day in Pittsburgh 22
Bar Hop Like a Local 23
Out with the Parents. 24

Sights 25
Downtown. 27
Strip District 37
Oakland. 39
South Side 47
Mount Washington 50
North Side 52
Squirrel Hill and Point Breeze. 56
Bloomfield and Lawrenceville. 57
Greater Pittsburgh 61

Restaurants 65
Downtown. 67
Strip District 71
Oakland. 75
South Side 80
Mount Washington 87
North Side 89
Shadyside. 90
Squirrel Hill and Point Breeze. 96
Bloomfield and Lawrenceville. 101

Arts and Entertainment 106

Nightlife 108
The Arts 122
Festivals and Events 139

Shopping 147

Arts and Crafts 149
Books and Music 151
Clothing and Accessories for Women 154
Clothing and Accessories for Men 158
Furniture and Home Decor............................ 158
Gifts... 160
Health and Beauty 161
Kids' Stores 162
Pet Supplies and Grooming 163
Shoes.. 164
Shopping Centers and Chain Retailers 164
Vintage and Antiques 166

Recreation 167

Parks.. 169
Bicycling.. 171
Spectator Sports..................................... 173
Water Activities..................................... 183
Winter Recreation.................................... 187
Gyms and Health Clubs............................... 189
Guided and Walking Tours 191
Other Recreation..................................... 194

Accommodations..................................... 202

Downtown.. 204

Oakland... 207
South Side 209
North Side 211
Shadyside.. 212
Greater Pittsburgh 214

Excursions from Pittsburgh........................ 216
Laurel Highlands... 219
Altoona, State College, and Johnstown................. 225
Beaver County and Butler County 231

Background... 235
The Setting.. 235
History 237
Economy... 240
The People 242
Arts and Culture 243

Essentials 247
Getting There... 247
Getting Around 249
Tips for Travelers 251
Health and Safety....................................... 252
Information and Services................................ 253

Resources... 260
Suggested Reading...................................... 260
Internet Resources..................................... 261

Index... 264

Maps... 281

The Neighborhoods

While the city of Pittsburgh is technically a collection of 91 distinct neighborhoods spread out over 55 square miles, most areas of interest can be found close to Downtown and the East End.

DOWNTOWN

Pittsburgh's Downtown, also known as the Golden Triangle, essentially acts as one large financial district. Efforts to persuade city dwellers to live here have largely failed, which is why the area becomes devoid of almost all activity outside of the normal nine-to-five business hours. Recently, however, the local arts community has had a substantial impact in Downtown; installation and visual art galleries are opening at a surprisingly rapid clip. The area's **Cultural District,** which offers Broadway-style entertainment and the occasional concert, is also a draw. Aside from the grandeur of **Point State Park,** however, Downtown is essentially utilitarian; this is where you'll find the bus and train stations, and probably your hotel.

STRIP DISTRICT

Pittsburgh's international district begins on the northeastern border of Downtown, just south of the Allegheny River on 11th Street, and runs all the way to 33rd Street, where Lawrenceville begins. The Strip, an industrial area filled with warehouses and loft buildings, plays two separate but important roles in the life of the city. During the day, the area is visited largely for its produce dealers, ethnic restaurants, and Asian grocery stores. But once night falls, clubgoers fill the district's bars and dance clubs in full force. Saturday morning is the time to see the Strip at its best—this is when the greatest variety of tourists, locals, vendors, and street musicians can be found along the Strip's two parallel thoroughfares—**Penn Avenue** and **Smallman Street.**

OAKLAND

Sometimes referred to as Pennsylvania's third-largest "Downtown," Oakland is the city's main East End neighborhood and home to numerous institutions of higher learning, including **Carnegie Mellon University** and the **University of Pittsburgh.** Oakland acts as the city's cultural nucleus, and, like most university districts, it boasts a bounty of ethnic restaurants and cafés, as well as plenty of places for outdoor rest and relaxation. The main branch of the **Carnegie Library** is here, as are the **Carnegie Museums of Art and Natural History,** behind which you'll find the urban playground of **Schenley Park.** Oakland's main commercial arteries are the parallel Forbes and 5th Avenues, but for a quainter shopping experience, try **Craig Street,** which intersects Forbes and 5th Avenues near the art museum.

SOUTH SIDE

The South Side, one of Pittsburgh's most eclectic and interesting areas, stretches along the Monongahela River from **Station Square** to **SouthSide Works,** a former steel mill turned shopping mall. The area known as the **South Side Flats** is where most visitors find themselves; **East Carson Street,** also known as the country's longest uninterrupted stretch of bars, runs the length of the district. Vintage clothing stores, antique shops, art galleries, and ethnic eateries can all be found on East Carson Street. Many of the area's immigrant families and more established residents reside on the **South Side Slopes**—a steep hill, really, that rises south of East Carson Street and offers some of the city's best views.

MOUNT WASHINGTON

Sitting atop the city's South Side and generally known as Pittsburgh's most tourist-friendly neighborhood, Mount Washington exists in the mind of the average Pittsburgher for two reasons only: the breathtaking views along Grandview Avenue, which every visitor to the city should see, and the expensive eateries of Restaurant Row, which are technically located in the little-known district of Duquesne Heights. Near to the Monongahela Incline, which ferries its passengers from Station Square to Mount Washington, is the mini-commercial district of Shiloh Street. Grandview Park, located about 20 minutes from Shiloh Street on foot, provides a different but still stunning view of the city skyline.

NORTH SIDE

Lying just across the Allegheny River from Downtown, the North Side was originally an independent city known as Allegheny; it was annexed to the City of Pittsburgh in 1907. It's also an area rife with history: The Jehovah's Witnesses were founded in a now-demolished home here, and the first World Series was played in long-gone Exposition Park. The North Side is also where you'll find the decidedly upscale Mexican War Streets, as well as the Andy Warhol Museum and the world-class Mattress Factory museum. Sports fans will find the Pirates and Steelers battling it out on their respective fields here. A word of warning: Much of the area north of the Andy Warhol Museum shouldn't be explored after dark.

SHADYSIDE

Often called Pittsburgh's Haight-Ashbury in the 1960s, Shadyside, just east of Oakland, is now one of the city's most prestigious and image-conscious neighborhoods. Walnut Street forms the area's commercial core; here you'll find both big-name and boutique shopping and a near-steady stream of pedestrian traffic. Running parallel to Walnut Street is Ellsworth Avenue, where most of Shadyside's better bars and restaurants can be found. Shadyside residents tend to be liberal, affluent, and arts-minded; the area is also known as being particularly queer-friendly.

SQUIRREL HILL AND POINT BREEZE

Squirrel Hill has one of the largest Jewish communities in the mid-Atlantic region. The neighborhood begins at the eastern end of **Carnegie Mellon University** and is sandwiched comfortably between **Schenley Park** and **Frick Park.** Its two major thoroughfares, **Forbes Avenue** and **Murray Avenue,** offer grocers, movie theaters, synagogues, and kosher eateries.

On the opposite side of Frick Park, Point Breeze and the small district of **Regent Square** are Squirrel Hill's somewhat upscale neighbors to the east. Although largely residential, both areas have decent-sized commercial strips. Simply explore the length of **Penn Avenue** in between 5th and Braddock Avenues to see what Point Breeze has to offer. In Regent Square, **South Braddock Avenue** is the main drag.

BLOOMFIELD AND LAWRENCEVILLE

Also known as Pittsburgh's **Little Italy,** the East End neighborhood of Bloomfield took its name from the flowers that once grew wild in the area. Today, Bloomfield is both a tightly knit residential community as well as a popular shopping district where parking meters are hand-painted to resemble the Italian flag. **Liberty Avenue,** the neighborhood's heart and soul, is home to a charming medley of boutiques, cafés, grocery stores, and restaurants.

Lawrenceville, one of Pittsburgh's largest neighborhoods, stretches along the river from the Strip District to Morningside. The neighborhood is still largely working class, although a recent influx of gay and lesbian residents, art galleries, and boutiques along the main drag of **Butler Street** has been raising Lawrenceville's profile considerably.

Planning Your Trip

Thanks to Pittsburgh's convenient mid-Atlantic location, a decent number of major metropolitan cities are located within an easy day-long drive, or less. Visitors from Cleveland, Washington, D.C., or Baltimore can reach Pittsburgh in three to five hours, while the borders of Chicago, Detroit, Buffalo, Toronto, Philadelphia, and New York City all sit somewhere within the six- to 10-hour range. Keep in mind that if you're already in or near a large North American city, round-trip airfare may be less expensive than the gas required to drive.

While planning your visit, don't make the common mistake of assuming that because Pittsburgh isn't a top tourist draw, hotel rooms will be easy to come by. On the contrary, because of the many universities and top hospitals scattered throughout the city, accommodations are quite often scarce. Unless you'll be arriving with your own transportation and plan to stay at a chain hotel somewhere off a major highway, you'll want to do a bit of pre-trip research so as not to be unpleasantly surprised upon your arrival. The *Accommodations* chapter of this book is a good place to start. And should your visit coincide with the beginning or ending of a college school year (August and September or April and May), booking well in advance is strongly advised, especially if you've got your heart set on a central Oakland location.

Although carefully choosing a neighborhood in which to hang your hat will undoubtedly improve the quality of your experience in Pittsburgh, it's worth noting that within the actual city limits, no one neighborhood is really all that far from any other. The fact, however, is that most visitors and nearly all business travelers end up staying in one of Downtown's nine hotels or at nearby Station Square, which has one hotel.

Aside from Downtown, the university district of Oakland is Pittsburgh's other major hotel district. If nightlife and typical urban conveniences are what you're after, Oakland is a far smarter choice than the Downtown area. Much like the financial districts of larger cities, Pittsburgh's entire Downtown is largely abandoned on weekends and after-work hours on weekdays. Out-of-towners in search of the action should hop in a taxi and ask to be taken to the South Side's East Carson Street (16th and E. Carson Sts. is a good place to begin).

Many visitors do arrive in Pittsburgh with their own transportation, and while it's certainly possible—and sometimes fun—to traverse the city with nothing but a bus pass, it's an undeniable fact that Pittsburgh is a driving town. If you're planning to explore the outer suburbs or some of the city's popular excursions, such as Fallingwater or Ohiopyle, definitely bring a car if you can manage to do so. Nearly every city B&B offers free parking, and many hotels have impressively large lots. However some of the chain hotels have the tactlessness to charge their own guests rather high rates for parking access, so it's worth calling ahead to request that information.

Unlike some midsize cities, Pittsburgh's major sites and most important neighborhoods aren't all within walking distance of each other. But nonetheless, a relatively comprehensive survey of the town can be accomplished in three days, assuming you only intend to visit the most obvious sights. Allow five days if you plan to mix in a medley of creative entertainment and dining excursions. A full week should allow enough time to add in an out-of-town trip or two, and some leisurely shopping.

WHEN TO GO

Pittsburghers like to brag about the fact that Southwestern Pennsylvania fully experiences all four seasons, and, indeed, observing the changing colors of the natural landscape here is quite a joy—especially for Californians and other West Coasters who've grown accustomed to passing annually through two seasons only: hot and cold.

Choosing the perfect time to visit is really nothing more than a matter of personal inclination. When snow falls, the winter season here (late December–early April) is absolutely gorgeous, yet the months of January and February can be unbearably cold; even native Pittsburghers tend to hibernate during this time of the year.

Pittsburgh summers are often scorching hot and dripping with humidity, although this is also the season during which the city comes alive with the most vigor and excitability. What's more, a score of important festivals and events takes place during the summer. To see exactly what's on offer, see the *Festivals and Events* section in this book.

Fall is a particularly lovely time to visit Pittsburgh. There's nothing quite like the sight of the city's green leaves turning to shades of yellow, red, and brown before falling to the sidewalks. The weather is also evenly pleasant, with days that are cool but not cold and evenings that might best be described as light-jacket weather: sharp and brisk.

WHAT TO TAKE

As is the case throughout most of Middle America, casual dress is acceptable in just about every social situation in Pittsburgh. Even at affairs during which the majority of the crowd will likely be sporting more formal attire, such as Sunday morning church services or the dinner hour at a four-star restaurant, you're unlikely to be the victim of disapproving glares as long as your denim isn't torn and your shirt comes complete with buttons.

It's rather simple to be considered well dressed and fashionable in the Steel City, a place where nearly half the populace seems to don football or hockey jerseys during game days. As far as practical clothing is concerned, packing for a trip to Pittsburgh is really a matter of simply checking the upcoming week's weather forecast. And should you forget an essential item, just about anything can be purchased upon arrival.

The prudent packer, however, should take care to bring the following: a compact umbrella, as sudden showers can take place during any season; comfortable and sensible walking shoes (if arriving in wet or snowy weather, you'll want waterproof shoes—preferably cross-trainers—with a decent tread); sunglasses, sunscreen, and a wide-brimmed hat during the summer months; and, if you plan to attend any of the events or festivals at Point State Park, a sweater or light jacket, as breezes coming off the rivers can sometimes make for chilly evenings.

Summer visitors might also consider packing swimwear, as public pools, the Youghiogheny River, and Sandcastle Waterpark are all popular warm-weather diversions. Winter visitors should bring tight-fitting thermal underwear (long-sleeved tops and bottoms are best), insulated gloves or mittens, and a wool scarf and beanie-style cap.

Explore Pittsburgh

THE TWO-DAY BEST OF PITTSBURGH

Although a thorough exploration of Pittsburgh and its environs would require at least a week, the city is compact enough that its most important sights and activities can be experienced easily in two days. The following itinerary assumes a Saturday-morning arrival in Pittsburgh, but with the exception of a visit to the Strip District, which is at its best on Saturday mornings, all the activities below can easily be shuffled around at will. Thankfully, getting around Pittsburgh is also a snap. The Downtown district is walkable, and a fleet of public buses originating in the Golden Triangle serves nearly every obscure outpost in town. To gather your own collection of bus schedules, visit the Downtown Wood Street or Steel Plaza "T" stations, or stop by the Port Authority Downtown Service Center.

Day 1

Start your visit with an early-morning trip to the **Strip District.** Stop by **Pamela's Diner** for breakfast and then join the throngs of shoppers searching for kitschy souvenirs along **Penn Avenue.** Afterward, spend an hour or two at the **Senator John Heinz Pittsburgh Regional History Center.** If it isn't a Saturday, treat yourself instead to the most exciting ride in the city—a trip up **Mount Washington** on one of the two inclines—and then to the best view of the city, from the lookout platforms along **Grandview Avenue.** If you take the **Monongahela Incline** back down to street level, you'll see **Station Square** just ahead—it's a perfect pit stop for coffee or lunch. Should you find yourself in the mood for fine dining, head to the historic **Grand Concourse,** but be sure to bring the AmEx along! Afterward, make your way down East Carson Street toward the South Side Flats for a bit of late-afternoon shopping. Eco warriors will be thrilled with the selection of natural gifts at **E House,** while women on the prowl for quality denim would be wise to check out the selection at **Pittsburgh Jeans Company.** Globetrotters will appreciate the quirky Asian imports at the **Culture Shop.** For more mainstream window shopping, continue on to **SouthSide Works** at the far end of East Carson Street, where popular chain stores like REI, Benetton, and Urban Outfitters are located. Then, head back to the heart of the Flats and end your day with a nightcap. **Dee's Café** is one of Pittsburgh's best dive bars, but for a great selection of microbrews and a more clean-cut atmosphere, try **Fat Heads,** which also serves wonderful salads and sandwiches.

Day 2

If you're staying Downtown, walk to the nearby Strip District for breakfast. Locals will warn you not to miss **DeLuca's Restaurant,** which is without a doubt the city's most legendary breakfast spot. But if you're looking for a healthier, less greasy spoon experience, try **Pamela's** and order yourself an omelet. After your umpteenth cup of bottomless coffee, work off some of those carbs by taking a stroll through Downtown and into **Point State Park.** Use the pedestrian walkway on the **Fort Duquesne Bridge** to cross over the Allegheny River. If you've got

Park, eat lunch at the attached **Outback Steakhouse**—diners can actually take in the game while eating. (You'll need to book ahead to reserve the best window-side seats.) After lunch, walk to the **National Aviary** in West Park—with a family of more than 600 feathery friends, it's the only nonprofit bird zoo in the country. If you still have energy, spend the rest of the afternoon exploring the Oakland neighborhood. Spend some time at the **Carnegie Museums of Art and Natural History,** and, if the sun is shining, visit **Schenley Park** and its **Phipps Conservatory.** For dinner, head back into Downtown. Take a cab if the weather is chilly, or go by foot across one of the **Three Sisters Bridges**—also known as the only trio of near-identical bridges in the country. All three are self-anchored suspension bridges and are painted Aztec gold. Your destination is **Cafe Zao,** located next door to the O'Reilly Theater. Owned by the same people responsible for the legendary but now shuttered Baum Vivant, Cafe Zao is a perennial hit with the theater crowd for good reason— the Portuguese entrées here are probably the finest in the tri-state area. After dinner, take in a show in the **Cultural District.** Pick up a free copy of *Pittsburgh City Paper* to see what is in production. If nothing grabs your interest or you'd prefer a less expensive and more intimate entertainment option, head back to the South Side via taxi and stop in at **Club Café,** which usually offers two pop or folk concerts nightly. (Ask your cabbie to take the 10th Street Bridge from Downtown, which can also be crossed on foot.)

Andy Warhol Museum

the energy for a long walk, follow the **Three Rivers Heritage Trail** as far as your heart desires. (The path ends near the 40th Street Bridge.) Descend the stairs at the opposite end of the Fort Duquesne Bridge, and you'll be in the **North Shore.** Head to the nearby Andy Warhol Museum, which, aside from having a great gift shop and a rotating schedule of fascinating temporary exhibits, is the largest single-artist museum in the United States. The Warhol also has a surprisingly good basement café, which is a decent choice for lunch. Before leaving, get directions to the nearby **Mattress Factory,** a world-renowned installation museum. If the Pirates happen to be playing down the street at PNC

FUN AND CHEAP: PITTSBURGH ON A BUDGET

Operating strictly on a shoestring budget? You've come to exactly the right city. Budget living is practically a religion in some quarters of Pittsburgh, where a night on the town can be accomplished for as little as $20, and a day exploring the urban jungle can be had for almost nothing at all.

Sightseeing

For budget sightseeing, Oakland is more or less your best bet. Take a free, self-guided tour of the **Nationality Rooms,** located inside Pitt's **Cathedral of Learning,** and then explore **Schenley Park.** Other freebie sights abound, from the ruins of the historic **Forbes Field** to the **University Art Gallery** in the Student Union.

Looking for a cheap city tour? Try the **54-C,** a public bus that passes through Oakland on its way to the South Side, Bloomfield, the Strip District, and the North Side; it's a bargain at $1.75. Strolling the various paths of the **Three Rivers Heritage Trail** on foot is another fun and cheap way to see often unseen parts of Pittsburgh; many visitors enjoy walking the 2.6-mile-long **Eliza Furnace Trail.** Also known as the **Jail Trail,** it begins Downtown at the PNC Center alongside the Monongahela River and has a convenient exit point in Oakland, just steps from the commercial strip of North Craig Street.

Food

For cheap eating, think Indian buffets and half-price deals. **People's Indian Restaurant** in Garfield offers a $6.95 all-you-can-eat lunch spread daily (closed Sundays). It's the same deal at Highland Park's **Taj Majal.** Eat enough and you won't be hungry again until, say, 11 P.M., which coincidentally is when the half-price feeding frenzy starts at **Mad Mex, Fuel and Fuddle,** and **India Garden,** all located in Oakland. **The Sharp Edge Beer Emporium** in Friendship/East Liberty serves half-off American-style pub grub 10 P.M.–midnight, Monday–Friday. Other cheap eats can be had in and around Oakland; some restaurants offer discounts to students with ID.

For über-cheap vegan dining, **Sree's Indian Food** simply can't be beat. For a mere $4, Sree's offers a massive plate of authentic Indian food; non-vegetarians can choose to add meat for an extra dollar. The restaurant's main locations are in Squirrel Hill and Downtown.

You know what they say about pizza: Even when it's bad, it's still good. Bloomfield's **Pizza Italia,** however, serves a surprisingly toothsome pie for less than $7, tax included (large, cheese only). It's takeout only, but trust me: It's worth it.

Nightlife

Pittsburgh simply abounds with cheap nightlife options and great dive bars; some of the most popular include **Gooski's** on Polish Hill, the South Side's **Dee's Café,** and **Jack's Bar.** On Thursdays, the budget beer crowd heads to the **Bloomfield Bridge Tavern** in Bloomfield for Dollar Night, when a wide selection of obscure imports and microbrews go for just a buck.

Some South Side taverns even offer live music for nothing more than the cost of a cheap pint. At **The Smiling Moose,** vicious punk and metal bands whip the small pub into a frenzy every weekend (and occasionally on weekdays). Down the street at **Piper's Pub,** traditional Irish duos or trios can be found tucked into the bar's front corner most weekends.

If you'd prefer to mix with the college crowd, head to **Peter's Pub** in Oakland, where a deejay, a dance floor—and, if you're lucky, a swarm of comely youngsters—can be found upstairs. There's no cover charge. Also in Oakland is **The Upstage,** a former punk club that now hosts a diverse slew of parties and deejay nights, including the hugely popular **'80s Night** and **Panty Raid,** where fans of Brit-pop dance to the sounds of Suede and Oasis in their underwear. Seriously.

Shopping

For decent but cheap shopping of all sorts, try not to miss the **Red White & Blue Thrift Store,** where you'll find one of the best collections of clothing and flatware in the 'Burgh.

For shoestring-budget souvenir shopping, make the scene on **Penn Avenue** in the Strip District, where everything from fake Steelers T-shirts to Peruvian finger puppets are on offer. Try to go on a Saturday morning, when the sidewalks are jam-packed with vendors.

The Arts

You'll want to jumpstart your exploration of the arts with a bit of research. Pick up a copy of *Pittsburgh City Paper* (www.pghcitypaper.com), a free alternative weekly with a useful events listing section. Next, look up a few of the better-known events websites: **This Is Happening** (www.thisishappening.com) lists free and low-cost cultural and political goings-on, while the more mainstream *Pittsburgh Post-Gazette* **Events Calendar** (www.post-gazette.com/events) is fairly all-encompassing. No computer? Stop by any branch of the **Carnegie Library** (www.clpgh.org) for high-speed access; a driver's license or passport is required to apply for a temporary membership.

During the summer season, **free movies** are screened outdoors in seven different parks, including Schenley Park in Oakland (Sundays and Wednesdays at dusk), Arsenal Park in Lawrenceville (Fridays at dusk), and Grandview Park in Mount Washington (Saturdays at dusk). For movie listings and times, call 412/937-3039 or visit www.city.pittsburgh.pa.us.

Recreation

The most obvious free recreation activity in Pittsburgh—and probably the most popular—would have to be walking, jogging, or just generally goofing around in one of the many city parks. Yet slightly more arresting activities can be experienced for just a small amount of cash.

Kayak Pittsburgh, for instance, offers a fantastic way to experience the city from a duck's-eye view, assuming you're willing to part with $15 or so. Canoes, kayaks, and even hydrobikes can be rented by the hour. Grab a *Venture Outdoors* newsletter while you're there; the organization sponsors all manner of unusual outdoor activities and classes throughout the year.

To tour Pittsburgh via bicycle, visit **Friends of the Riverfront.** There, you can sign up for the free **Dasani Blue Bikes** program; trail riders can pedal the company's bicycles gratis along the paths lining the Allegheny and Ohio Rivers.

A RAINY DAY IN PITTSBURGH

On average, the city of Seattle, well-known as one of the wettest in the United States, sees a little more than 34 inches of rain each year. And Pittsburgh? Try approximately 37. That's right: You've come to a seriously rainy place. But not to worry—there's more than enough going on here underneath the protection of a solid roof.

Think Museums

In Oakland, the **Carnegie Museums of Art and Natural History** both lie within the same building. What's more, the entrance fee includes admission to both. It's an interesting juxtaposition: If you grow tired of the Monets or Jackson Pollacks, for instance, there's always the Hall of African Wildlife next door. And there's no need to hunt outside for lunch, either—the Museum of Art Café and the Fossil Fuels Café both have you covered. When the museums get old, take a pit stop at the main branch of the **Carnegie Library,** which is also under the same roof. It can be accessed through a door located in Sculpture Hall. (Both museums are closed on Monday.) Also, don't forget the **Nationality Rooms** at Pitt's **Cathedral of Learning,** which is about a two-minute walk away.

Should you find yourself on the North Side, the **Andy Warhol Museum** offers not just a stunning collection of the artist's work, but also various temporary exhibitions, a movie theater screening Warhol films daily, a café, a vintage, black-and-white photo booth, and a fantastic gift shop. There is also the Weekend Factory, where visitors can create their own Warhol-esque art on Saturdays and Sundays. A bit further north and in the heart of the Mexican War Streets is the **Mattress Factory,** a stunning installation art museum featuring a number of permanent exhibitions by James Turrell.

Take in a Show

Pittsburgh has a surprisingly vibrant theater scene; independent productions and mainstream fare can be found throughout the city. The ever-popular **City Theatre** on the South Side offers everything from one-person shows to Broadway productions; the CMU drama department consistently produces quality work at the **Purnell Center for the Arts**; the **Pittsburgh Public Theater** in the city's Cultural District presents Broadway-style plays in an intimate setting; and the **Pittsburgh Playhouse** is home to three acclaimed theater companies.

Not a fan of the boards? Check out one of Pittsburgh's independent film houses: Local favorites include the **Melwood Screening Room** in North Oakland, Downtown's **Harris Theater,** the **Oaks Theater** in Oakmont, and the **Regent Square Theater** in Edgewood.

Flex Your Mind

Assuming you're at least somewhat literarily inclined, you've probably passed more than your fair share of rainy days sunken deep in a comfy couch with a stack of good books and a cup of hot chocolate by your side. Conveniently enough, **Joseph-Beth Booksellers** at **SouthSide Works,** the city's largest bookstore, has a super-secret door in the far corner of its music department that leads directly to **Caribou Coffee.** Caribou offers all manner of snacks and caffeinated beverages. Joseph-Beth's magazine selection alone will make your jaw drop, and some of the chairs and couches are comfortable enough to pass out in. Author readings take place quite often, so grab a schedule at the checkout counter to see what's going on.

BAR HOP LIKE A LOCAL

The Steel City doesn't call itself "a drinking town with a football problem" for no good reason: Most Pittsburghers like to drink. A *lot.* So if your aim is fitting in, you'll want to plan on regularly touring some of the city's finest taprooms and alehouses.

Best to start on the South Side's East Carson Street, which essentially transforms the neighborhood into a gigantic pubcrawl every Friday and Saturday night. **Jack's** is a perennial favorite, and it's cheap, too; former frat party attendees will feel right at home. The South Side does a particularly good trade in hipster bars, the oldest being **Dee's Café,** where the glory days of '90s alt-rock never faded away. Nearby, the Scottish-Irish **Piper's Pub** has a refined feel, not to mention a decent pub grub menu and the occasional Irish folk singer wailing away in the corner. Even better, British expats can be spotted here taking in a game of footie on Saturday mornings. True beer snobs will find their appetites satiated at **Fat Heads** and **Smokin' Joe's,** both with dozens of imports and craft brews on tap. The Polynesian-themed **Tiki Lounge** and the cave-themed **Lava Lounge** both attract a slightly older and more moneyed hipster crowd, while **Z Lounge** pulls in the BPM set with its frequent deejay nights.

Pittsburgh's other favorite pubs are scattered widely throughout the city. In the East End, there's **Kelly's Bar** in East Liberty with a retro-cool vibe and phenomenal bar food. **The Sharp Edge,** located on the border of Friendship and East Liberty, is known for its near-exhaustive selection of Belgian beers. Straddling the Bloomfield–Lawrenceville border is the city's newest home for hipsters, **Brillobox,** which frequently hosts indie-rock shows and art events. The **Bloomfield Bridge Tavern**

Piper's Pub

© FABIAN BAUTISTA

is well loved for its Polish dishes and also for its Thursday evening dollar beer specials. Although located in slightly out-of-the-way Polish Hill, **Gooski's** pulls in the hipster dive-bar crowd, as well as the occasional touring rock star. The grad school set kicks back at the cozy **Squirrel Hill Café** or at **Silky's Sports Bar & Grill,** also located in Squirrel Hill. For a favorite brewpub that serves phenomenal wood-fired pizzas, try **The Church Brew Works** in Lawrenceville, which is located inside an actual church. There's also the North Side's **Penn Brewery,** which offers a carb-heavy menu of wonderfully prepared German fare.

Need a break from the beer? End the night with burgers or sandwiches at the legendary, 24-hour **Primanti Brothers.** Open until 2 A.M. on the weekends, the **Beehive** is a popular spot for a late-night cup of organic coffee.

OUT WITH THE PARENTS

If you've come to town to attend one of the area's colleges or universities, it's a good bet that at some stage of your matriculation, the parents will be paying Pittsburgh a visit. So, how exactly do you keep them entertained? Here's a hint: They aren't interested in seeing the slums of South Oakland. Take a look at this two-day itinerary instead.

Day 1

Mom and Dad have to eat, right? Bring 'em straight to **DeLuca's** in the Strip; it's old-school Pittsburgh at its finest. Afterward, do a bit of light shopping: Take Mom to **Hot Haute Hot** for unique gifts and home furnishings. Dad may prefer to be left to his own devices, but you should steer him instead toward **La Prima Espresso Company,** one of the most authentic Italian coffee shops in town. If it's midday and everyone has worked up an appetite, head to **Klavon's Ice Cream Parlor** for sundaes and milkshakes. If your folks are interested in the arts, they'll love the **Society for Contemporary Craft;** don't miss the gift shop, where jewelry and modern folk art can be found. For dinner, head to **Sushi Kim,** also in the Strip, or wander Downtown for a bite at **Six Penn Kitchen,** an upscale bistro specializing in comfort food.

Day 2

No visit to Pittsburgh is complete without a ride to the top of **Mount Washington.** If your parents are staying Downtown, it's a cinch to do the trip on public transport. But first, you have to eat. For a memorable experience, take a train from any Downtown "T" station to Station Square. If it happens to be a Sunday, dig into the legendary all-you-can-eat buffet brunch at the **Grand Concourse** from 10 A.M.–3 P.M.

At Station Square, you'll notice the entrance of the **Monongahela Incline** right across the street. The incline will shuttle you up Mount Washington and onto must-see **Grandview Avenue.** If you're up for a stroll, ask the incline booth employees for directions to **Grandview Park;** it's roughly a 20-minute walk, and it offers an alternate city skyline view. A trip down Grandview Avenue to the historic **Duquesne Incline** is also a wonderful idea, if only to explore the patched-together but informative **Incline Museum** inside. For lunch, hit the **Grandview Saloon.** Located close to the Duquesne Incline, it offers surprisingly decent pub grub and one of the best outdoor patio views in all of Pittsburgh.

Afterward, head back to Station Square. Share a bit of Pittsburgh history with your family by showing them the retired blast furnace in **Bessemer Court**—it's right behind Station Square's Waltzing Waters fountain, which, amusingly enough, is choreographed to music. Next, hail a cab to the North Side, or if the folks are feeling particularly vigorous, walk across the Smithfield Street Bridge, through Downtown, and then over the 6th Street Bridge, which will deposit you in front of PNC Park. Pass an hour or two at the **National Aviary,** or take in a film at the **Carnegie Science Center's IMAX theater.** For dinner, head to **Tessaro's** in Bloomfield; its burgers and chicken are both well known for being among the city's best.

SIGHTS

Before beginning your exploration of the hilly and often-circuitous city of Pittsburgh, consider this: Even *natives* enjoy joking about how easy it is to get hopelessly lost on the town's twisting and turning roads. The war correspondent Ernie Pyle probably explained it best in a 1937 column that appeared in the *Pittsburgh Press:* "Pittsburgh is undoubtedly the cockeyedest city in the United States," he wrote. "Physically, it is absolutely irrational. It must have been laid out by a mountain goat."

There's a perfectly good reason for all this, of course: Pittsburgh's topography consists largely of steep hills, deep valleys, and three proud rivers—the Allegheny, the Monongahela, and the Ohio—all of which weave their way in and out of Pittsburgh's multi-hued quilt of neighborhoods, creating chaos and confusion for motorists and pedestrians alike. But spend a day or two exploring the nearly vertical neighborhood of the South Side Slopes, or strolling the historic bridges that span the Allegheny and Monongahela Rivers, or breathing in the natural beauty of Schenley and Frick Parks, and decide for yourself if all the confusion isn't actually worth it. Because while Pittsburgh's sights and scenery may at first appear to be little more than a jumbled-together collection of

HIGHLIGHTS

LOOK FOR ◖ TO FIND RECOMMENDED SIGHTS.

◖ **Best History Lesson:** Most Pittsburghers agree that the **Senator John Heinz Pittsburgh Regional History Center** has done a fantastic job of documenting and presenting the history, culture, and attendant struggles of the Southwestern Pennsylvania region. And while much of the museum is serious business, there's more than enough here to keep kids amused (page 37).

◖ **Best Gothic Landmark:** Certainly one of Pittsburgh's most beloved structures, the **Cathedral of Learning,** which happens to be the second-tallest educational building in the world, can be spotted from hundreds of different vantage points throughout the city (page 42).

◖ **Best Park:** If you haven't been to **Schenley Park,** you haven't witnessed the full diversity of the student-filled district of Oakland. Free films are screened on the park's **Flagstaff Hill** throughout the summer, paths for walking and jogging are plentiful, and the café next to Phipps Conservatory is probably the most peaceful in the entire East End (page 45).

◖ **Best Way to Enjoy the Three Rivers:** The many vessels of the **Gateway Clipper Fleet** ferry tourists and locals alike throughout the farthest stretches of the Allegheny, Ohio, and Monongahela Rivers – even during the depths of winter (page 47).

◖ **Best Skyline Views:** A historic hillside neighborhood packed tight with rickety row houses, the **South Side Slopes** was built for the Eastern European immigrants who toiled in the riverside mills below. Not only does a stroll through the area provide a great workout, it also offers some of the city's most incredible skyline views (page 48).

◖ **Best Mountainside Ride:** Pittsburgh's cable-powered **Duquesne and Monongahela Inclines** shuttle passengers back and forth between Mount Washington and the South Side. Definitely not a journey for the faint of heart (page 50).

◖ **Best Museum:** Controversial, shocking, and endlessly entertaining, the North Side's **Andy Warhol Museum** is the largest official space dedicated to a single artist in the United States. The novelty-packed gift shop is practically a pop art museum in its own right (page 52).

◖ **Best Church:** With its jaw-dropping collection of stained-glass windows and frightfully lifelike gargoyle busts, the North Side's **Calvary United Methodist Church** is a near-masterpiece of late 19th-century Gothic architecture (page 52).

◖ **Best Body and Mind Workout:** A parking lot on the North Shore separates kid-friendly but intellectual **Carnegie Science Center** and **UPMC SportsWorks,** an entirely interactive museum where young and old alike can learn how the body works by working out themselves (page 54).

◖ **Most Historic Amusement Park:** One of the oldest operating amusement parks in the United States – and now a designated National Historic Landmark – **Kennywood Amusement Park** features acres of thrill rides, an unmatched collection of wooden and steel coasters, and oodles of deep-fried junk food (page 62).

industrial-era ephemera, a closer inspection reveals something much more uncommon: one of America's most charming small cities that just happens to offer all the amenities of a major metropolitan town.

Which isn't to say that the Steel City's charms are intended to be any sort of a well-kept secret. On the contrary, since the early 1980s Pittsburgh has been consistently ranked as one of America's most livable towns. And much to the contentment of locals, who knew it all along, *USA Week-end* magazine recently graded the nighttime view from Mount Washington's Grandview Avenue as the second most beautiful sight in the country.

In fact, it might make sense to think of poking around Pittsburgh as something akin to an urban scavenger hunt. It's true that finding what you're looking for won't always be easy. Getting from here to there may be even tougher still. But once you arrive, your reward will almost always be singularly unique.

Downtown   Map 1

ALLEGHENY COUNTY COURTHOUSE
436 Grant St., 412/350-4636
HOURS: Mon.-Fri. 8:30 A.M.-4:30 P.M.
COST: Free

Designed in 1883 by the much-imitated architect Henry Hobson Richardson, the Allegheny County Courthouse, which was the third courthouse to be built in the county, is one of Downtown Pittsburgh's most recognizable and historic sights. The granite structure is virtually unmissable—just keep your eyes peeled for the truly ancient-looking block building that sticks out like a sore thumb—albeit a very attractive and smartly designed thumb—among Grant Street's more modern skyscrapers.

One of the building's most interesting features is its arching stone bridge, which locals frequently refer to as the **Bridge of Sighs.** This bridge connects the courthouse to the adjoining jail, which is no longer in operation. Yet during its time, convicts were simply transferred to the jail by means of the bridge following their courthouse sentencing. It's also worth noting that some of the old jail's individual granite blocks weighed more than five tons each. Prison breaks, we can assume, were rare. (The new jail, should you care to see it, is also located Downtown, at 950 2nd Avenue, not far from the 1st Avenue "T" Station and the temporary Greyhound bus terminal.)

It's possible to enter the courthouse for a look-round, although you will be required to pass through a metal detector first. A model of the entire courthouse complex is on display beneath glass on the second floor; also take note of the many rounded arches built into the courthouse's interior. Construction of the complex cost approximately $2.25 million; not a particularly small sum in the late nineteenth century.

Interestingly, the main building was designed with an interior courtyard at its center. Richardson considered this detail of his design to be particularly clever, as fresh air and light could then reach even the offices that weren't lucky enough to have street-facing windows. Today, the courthouse is a decent location for a midday picnic; anyone is welcome to join the nine-to-fivers who gather around the outdoor fountain in the courtyard.

PITTSBURGH: CITY OF FIRSTS

1st Drive-In Filling Station
At this site in Dec. 1913, Gulf Refining Co. opened the first drive-in facility designed and built to provide gasoline, oils, & lubricants to the motoring public. Its success led to construction of thousands of gas stations by different oil companies across the nation.

© DAN ELDRIDGE

The country's first drive-in gas station is now a parking lot behind the Spinning Plate Artist Lofts in Friendship.

When Pittsburgh bridge-builder George W. Ferris built his very first wheel – a Ferris wheel, for the 1893 Chicago World's Fair – he couldn't have possibly imagined that he'd given birth to a Steel City tradition of invention and innovation that continues today. A Latrobe-area pharmacist by the name of Dr. David Strickler, for instance, is responsible for building the country's first banana split. That was way back in 1904. And Pittsburgh is also to blame for the now ubiquitous Big Mac – franchise owner Jim Delligatti created the sandwich at his Uniontown McDonald's store in 1967. Even the very first Internet emoticon, The Smiley, was created by a Carnegie Mellon University computer scientist in 1980. Here's a look at a few other Pittsburgh famous firsts:

FIRST WORLD SERIES – 1903
The Pirates were bested by the Boston Pilgrims in the eight-game series, four of which were played in a field not far from the current location of PNC Park.

FIRST MOTION PICTURE THEATER – 1905
The Nickelodeon on Smithfield Street, Downtown, was the world's first theater devoted exclusively to the moving motion picture.

FIRST GAS STATION – 1913
Gulf Refining Company built the country's first auto service station, which still sits in Friendship today. Look for it on Baum Boulevard.

FIRST COMMERCIAL RADIO STATION BROADCAST – 1920
After first installing a radio transmitter in his Wilkinsburg garage, a Westinghouse engineer sent a KDKA signal from a location in East Pittsburgh. The station still transmits today.

FIRST BINGO GAME – early 1920s
After creating the game and then taking it to carnivals nationwide in 1924, Pittsburgher Hugh J. Ward penned an official book of bingo rules in 1933.

POLIO VACCINE – 1953
Dr. Jonas Salk and his staff developed the critical vaccine while at the University of Pittsburgh.

© FABIAN BAUTISTA

eyeball seats in Agnes R. Katz Plaza, Downtown, designed by sculptor Louise Bourgeois

AUGUST WILSON CENTER FOR AFRICAN AMERICAN CULTURE

Regional Enterprise Tower, 425 6th Ave., Ste. 1750, 412/258-2700, www.africanaculture.org

COST: Free

Currently, the nonprofit August Wilson Center for African American Culture, which was formerly known as the African American Cultural Center of Greater Pittsburgh, acts as a sort of performing and visual arts organization without a proper home. Since 2003, the group has been offering a wide-ranging schedule of educational and performance programs throughout the city—including dance, music, and spoken word—that celebrate the cultural advancements and achievements of all African Americans. Sometime in early 2008, however, the organization will see a two-story, state-of-the-art, ultramod-ern facility erected on Liberty Avenue, on the corner of 10th Street and William Penn Way, Downtown. Appropriately enough, that location will position the center right in the heart of the Cultural District.

Along with an exhibition gallery and a 500-seat theater, the 67,000-square-foot center will have a café featuring live music and African food, a gift shop, a multipurpose room, and a number of classrooms and educational activity spaces. An artist-in-residence program is currently in the works for the center. Anyone interested in making a financial contribution should call the development office at the number listed, or simply visit the website, where contributions can be made online.

THE CULTURAL DISTRICT

Bordered by Fort Duquesne Blvd., 10th St., Liberty Ave., and Stanwix St., www.pgharts.org

A 14-square-block area in the heart of the Golden Triangle, Pittsburgh's Cultural District encompasses a total of 47 restaurants, 88 retail establishments, and eight public parks. Yet none of those amenities have much to do with why tourists and locals alike flock here in droves on weekend afternoons and evenings. Instead, the expensively dressed crowds you'll spot clutching playbills in this compact region of Downtown come mostly to visit the area's four performing arts theaters. Each year, in fact, roughly 1,400 performances take place in the area—everything from chamber music and ballet performances to opera, drama, film screenings, pop concerts, and more.

Some of the district's most historically popular events are the concerts given by the Pittsburgh Symphony Orchestra at **Heinz Hall** (600 Penn Ave., 412/392-4900,

MERCIFUL PITTSBURGH

The religious order of Catholic women known as the Sisters of Mercy were founded by Catherine McAuley in Dublin, Ireland, in 1831, and they were apparently a rather prolific and hard-working coalition. By December 21, 1843, a group of seven sisters from Carlow, Ireland, had already established their first convent in the United States; it was located in the Pittsburgh area known today as Downtown. If you wander to 800 Penn Avenue, you'll see a historical marker posted just outside the building.

Aside from taking vows of poverty, chastity, and obedience, the Sisters concern themselves largely with providing educational and social services for the poor, the sick, and the needy. This explains why so many schools and hospitals use the word "Mercy" in their names; these were institutions run by the sisters, or somehow affiliated with them. In fact, the first hospital in the world established by the sisters was Pittsburgh's Mercy Hospital, which opened its doors in 1847.

The sisters were also responsible for establishing Oakland's Carlow University, which was known as Mount Mercy College when it opened in 1929.

Currently, the Sisters of Mercy of the Americas have around 4,500 members; there are more than 10,000 Sisters of Mercy located worldwide.

www.pittsburghsymphony.org). The orchestra has long been noted by both domestic and international music critics as being one of the best orchestras in the country, and any visitor to Pittsburgh with the time and money to do so would be wise to squeeze in a performance. In fact, merely sitting alone in an empty Heinz Hall could qualify as a cultural experience—the theater, which today has 2,261 seats, has a rather unique history.

The first structure to be built on the site was the St. Clair Hotel, which in 1880 changed its name to the Hotel Anderson. And although that hotel existed until 1927, during the end of the 19th century it was known for hosting mostly traveling theater companies, including Shakespearean actors.

The Anderson next became the Loews Penn Theater. One of the great American movie houses, the Penn Theater was known locally as the "Temple of the Cinema" and was considered the best and most ornate cinema between Chicago and New York City.

But thanks in part to the invention of television, the theater was forced to call it a day in 1964. Slated to become a parking lot, the building was saved only by the intervention of the Pittsburgh Symphony itself, which at the time was performing in too-small halls located in the university district of Oakland. Five years and $10 million later, construction was completed at the newly named Heinz Hall for the Performing Arts. An open-air Grand Plaza, complete with a small waterfall, was built adjacent to the hall in 1982. And then in 1995, the hall was given the gift of yet another facelift, during which it received a new orchestra shell, new wallpaper, paint and carpeting, and new acoustical risers, among other improvements. The total cost: $6.5 million.

Of course, the Cultural District doesn't consist of simply old and historical structures. Modern architecture buffs in particular will want to pay a visit to the recently built **O'Reilly Theater** (621 Penn Ave.,

412/316-1600, www.pgharts.org/venues/ oreilly.aspx), a $25 million state-of-the-art performance venue designed by the ultrafamous Michael Graves, who has since given up on buildings and today focuses almost entirely on product design.

The O'Reilly sits on the former site of the Lyceum Theater, a vaudeville house that was deemed unusable following a 1936 flood. The new structure, where the Pittsburgh Public Theater as well as touring stage actors perform, is especially notable for its unique thrust stage, which is surrounded by the audience on three sides. The effect is such that shows here feel particularly intimate, sometimes uncomfortably so.

After observing the O'Reilly, followers of Michael Graves's work should examine the nearby **Agnes R. Katz Plaza,** which sits at the corner of Penn Avenue and 7th Street. Featuring possibly the most eclectic public sculptures in the Golden Triangle, the plaza is a striking example of Pittsburgh's ongoing bid to become a serious arts town. It's also rather tough to miss: Just look for the open square filled with a half dozen granite benches that resemble giant human eyes.

A collaboration with artist Louise Bourgeois (who created the eyeball seats), landscape architect Daniel Urban Kiley (who designed the plaza's backless granite benches), and the aforementioned Michael Graves, the square's focal point is a 25-foot bronze fountain, also designed by Bourgeois.

But even those who couldn't care less about fine art and design will find much to like about the plaza. Not only is it perfect for people-watching, it's also a convenient place to take a break or meet friends in between theater- or restaurant-going.

Also notable in the Cultural District is the **Byham Theater** (101 6th Ave., 412/456-6666, www.pgharts.org/venues/byham .aspx), a structure built in 1903 that was originally known as the Gayety Theater. Like the Lyceum, the Gayety was a vaudeville house—one of the country's most well known, in fact. Although somewhat faded, a masterfully designed tile mosaic featuring what must have been the Gayety's logo can still be seen on the floor of the Byham's entry. Sometime in the 1930s, the Gayety became known as the Fulton, which soon after transformed into a movie house. The building didn't become known as the Byham until the mid-1990s.

The **Benedum Center for the Performing Arts** (719 Liberty Ave., 412/456-2600, www .pgharts.org/venues/benedum.aspx), however, holds a distinction entirely unique from the district's other venues: After a $43 million restoration by H. J. Heinz II, who restored the center to its former 1928 glory when it was known as the Stanley Theater, the Benedum was added to the National Register of Historic Places.

Other venues located in the Cultural District include **SPACE** (812 Liberty Ave., 412/325-7723, www.spacepittsburgh.org), a contemporary arts gallery, and the **Harris Theater** (809 Liberty Ave., 412/682-4111, www.pghfilmmakers.org), an independent cinema house where stage performances occasionally take place.

MARKET SQUARE

Bordered by Stanwix, Wood, 4th, and 5th Sts. Today, the relatively small area known as Market Square isn't much more than an open-air square-shaped block of restaurants and retail establishments with a small park at its center. What's more, the majority of the square's historic businesses have long since fled for the suburbs. And aside from the lunch hour, when business types descend upon Starbucks and Subway, the only returning visitors are a small gathering of homeless people and the occasional cop on horseback. Yet the square is still worth a look, if only to imagine what it might have felt like to be a part of the action in the late 1700s, when John Campbell first designed the city's Downtown street plan.

The original market was a covered and enclosed building generally referred to as the Diamond. It soon became the commercial center of the city. The buying and selling of foodstuffs took place there, and the city's courthouse, its jail, and its first newspaper, *The Pittsburgh Gazette,* were also housed inside.

Business continued as usual until the early 1900s, when a fire permanently destroyed the Diamond. A new market house was soon built in its place; it encompassed 11,000 square feet and reached all the way to the road now known as Forbes Avenue. Yet five days after the Christmas of 1960, the final enclosed market house was demolished, due largely to unbearable overhead expenses.

The existing open-air Market Square that we see today, which certainly lacks the small-town vibe that existed before the disaster of former mayor Tom Murphy's 5th-Forbes redevelopment scheme, completed its construction in 1977. Adding a rather interesting contrast to the area after its own completion in 1980 was the postmodern **PPG Place;** the main tower of that building complex rises just south of the market.

Thankfully, a small number of the market's older businesses have been restored and may be visited. If you have the time to visit only one, make it the 136-year-old **Original** **Oyster House** (20 Market Sq., 412/566-7925, Mon.–Sat. 9 A.M.–11 P.M.), a veritable Pittsburgh tradition offering enormous fish sandwiches and fried oysters. You might also try the much newer local legend known as **Primanti Brothers** (2 S. Market Pl., 412/261-1599, daily 10 A.M.–11 P.M., www.primantibros.com), where hearty meat sandwiches are served with french fries *inside.*

POINT STATE PARK

101 Commonwealth Pl., 412/471-0235 (park),
412/281-9284 (museum),
www.fortpittmuseum.com,
www.denr.state.pa.us/stateparks
HOURS: Wed.–Sun. 9 A.M.–5 P.M. (museum)
COST: $5 adult, $4 senior (museum)

It's easy enough to think of the triangle-shaped Point State Park as Pittsburgh's answer to Central Park: a grassy, seemingly secluded respite from the urban grind. But the 36-acre area now used solely as a recreational park—and also as an outdoor concert, theater, and visual arts gallery during Pittsburgh's annual Three Rivers Arts Festival—has a bloody history of some national significance.

Originally known as Fort Pitt, this was the site of the French and Indian War, which was won by General John Forbes (and an army of 6,000) for the British Empire in 1758. The **Fort Pitt Museum** and its accompanying **Fort Pitt Blockhouse** (Tue.–Sat. 9:30 A.M.–4 P.M., Sun. noon–4 P.M.), both located inside the park, tell the story of this crucial epoch in American history.

No interest in battlefield lore, however, is necessary to appreciate Point State Park's pivotal location at the axis of the city's three rivers: Not only do the Allegheny, the Monongahela, and the Ohio converge where the park begins, but a hidden "fourth river"—prop-

COURTESY OF VISITPITTSBURGH

enjoying the fountain at Point State Park

erly known as the Wisconsin Glacial Flow—streams lazily underneath them all. In fact, visitors who make their way to the western-most tip of the park when its **fountain** is in operation will be able to view the fourth river themselves: That's it, shooting into a 30-foot-tall plume above the fountain's 200-foot-diameter concave bowl, in which children can often be seen frolicking. During the spring, summer, and fall, the fountain, which was dedicated in 1974, is in operation 7:30 A.M.–10 P.M., weather permitting.

The Point is also a place where Pittsburgh comes to play, especially during the summer months. Aside from the Three Rivers Arts Festival, the Three Rivers Regatta and the Fourth of July Fireworks take place here. During your exploration of the park, look out for the 23 monuments and commemorative markers detailing spots of historic importance within the park.

The park, however, is currently undergoing major renovations and the majority of the park will be closed until its expected completion in December 2007. During the renovation period visitors will be able to access the Fort Pitt Museum, the Allegheny Wharf by the Lower Allegheny River Front Park, and the Mon Wharf through the tunnel from the parking garage along Commonwealth Place.

PPG PLACE
200 Three PPG Place, 412/434-1900 (events), 412/394-3641 (ice skating rink), www.ppgplace.com
Completed in 1984 and designed by the legendarily influential architect Philip Johnson, PPG Place is easily the most noticeable and modern complex (some would say post-modern) located within the confines of the Golden Triangle. Wander toward Downtown's Market Square to separately view

the six structures of PPG Place, or simply look skyward as you approach: PPG's massive tower, covered in a reflective glass skin, rises skyward. At its top are a series of jagged, "Glassy Gothic" spires with triangular and pointed tips. The remaining five buildings, while of a much smaller stature, are also covered in a glass skin and sport gothic spires; in total, there are 231 spires in the complex.

PPG Place is an unusual and a somewhat bizarre series of edifices, to be sure, especially when considered with the immediate area's other corporate buildings, the majority of which are largely uninspired and architecturally plain (except, of course, the few remaining historic structures, such as Henry Hobson Richardson's Allegheny County Courthouse).

So how exactly *did* the design for PPG Place come about? As critic Peter Blake put forth in the February 1984 issue of *Progressive Architecture:*

> If you are an architect asked to design a complex that will house the Corporate Headquarters of the Pittsburgh Plate Glass Company (plus other tenants), you will, obviously, design a glass building. The question is – what sort of glass building? And what sort of image will you try to project?

Blake goes on to suggest that Johnson might have designed something resembling one of Mies van der Rohe's sketches for skyscrapers in glass. But instead, Johnson chose to essentially create a miniature Rockefeller Center, complete with arcaded sidewalks that join all six buildings. Yet the complex also includes a magnificent, glass-enclosed Winter Garden, clearly a nod to the 17th-century gardens of Italy and

Philip Johnson's PPG Place, Downtown

France. And perhaps most exciting (and most interactive) for tourists are the 60- and 90-degree angles of glass that cover the facades of each face: Because of the way the plates of glass reflect upon each other, and upon the gritty scene of urban Pittsburgh surrounding them, the images appearing in the structure's reflections make for incredible photographs. Should you grow tired after exploring the structure, simply drop into any of the adjoining cafés, or descend to the ground floor of the complex where a food court can be found.

As an interesting trivial aside, PPG Place almost became the mansion of the fictional vigilante Bruce Wayne, a.k.a. Batman, until the production company in charge of the recent Batman films decided not to shoot in the city.

SMITHFIELD STREET BRIDGE

www.pghbridges.com

Anyone walking from Downtown Pittsburgh to Station Square, which sits on the opposite side of the Monongahela River, does so by strolling along one of the two footpaths of the Smithfield Street Bridge, a span often referred to locally as the "Kissing Fish Bridge" (view the bridge from afar and you'll understand the reference). Yet even if the idea of a walk across the bridge doesn't necessarily appeal, anyone interested in viewing a particularly striking Pittsburgh city skyline should nonetheless give it a shot. As you cross, take the time to pause periodically along the way and observe the view in front of you, behind you, and even beneath you; assuming your timing is right, a tugboat or even a coal barge might pass.

Constructed between the years 1881 and 1883, the Smithfield Street Bridge is actually the third such structure to exist on the site. The first to be built here, in 1818, was

the Monongahela Bridge, which was also the very first river crossing in Pittsburgh. Its construction put the city back only $102,000, although it was rendered unusable during the Great Fire of 1845.

The second bridge constructed on the site was designed by John Roebling, who also created both the Brooklyn Bridge and the span that was replaced by Pittsburgh's Roberto Clemente Bridge. Increasing loads of heavy traffic soon led to this second bridge's closure and then to the construction of the bridge we see today, which has been designated a Historic Landmark by the Department of the Interior, the American Society of Civil Engineers, and the Pittsburgh History and Landmarks Foundation.

Designed by Gustav Lindenthal—who was also responsible for creation of Hell Gate Bridge, which connects Astoria, Queens, to Randalls Island in New York City—the Smithfield Street Bridge is a truss-style span over which streetcars once passed. But in order to create room for more traffic flow, that practice ended in the summer of 1985, and the streetcars were moved to the nearby Panhandle Bridge, which you'll cross today should you ride the "T" from any of Downtown's four streetcar stops to Station Square.

As you cross beneath the portals of the Smithfield Street Bridge on foot, pay close attention to the detailed lamps, as well as to small, intricate moldings representing the city's legendary industrial prowess.

THE THREE SISTERS

www.pghbridges.com

Although nearly all of Pittsburgh's Downtown spans are visually striking and historically significant, probably no trio of bridges means more to the city than those known

© FABIAN BAUTISTA

the Roberto Clemente Bridge, one of the legendary Three Sisters

collectively as the Three Sisters. And because all are identically designed, it's quite likely that these bridges are the first you'll notice when exploring the Golden Triangle. The Three Sisters, in fact, all of them painted a rather striking shade of yellow known as Aztec gold, are today the only identical trio of side-by-side bridges in the world. They were also the very first self-anchored suspension spans built in the United States.

Today known as the **Roberto Clemente Bridge** (formerly the 6th Street Bridge, built in 1928), the **Andy Warhol Bridge** (formerly the 7th Street Bridge, built in 1926), and the **Rachel Carson Bridge** (formerly the 9th Street Bridge, built in 1927), all three bridges cross the Allegheny River to reach the North Side.

Renamed on March 18, 2005 was the Andy Warhol Bridge. It earned its new name as part of a 10th anniversary celebration for

the Andy Warhol Museum, which sits just steps from the north end of the bridge. The celebration for the renaming of the Warhol Bridge was, appropriately enough, probably the most Dionysian of the three. A number of the city's most left-of-center artists were in attendance, and a brief dance and drama event by students attending a nearby performing arts high school took place.

Perhaps even more interesting, though, is the Warhol Bridge's immediate neighbor to the west, the Roberto Clemente Bridge. The Roberto Clemente gained its new name on April 8, 1999, which was the day after a groundbreaking ceremony took place on the bridge's northern end for PNC Park, which became the new home of the Pittsburgh baseball club two years later (Clemente was a legendary Pirate who played from 1955 until his death by plane crash in 1972). The bridge's proudest moment probably came as early as

1928, the year it was erected. This was when the American Institute of Steel Construction named it the year's most beautiful steel bridge. And while each of the Three Sisters replaced former bridges, the Roberto Clemente replaced a notable span built by the once-famous John Roebling, probably best known for creating New York City's Brooklyn Bridge.

The Rachel Carson Bridge was renamed on April 22, 2006. This was also the day during which the environmental celebration known as Earth Day took place. It was quite an appropriate time for the renaming, as Carson, author of the classic *Silent Spring,* is still known today as the most famous environmentalist to hail from Southwestern Pennsylvania. (Born in 1907, Carson was raised in Springdale at a site now known as the Rachel Carson Homestead, which is open to tourism.)

The renaming of the bridge happened largely due to the efforts of Esther Barazzone, the president of Chatham College, where Carson matriculated in the 1920s, when Chatham was still known as the Pennsylvania College for Women. Barazzone initially had her sights set on a statue of Carson, which would have been the city's first statue of a woman, but those plans were dashed due to Pittsburgh's financial problems.

Strip District   Map 1

SENATOR JOHN HEINZ PITTSBURGH REGIONAL HISTORY CENTER

1212 Smallman St., 412/454-6000,
www.pghhistory.org

HOURS: Daily 10 A.M.–5 P.M.

COST: $7.50 adult, $5 student, $3.50 child (ages 6-18), free for children ages 5 and under, $6 senior

Certainly one of the city's most educational and culturally viable additions to the museum scene, the seven-story Pittsburgh Regional History Center acts as a nearly exhaustive record of Western Pennsylvania life and culture spanning more than 250 years. And because so many exhibitions are hands-on and creatively curated, the museum—which is housed inside the former headquarters and warehouse of the Chautauqua Lake Ice Company—is also attractive to children. Underage visitors will find much to capture their attention in the **Western Pennsylvania Sports Museum,** which celebrates the achievements of area athletes and allows youngsters to play along. And on the museum's third floor is Discovery Place, a hands-on historical exhibit specifically designed for younger guests. Kids also love sitting in the driver's seat of the restored 1949 streetcar trolley, which is located in the ground floor's Great Hall, which is also where you'll find Kidsburgh, a small play area built above Reymer's Old-Fashioned Deli. And yet the History Center might best be described as a can't-miss attraction for folks of any age, assuming they carry even a passing interest in the development of the region and its people.

Although the museum opened its doors to the public in 1996, it didn't come into its full glory until late 2004, when a new wing affiliated with the Smithsonian Institution was completed. That process also established the center as the largest history museum in the state. Two recent additions to the Smithsonian wing are the aforementioned Sports Museum and the superbly curated Special

© FABIAN BAUTISTA

a goalpost from Three Rivers Stadium outside the Senator John Heinz Pittsburgh Regional History Center

Collections Gallery, which takes an especially close look at the immigrant communities that flocked to Pittsburgh at the turn of the 20th century. Here you'll find artifacts used by the immigrant laborers, such as cigar-rolling supplies and tools that were used in the area's mines. There's also a life-size recreation of the inside of a typical laborer's home. Some of the more recent artifacts include the head gear and uniforms used by the steel miners of the 1970s; you'll also see an actual steel miner's locker, decorated in now-faded Pittsburgh Steelers stickers.

ST. PATRICK'S CHURCH

57 21st St., 412/471-4767

HOURS: Daily 8 A.M.-3:30 P.M.

COST: Free

Known to area residents as "Old St. Patrick's," this was Pittsburgh's very first Catholic parish. And while the church building itself wasn't constructed until 1936, the parish was founded way back in 1808 by a group of Irish immigrants. This most likely explains the structure's stone tower, built to resemble the towers of Irish monasteries in medieval times.

Today, St. Patrick's is probably best remembered by older generations of Pittsburghers because of Father Cox, an astonishingly altruistic man who acted as the church's priest throughout the Great Depression. Among other good deeds, Cox helped the city's homeless and unemployed population construct a ragged but livable Shantytown along stretches of Liberty Avenue.

Old St. Patrick's also has something of a national reputation; it's one of the very few churches in the world to own a replica of the famous **Holy Stairs,** which represent the number of steps Jesus climbed on the day Pontius Pilate condemned him to death. Visitors may climb the steps during normal church hours, except during Monday and Thursday Mass at 12:10 P.M. Do keep in mind, however, that ascending the steps must be done on one's knees. (Walking *down* the steps is allowed.) The set of steps believed by many to be the authentic *Scala Pilati* (Pilate's Stairway), which is also known as the *Scala Sancti* (Holy Stairway), is located in a papal sanctuary next to the Basilica of St. John Lateran in Rome.

Oakland   Map 2

CARNEGIE MELLON UNIVERSITY
5000 Forbes Ave., 412/268-2000,
www.cmu.edu

After Scottish immigrant Andrew Carnegie made his fortune in the steel industry and then became one of the world's most famous philanthropists, he gave quite a bit back to the city of Pittsburgh, where buildings and institutions named after him seem nearly ubiquitous in some quarters.

Carnegie Mellon University was founded by Carnegie himself in 1900, who first dubbed it Carnegie Technical School; it later became known as the Carnegie Institute of Technology. Today, the university is considered a worldwide leader in the fields of robotics and computer engineering and, to a lesser extent, in fine arts and business administration.

To pay a visit to the campus, which is located on Forbes Avenue just up the hill from the University of Pittsburgh, start by wandering the grassy, parklike expanse known as "the cut"; to its left sits the **University Center,** where a convenience store, the student bookstore, a food court, and a café can be found. Once inside the University Center, the **Information Desk** (412/268-2107, daily 8 A.M.–10 P.M.), which is actually a walk-up window, should be your very first stop. Here you can speak to an actual CMU student who will respond to queries about where to go, what to see, and what to do while on campus. Detailed campus maps and handbills advertising upcoming events are available here. To view an even wider collection of notices, such as flyers announcing upcoming rock concerts, cars for sale, and roommates wanted, ask the Info Desk student to point you in the direction of the bulletin board down the hall.

In total, CMU has a collection of seven colleges and schools, and since the campus

© DAN ELDRIDGE

University of Pittsburgh student dormitories, known as the Towers in Oakland

is relatively small and quite walkable, a stroll across the grounds shouldn't take much longer than a half hour.

Should you care to extend your stay, you might consider taking in a performance by the world-renowned **School of Drama** (www .cmu.edu/cfa/drama). Not only was CMU the first university in the country to offer academic drama degrees, but the majority of performances today receive high marks from local theater critics. Carnegie Mellon Drama School graduates include Ted Danson, Holly Hunter, George Peppard, Blair Underwood, and Steven Bochco. Tickets can be purchased at the box office of the **Purnell Center** (412/268-2407) noon–5 P.M. Mondays and Fridays, noon–5 P.M. and 6–8 P.M. on weekdays when a performance takes place, and two hours before curtain on Saturdays prior to a performance.

Visitors interested in computer technology might be interested in strolling the halls of Carnegie Mellon's **School of Computer Science** (www.cs.cmu.edu); its graduate program was ranked the top such program in the country by *U.S. News & World Report*. In 2000 and 2001, *Yahoo! Internet Life* magazine ranked CMU the "most wired" university in the United States. The university's **Robotics Institute** (www.ri.cmu.edu) is also notable. Founded in 1979, it's the largest college research facility of its type in the United States, and its faculty, students, and the innovations of both frequently appear in the local and national press.

Any visitor to the Carnegie Mellon campus not particularly impressed by technological advancements should consider this: Beginning in 1937 with physics professor Clinton Davisson, 15 graduates or faculty

---

THE RUINS OF FORBES FIELD

Long before the existence of PNC Park and even the historic Three Rivers Stadium – which was imploded and turned into a parking lot in 2001 – the Pittsburgh Pirates baseball club battled its rivals at **Forbes Field,** a park located in South Oakland. Not much remains of the old field, which saw its first match in 1909 and its last on June 28, 1970. Nonetheless, baseball history buffs may appreciate seeing the park's original home plate; it lies under a slightly foggy slab of plastic on the ground floor of the University of Pittsburgh's Wesley Posvar Hall, just outside the men's restroom. (Posvar itself sits next door to the Hillman Library, where employees at the checkout counter will be more than happy to provide you with a campus map.)

Even more exciting is the remaining portion of the right field wall, which sits just across the street from Posvar and stretches all the way to the building that houses that Katz Graduate School of Business. Even though the wall is slightly vine-covered, it's fairly easy to find: Just look for the hand-painted numbers indicating the distance in feet between the wall and home plate. And while you won't often find fans gathered around the historic artifact inside Posvar, hardcore Pirates obsessives do occasionally set up shop – complete with patio chairs and radios – alongside the old stadium wall. It's a rather moving sight to see the fans, most of them old-timers, sitting perfectly still with wool blankets over their legs and battered boomboxes atop their laps.

ANDREW CARNEGIE, SELF-HELP ENTHUSIAST?

Most everyone knows that the Scottish-born Andrew Carnegie, who built his fortune in Pittsburgh, was a famous industrialist, capitalist, and philanthropist. But very little has been written about Carnegie's fourth passion: self-improvement culture.

Carnegie had a strict belief in the concept that acquiring massive financial wealth was little more than a multistep process that could easily be whittled into a simple-to-follow formula. Not knowing exactly what that formula was, however, he hired the soon-to-be-legendary self-help author Napoleon Hill, who at the time was an unknown journalist, to interviews hundreds of wealthy and famous men, some of them millionaires. Carnegie's assumption was that most of the men, if not all, would have many traits in common, and that those traits could be used as clues for the rest of us in our own pursuits of excellence.

In 1928, the information gleaned from Hill's interviews became a book entitled *The Laws of Success*. Almost a decade later, Hill published the tome that today he is best remembered for: *Think and Grow Rich*. Some copies of that book were edited and abridged by Hill himself, who included with the revised text Carnegie's own formula for the creation of wealth, also known as "The Carnegie Secret." So what was the secret? Carnegie suggested that it had everything to do with desire. Whatever a mind truly focuses on and honestly desires, he believed, it would eventually get.

Of course, no one should conclude from Carnegie's significant interest in wealth- and success-building that the man was a simple narcissist, concerned only with his own well-being. On the contrary, in 1889 Carnegie published an essay titled "The Gospel of Wealth"; in it he argued that philanthropy was nothing less than a responsibility of the wealthy, regardless of whether they'd been born rich or were self-made millionaires.

members of Carnegie Mellon have had the very prestigious honor of being awarded the Nobel Prize.

CARNEGIE MUSEUM OF ART

4400 Forbes Ave., 412/622-3131, www.cmoa.org
HOURS: Tue.-Sat. 10 A.M.-5 P.M., Sun. noon-5 P.M., closed Mon.
COST: $10 adult, $6 child, $7 senior

Pittsburgh's premiere museum of modern art, the Carnegie Museum of Art also maintains a noted collection of contemporary pieces, post-Impressionist paintings, late 19th-century American art, and both European and American decorative arts from the past 200 years. Paintings and furniture certainly aren't the entire story, however. There's also the Hall of Sculpture, filled with Greek and Roman reproductions (including a scaled-down Parthenon). There's the Hall of Architecture and the Heinz Architectural Center, both of which see a good number of special exhibitions featuring modern masters. The acclaimed Carnegie International takes place here every three years—it's Pittsburgh's version of the Whitney Biennial. The next show is scheduled to open sometime in the fall of 2007; if you can't make it, you'll

the Grand Staircase inside Oakland's Carnegie Museum of Art

have to satiate yourself instead by perusing the museum's Scaife Gallery, where all manner of Warhols, Pollacks, and de Koonings can be found.

CARNEGIE MUSEUM OF NATURAL HISTORY

4400 Forbes Ave., 412/622-3131, www.carnegiemnh.org

HOURS: Tue.-Sat. 10 A.M.-5 P.M., Sun. noon-5 P.M., closed Mon.

COST: $10 adult, $6 child, $7 senior

Located underneath the same roof as the affiliated Carnegie Museum of Art, the Carnegie Museum of Natural History is home to a wealth of scientific and environmental exhibitions, including the world-renowned Dinosaur Hall (which you may recognize from its cameo in *Silence of the Lambs*). Some of the museum's other permanent displays include the Walton Hall of Ancient Egypt (mum-

mies!); the Hall of African Wildlife, which is complete with stunning lifelike dioramas and jungle creatures; and the Botany Hall, where plantlife can be contemplated. Area scientists and archaeologists work daily in the museum's on-site PaleoLab.

◖ CATHEDRAL OF LEARNING

Corner of 5th Ave. and Bigelow Blvd., 412/624-4141, www.pitt.edu

COST: Free

Aside from its hallowed status as one of the most majestic structures in the city, the Gothic-style Cathedral of Learning, which acts as the symbolic nucleus of the University of Pittsburgh campus, is also the second-tallest educational building in the world. (A structure at Moscow State University, in Russia, currently holds the title.)

Appropriately enough, the story of the Cathedral's construction is substantially grandiose. In 1925, Chancellor John Bowman divulged his vision of a tower whose soaring-to-the-heavens architecture would send a subtle message to the varied citizens of Pittsburgh: namely, that a higher education could be considered just as essential and dignified as a higher power. Bowman enlisted a virtual army to raise the $10 million necessary to complete the project; during the Great Depression, when charitable contributions dried up, area schoolchildren took to kicking in a dime each to "buy a brick for Pitt."

The Cathedral was finally dedicated in 1937, and even today it cuts an impressive sight. A 42-story Indiana-limestone structure on the outside, the building's inside denotes a considerably more intimate feel. Filling a cavernous but churchly first floor is the 100-foot-wide-by-200-foot-long Commons Room;

the 42-story Cathedral of Learning on the University of Pittsburgh campus

COURTESY OF VISITPITTSBURGH

students can be found tapping on laptops and sipping coffee at its long wooden benches all hours of the day and night.

Running a ring around the first floor are the fabled **Nationality Classrooms** (1209 Cathedral of Learning, 412/624-6000, www.pitt.edu/~natrooms); collectively they are easily the building's most fascinating feature. Designed to represent specific periods from various nations of the world—including many whose citizens have created enclaves in Pittsburgh—both original and recreated accoutrements were joined together as each successive room was built.

Twenty-six rooms in all can be viewed independently or as part of a guided or taped tour, including a 10th-century Armenian classroom, a folk-style Norwegian classroom, and a Byzantine-era Romanian classroom. Take care not to miss the resplendent Damascus-style Syria-Lebanon room (which unfortunately can only be viewed through a glass partition) or the many rooms on the third floor, especially the Minka-style Japanese classroom and the Israeli and African Heritage classrooms. Tours take place Monday–Saturday 9 A.M.–2:30 P.M. and on Sunday and holidays 11 A.M.–2:30 P.M. No tours are offered on Thanksgiving Day, December 24–26, or January 1. Tours are $3 for adults and $1 for children ages 8–18.

PHIPPS CONSERVATORY AND BOTANICAL GARDENS

1 Schenley Park, 412/622-6914, www.phipps.conservatory.org
HOURS: Sat.-Thurs. 9:30 A.M.-5 P.M., Fri. 9:30 A.M.-9 P.M.
COST: $7.50 adult, $4.50 child, $6.50 senior

Since its opening in 1893, Phipps Conservatory has been the nerve center of horticulture

© PAUL WIEGMAN

Phipps Conservatory Welcome Center at dusk

education in Southwestern Pennsylvania. Located just past the main entrance of Schenley Park in Oakland, the 13 rooms of the conservatory sit inside a Victorian-style glasshouse, where orchids, palm trees, ferns, a Japanese garden, a medicinal plant garden, and an assortment of floating water plants—to name just a sampling of the varieties on-site—await your discovery. Staying true to its fundamental mission as an education center, Phipps also hosts annual flower shows as well as occasional exhibits, lectures, and events.

Henry Phipps, a close friend of Andrew Carnegie's and, in his later years, a philanthropist, built the conservatory as a gift to the city of Pittsburgh. His explanation? He wanted to "erect something that will prove a source of instruction as well as pleasure to the people." Phipps even took pains to ensure that the conservatory would remain open on Sundays so that workers could stop by on what was their only day off.

At the time of writing, the conservatory was in the midst of a massive, $36 million renovation and expansion project. Already an environmentally friendly welcome center has opened its doors, and soon, the Tropical Forest Conservatory will be unveiled. The 12,000-square-foot display room will feature a different horticultural theme every two years.

RODEF SHALOM BIBLICAL BOTANICAL GARDEN

4905 5th Ave., 412/621-6566, www.biblicalgardenpittsburgh.org

HOURS: Sun.-Thurs. 10 A.M.-2 P.M., Sat. noon-1 P.M., closed during winter

COST: Free

With a collection of more than 100 temperate and tropical plants, a small waterfall, a stream representing the River Jordan, and a desert scene depicting the biblical lands from Lake Galilee to the Dead Sea, the Biblical Botanical Garden at Rodef Shalom Temple is meant to symbolize the universal love of the Bible. Many of the plants here have Biblical names (Moses in a Basket, Biblical Coat), and during each season, the garden focuses on a differing theme of Near Eastern horticulture. The experience of wandering the garden is meant to be something akin to a stroll through the Holy Land of ancient Israel, but even nonbelievers will enjoy relaxing among the beauty of nature here; the Temple is within walking distance of both the Carnegie Mellon and Pitt campuses and sits across the street from the WQED studios.

New special displays and educational programs are scheduled most seasons; call or visit the garden's website for updated information. Free public tours are given with a trained docent on the first Wednesday of June, July, August, and September; tours can also be arranged for groups of eight or more, although it is highly recommended to make reservations two weeks in advance. A number of educational books and brochures about the art of horticulture are available for purchase on-site.

◖ SCHENLEY PARK AND FLAGSTAFF HILL

Schenley Park Visitors Center, Panther Hollow Rd., 412/687-1800, www.pittsburghparks.org
HOURS: Daily 10 A.M.-4 P.M.

A virtual oasis in the center of the city, the 456-acre Schenley Park sits on hundreds of acres of prime urban real estate in between Oakland's university district and Squirrel Hill. Donated to the city by Mary Schenley in 1889, the park's wooded trails are particu-

larly popular with after-work and weekend joggers. The park also boasts a soccer field, an ice skating rink, 13 tennis courts, a public swimming pool, and its very own lake. You'll also find **Phipps Conservatory** and **Botanical Gardens** here and, across the street, another perennial favorite, Flagstaff Hill.

From the beginning of June through the end of August each year, free movies are shown on Flagstaff Hill, projected onto a theater-size outdoor screen. Show up on Wednesdays at sundown (usually around 9 P.M.) with a blanket and picnic foods. No alcohol is allowed. On Sundays at sundown, family-friendly films are screened.

If your plans include exploring the park in depth, stop first at the informative Schenley Park Visitors Center, where a guide can suggest walking routes or jogging trails. Ask about free historical walks of Schenley Park, which are led on the first and third Sunday of every month at 1 P.M. The visitors center will also have scheduling information about the free kids storytelling events and puppet shows, and the free National Geographic Film Festival, both of which take place throughout the summer.

Right next door is the **Schenley Park Cafe** (101 Panther Hollow Rd., 412/687-1800, www.pittsburghparks.org/VisitorCenter76 .php, 10 A.M.–4 P.M. with extended summer hours), which offers free wireless Internet access and live folk and blues music on Sundays 12:30–3:30 P.M. (July 2–Oct. 15 only). The café offers trail maps of the park as well as coffee, light lunches, desserts, and a gift shop.

SCHENLEY PLAZA

4100 Forbes Ave., www.schenleyplaza.org
Modeled after Manhattan's Bryant Park and

© DAN ELDRIDGE

a Victorian-style carousel in Schenley Plaza

quickly on its way to becoming the Oakland area's most popular outdoor socializing spot, it's hard to believe that Schenley Plaza—which sits directly in between the main branch of the Carnegie Library and Pitt's Hillman Library—was very recently a medium-size parking lot. Now a lush and inviting town square of sorts with a one-acre lawn, the plaza acts as a gateway to Schenley Park itself. Coincidentally, that was exactly the land's intended use when Mary Schenley donated the acreage to the city in 1890.

The plaza today is filled with movable chairs and café tables designed for socializing, food vendors, free wireless Internet access, a large tented area to provide protection from the elements, 24-hour security, and an entertainment schedule that includes author appearances and live music year-round. Perhaps the plaza's most exciting amenity, how-

ever, is its Victorian-style carousel. Featuring a colorful herd of animals that round the carousel to the accompaniment of old-fashioned pipe organ music, the ride is open to all ages and is wheelchair accessible. Tickets are $1.25.

SOLDIERS AND SAILORS MEMORIAL

4141 5th Ave., 412/621-4253,
www.soldiersandsailorshall.org
HOURS: Mon.-Sat. 10 A.M.-4 P.M.
COST: $5 adult, $3 child, senior, and veteran

One of America's largest museums dedicated to honoring and remembering its veterans, Soldiers and Sailors Memorial began life in the early 1900s with a much more local focus: It was originally intended only to recognize the sacrifice and patriotism of the Civil War veterans of Allegheny County. Today however, the memorial represents all branches of service.

The building's massive Greco-Roman grand edifice—look for it on the corner of 5th and Bigelow across from Pitt's student union—was designed to resemble the mausoleum of Halicarnassus, one of the Seven Wonders of the Ancient World. It's the memorial's museum, however, that will be of most interest to guests. Curios, uniforms, bric-a-brac, and other assorted gewgaws related to American-led battles—starting with the Civil War era and stretching all the way to Operation Iraqi Freedom—are displayed in glass cases. A special exhibition is dedicated to area women who've served in American wars.

ST. PAUL CATHEDRAL

Corner of Craig St. and Fifth Ave., 412/621-4951, www.catholic-church.org/st.paulcathedralpgh

COST: Free

Known as the Mother Church of the Diocese of Pittsburgh, the Gothic-style St. Paul Cathedral in Oakland celebrated its 100th birthday in 2006. The 1,800-capacity church, with a 75-foot ceiling designed to resemble the hull of a ship, is undoubtedly one of Pittsburgh's most breathtaking. But the cathedral's true treasure is its massive organ, manufactured by the Rudolf von Beckerath Co. of Germany and generally considered to be one of the finest pipe organs in the world. At the time of writing, however, St. Paul was undergoing a massive reconstruction project that included a restoration of the organ and its pipes. Once the instrument is fully repaired, a schedule of free-to-the-public organ concerts will resume; call for updated information.

Also impressive are the church's stained-glass windows, some of which represent Bible stories and the church's history in pictures. Take note of the large windows above the side doors, which document the life—and eventual martyrdom—of St. Paul himself.

Sunday Masses take place at 6:30 A.M., 8 A.M., 10 A.M., noon, and 6 P.M. Weekday Masses happen Monday–Saturday at 6:45 A.M., 8:15 A.M., and 12:05 P.M. To schedule a free tour of the cathedral, call the parish office at 412/621-4951 between 8 A.M. and 4 P.M. (Tour guides will only be granted to groups of five or more.)

South Side   Map 3

◖ GATEWAY CLIPPER FLEET

412/355-7980, www.gatewayclipper.com

COST: Cruise prices vary

Located next to Station Square's Sheraton Hotel is a sloping dock that leads to the Gateway Clipper Fleet, a riverboat operation that for nearly 50 years has been providing cruise tours both luxuriously elaborate and relatively simple along the city's three rivers.

As the most popular attraction in Pittsburgh, the Gateway Clipper Fleet claims to be the largest inland riverboat fleet in the country today. Yet the company began in 1958 with just one solitary boat—a vessel purchased in Erie for $50. By 1959, the river tours on the 100-passenger capacity *Gateway Clipper* had proved so popular that two more 100-passenger vessels, the *Good Ship Lollipop* and the *Gateway Clipper II,* were added.

The fleet now contains five boats, all of them authentic reproductions of old working riverboats. Cruises happen throughout the year and in all sorts of weather. Passengers can experience a cruise tailored specifically for children, a formal evening cruise with dinner included, or dozens of other voyages. Visit the fleet online for more detailed information or to learn about chartering an entire ship.

◀ SOUTH SIDE SLOPES
www.southsideslopes.org

Just minutes away from the hustle and energy of East Carson Street, the South Side Slopes neighborhood is Pittsburgh to the core. A winding maze of narrow traffic lanes and hillside steps weaves throughout this mostly blue-collar neighborhood, which was originally built for the immigrant workers who labored at the steel mills along the Monongahela River below.

The main attraction on the slopes is the view itself; many roads rival even the view of Downtown seen from Mount Washington's Grandview Avenue; beautiful views of Oakland and the South Side can also be seen. To experience the various views for yourself, simply wander up 18th Street and poke around. The dozens of differing views will become clearly apparent as you stroll higher into the Upper Slopes, where you'll also see mixed-use development and upscale condos being built alongside the decrepit and decades-old row houses. Built mostly in the mid-1800s, the majority of houses in this particularly cramped region of Pittsburgh are only one room wide, two rooms deep, and up to three or four stories high. Should you find yourself truly turned around while exploring, simply head down any hill; nearly all roads lead back to East Carson Street. And as you climb up 18th Street, take note of the mural on the road's right-hand-side retaining wall by local artist Rick Bach, who is

also responsible for many of the metal sculptures and interiors found in the city's Mad Mex restaurants, as well as illustration work inside many of the older bars and restaurants of the South Side Flats.

The **St. Paul of the Cross Retreat Center** (148 Monastery Ave., 412/381-7676, www.catholic-church.org/stpaulsretreatcenter) is one of the more curious points of interest on the Slopes. The church was founded in the mid-1800s by four members of the Passionist Congregation who traveled to Pittsburgh from Italy. Today it acts as a spiritual facility open to anyone interested in deeply studying the Christian relationship with God. Traditional weekend retreats cost $160 and cover two nights' accommodations, six meals, and all programs. Call for scheduling information, as men's and women's retreats take place on differing weekends throughout the year.

St. Michael's Rectory, also located in the Slopes, is the location where the historical Lenten drama *Veronica's Veil* (44 Pius St., 412/431-5550, www.veronicasveilplayers.org) has been staged on and off since 1910. The play explores the passion and death of Jesus Christ.

Another particularly popular event is the annual **Pittsburgh Step Trek** (www.steptrek.org), a leisurely but organized walk through some of the most picturesque reaches of the Slopes. The trek takes place every autumn; you can register online. To take a self-guided tour, purchase a copy of Bob Regan's *The Steps of Pittsburgh* (The Local History Co.), available from most local booksellers.

STATION SQUARE
Carson St. at the Smithfield Street Bridge, www.stationsquare.com

Previously a cluster of railroad yards utilized by the Pittsburgh & Lake Erie Railroad

Company, the 52-acre indoor shopping center and open-air entertainment complex known collectively as Station Square was converted into a center of commerce thanks to the midcentury decline in railway usage. The **Pittsburgh History and Landmarks Foundation** (100 W. Station Square Dr., Ste. 450, 412/471-5808, Mon.–Fri. 9 A.M.–5 P.M., www.phlf.org) spearheaded the renewal, which is likely the sole reason so many historic artifacts remain on-site. Of particular interest to those fascinated by Pittsburgh's industrial past is the massive, steel-purifying **Bessemer converter;** only two such converters exist in the United States. Look for Bessemer Court behind the Hard Rock Cafe. A fascinating selection of archival photographs can be viewed in the lobbies of the **Grand Concourse** restaurant and its adjacent **Gandy Dancer Saloon** (412/261-1717, www.stationsquare.com/grandconcourse). The main entrance of the restaurant is located on what was once the lower level of the P&LE Railroad Station, while the Gandy Dancer itself was formerly the P&LE's waiting room.

The complex's **Guest Services booth** is located inside the Freight House Shops building and next to the **Station Square Express** (Mon.–Thurs. 4–9 P.M., Fri.–Sat. noon–9 P.M., Sun. noon–5 P.M., ticket $1), a small train ride for kids. A wealth of brochures containing information about the Greater Pittsburgh area can be picked up for free at the booth.

Although still a relatively popular shopping and entertainment complex, Station Square has certainly seen happier days. Retail establishments and eateries in the main terminus have lately been closing with a depressing frequency, although across the Smithfield Street Bridge in the square's nightlife sphere, new businesses appear to open just as quickly as old ones fade away. Currently, club-hoppers can visit a multi-themed dance club, a Hooters restaurant, and a country-and-western club complete with line dancing and a mechanical bull.

At Station Square's outdoor **Bessemer Court,** you'll find the usual assortment of suburban chain restaurants. Those looking for an affordable and somewhat goofy way to explore Pittsburgh's waterways should stop by the **Just Ducky Tours booth** (125 W. Station Square Dr., 412/402-3825, Apr. 10–Oct., weekends only in Nov., $19 general, $18 senior, $15 child, www.justduckytours.com), also in Bessemer Court. The company's vintage WWII amphibious vehicles circle through the historical sites of Downtown before plunging into the water.

Mount Washington   Map 3

◖ THE DUQUESNE AND MONONGAHELA INCLINES

1220 Grandview Ave., 412/381-1665, www.incline.cc (Duquesne Incline); Carson St. at Smithfield Street Bridge, 412/442-2000, www.ridegold.com/ride/pgincline.asp (Monongahela Incline)

DUQUESNE INCLINE HOURS: Mon.-Sat. 5:30 A.M.-12:45 A.M., Sun. and holidays 7 A.M.-12:45 A.M.

MONONGAHELA INCLINE HOURS: Mon.-Sat. 5:30 A.M.-12:45 A.M., Sun. and holidays 8:45 A.M.-midnight

COST: Tickets $1.75, $2.25 with a transfer

Definitely skip the taxi if you're planning an outing to Mount Washington; the most interesting way to arrive is certainly via one of the city's two remaining inclines—the hillside cable cars you may have seen inching up and down the mountain.

The Monongahela Incline is the easier of the two to reach on foot. The incline will scurry you up the hill and deposit you atop Grandview Avenue. Just a block away is Shiloh Street, home to a charming assortment of informal restaurants and cafés. From the corner of Grandview Avenue and Shiloh Street, make your way along the pedestrian path and look for the entrance to the Duquesne Incline, which would have been demolished in the mid-1960s if not for the efforts of the nonprofit Society for the Preservation of the Duquesne Incline; the society's volunteers have been operating the station since 1963.

Even if you don't plan to ride the Duquesne back down to Carson Street, don't miss the station itself, which is filled with historical newspaper accounts of Pittsburgh's incline system and archival photos and postcards of funiculars around the world. The view from the station's observation deck is absolutely jaw dropping, and also worth a look is the Gear Room, where $0.50 gets you up-close-and-personal with the machinery that makes the incline go 'round.

The inclines are certainly one of the city's most popular attractions for tourists, and for good reason. The two-minute, six-mile-per-hour ride, while a touch frightening for first-timers, is also exhilarating. As the cars slowly rise from their lower stations, Downtown Pittsburgh and the suburbs to the east and west appear into view. The Duquesne travels a total of 400 feet up the hillside to reach an elevation of 800 feet, while the Monongahela travels 635 feet to reach a much lower 369-foot elevation. And given their ages (the Monongahela Incline has existed since 1870, although it was renovated in 1983 and '94, while the Duquesne Incline was built in 1877), it's surprising to note just how smooth and unjarring the experience is. Small children, however, often grow increasingly worried as the cars end their descent and gain traction toward the station houses; you might mention to any youngsters in your group that the car slows to a near dead stop about 10 feet from the bottom. It then easily inches its way home.

Keep in mind too that while the city refers to the inclines as "working museums," which is certainly an accurate descriptor, their primary function is that of public transport. You will almost always see more locals than tourists inside the cars, many of whom are Mount Washington residents who ride the inclines up and down the hillside each day (as this author did while briefly living on Mount Washington's Wyoming Street).

Bicycles may be taken on the Duquesne Incline only, although a double fare is required.

PITTSBURGH'S DISAPPEARING INCLINES

COURTESY OF VISITPITTSBURGH

the historic Duquesne Incline overlooking the Point, where Pittsburgh's three rivers converge

It was the late 1800s, and as the population of Pittsburgh's mill workers and coal miners quickly began to grow in number, the city also began to recognize a troubling site-specific problem: The precipitously steep hilltop neighborhoods – especially those above the South Side – were virtually inaccessible by either foot or horse. And since the land along the Monongahela River consisted mostly of mills and factories, the European migrants who worked there found it necessary to make their homes on the hills above. So in 1870, the two-car Monongahela Incline was constructed.

It rose from the base of the Smithfield Street Bridge and traveled up Mount Washington to what is now Grandview Avenue, operated by a relatively simple cable-pulley system: When one car traveled down, gravity pulled the other car up.

Eventually, more than 17 inclined planes – out-of-towners might refer to them as funiculars – were serving the city of Pittsburgh. But not only foot passengers utilized the hillside cable cars – light freight, horses, and wagons were also shuttled to and fro. Passenger fares ranged from one to five cents among the different inclines; heavy loads required extra payment.

The civil engineer responsible for the design and construction of the majority of the inclines in Pittsburgh was a Hungarian immigrant by the name of Samuel Diescher. After first settling in Cincinnati in 1866, where he built his first incline, Diescher eventually moved to Pittsburgh. He continued to build inclines elsewhere, however, including one in Johnston, Pennsylvania, one in Wheeling, West Virginia, and two in South America.

Very few inclines exist today in the United States, although two shining examples remain in Pittsburgh: The Monongahela Incline and the Duquesne Incline. The Duquesne offers the superior view, although the Monongahela is much easier to access on foot; you'll find its entrance just across the street from Station Square on the South Side. Both inclines climb Mount Washington and dispatch passengers atop Grandview Avenue.

North Side   Map 4

◖ ANDY WARHOL MUSEUM

117 Sandusky St., 412/237-8300,
www.warhol.org

HOURS: Tue.-Thurs. and Sat.-Sun. 10 A.M.–5 P.M.,
Fri. 10 A.M.–10 P.M., closed Mon.

COST: $10 adult, $6 child, $7 senior

As the country's largest museum dedicated
to a single artist, the Andy Warhol Museum
seum is a particularly unique feather in
Pittsburgh's modern art cap. To explore the
building properly, start on the top floor; this
is where temporary exhibitions are generally
held. As you work your way slowly down,
you'll encounter work both obscure (Jesus
punching bags, oxidation paintings made of
urine) and familiar (Campbell's soup cans,
Brillo boxes). Definitely don't miss the Silver

Cloud Room, where aluminum balloons are
kept afloat by fans. A theater that regularly
screens films by and about Warhol and his
entourage is on the ground level; in the basement sits a café and the city's only vintage
photo booth. An archival collection housing thousands of pieces of Warhol's personal
ephemera is also on-site.

◖ CALVARY UNITED METHODIST CHURCH

971 Beech Ave., 412/231-2007,
www.gbgm-umc.org/calvarypgh

HOURS: Group tours given by appointment only

COST: Free

Built in 1890 by residents of the North
Side's so-called Millionaires Row, which
can still be visited today in the **Allegheny
West Historic District** (www.city.pittsburgh
.pa.us/wt/html/allegheny_west.html), Calvary United Methodist Church is probably
best known for its stained-glass windows.
Large and wonderfully gorgeous, the triple-
lancet, Tiffany-produced windows are still
considered the finest and most elaborately
detailed examples of religious stained glass
ever created by the company. Calvary's exterior is also notable: Many claim its set of
gargoyles to be among the city's best.

Also interesting is the architecture of
the Gothic-styled church, which was constructed in the shape of a cross. The famous industrialist Charles Scaife, among
scores of wealthy Pittsburgh merchants,
was a member of the church's building
committee. The uniquely curved pews, in
fact, were constructed by the Joseph Horne
Company, which sold dry goods in the city
for decades.

COURTESY OF VISITPITTSBURGH

the Andy Warhol Museum, a memorial to one
of the city's most eccentric souls

ANDY WARHOL'S PITTSBURGH

So you've come from far and wide to visit the Andy Warhol Museum, and now you'd like to discover some of the sites that transformed the shy Pittsburgh boy into a pop art superstar? The following suggestions, adapted from a tour formerly offered by the Greater Pittsburgh Convention and Visitor's Bureau, will take you to a number of locations essential to young Andy Warhola's growth as an artist.

A sign welcomes visitors to the formerly star-studded South Oakland neighborhood.

Your first stop on the DIY Warhol Tour should absolutely be the **Warhola family home** in South Oakland, which still sits at 3252 Dawson Street. Don't expect much, just a typical rowhouse with a green and white striped awning and a collection of hedges. The Warholas were a family of especially modest means – Andy's father Andrei toiled as a construction worker during the Depression and was often without gainful employment.

An easy walk from the Warhola home is **Schenley High School,** at 4101 Bigelow Boulevard. Warhol was a student here, and this is also where some of his earlier artistic impulses first flourished.

Near the Jewish neighborhood of Squirrel Hill is Greenfield, where you'll find **St. John Chrysostom Byzantine Catholic Church.** The church, at 506 Saline Street, is where the Warhola family worshipped regularly. Call 412/421-0243 for service schedules.

In between Oakland and Squirrel Hill is the campus of **Carnegie Mellon University,** which was known as Carnegie Tech when Andy Warhol attended as a student in the department of painting and design.

You'll need a car for this one: **St. John the Baptist Cemetery** is located in the South Hills neighborhood of Bethel Park, at the corner of Route 88 and Conner Road and not far from South Hills Village Mall. Warhol is buried here next to his parents. The tombstone, located on a sloping hillside, is very modest and is sometimes decorated with a Campbell's soup can or two.

In the somewhat rough-and-ready neighborhood of McKees Rocks is the **Holy Ghost Byzantine Catholic Church,** where Warhol's funeral service took place. Feel the need to pay your own belated respects? The church is located at 1437 Superior Avenue.

Two of Andy Warhol's nephews, George and Marty Warhola, who both continue to live in Pittsburgh, are currently operating competing scrap metal businesses within three miles of each other on the North Side. Marty runs **Paul Warhola Scrap Metals** at 825 Pennsylvania Avenue, and George owns **AJ Warhola Recycling Inc.,** located at 203 Chesboro Street.

On March 18, 2005, the 7th Street Bridge was renamed (with much fanfare) the **Andy Warhol Bridge.** Start on the Downtown end and walk across for a beautiful view of the city and the Allegheny River. Once you reach the North Side you'll be within spitting distance of the **Andy Warhol Museum** itself.

Wrote Franklin Toker about Calvary United in *Pittsburgh: An Urban Portrait:* "Everything about the church inside and out is rich, textured, and above all, comfortable. To enter it is to intrude on a sumptuous private drawing room."

Currently, the **Allegheny Historic Preservation Society** is working to preserve the sections of this national landmark that have fallen into disrepair. To make a contribution, contact the AHPS at 412/323-1070.

◖ CARNEGIE SCIENCE CENTER AND UPMC SPORTSWORKS

1 Allegheny Ave., 412/237-3400, www.carnegiescience.org
HOURS: Sun.-Fri. 10 A.M.-5 P.M., Sat. 10 A.M.-7 P.M.
COST: $14 adult, $10 child and senior (including Science Center exhibits, UPMC SportsWorks, Buhl Planetarium, and USS *Requin,* Omnimax films and laser shows are extra)

Filled with kid-friendly and hands-on exhibits, the Carnegie Science Center approaches an often-tedious subject with a rather honorable mission: "To [inspire] learning and curiosity by connecting science and technology with everyday life." In other words, gaining an understanding of the world in which we live can be a blast here, where permanent displays include the Kitchen Theater, which looks at science through the art of cooking, and SeaScape, a 2,000-square-foot aquarium. Visitors also flock to the Science Center for its four-story **Rangos Omnimax Theater,** as well as for its **Buhl Planetarium & Observatory,** regarded as one of the world's most technologically sophisticated. (On Friday and Saturday nights, the planetarium plays host to a series of laser shows accompanied by classic rock soundtracks.) And

docked in the Allegheny River just behind the Science Center is the World War II–era USS *Requin,* a Navy submarine that can be boarded and explored.

On the opposite side of the parking lot you'll find the Science Center's phenomenal UPMC SportsWorks, a wonderfully interactive experience where kids young and old are encouraged to learn about the mysterious workings of the body by engaging in physical activity. Visitors can race a virtual Olympic sprinter, climb a 25-foot rock wall, or attempt to pitch a fastball. SportsWorks, in fact, is the very best sort of museum: It's practically a guaranteed good time.

NATIONAL AVIARY

Allegheny Commons West Park, 412/323-7235, www.aviary.org
HOURS: Daily 9 A.M.-5 P.M.
COST: $8 adult, $6.50 child, $7 senior

As home to more than 600 exotic birds of more than 200 species—many of them endangered—it's no wonder the National Aviary is known as one of the most important bird collections in the country. Along with its extensive and many-hued flock, however, much of the Aviary's deserved popularity is derived from the glass building's interior design: Visitors can choose to stroll through the two open rooms where birds fly freely among them, or they can venture into a more traditional viewing locale where birds and humans don't mix. (In these areas, a thin mesh-wire sheet is used to cage the creatures.) Yet completely unlike the traditional zoo environment, it is possible here to literally get face-to-beak with a flamingo or a parrot. And while some visitors may find this setup surprising, or even frightening, young children often seem to mix quite naturally with the animals. What could possibly be a more exciting way to educate a preschooler or elementary school–age child about the wonders of the natural world?

Some of the many birds you may see here include the bald eagle, the gray-winged trumpeter, the king vulture, the military macaw, the toco toucan, the African penguin, the speckled mousebird, and the white-crested laughing thrush. Feedings and various demonstrations take place throughout the day; especially curious visitors may even inspect specific menu items prior to mealtime.

NORTH SHORE AND
THE THREE RIVERS HERITAGE TRAIL

Heinz Field to the 40th Street Bridge, alongside the Allegheny River

Essentially a developer-created enclave that was once known simply as a portion of the North Side, the eateries and sports bars of the North Shore first began sprouting up around 2001. That was when the nearby **Heinz Field** (home of the Pittsburgh Steelers) and **PNC Park** (home of the Pittsburgh Pirates) officially opened for business.

The majority of the area's amenities are clustered on and around Federal Street; PNC Park sits at 115 Federal Street. To reach the area on foot from Downtown, follow 6th Street to the 6th Street Bridge, also know as the Roberto Clemente Bridge. Conveniently, the bridge is restricted to pedestrian-only traffic during baseball games. The North Shore is also where you'll find the **Carnegie Science Center, UPMC SportsWorks,** and the **Andy Warhol Museum.**

Stretching for nearly 40 miles along both sides of the Allegheny, Monongahela, and Ohio Rivers is the well-maintained **Three Rivers Heritage Trail**. It begins as a concrete path on the North Shore, where it runs right alongside the Allegheny River. The trail is an absolute boon for urban cyclists, joggers, and walkers. The length of the trail running through the North Shore is also where you'll find the Vietnam Veterans Monument and the Korean Veterans Memorial.

The Vietnam memorial, which features life-size statues of soldiers returning home from war to greet their families, stands mere feet from the Allegheny shoreline and almost exactly between Heinz Field and PNC Park. It's capped by an egg-shaped canopy meant to symbolize a hibiscus flower, which represents rebirth and regeneration and is native to tropical regions throughout the world, including Southeast Asia. The Korean War memorial is a bit farther east; it represents the 2,401 Pennsylvanians who died during the war. (California is the only state in the country that suffered more losses.) The memorial features a number of tall but thin blocks, fanned into a semicircle design. During certain times of the day, columns of sunlight, which the memorial's designer hoped would represent aspects of both shared and individual experiences, stream through the blocks. There are also commemorative plaques on the site documenting the war's chronology and a memorial wall engraved with names of the fallen soldiers.

Continue east along the path, with the river on your right, and soon the walkway will turn to dirt. Eventually the massive Heinz factory will appear on your left; much of it was recently converted into loft apartments.

The dirt trail turns to rock and begins to peter out around the 40th Street Bridge, at which point you'll have to turn around and head back to the city. Another option would be to explore the 13-acre **Millvale Riverfront**

Park, which sits underneath the bridge. The park is home to a gazebo, a covered picnic pavilion, and the training facility of the Three Rivers Rowing Association.

To discover the route's other stretches, take note of the maps-covered plaques that line the trail. Maps can also be found online at www.friendsoftheriverfront.org.

Squirrel Hill and Point Breeze   Map 5

FRICK PARK

Corner of S. Braddock Ave. and Beechwood Blvd.,
www.pittsburghparks.org

Popular with bird-watchers and urban dog walkers alike, the 600-acre Frick Park is not only the city's largest, but also its most varied. Stretching in between the neighborhoods of Squirrel Hill and Point Breeze, the park is filled with playgrounds, various recreational facilities, dog runs, winding footpaths, red clay tennis counts, and even a bowling green.

Lesser known are the park's nearly two-dozen phenomenal mountain biking paths.

With names like the Rollercoaster and the Worm Trail, it probably goes without saying that many of these routes are significantly challenging; even experienced cyclists are urged to stay away on rainy or poor-weather days.

JEWISH COMMUNITY CENTER
AND THE AMERICAN JEWISH MUSEUM

5738 Forbes Ave., 412/521-8010,
www.jccpgh.org

HOURS: Mon.-Thurs. 5:30 A.M.-10 P.M., Fri. 5:30 A.M.-6 P.M., Sat. 1-7 P.M., Sun 7:45 A.M.-6 P.M.

COST: Free

© MELISSA MCMASTERS, PITTSBURGH PARKS CONSERVANCY

Beechwood Boulevard gatehouse entrance to Frick Park

Something of an all-inclusive recreational clubhouse where both Jews and gentiles congregate, the Jewish Community Center features a state-of-the-art fitness center, a regular schedule of art classes, seminars, educational lectures, and theater performances, as well as the wonderfully contemporary American Jewish Museum, which is the only museum in the western half of the state dedicated to preserving the art, history, and culture of the Jewish diaspora.

The JCC, as it's often referred to locally, opened its doors way back in 1895 and was originally known as the Irene Kaufmann Settlement. The Kaufmann family and the National Council of Jewish Women were both responsible for the center, which was built in response to the rapidly growing number of Jewish immigrants settling in Pittsburgh. Today, people of all backgrounds are improving their bodies and their minds at the JCC. In fact, the center has proven so popular that a second facility now operates inside the **Henry Kaufmann Building** (345 Kane Blvd. off Bower Hill Rd., Scott Township) in the South Hills. Visit the JCC's website to download a coupon offering a one-week trial gym membership.

Bloomfield and Lawrenceville   Map 6

ALLEGHENY CEMETERY
4734 Butler St., 412/682-1624,
www.alleghenycemetery.com
HOURS: Sept.-Apr. daily 7 A.M.-5:30 P.M., May daily 7 A.M.-8 P.M., June-Aug. daily 7 A.M.-7 P.M.
More than 120,000 dead are currently at rest in the gorgeously landscaped Allegheny Cemetery, which covers some 300 acres smack-dab in the middle of Bloomfield and Lawrenceville. Composer **Stephen Foster** ("Oh! Susanna," "My Old Kentucky Home") is undoubtedly the cemetery's most recognizable name; a collection of difficult-to-follow signs point the way to his grave, which can be found in Section 21, Lot 30. (Stephen Foster's boyhood home is located just a five-minute drive away at 3600 Penn Avenue, also in Lawrenceville, although it unfortunately is not open to the public. A historical marker can be seen on the house's front lawn.) Other Allegheny Cemetery notables include Don Brockett (Chef Brockett of *Mister Rogers' Neighborhood*), Thomas Mellon, and General Alexander Hays.

Chartered as a nonprofit organization in April 1844, Allegheny Cemetery is the country's sixth-oldest rural cemetery. And probably because it was modeled on the landscapes of fashionable English parks, the experience of strolling the grounds is rather pleasant, and during the sunlight hours, not the least bit creepy. Nonetheless, it's all too easy to get lost in the cemetery; even locals who jog or walk here sometimes find themselves turned around. The roads are winding and the grounds are quite hilly, so even though posted signs point the way to various plots and sections, things can get confusing. But not to worry: Both the Bloomfield and Lawrenceville ends of the cemetery have separate entry points, and groundskeepers patrol regularly in private cars.

ARSENAL FIELD
40th and Butler Sts., Arsenal Middle School
Talk about standing on the shoulders of a giant: The footballers at Lawrenceville's

© DAN ELDRIDGE

the 300-acre Allegheny Cemetery, where songwriter Stephen Foster is buried

Arsenal Middle School must be some of the country's only students to have the privilege of playing on the same field as a former sports hero—in this case, NFL legend Johnny Unitas.

A Pittsburgh native who grew up in Brookline and on Mount Washington, Unitas was recruited in the ninth round by the Pittsburgh Steelers in 1955 but, as a fourth-string quarterback, was never once given a chance to play. Eventually, he was cut from the team and soon after agreed to join the semi-pro Bloomfield Rams, who competed in pools of oil on Arsenal Field. (The oil was sprayed on the field to keep dust off the players.)

Unitas, who passed away in September 2002, was offered a spot on the professional Baltimore Colts squad after leading the Bloomfield Rams to the Steel Bowl Conference championship. During his stint with Bloomfield, Unitas was paid the princely sum of $6 a game. A plaque outside the Arsenal Field fence on Butler Street commemorates Unitas's contribution to the city's sports legacy.

ARSENAL PARK
40th and Butler Sts., behind Arsenal Middle School

Today it's a pleasant and sprawling green space filled with playgrounds, sporting facilities, and, of course, many of the young families who've been drawn to Lawrenceville because of its generally affordable real estate and convenient East End location. But Arsenal Park from 1814 until 1913 was known as the Allegheny Arsenal. Designed by Benjamin H. Latrobe, the arsenal functioned as a military barracks during the Civil War, the War of 1812, and the Mexican War. At one point during the Civil War, more that 1,100 civilian workers toiled here.

The arsenal was also a manufacturing site for weapons, and on September 17, 1862, somewhere between 70 and 100 men, women, and children perished when barrels of powder exploded. A bronze marker outside the park's restrooms now memorializes the victims of the blast, and next to the fence separating the park and the middle school sits an authentic IX Shell Gun Cannon that was constructed in 1865; a marker atop the cannon notes that it fired a total of 1,681 rounds. The arsenal's powder magazine now functions as a maintenance shed.

Popular with picnickers, area teenagers, and recreational sports leagues, Arsenal Park also offers tennis and basketball courts, two baseball fields, and plenty of space for a casual jog or walk.

© DAN ELDRIDGE

an authentic IX Shell Gun Cannon in Arsenal Park, Lawrenceville

DOUGHBOY SQUARE

East of 34th St., where Butler St. forks off from Penn Ave.

Doughboy Square, an arresting war monument celebrating area soldiers who gave their lives in World War I, is actually a triangle. At its base stands a statue of—what else?—a Doughboy. Most war historians agree that the nickname for WWI soldiers was derived from the white adobe soil that often coated them during training at a camp in Texas.

There's also a plaque at the statue's base listing the names of hundreds who perished not only in WWI, but also in WWII, the Korean War, and the Vietnam War. And just behind the statue sits the historic **Pennsylvania National Bank** building, a beautiful beaux arts structure that was built in 1902 and restored in the early 1990s.

IRON CITY BREWERY

3340 Liberty Ave., 412/692-1161,
www.pittsburghbrewingco.com

Founded in 1861 by Edward Fraueheim, a German immigrant, Iron City Brewery holds the distinction of being the first brewery in America to produce a lager. (Heavier ales and porters were much more popular at the time.) Approximately 10,000 barrels are brewed annually inside Iron City's two buildings today, which are located almost directly across the street from The Church Brew Works.

And like the city of Pittsburgh itself, Pittsburgh Brewing is famed in professional brewing circles for an astounding number of industry firsts. Pittsburgh Brewing was the first company ever, in 1962, to offer a Snap Top can, which was produced in conjunction with Alcoa, an aluminum-production company also based in Pittsburgh. In 1963,

Pittsburgh Brewing created the first twist-off resealable cap and, in 1976, the company introduced the first light beer, Mark V.

Recently however, Pittsburgh Brewing has been suffering from serious financial difficulties, and only time will tell if Iron City Beer makes it to the next decade. Also unfortunate is that tours of the facility, which take place on Tuesdays, are limited to groups of 15 people or more. I suspect, however, that a convincing out-of-towner might be able to persuade the company to accommodate a slightly smaller group.

PITTSBURGH ZOO AND PPG AQUARIUM

1 Wild Pl., Highland Park, 412/365-3640, www.pittsburghzoo.com

HOURS: summer 10 A.M.-6 P.M., fall 9 A.M.-5 P.M., winter 9 A.M.-4 P.M., spring 9 A.M.-5 P.M.

COST: $9 adult, $7 child, $8 senior

Much more than just a randomly selected menagerie, the 77-acre Pittsburgh Zoo and PPG Aquarium has been renovating and upgrading its facilities since 1980, when the once-staid exhibits first began their transformation into natural habitats. As a result, you won't see an abundance of depressing cages here. Instead, winding pedestrian paths take visitors past the African Savanna and the Asian Forest, and even into a five-acre indoor rainforest housing 150 different plant species and more than 90 primates, including orang-utans, cotton-top tamarins, and western lowland gorillas. Other naturalistic habitats include Cheetah Valley and a bear habitat, where Kodiak bears and black bears can be seen rummaging through rocky hills.

In fact, there are now literally thousands of animals representing hundreds of species here. Don't miss the rare komodo dragon and the gila monster, both of which can be found in the Reptile House. And if children

© MARA RAGO

You'll encounter many exotic underwater creatures at PPG Aquarium.

are a part of your group, visit Kids Kingdom, an interactive facility with playground equipment that replicates animal motions, thereby teaching children to play just as a mole-rat or a penguin might play.

Take care not to miss the PPG Aquarium, where polar bears, sea otters, and walruses can be found frolicking underwater. Keep in mind that balloons, pets, and tobacco products of any sort are banned from zoo premises.

Greater Pittsburgh   Map 7

ALLEGHENY OBSERVATORY
159 Riverview Ave., 412/321-2400,
www.pitt.edu/~aobsvtyr

Although it was founded in 1859 for the purpose of educating the citizens of the City of Allegheny (which later became incorporated into the City of Pittsburgh), the Allegheny Observatory eventually ran out of funds and was donated to the University of Pittsburgh, which today uses it as a research lab for its Department of Physics and Astronomy.

Located four miles north of Downtown in the 251-acre **Riverview Park** (www.city .pittsburgh.pa.us/district1/html/riverview_ park.html), free public tours of the observatory are offered from April through October of each year. Advance reservations are required. The highlight of the tour is a stop at the 13-inch Fitz-Clark refractor, through which visitors may view any number of celestial wonders, assuming the night sky is clear. Before viewing the refractor, a short film is screened, and visitors are then taken on a walking tour of the building. The 8–10 P.M. tours take place on Thursday nights from May 1 through the third week of August, and on Friday nights from April 1 through November 1. Because of the private research going on at the observatory, visitors can only tour the facilities during the designated tour schedule. Once a year, however, an open house is held during which visitors are al-lowed to tour the observatory by following a designated path throughout the building; tour guides are not present. The event, which is also free and requires advance reservations, generally takes place toward the end of September.

The observatory also maintains a regular schedule of free astronomy lectures delivered by area scholars; regularly updated information is available at the observatory's website.

BEECHWOOD FARMS NATURE RESERVE
614 Dorseyville Rd., Fox Chapel, 412/963-6100,
www.aswp.org/beechwood.html
HOURS: Tue.-Sat. 9 A.M.-5 P.M., Sun. 1-5 P.M.
(Evans Nature Center)
COST: Free

Considering it's the headquarters of the Audubon Society of Western Pennsylvania, it probably goes without saying that the Beechwood Farms Nature Reserve, which consists of five miles of walking trails and 134 acres of wilderness sanctuary, is a rather lovely and peaceful place. The trails here are open to the public from dawn until dusk every day of the year.

The reserve is also home to the 125-seat **Evans Nature Center auditorium,** an **Audobon Nature Store,** a **bird feeder observation room,** and a **Natural History and Teacher Resource Library.**

Wildlife exists in abundance on the reserve; be prepared to spot deer, screech owls, and even red fox. An artificially constructed pond built in 1981 is home to mallards and Canada geese. Visitors should also stop by the **Audobon Center for Native Plants,** a greenhouse and nursery complex whose mission is to educate gardeners and landscapers about the importance of working with native plants.

K KENNYWOOD AMUSEMENT PARK

4800 Kennywood Blvd., West Mifflin, 412/461-0500, www.kennywood.com

HOURS: Memorial Day–Labor Day daily 10:30 A.M.–10 P.M.

COST: $28.95 adult, $18 child under 46 inches, $14.95 senior

Founded in 1898, the long-lasting and much-loved Kennywood Amusement Park has since become practically synonymous with the city of Pittsburgh itself. Over the past century, the park has survived fierce corporate battles, major changes in the industry, and even the Great Depression. But good ol' fashioned fun trumps all, it seems, and today the park is still a hugely popular Pittsburgh-area attraction. New rides continue to be added each summer season, and, in 1987, Kennywood was awarded National Historic Landmark status.

History aside, however, Kennywood is a can't-miss choice for Pittsburgh visitors both young and mature. Roller coasters continue to be a favorite here, especially the historical Thunderbolt and Jack Rabbit rides, as well as the terrifyingly fast Phantom's Revenge, which reaches speeds of 85 mph. The park also has its share of water rides and thrill rides, such as the catapulting SwingShot and the PittFall, a ride that simply drops its riders from a height of 251 feet to the ground below. But the fact that a decent number of classic rides are still in operation—like

the historic Kennywood Amusement Park, West Mifflin

the paddleboats, the bumper cars, and the merry-go-round—probably lends the park its most authentic sense of classic greatness.

Live entertainment occasionally takes place at Kennywood, and operating hours and admission prices change according to season. Call or visit the park's website for the most up-to-date information.

MONROEVILLE MALL

300 Monroeville Mall Blvd. (Exit #57 on Business Rte. 22), 412/243-8511, www.monroevillemall.com

HOURS: Mon.–Sat. 10 A.M.–9:30 P.M., Sun. noon–6 P.M.

Cinephiles and horror fans in particular have for years been journeying to Pittsburgh with the intention of visiting just one solitary attraction: the Monroeville Mall. Built in 1969, the mall today consists of four anchor stores, more than 120 shops and restaurants, and 6,800 parking spots spread out over 1,128,747 square feet. But to splatter-film obsessives, it's more popularly known as the filming location of the original *Dawn of the Dead,* George Romero's hugely popular follow-up to his 1968 classic, *Night of the Living Dead.*

Generally agreed upon as Romero's best film, and certainly one of the best zombie movies ever produced, filming began in late 1977 and ended in February 1978. Romero's inspiration for the film happened during a visit to the mall in the early 1970s, when it was still one of the largest shopping centers of its type in the United States. He noticed the vacant faces and glazed-over eyes of the mall's shoppers, dutifully marching from store to store, and couldn't help comparing them to the living dead. A deal was struck with the mall's development company: Filming could take place between the hours of 10 P.M. and 6 A.M., when the mall was closed to the public.

Thousands of fans visit what is essentially a historical film set each year, and mall security has responded by tightening up considerably. Some visitors have even had their film or cameras confiscated after photographing memorable film locations, so consider yourself forewarned. Should you still care to brave the wilds of Monroeville Mall, however, do yourself a favor by first doing a quick Internet search; numerous fan sites list the exact locations of the film's most memorable scenes.

Horror fans might also consider making a pilgrimage to the borough of Evans City in Butler County; the opening graveyard scene in Romero's *Night of the Living Dead* was shot at the Evans City Cemetery. Much closer to the center of town is the East End neighborhood of Bloomfield, where legendary makeup artist and special effects man Tom Savini hangs his hat. Savini, who can often be seen around town, has worked on nearly every one of George Romero's films and today is a horror-film actor and director as well.

ST. ANTHONY'S CHAPEL

1700 Harpster St., Troy Hill, 412/323-9504
HOURS: Tue., Thurs., Sat.-Sun. 1-4 P.M.
COST: Free

Although technically located in the northern neighborhood of Troy Hill, which isn't within walking distance of the North Side's more well-known attractions, the legendary St. Anthony's Chapel is nevertheless worth the trek. Tourists and other out-of-towners don't often come here to pray, but instead to examine the church's incredible collection of sacred Catholic relics. The collection, in fact, is said to be the largest of its kind in the world, outside of the collection found at the Vatican in Rome. St. Anthony's now owns approximately 4,200 pieces that are kept in 800 separate cases.

The chapel was founded in 1883 by a Belgian known as Father Mollinger; the current collection began when he rescued a number of reliquaries from Germany. Some he discovered in European pawnshops in the late 1800s, a time when many monasteries had splintered, and the relics protected by those monasteries were stolen, lost, or otherwise misplaced.

The chapel itself is rather lovely, if not particularly large. Dark wood and stained-glass windows fill the interior, and the Stations of the Cross, beautifully carved out of wood, are remarkable.

As is the case with most collections of saints' relics, many of the pieces here come complete with a touch of creepiness: You'll see saints' teeth, skulls, and bone fragments, for instance, although it's worth noting that gnarly body parts do not make up the bulk of the collection. There are also photographs, scraps of clothing, and other interesting bits.

Don't miss the small museum dedicated to Father Mollinger, which contains medicines and other items he used when curing the sick and dying. There's also a small gift shop, and guided tours of the church are given every Sunday at 1, 2 and 3 P.M. Tours, museum admission, and church admission are all free.

ST. NICHOLAS CROATIAN
CATHOLIC CHURCH

24 Maryland Ave., Millvale, 412-821-3438
HOURS: Call in advance to set up an appointment to view the interior.   ●
COST: Free

A tiny parish whose now-shuttered sister church on the North Side was the first Catholic Croatian church in the United States, St. Nicholas Croatian Catholic Church has since been awarded status as both a National Landmark and a Pittsburgh Historical Landmark. Twenty murals by the Croatian artist Maxo Vanka are the church's claim to fame; many critics consider them to be his greatest masterpieces.

Painted in 1937 and 1941, and commissioned by the Rev. Albert Zagar, a fellow Croation who at the time worked as the church's pastor, the murals depict mostly secular scenes of cultural and political significance: Croatian mothers grieving over their war-dead sons and the images depicting the oppressed nations of Eastern Europe. According to Vanka, the majority of the images, of which only a few contain religious symbolism, were inspired by Hitler's Nazi occupation.

Oddly enough, St. Nicholas is equally famous for a rather unsettling reason: The church is widely believed to be haunted by the ghost of a former priest; church members and employees claim to have seen him tending the altar. When the North Side's St. Nicholas parish was closed and the congregation transferred to Millvale, many members refused to show up because of the rumored haunting. Even Vanka himself claimed to have spotted the priest while painting his famous murals.

RESTAURANTS

In Pittsburgh, hunting down civilized dining options can sometimes feel like a bit of an up-hill battle. It's not exactly a foodie's paradise; eating well here often means embracing calories and comfort food. Historically, this makes good sense: You wouldn't have expected those steel miners to tackle the mills on a diet of haute cuisine and foie gras, would you?

This is a town where both salads and sandwiches are frequently served with french fries on top, and where the double-carb nightmare known as a pierogi—a pasta dumpling filled with mashed potatoes—is considered something of a delicacy.

Which isn't to say that no interesting options exist. On the contrary, Pittsburgh today is rich in ethnic eateries and not only of the Italian and Eastern European varieties. A number of master sushi chefs now call Pittsburgh home, for instance. And throughout the East End alone, locals flock on a daily basis to affordable Thai, Vietnamese, Indian, Ethiopian, and Filipino restaurants. And contemporary cuisine, if a bit sparse, can certainly be found.

Your best bet, however, is to think of each neighborhood as a separate and unique dining experience: Bloomfield for Italian restaurants, Oakland for ethnic and late-night bites, and Mount Washington for romantic

© MARA RAGO

RESTAURANTS

HIGHLIGHTS

LOOK FOR ◖ TO FIND RECOMMENDED DINING.

◖ **Best Breakfast:** Forget about Eat 'n Park. For an old-school, completely authentic Pittsburgh breakfast, go clog your arteries at **DeLuca's Restaurant** in the Strip District, where Pittsburgh accents and gum-snapping waitresses are still delightfully in style (page 71).

◖ **Best Diner:** Although not technically an *authentic* greasy spoon, **Pamela's Diner** serves affordable American grub that tastes great. Plus, they have five locations citywide (page 72).

◖ **Best Patio:** For prime people-watching and a party atmosphere, set up shop at **Roland's Seafood Grill** in the heart of the Strip District (page 72).

◖ **Best Restaurant for a First Date:** Show off your worldly and adventurous side by taking that possible Mr. or Ms. Right to **Spice Island Tea House,** where cuisine from throughout Southeast Asia makes conversation starters a breeze (page 76).

◖ **Best Sunday Brunches:** Join the city's tattooed and pierced contingent for the phenomenally creative prix fixe Sunday brunch at the **The Zenith** (page 81). Browse through the antique room on your way out. Looking for something a bit classier? Station Square's **Grand Concourse** offers a luxurious (if slightly pricey) brunch experience (page 80).

◖ **Best View:** To dine and drink while taking in one of America's best-looking city skylines, head to Mount Washington's **Grandview Saloon** sometime after dark (page 87).

◖ **Best Beer Selection:** Find your favorite import or craft-brewed beer at Regent Square's **D's Six-Pax and Dogs** (page 96).

◖ **Best Neighborhood Restaurant:** Pittsburgh's East End residents converge at **Point Brugge Café,** a cozy bistro spot with European panache (page 100).

◖ **Best Coffee Shops:** With seven Pittsburgh locations, free wireless access, and wonderfully eclectic atmospheres, locals flock to the nearest **Crazy Mocha** (page 103). For a more refined and artistic experience, hit **COCA Café**, which serves an upscale Sunday brunch (page 102).

© DAN ELDRIDGE

fine dining. And in the South Side you can always head to a bar after dinner if it's not quite time for the evening to end.

In other words, gastronomic delights can be found in even the furthest reaches of Pittsburgh, as long as you're willing to peak around the proverbial corner.

PRICE KEY

$	Entrées under $10
$$	Entrées $10-20
$$$	Entrées over $20

Downtown   Map 1

RESTAURANTS

Attempting to eat Downtown with any sort of creativity can be an exercise in frustration to say the least; there simply isn't a lot to choose from. And should you find yourself working nine to five and searching out budget options, things get even stickier still. If you're truly in a bind, there's an abundance of fast food joints, chain cafés and sandwich shops in the area. You'll also find that a good number of the Cultural District's pricier places stay open late on weekends—and some weekdays—for the theater crowd.

AMERICAN

COMMON PLEA RESTAURANT $$$
310 Ross St., 412/281-5140
HOURS: Tue.-Fri. 11:30 A.M.-10 P.M., Sat. 5-10 P.M., closed Sun.-Mon.

A longtime Ross Street stalwart, the Common Plea caters mostly to Pittsburgh's law community, the majority of whom toil at the nearby courthouse or the area law offices. The atmosphere here is strictly white tablecloth, so don't arrive expecting too many surprises; entrées include fairly standard fish, meat, and pasta dishes. Show up during the evening hours, however, and the scene is slightly more exciting, with less lawyers and more moneyed urban achiever types in attendance. Particularly impressive is the Common Plea wine cellar, which features a decent collection of older vintages.

FRANKTUARY $
325 Oliver Ave., 412/288-0322,
http://franktuary.com
HOURS: Mon.-Fri. 8:30 A.M.-5 P.M.

Located on the ground floor of Trinity Episcopal Cathedral, the pious-minded young entrepreneurs of Franktuary serve a beguiling blend of New York–style hot dogs, gourmet dogs, and fruit shakes. The prices lean a bit on the steep side, but the quality simply speaks for itself, and only 100 percent beef franks and Boar's Head meats are sold. Might as well try something creative, like the The Mexico (a dog served in a tortilla with guacamole) or The El Greco (with feta and artichoke hearts). Soups, salads, and veggie dogs are on offer for vegetarians, and wireless access is free. As they say at Franktuary, "Franks Be to God!"

ORIGINAL OYSTER HOUSE $
20 Market Sq., 412/566-7925
HOURS: Mon.-Sat. 9 A.M.-11 P.M., closed Sun.

As the oldest bar and restaurant in the city, the men behind the counter at the historic Original Oyster House have been serving up giant fish sandwiches, breaded oysters, and cold mugs of beer for more than 130

MAKING SENSE OF PITTSBURGH CUISINE

There really is such a thing as Pittsburgh-specific cuisine. And while none of it is very good for you, all of it is almost addictively delicious. For starters, there's the legendary **Primanti Brothers sandwich,** which comes complete with french fries and coleslaw *inside*. The experience of gnawing on a roast beef sandwich at the counter and washing it down with a pint of Iron is authentic Pittsburgh to the core. According to Primanti's lore, the sandwich was created specifically for the hardworking men who unload produce trucks in the Strip District in the middle of the night. The idea was that they could eat an entire meal with one hand while still continuing to work with the other.

Pierogi and **kielbasa** are also considered regional staples. Both are of Polish origin; a pierogi is a boiled potato dumpling deep-fried in butter, and a kielbasa (pronounced "kiel-bah-see" in Pittsburghese) is a smoked sausage, usually made of pork. The **Bloomfield Bridge Tavern** is the place to go to sample locally prepared Polish food at its finest – try the sampler dish known as the Polish Platter. To buy your own pierogi, make the scene at **Pierogies Plus** (342 Island Ave., 412/331-2224, McKees Rocks), where Eastern European cooks fry 'em up Old World–style in a renovated gas station.

Order a steak salad at just about any restaurant in Southwestern Pennsylvania, and you'll likely find a generous bed of fries scattered atop. This is a regional riddle that even local culinary experts don't understand, but how can you not love a city that loads its salads with red meat and fried carbs?

And speaking of beef, what better time than now to order your next T-bone or porterhouse steak **"Pittsburgh rare?"** Do just that, and your meat will come charred on the outside and blood red on the inside. Allegedly, this trend reaches all the way back to Pittsburgh's steel-making era, when steelworkers would bring raw steaks to work, and then sear them on the nearest piece of burning hot metal just before lunchtime.

If you'd rather try a lighter local lunch fare, go for a **Devonshire sandwich.** The open-faced sandwich, made with either chicken or turkey, was invented here in 1936 by restaurateur Frank Blandi. Blandi is also responsible for the creation of Mount Washington's swanky Le Mont eatery.

Most folks are aware that **Heinz Ketchup** has its roots in the Steel City. H. J. Heinz himself even taught Sunday School at the Grace Methodist Church in Sharpsburg. But few are aware that the **Clark Bar** and the **Klondike Bar** were born here as well. The Clark Bar was invented way back in 1886 on the city's North Side, where the Clark Building still stands. Today it houses the editorial team of the *Pittsburgh Tribune-Review.* The Klondike Bar was created by **Isaly's,** a company whose ice cream in particular remains legendary throughout the region. And should you care to pass yourself off as a local, order another Islay's creation – **chipped ham** – the next time you're at the deli counter in a Pittsburgh grocery store. Chipped ham is very thinly sliced; you can also order it "chipped chopped," which is small clumps of the thinly sliced stuff. Enjoy!

years. So popular is this eatery locally, it's even been designated a historic landmark by the Pittsburgh History and Landmarks Foundation. With its location in the heart of Market Square, the atmosphere here—and the fast food—is much as it has been since the Oyster House's opening in 1870. Even Hollywood considers the restaurant particularly quaint: Scenes from 25 films, including *Striking Distance* and *Innocent Blood,* have been shot here.

TAP ROOM $$
530 William Penn Pl., 412/281-7100
HOURS: Sun.-Thurs. 11:30 A.M.-1 A.M., Fri.-Sat. 11:30 A.M.-2 A.M.

An English-style pub located in the lobby of the upmarket Omni William Penn Hotel, the Tap Room is the perfect spot to hold a casual business meeting. The menu here isn't anything special—just typical tavern-style food and plenty of beer—but the cozy country ambience is unlike anything else Downtown. If it's chilly outside, try a bowl of the locally legendary chili.

ASIAN
LEMON GRASS CAFÉ $$
124 6th St., 412/765-2222
HOURS: Mon.-Fri. 11 A.M.-9 P.M., Sat. 11 A.M.-1 P.M., Sun. 4-9 P.M.

No need to shed a tear about the closing of the crosstown Cambodian restaurant Phnom Penh; Lemon Grass Café is its sister restaurant and offers essentially the same menu but in a somewhat classier setting. (And with somewhat pricier entrées.) Curries seem to be winning the popularity contest here, but it's definitely worth the effort to try something slightly more adventurous, like the spicy mussels or the Haw

Mook (steamed fish with coconut milk). Some Chinese and Thai entrées are also on offer here; the pad thai frequently earns approving nods. Don't fancy a sit-down meal? Try the take-away stand out front, which is always open for business during Pirates home games.

SUKHOTHAI $
410 1st Ave., 412/261-4166
HOURS: Mon.-Fri. 11 A.M.-3 P.M. and 5-9 P.M.

Located in the former storefront of the much-loved Cambodian restaurant Phnom Penh, Sukhothai serves up simple but lovingly prepared Thai dishes, most often to office workers who take their lunch orders to go. The red and green curries are probably the most popular dishes here, but don't miss the especially toothsome ginger chicken, or for that matter, the homemade Thai Custard dessert.

INDIAN
SREE'S INDIAN FOOD $
701 Smithfield St., 412/288-9992, www.srees.com
HOURS: Mon.-Fri. 11:30 A.M.-3 P.M.

It doesn't get much simpler—or much cheaper—than Sree's, where flavorful and all-vegan South Indian food is served cafeteria-style. All meals are $4, and include a choice of three veggie selections on top of a massive bed of rice. The menu rotates daily, and chicken is available for an extra fee. Finishing a Sree's meal in one sitting is no easy task, and because of its substantial value, dining here daily has become almost religion to some Downtown desk jockeys, not to mention half the city's fleet of bike messengers. Sree's also has locations on Murray Avenue in Squirrel Hill and on CMU's campus.

MEDITERRANEAN

CASABLANCA BISTRO $$$

212 6th St., 412/281-3090,
www.casablanca212.com

HOURS: Tue.-Sun. 11:30 A.M.-2:30 P.M. and
4:30 P.M.-close

Presided over by the ebullient chef Omar Mediouni, Casablanca Bistro likes to refer to itself as an oasis within the Cultural District. And how! An inventive fusion of French, Spanish, and Moroccan cuisine, main courses here are organized as "tasting menus"; selections may include anything from paella to a Mediterranean-infused filet mignon to a traditional Moroccan casserole or couscous. And if you're in the mood for a bit of after-dinner repose, try stopping by on a Friday or Saturday night, when martini specials last until midnight. Even better, Saturday dinners come complete with live belly dancing.

MEXICAN

MADONNA'S RESTAURANT $

336 4th Ave., 412/281-4686

HOURS: Daily 11 A.M.-10 P.M.

Best of luck tracking down Madonna's. It's tucked away inside an office tower that you'll need to enter before reaching the restaurant itself. Once you make your way inside, be prepared to be greeted by all the usual suspects: office jockeys in full bummed-out repose, most with their noses in a newspaper. But no matter—it's the burritos you're here for, and Madonna's is well known for its generous portions and reasonable prices. This is the closest you'll get to a San Francisco–style burrito inside the city limits.

CONTEMPORARY AND NEW AMERICAN

CAFE ZAO $$$

649 Penn Ave., 412/325-7007

HOURS: Mon.-Fri. 11:30 A.M.-2:30 P.M. and
5-9 P.M., Sat. 5-10 P.M., Sun. 4-9 P.M.

Located next door to the O'Reilly Theater complex in Downtown's Cultural District, Cafe Zao boasts a modern Mediterranean fusion menu assembled with a strong Portuguese influence (including an impressively curated Portuguese wine list). This should come as quite a pleasant surprise to any foodie who has previously dined at chef and owner Toni Pais's now-defunct eatery, Baum Vivant, a Portuguese restaurant that for years was one of the city's consistent top draws. The majority of entrées here are stunningly prepared; meat, fish, and poultry are served with light Asian touches, and all dinners are served with a sweet potato puree and vegetable side. For a less ostentatious and more affordable example of Pais's culinary genius, check out Cafe Zinho (see listing under *Shadyside* restaurants), a hidden gem located not far from the East Liberty border.

NINE ON NINE $$$

900 Penn Ave., 412/338-6463

HOURS: Tue.-Sat. 5-10 P.M.

One of the most recent (and most welcome) additions to the Cultural District's contemporary dining scene, Nine on Nine is the sort of elegant and rarified establishment not often found in Midwestern or Rust Belt locales. Both the menu and the ambience here are striking; grilled quail, wing of stingray, and Amish chicken are just a few of the unusual offerings. The wine list is 29 names long, and the artfully prepared dessert list is said to be as august and grand as the entrées.

OPUS $$$
107 6th St., 412/992-2005

HOURS: Daily 6:30 A.M.-2 P.M. and 5 P.M.-midnight
Located inside the Renaissance Hotel, it probably makes good sense that Opus is not the sort of place where you'll be running into a lot of locals. This is contemporary dining for out-of-towners with expense accounts, mostly, but even if you call Pittsburgh home, it's worth a second look: Starting with its contemporary interior design and ending with its inventive menu of fish and meat entrées, Opus is one of the Downtown area's wisest choices for diners looking to kick the quality and ambience scale up a notch. And as an added bonus, Opus and the Renaissance are both known as not-shabby spots for celebrity spotting.

SIX PENN KITCHEN $$$
146 6th St., 412/566-7366,
www.sixpennkitchen.com

HOURS: Mon.-Thurs. 11 A.M.-11 P.M., Fri. 11 A.M.-midnight, Sat. 3 P.M.-midnight
The Six Penn Kitchen management team had a simple goal when designing the look and feel of this recent addition to the Cultural District: Create a modern and casually sophisticated American bistro, but let the service be casual enough and the food be comfortable enough so as to not frighten away the locals. Talk about successfully studying your target market! The menu changes frequently here; expect some variation of what might be called American Classic: Grilled chicken sandwiches, four-cheese pastas, wood oven-roasted pizzas. Also, keep your eyes peeled for Six Penn Kitchen's more eclectic offerings, like the lobster mac 'n' cheese.

SEAFOOD

ORIGINAL FISH MARKET $$$
1001 Liberty Ave., 412/227-3657,
www.originalfishmarket.com

HOURS: Mon.-Fri. 11 A.M.-1 A.M., Sat.-Sun. 4 P.M.-1 A.M.
Tucked deep inside Downtown's Westin Hotel, the Original Fish Market serves what many claim to be some of the city's best sushi. (And for what it's worth, this author concurs.) A fantastic fresh seafood menu is also on offer—on it you'll find grouper, seared king salmon, ahi tuna, grilled swordfish, and the daily catch, among other house specialties. Better still is the fact that the Fish Market keeps such late hours; aside from a few greasy spoons on the South Side and the East End, this is one of Pittsburgh's very few late-night dining options.

RESTAURANTS

Strip District   Map 1

Pittsburgh may not have a Chinatown, but it does have the Strip District—an international neighborhood filled with everything from Asian grocery stores to Italian delis.

AMERICAN

◖ DELUCA'S RESTAURANT $$
2015 Penn Ave., 412/566-2195

HOURS: Mon.-Sat. 6 A.M.-3 P.M., Sun. 7 A.M.-3 P.M.
A truly rough-around-the-edges diner in the finest greasy spoon tradition, De-Luca's has held legendary status among Pittsburgh's breakfast aficionados for eons now; this is the place to bring an out-of-town visitor who wants to experience the *real* Steel City. The menu is exactly what

you'd expect: massive plates full of eggs, bacon, and buttered toast. For something a bit different, try the fruit-filled pancakes; a regular order is so large you may not be able to finish it in one sitting. Or go for the breakfast burrito, but try not to snicker at the slices of processed American cheese melted on top. Remember: You've come for the *experience*.

【 PAMELA'S DINER $$
60 21st St., 412/281-6366

HOURS: Mon.-Fri. 7 A.M.-3 P.M., Sat. 7 A.M.-4 P.M., Sun. 8 A.M.-3 P.M.

A much loved mini-chain with five locations throughout the city (Shadyside, Squirrel Hill, Oakland, Millvale, and the Strip), Pamela's Diner is your best bet for a quality, even-tempered breakfast experience; last night's date will feel just as comfortable munching on toast here as will your visiting parents. Truthfully though, the fare at any given Pamela's isn't much different than your average greasy spoon—it's the crowd you'll run into here that makes the difference: students, hipsters, and young parents, mostly. The pancakes here are what most folks rave about, although egg obsessives should take care not to miss the omelets, which are some of the most satisfying in the city.

PRIMANTI BROTHERS $
46 18th St., 412/263-2142, www.primantibros.com

HOURS: Daily 24 hours

Much more than just a restaurant, the original Primanti Brothers location in the Strip is a destination, a tourist attraction, and a very proud chapter of Pittsburgh history. The rumors you've heard are true: A huge pile of

© MARA RAGO

preparing for the lunchtime rush at Primanti Brothers, where sandwiches come with french fries inside

french fries, and sometimes a fried egg, go *inside* the sandwich, which is already stacked sky-high with coleslaw and your choice of artery-clogging meat (roast beef and pastrami are favorites). Soups and salads can also be ordered, but most folks don't bother. With five city locations and six more in the suburbs, you've got few excuses to miss this venerable Pittsburgh institution. And yes, vegetarians can always order sandwiches without meat.

【 ROLAND'S SEAFOOD GRILL $$
1904 Penn Ave., 412/261-3401, www.rolandsseafoodgrill.com

HOURS: Sun.-Thurs. 11 A.M.-1 A.M., Fri.-Sat. 11 A.M.-2 A.M.

A little nervous to try seafood in a landlocked locale like the 'Burgh? Don't be. Roland's serves an especially fresh and varied selection of all things oceanic at its nearly always-packed seafood bar—everything from lobster tails to the universally popular beer-battered fish sandwich. Arrive later in the evening, and you'll find Roland's transformed into a rowdy nightspot. The two-level deck is especially popular; wander by on a weekend night and you won't be able to miss the roaring hoards holding court high above Penn Avenue.

ASIAN

SUSHI KIM $$
1241 Penn Ave., 412/281-9956,
www.sushikim.com

HOURS: Tue.-Thurs. 11:30 A.M.-10 P.M., Fri.-Sat. 11:30 A.M.-10:30 P.M., Sun. 5-9 P.M.

Tucked into a depressing stretch of Penn Avenue between Downtown and the Strip, Sushi Kim is a local diamond in the rough: The decor exists somewhere between Asian pop culture and hipster kitsch, and the entrée list is split evenly between traditional Japanese and Korean dishes—about 40 in all. But most come here for the sushi, which is some of the best in the Strip. (Other smart options include the take-away counter at Wholey's on Penn Avenue and at Benkovitz Seafoods on Smallman Street.) Particularly amusing are the massive sushi boats, a sort of combo platter for the young-at-heart fresh-fish lover.

CAFÉS

LA PRIMA ESPRESSO COMPANY $
205 21st St., 412/281-1922, www.laprima.com

HOURS: Mon.-Sat. 6A.M.-4 P.M., Sun. 8 A.M.-3 P.M.

Some call La Prima the most authentic espresso shop in Pittsburgh, and if you show up during the morning rush,

---

SMOKING BAN

The county of Allegheny, which includes the city of Pittsburgh, recently voted to pass a ban on smoking inside bars and restaurants, but a number of rather confusing amendments to the law have been introduced. As a result, no one seems to be quite clear on exactly when the ban will begin. At the time of writing, the ruling was scheduled to go into effect sometime during the summer of 2007. According to the written ordinance, however, a number of rather curious loopholes exist; the strangest of which states that smoking will be completely legal throughout the ban's first two years at any bar that has less than 10 employees and receives less than 10 percent of its revenue from food sales.

Other unusual amendments have also been introduced. Smokers will still be allowed to light up at volunteer-staffed events, for instance. But if that same smoker happens to come within 15 feet of any business where smoking is banned, he or she can be legally fined.

For the time being, smokers would probably be wise to simply play it safe. While drinking or dining at a Pittsburgh-area bar or restaurant, take a quick look around you to make sure others are smoking before lighting up. If you see no cigarettes in action, ask your server if smoking is permitted.

---

you'll see why. Clusters of middle-aged men gather around the front counter with espresso and Italian-language newspapers, and the baristas are consistently at the top of their game. (Look for the leaf or heart design that'll likely be poured onto the

RESTAURANTS

RESTAURANTS

top of your latte or cappuccino.) Even drip coffee is something special here; there's almost always a Central American fair-trade or shade-grown selection on offer.

CARIBBEAN

KAYA $$
2000 Smallman St., 412/261-6565,
www.bigburrito.com/kaya
HOURS: Mon.-Wed. 11:30 A.M.-10 P.M., Thurs.-Sat. 11:30 A.M.-11 P.M., Sun. noon-9 P.M.

An island paradise in the heart of the Strip's warehouse district, Kaya represents the Caribbean arm of the local Big Burrito restaurant group. This is certainly Pittsburgh's premiere locale for Jamaican jerk chicken and Cuban sandwiches, and what's more, the menu changes daily, so dining here often feels as much like a vicarious travel experience as it does a culinary adventure. The clientele leans toward the young, beautiful, and trust-funded, and the happy hour is a scene unto itself; saddle up for tropical island drinks or a martini.

CONTEMPORARY AND NEW AMERICAN

ELEVEN $$$
1150 Smallman St., 412/201-5656,
www.bigburrito.com/eleven
HOURS: lunch Mon.-Fri. 11:30 A.M.-2 P.M., dinner Mon.-Thurs. 5-10 P.M., Fri.-Sat. 5-11 P.M., Sun. 5-9 P.M.

The aptly named Eleven (it's the 11th cre-

ation of the Big Burrito restaurant group) has lately become an especially strong cornerstone of the fine contemporary dining scene in Pittsburgh. The philosophy is contemporary, too: As a serious adherent to the slow food movement, Chef Greg Alauzen and his four-star charges take pains to include seasonal, regional items to most dishes. You can expect all the usual suspects, of course: Elysian Fields lamb, pulled pork. But it's the gracefully prepared plates that truly make the food at Eleven such a high edible art. The wine list here is nearly 150 names long.

SNACKS AND DESSERTS

KLAVON'S ICE CREAM PARLOR $
2801 Penn Ave., 412-434/0451,
www.klavonsicecream.com
HOURS: Mon.-Tue. 10 A.M.-5 P.M., Wed.-Fri. 10 A.M.-9 P.M., Sat.-Sun. noon-9 P.M.

You wouldn't necessarily know it from walking past the uninspiring facade, but this art deco drugstore and ice cream shop is the real deal. It opened way back in 1925, and all the trimmings are original, including the marble soda fountain and its attendant swivel stools, which are designed to look like soda bottle caps. Along with the regular assortment of sundaes and banana splits, Klavon's also stocks a wide array of old school–style candy and even boasts a sandwich and soup menu for the sugar-phobic.

Oakland   Map 2

This is Pittsburgh's university district, which means affordable pub grub, fast food, and wonderful ethnic restaurants can be found almost anywhere. Try to avoid the chains, however, and instead try something new and different that grabs your interest. Oakland is a literal bounty for the food lover, and new spots serving unusual fare open quite frequently.

AMERICAN

FUEL AND FUDDLE $
212 Oakland Ave., 412/682-3473,
www.fuelandfuddle.com
HOURS: Daily 11 A.M.-2 A.M.

A popular college eatery centered around the dual themes of bar food and good beer, Fuel and Fuddle is the perfect place to eat when you can't quite decide what you're in the mood for. The menu consists of large plates of pub grub and finger foods, such as chicken wings, Thai skewers, jack cheese quesadillas, and nacho plates. Beer specials change daily.

HEMINGWAY'S $
3911 Forbes Ave., 412/621-4100
HOURS: Mon.-Sat. 11 A.M.-2 P.M., closed Sun.

Once a must-see stop on the city's bohemian café circuit, Hemingway's is now more of an epicenter for observing primal meathead behavior. The beer doth flow here, and boy is it cheap. But get here before dark falls, and you might just find the English-pub atmosphere and its attendant pub-grub menu rather charming. What's more, Hemingway's commands an enviable location on the University of Pittsburgh campus, making it a perfect place to meet up for a burger

or sandwich before a raging night out. Just make sure you go easy on the $1 Miller Lites, bro.

UNION GRILL $$
413 S. Craig St., 412/681-8620
HOURS: Mon.-Thurs. 11:30 A.M.-10 P.M., Fri.-Sat. 11:30 A.M.-midnight, Sun. 11:30 A.M.-9 P.M.

If it's simple, hearty American fare you're after, you won't do much better in this stretch of town than the Union Grill. Burgers are the really big mover here, clocking in at around a half pound after cooking. Just about every entrée includes more food than the average person can consume in one sitting, though, from the sandwiches and veggie wraps to the chicken entrées and crab cakes. If you've managed to save room for dessert, make it a slice of the homemade pie, and when the weather's warm, request a sidewalk table for optimum Craig Street people-watching.

ASIAN

★LULU'S NOODLES $
400 S. Craig St., 412/681-3333
HOURS: Daily 11 A.M.-10 P.M.

Living somewhere in between cafeteria-style casual dining and chic urban café, Lulu's Noodles is a favorite destination for budget-conscious Pitt and CMU undergrads looking for good value in a stylish setting. Portion sizes are generous, too: Order a noodle dish—the Singapore rice noodles are a good bet—and you'll have a tough time cleaning your plate. Noodle soups are also recommended, and since Lulu's shares a counter and a kitchen with its sister restaurant, Yum Wok Pan Asian Diner, you're practically guaranteed to find something on one of the two menus that appeals—even if it's just a take-away bubble tea.

OISHII BENTO $$

119 Oakland Ave., 412/687-3335,
www.oishiibento.com

HOURS: Mon.-Sat. 11 A.M.-8:30 P.M.

What a concept: A traditional Japanese *bento* restaurant right in the heart of the university district, featuring a mini sushi counter, Japanese-style floor seating, and even a selection of Korean dishes. No wonder Oishii Bento—the name means "Yummy Lunchbox"—is such a raging success. Prices are reasonable, the menu is completely unique, and each order of food is its very own work of art. For a truly filling lunch, go with one of the meat or veggie rice bowls. For pure fun, though, simply pick and choose at random; aside from sleeping in and skipping class, Oishii Bento is certainly one of Oakland's most amusing midday distractions.

◖ SPICE ISLAND TEA HOUSE $$

253 Atwood St., 412/687-8821,
www.spiceislandtea.com

HOURS: Mon.-Thurs. 11:30 A.M.-9 P.M., Fri.-Sat. 11:30 A.M.-10 P.M.

A pan-Asian legend that for eons now has been introducing the Oakland college community to Indonesian, Burmese, Thai, Cambodian, and Filipino food, Spice Island Tea House is one of the area's few can't-miss institutions. Even a bad meal here would still be fun, what with the charming mismatched furniture and thatched-roof vibe. But nearly every Spice Island entrée is a crowd pleaser, especially the Indonesian and Thai rice dishes. (Some

of the Burmese soups can be a bit scary.) Sadly, management has recently changed the formerly liberal BYOB policy, so prepare to pay a corkage fee. Or, consider choosing a loose-leaf tea from the front counter's impressive collection.

SUSHI BOAT $$

128 Oakland Ave., 412/681-1818

HOURS: Mon.-Fri. 10:30 A.M.-9 P.M., Sat. 11 A.M.-9 P.M., closed Sun.

Slightly cheaper than Oishii Bento across the street (and with a bit more of a low-rent cafeteria vibe), Sushi Boat tends to fill up fast during peak lunch hours, especially with Pitt students grabbing a bite between classes. Both Chinese and Japanese dishes are served here, although maki, nigiri, and sashimi sushi is the big draw; expect to pay around $1.50 per piece. For the biggest bang for your buck, go with the vegetarian rice bowl or the seafood fried rice platter.

CAFÉS

KIVA HAN $

420 S. Craig St., 412/687-6355 and 3533 Forbes Ave., 412/697-3391, www.kivahan.com

HOURS: Mon.-Thurs. 7 A.M.-11 P.M., Fri. 7 A.M.-midnight, Sun. 8 A.M.-11 P.M.

With two locations in Oakland, Kiva Han is the neighborhood's only choice for non-chain coffee. Good thing its espresso, sandwiches, and pastries are so good, huh? If you're choosing between the two locations, head to Craig Street if you want big crowds, people-watching, original art on the walls, and the occasional late-evening folk or electronic music event. The smaller Forbes location is generally quieter, emptier, and more appropriate for serious studying.

CAFÉ CULTURE IN SHARPSBURG

Whether you're planning on staying in Pittsburgh for two weeks or two years, it's quite likely that the somewhat secluded neighborhood of Sharpsburg hasn't yet found its way onto your itinerary. But if it's quality cuisine you're after, you'd be wise to pay the area a visit. Unassuming and somewhat hardscrabble, Sharpsburg and a number of its surrounding communities have lately sprouted large numbers of phenomenal cafés and restaurants, many of them largely undiscovered even by locals.

The most popular of all is probably Sharpsburg's **Bona Terra** (908 Main St., 412/781-8210, Tue.-Thurs. 5-10 P.M., Fri.-Sat. 5-11 P.M.), a small and expensive fine-dining establishment with just over a dozen tables and contemporary American cuisine on the menu. If the name rings a bell, you may have seen it mentioned in *Apple's America*, a travel book penned by legendary *New York Times* reporter R. W. Apple, Jr. We recommend making reservations at least two weeks in advance.

Practically right next door is the aptly named **Cafe on Main** (914 Main St., 412/782-2248), which serves some of best-tasting (and best-looking) breakfasts in town. Not far from Bona Terra and across the street is **Club Sandwich & Deli** (711 Main St., 412/781-6860), which boasts a truly impressive menu of high-quality deli sandwiches, with a number of house specialty sandwiches and signature sauces to choose from.

Located just up the street a stretch, in a building that formerly housed a pet grooming business, is **The Gran Canal Caffe** (1014 N. Canal St., 412/781-2546, Tue.-Sat. 5:30-10:30 P.M., closed Sun.-Mon.), a tiny pasta shop noted for its authenticity and its to-die-for desserts. Although Gran Canal likes to refer to itself as "Pittsburgh's best-kept culinary secret," this is another spot at which you'd be wise to call ahead and reserve a seat (apparently, the secret's out).

Finally, there's **CC's** (2218 Main St., 412/784-8338), where homemade pasta, garlic bread, and homemade key lime pie are offered. (And by the way, don't be fooled by CC's modest exterior, which looks not unlike a crumbling biker bar.)

If you travel a bit farther past CC's and toward the Waterworks outdoor shopping center in Aspinwall, you'll pass two more eateries of note: The **Aspinwall Grille** (211 Commercial Ave., 412/782-6542, www.aspinwallgrille.com), which is known for its hamburgers, huge sandwiches, and gourmet entrées, and **Luma** (8 Brilliant Ave., 412/781-0355, www .lumapgh.com, Mon.-Thurs. 11 A.M.-10 P.M., Fri.-Sat. 11 A.M.-11 P.M., Sun. 4-9 P.M.), which offers a lunch, dinner, and banquet menu with contemporary American and Asian fusion choices coexisting beautifully side by side.

INDIAN
INDIA GARDEN $$
328 Atwood St., 412/682-3000,
www.indiagarden.net
HOURS: Daily 11:30 A.M.-1 A.M.

Expect a somewhat chaotic atmosphere at India Garden, one of Oakland's most popular Indian joints (and most authentic, according to some). Every year, it seems, the food here pulls some sort of award from a Pittsburgh publication (including the *Pittsburgh City Paper*'s Best Indian award), and you'll certainly understand the hype after trying any of the toothsome curries, chicken tandooris, or *tikka masalas*. Vegetarians also have cause to rejoice, as the nonmeat dishes are absolutely celestial. (Try the eggplant.) Dinners are 50 percent off daily 4–6 P.M. and 10 P.M.–1 A.M.

STAR OF INDIA $$
412 S. Craig St., 412/681-5700
HOURS: lunch daily 11:30 A.M.-2:30 P.M., dinner Sun.-Thurs. 5-10 P.M., Fri.-Sat. 5-10:30 P.M.

Northern Indian fare is served almost exclusively here, meaning curries and tandoors especially. But unlike at Atwood Street's slightly more jubilant India Garden, the scene can be a bit staid. That said, Star of India is a decent place to bring your parents, or a date that you're trying to impress. Definitely order appetizers of samosas and *nan* (flatbread); both are particularly toasty and crispy, but with a nice softness on the inside. The lamb and vegetarian entrées here are also popular, and when dinner's done, take a stroll through the Indian grocery store across the street for imported soft drinks.

ITALIAN
LUCCA $$$
317 S. Craig St., 412/682-3310
HOURS: Mon.-Thu 11:30 A.M.-2 P.M. and 5-10 P.M., Fri.-Sat. 5-11 P.M., Sun. 4:30-9 P.M.

Assuming you aren't bothered by the chants of the Animal Liberation activists out front, who frequently enjoy protesting the restaurant's use of foie gras, you'll likely fall in love with Lucca, one of the city's more luxurious Italian experiences. Young movers and shakers and swooning couples on dates flock here for the fettuccine, couscous, and caramelized onions and also for the quaint decor and the staff's unmatchable attention to detail. If money's not an issue and you've got a discriminating palate to impress, Lucca's your place.

ZARRA'S $$
3887 Bigelow Blvd., 412/682-8296
HOURS: Mon.-Sat. 5-11 P.M.

Formerly an infamous punk nightclub known as the Electric Banana, Zarra's is now the sort of place that feels something like an episode of *The Sopranos* come to life. Fans of eclectic dining will be especially pleased; the atmosphere here is probably best described as "grandma's kitchen meets mafioso." Interestingly, many of the menu items are old family recipes, including an especially well-made hand-rolled ravioli. And if you can't manage to pick just one entrée from the massive menu, go with a sampler plate that offers a curious but delectable blend of meats and pastas.

MEXICAN
MAD MEX $$
370 Atwood St., 412/681-5656,
www.madmex.com
HOURS: Daily 11 A.M.-1 A.M.

For lovers of quality Tex-Mex and massive food portions, it doesn't get much better than Mad Mex, a locally based restaurant-and-bar chain. The menu here is an inventive collection of burritos, enchiladas, or quesadillas with a twist: portobello mushrooms inside, say, or tofu or chickpea chili. If it's the truly sublime you're after, go with the Dance Marathon Burrito (spinach, portobellos, and marinated chicken) or the Kristy's Big Sister's Red Velvet Burrito, complete with *pico de gallo* and zucchini inside. Graciously, food is half-off every night 11 P.M.–1 A.M.; expect long lines. Other locations are in Monroeville, Robinson, the South Hills, and the North Hills.

MIDDLE EASTERN

ALI BABA $$
404 S. Craig St., 412/682-2829,
www.ibp.com/pit/ali-baba
HOURS: Mon.-Fri. 11:30 A.M.-2:30 P.M. and 4:30-
9:45 P.M.

A longtime Craig Street favorite, Ali Baba is the Steel City's preeminent Middle Eastern deal. ("The best Middle Eastern restaurant in Pittsburgh," according to *Pittsburgh* magazine.) And while prices may indeed be fit for a college-style budget, it's easy to pretend you're living large here, what with the decidedly classy decor and ambience. In other words, a student dive this most definitely is not, although Pitt and CMU types (and their parents and professors) are almost always in attendance. Food-wise, it's tough to go wrong, although the Shish Kebab Dinner is particularly inviting, as is the Shiek El-Mahshi (roasted eggplant with seasoned lamb). The baklava is an especially agreeable dessert; be aware that the BYO policy extends to wine only.

SNACKS AND DESSERTS

DAVE AND ANDY'S $
207 Atwood St., 412/681-9906
HOURS: Mon.-Fri. 11:30 A.M.-10 P.M., Sat.-Sun.
noon-10 P.M.

Without a doubt, this non-chain store is the finest purveyor of ice cream in Pittsburgh. The confections at Dave and Andy's are good for a reason: Ice cream is made the old-fashioned way, with wooden churns and rock salt. The result? Fresh, perfectly creamy cones offered in a regularly rotating selection of flavors. Ask for yours in a homemade waffle cone, which includes a handful of M&Ms that plug up the hole on the bottom.

THE ORIGINAL HOT DOG SHOP $
3901 Forbes Ave., 412/621-7388,
www.originalhotdogshop.com
HOURS: Sun.-Thurs. 10 A.M.-3:30 A.M., Fri.-Sat.
10 A.M.-5 A.M.

Much more than just a corner hot dog and pizza shop, The O, as it's known locally, is nothing less than a Pittsburgh institution. Opened in 1960, it's probably safe to say that anyone who's ever spent time in the nearby Pitt dorms has a story to tell about The O. The natural dogs are world class, but most come here for the ridiculously large baskets of fries with melted cheese on top, or the cheap pizzas, or at least a six-pack. The O is always at its best after dark, when things are crowded and chaotic. And since rumors of the shop's impending demise have been floating around for months now, you'd do well to soak up the atmosphere while it's still cookin'.

RESTAURANTS

South Side   Map 3

The South Side is widely known as party central to most Pittsburghers, who fill the pubs and taverns here on weekends. East Carson is where you'll find most of the action, including the majority of good places to eat. You'll find some ethnic options here, including a wonderful French restaurant, a good number of Italian places, and two decent Japanese locales. Naturally, pizza shops abound.

AMERICAN

FAT HEADS $$

1805 E. Carson St., 412/431-7433,
www.fatheads.com

HOURS: Mon.-Thurs. 11 A.M.-midnight, Fri.-Sat.
11 A.M.-1 A.M., Sun. 11 A.M.-11 P.M.

Fat Heads is easily one of the South Side's best bar and grill joints, although it's more popularly known as a premiere East Carson locale in which to get good and tanked.

Clearly, that has much to do with the three dozen or so imports and craft brews on tap, but pick up a menu between pints and you'll find that Fat Heads has much more than just alcohol on offer: in short, a pub-grub-on-steroids menu featuring mostly burgers, sandwiches, and the massive (and massively popular) "headwiches." Diners watching their waistlines, in others words, will want to proceed to Fat Heads with extreme prejudice.

⟨ GRAND CONCOURSE $$$

100 W. Station Square Dr., 412/261-1717,
www.stationsquare.com/grandconcourse

HOURS: Mon.-Fri. 11:30 A.M.-2:30 P.M. and 4:30-10 P.M., Sat. 4:30-11 P.M., Sun. 10:30 A.M.-2:30 P.M.

Located in the concourse of the old P&LE Railway station, and with seating for 500, the Grand Concourse is quite accurately known as one of Pittsburgh's most elegant and stately

Fat Heads, a burger-and-microbrewed-beer joint, South Side

© FABIAN BAUTISTA

VEGAN AND VEGGIE-FRIENDLY OPTIONS

Just as the average Pittsburgher much prefers the taste of a cold IC Light over, say, that of a late vintage California Chardonnay, so too does the Steel City prefer meat over, well, no meat. But vegetarians, and even vegans, need not despair: Pittsburgh is also home to a reasonable number of quality, vegan and veggie-friendly eateries.

The Zenith on Pittsburgh's South Side is not only a vegetarian restaurant but also an antique shop and an art gallery. Certainly try the hugely popular Tofishy tofu sandwich, and don't miss the always-packed Sunday brunch (11 A.M.-3 P.M.), with its ever-rotating menu.

The formerly all-vegetarian **Hunan Kitchen** in Squirrel Hill still offers a decent selection of meat-free Asian dishes. A word to the wise: Steer clear of the tofu.

Any of the area's four **Mad Mex** locations are happy to veg-o-fy practically anything on the menu; the truly hardcore can even request soy cheese and soy sour cream! In fact, the entire family of eateries owned by the Big Burrito Restaurant Group – which includes **Kaya** in the Strip District and **Casbah, Umi,** and **Soba** in Shadyside – are quite good about catering to non-meat and -dairy eaters.

While meat is in plentiful distribution at Pittsburgh's only Ethiopian restaurant, **Abay Ethiopian Cuisine** in East Liberty (near Shadyside), vegetarians will find more than enough options on the menu to keep their jaws busy as well. Abay is also a great place for groups.

A number of cafés and coffeeshops in Pittsburgh serve vegetarian-friendly cuisine, including Oakland's **Kiva Han** for snacks and sandwiches, and the **Quiet Storm** (5430 Penn Ave., 412/661-9355) in Friendship, which offers a full menu and a fantastic Sunday brunch. Also try the café at the **East End Food Co-Op** (7516 Meade St., 412/242-3598) in Point Breeze for great soups.

RESTAURANTS

places in which to dine, complete with fully refurbished Edwardian-era architectural trimmings. It's also the largest restaurant in the city. The somewhat timid menu is largely seafood based; typical entrées include lobster ravioli, coconut shrimp, and Maryland crab cakes. For a slightly more informal experience, ask to be seated in the Gandy Dancer Bar, where oysters and clams can be ordered alongside olde-style cocktails.

◖ THE ZENITH $$
86 S. 26th St., 412/481-4833, www.zenithpgh.com
HOURS: Wed.-Sat. 11:30 A.M.-9 P.M., Sun. brunch 11 A.M.-3 P.M.

A vegetarian café, an art gallery, and an antique shop, all underneath the same roof? Believe it. The Zenith—formerly known as The Zenith Tea Room—is renowned locally for its $10 prix fixe Sunday brunch, where diners help themselves to an astounding spread of pastas, cakes, and breakfast-style entrées. But the weekly menu is equally interesting, consisting of creatively prepared casseroles, stews, and meat-free sandwiches. After your meal, stroll through Zenith's eclectic collection of collectibles and vintage clothing. And definitely don't miss the rest rooms, which are some of the most amusingly decorated in the city.

RESTAURANTS

ASIAN

CAMBOD-ICAN KITCHEN $

1701 E. Carson St., 412/381-6199,
www.cambodicankitchen.com

HOURS: Tue. 3-11 P.M., Wed.-Thurs. noon-11 P.M., Fri. noon-4 A.M., Sat. 2 P.M.-4 A.M., closed Sun.-Mon.

Originally a legendary street food cart that fed the hungry barhopping masses of East Carson Street until the wee hours of most mornings, Cambod-ican Kitchen—now reinvented as a sit-down restaurant—has returned to Pittsburgh after a nearly three-year hiatus. Cambod-ican purists need not fret, however—the original "Cat on a Stick" (chicken shish kabob) is still for sale. So too is a wonderfully adventurous menu of fried noodles and wontons, curry rolls and fresh spring rolls, and a sampler platter big enough to share with one or two friends.

NAKAMA JAPANESE
STEAK HOUSE $$$

1611 E. Carson St., 412/381-6000,
www.eatatnakama.com

HOURS: Mon.-Sat. 11 A.M.-1 A.M., Sun. 1 P.M.-9 P.M.

Depending on where you sit and what you order at the 200-seat, über-trendy Nakama, a culinary experience here can become just about anything you'd like. Large groups and parties, for instance, flock to the smokeless hibachi tables for filet mignon and hibachi scallops, while late-night arrivals and the happy hour crowd gather around the massive island bar for carafes of sake and pints of Japanese beer. Arriving solo? Try straddling up to the sushi bar, where along with a comprehensive menu of sashimi and veggie-based rolls, health-conscious diners can order raw fish with brown rice to go.

THAI ME UP $$

1925 E. Carson St., 412/488-8893

HOURS: Mon.-Thurs. 11 A.M.-10 P.M., Fri. 11 A.M.-10:30 P.M., Sat. noon-10:30 P.M.

A fairly recent addition to the city's newly trendy Thai restaurant scene, Thai Me Up is primarily a take-out joint with a reputation for moan-inducing pad thai, curries, and rice dishes. And while the menu offers a wide range of fusion-esque items for both vegetarians and meat-eaters alike, even ravenous carnivores should try the tofu with peanut sauce, not to mention the spicy basil noodles. Eating in is certainly allowed here—there's seating for about 20—and the atmosphere is contemporarily clean and even a bit sexy. Looking for a particularly sensual experience? Try dipping into the lemongrass soup, but please, try to keep the discernible outbursts to a minimum.

CAFÉS

BEEHIVE $

1327 E. Carson St., 412/488-4483

HOURS: Mon.-Thurs. 9 A.M.-1 A.M., Fri.-Sun. 9 A.M.-2 A.M.

One of Pittsburgh's most iconoclastic locales in which to sip organic coffee and suck down Camel Lights while discussing Sartre, the Beehive has been many different things to many different angst-ridden teens since its opening in 1991. What it remains, however, is a pleasantly comfortable way to immerse one's self into the city's bohemian subculture. And while the Beehive's interior decor vibe is strictly thrift store—think mismatched furniture and kitschy wall murals—more recent additions have included a nonsmoking room and an outdoor patio perfect for warm-weather days. What else? There's also pinball, wireless access, used

the much-loved Beehive, a favorite among the city's most eccentric and artistic caffeine fiends

paperbacks in the vending machine, and the best-pierced baristas in Pittsburgh. In other words, the spirit of the South Side, all beneath the same roof.

CONTEMPORARY AND NEW AMERICAN

CAFE ALLEGRO $$$

51 S. 12th St., 412/481-7788,
www.cafeallegropittsburgh.com

HOURS: Sun.-Thurs. 5-10 P.M., Fri.-Sat. 5-11 P.M.

Long known as a local barometer of excellence in elegant dining, Cafe Allegro is the place to arrive when you're looking for simple intimacy and understated professionalism. The seasonal, contemporary menu leans toward continental cuisine and Mediterranean-style dishes, with house specials such as stuffed salmon and filet mignon with gorgonzola cheese leading the charge. And

while your pocketbook might not be pleased by night's end, your palate most certainly will. Neither of which should come as too much of a surprise from a restaurant whose stated mission is to provide its customers with "excellent experiences... and the highest quality dining value available anywhere on the planet."

CAFE DU JOUR $$

1107 E. Carson St., 412/488-9695

HOURS: Tue.-Sat. 11:30 A.M.-10 P.M.

With the ambience of an intimate European bistro, the flavor of Cafe du Jour has lately been tweaked by its two new owners—both of them young chefs who've introduced to the menu an impressive array of inventive Californian cuisine. This may not sound like much, but in a city where contemporary dining always seems to revolve around dishes from the old country, Cafe du Jour stands out in spades. And don't be afraid to let the servers guide your choices here, as some are wont to do; after all, everything from the portobello soup to the cheese plates to the cassoulet is simply stunning. No credit cards.

DISH $$$
128 S. 17th St., 412/390-2012
HOURS: Mon.-Sat. 4 P.M.-1:45 A.M.

Popularly known as one of Pittsburgh's best choices for a first date, Dish is actually a bar that just happens to serve some of the best-prepared small plates and soups on the South Side. Pasta, meat, and fresh fish dishes—as well as a long list of wonderfully sinful desserts—are also on offer here. But for many, the real draw at Dish is its ambience: Lights are always turned down low, and the small tables and considerable lack of elbowroom tend to make for a rather cozy dining or drinking experience. Fair warning: Reservations are recommended during the always-busy weekends. No credit cards.

FRENCH
LE POMMIER $$$
2104 E. Carson St., 412/431-1901
HOURS: Mon.-Sat. 5:30-10 P.M.

A South Side stronghold for decades, Le Pommier is practically synonymous with fine French dining and quality cuisine among Pittsburghers. But don't expect a particularly intimate experience; the bistro sits inside a rather sizable storefront smack-dab in the bustle of East Carson Street. Do expect white tablecloth service, however, not to mention a truly attentive staff that is often willing to go above and beyond the call of duty for particularly discerning din-

ers. Thanks to chef Mark Collins, organic, locally grown produce and ingredients find their way into most every dish; diners who simply can't decide should try the four-course prix fixe menu, available Monday through Friday. Le Pommier is also well known for its extensive wine menu.

ITALIAN
ABRUZZI'S $$
20 S. 10th St., 412/431-4511
HOURS: Mon.-Thurs. 11:30 A.M.-10 P.M., Fri.-Sat. 11:30 A.M.-11 P.M., Sun. 4-9 P.M.

After finally settling into its new location in the Holiday Inn Express, there's no doubt that the much-loved Abruzzi's has lost at least a touch of its former shabby chic glory and coziness. Also gone is the former space's "smallest bar in the 'Burgh," which had only three stools. Abruzzi's Northern Italian dishes, however, remain as stunning as ever, especially the seafood and gnocchi. And thankfully, the personalized service and colorful atmosphere have remained largely unchanged. Patrons who weren't fond of the old space's slightly claustrophobic feel might appreciate giving the outdoor terrace here a try.

BRUSCHETTA'S $$
1831 E. Carson St., 412/431-3535,
www.bruschettas.com
HOURS: Mon.-Thurs. 11:30 A.M.-10 P.M., Fri.-Sat. 11:30 A.M.-11 P.M., closed Sun.

Certainly, the decade-old Bruschetta's isn't one of the South Side's newest or trendiest eateries. But it's longevity and continued popularity in such an ever-fickle neighborhood is undoubtedly a testament to its quality and good value. Dinners here, for instance, start with a sampling of—what else?—an order of fresh bruschetta; most folks then move on to one of the restaurant's famed pasta or veal dishes. Also popular is the "create your own pasta" option; Bruschetta's claims there are 118,632 possible combinations. Might want to skip lunch.

PIZZA VESUVIO $

1417 E. Carson St., 412/481-3888

HOURS: Mon.-Wed. 11:30 A.M.-midnight, Thurs.-Sat. 11:30 A.M.-3 A.M., Sun. 11:30 A.M.-9 P.M.

Hankering for a late-night slice? Pizza Vesuvio is hands-down your best bet on the South Side. The small storefront isn't much—just a few bar stools gathered in each corner and stereo speakers blasting old-school indie rock and punk. But the pies are pure genius: Very thin and very wide, just like you'd get in a New York shop, and perfect for eating on the go. Square, Sicilian-style slices are also available.

MEXICAN
TACO LOCO $

2700 Jane St., 412/488-8858

HOURS: Mon.-Thurs. 11 A.M.-10 P.M., Fri.-Sat. 11 A.M.-midnight, Sun. noon-9 P.M.

Understandably, it's taken a bit of time for Pittsburghers to get comfortable with the concept of an authentic Mexican taqueria in their midst. And the menu at Taco Loco, heavy with chorizo and jalapeños, doesn't much resemble that of other area Tex-Mex joints, which is exactly the point. Instead, expect refreshingly simple items like bean and cheese tacos and chicken enchiladas. Or, experiment with south-of-the-border standards like *alambres* (grilled steak) or *tortas* (a cross between a sandwich and a hoagie). And during the summer months, definitely request patio seating, where you may even forget what country you're in. If you're lucky.

MEDITERRANEAN
GYPSY CAFÉ $$

1330 Bingham St., 412/381-4977, www.gypsycafe.net

HOURS: Tue.-Fri. 11:30 A.M.-3 P.M., Tue. 5-10 P.M., Wed.-Thurs. 6-11 P.M., Fri. 6 P.M.-midnight, Sat. 5 P.M.-midnight, Sun. noon-3 P.M. and 4-9 P.M.

A cozy neighborhood café tucked safely away from the chaos of East Carson Street, Gypsy Café serves a clever sort of Mediterranean concept cuisine. That means Italy, Greece, and North Africa, but also Eastern Europe, Ireland, and Spain, to name but a few. Events are a popular draw here; *tamburitza* and jazz musicians occasionally perform, as do tarot card readers. Because of the occasional private party, hours are somewhat flexible, as is the seasonal menu, so it's always wise to call ahead. Reservations are practically a necessity during nights when nearby City Theatre is in session.

SNACKS AND DESSERTS
CHOCOLATE CELEBRATIONS AND THE MILKSHAKE FACTORY $

1705 E. Carson St., 412/488-1808, www.chocolatecelebrations.com

HOURS: Mon.-Wed. 11 A.M.-6 P.M., Thurs. 11 A.M.-8 P.M., Fri.-Sat. 10 A.M.-8 P.M., closed Sun.

Still operated by the same candy-making family that immigrated to Pittsburgh from Greece in the early 1990s, Chocolate Celebrations features fine confections and hand-dipped chocolates of all types. The majority of the candy is handmade right on the premises, including the particularly popular chocolate-covered pretzels. In the back of the store is The Milkshake Factory, which also serves ice cream in waffle cones. A wide selection of the company's gourmet confectionary gift baskets can be ordered online.

RESTAURANTS

THE PRETZEL SHOP $

2316 E. Carson St., 412/431-2574

HOURS: Mon.-Sat. 7 A.M.-4 P.M.

A veritable Pittsburgh legend, hundreds upon hundreds of soft pretzels are prepared at The Pretzel Shop by hand daily; hang around long enough in the lobby and you're sure to see the master pretzelers and their late 1800s-era beehive oven in action. Deli-style sandwiches can be ordered on the pretzels as well. And don't forget to request the house special: an absolutely addictive homemade honey mustard sauce.

SPANISH

IBIZA TAPAS AND WINE BAR $$

2224 E. Carson St., 412/325-2227,

www.ibizatapasrestaurant.com

HOURS: Mon.-Thurs. 4 P.M.-midnight, Fri.-Sat. 4 P.M.-1 A.M.

Owned and operated by local restaurateur Antonio Pereira, who is also responsible for next-door's Spanish-themed restaurant Mallorca, Ibiza boasts 45 small plates—some hot and some cold—from both continental Europe and South America. Style and creativity are in full force here, so be prepared to encounter an exceptional menu. Beef carpaccio, tuna tartar, and stuffed banana peppers with veal are just a few of the many offerings. Particularly obsessive foodies might consider requesting a table with a kitchen view, where the chefs toil on full display.

MALLORCA $$$

2228 E. Carson St., 412/488-1818,

www.mallorcarestaurant.com

HOURS: Mon.-Thurs. 11:30 A.M.-10:30 P.M., Fri.-Sat. 11:30 A.M.-11:30 P.M., Sun. noon-10 P.M.

A traditional Spanish restaurant in the

© FABIAN BAUTISTA

Head to the South Side for the best soft pretzels this side of Philly.

finest white tablecloth style, Mallorca offers a premiere dining experience that is simply unequaled elsewhere in the city. Families and young couples on dates crowd the gated outdoor terrace or the often-packed dining room here to gorge on Spanish- and Mediterranean-style seafood dishes or the exotic house specialties: roast sucking pig, say, or even goat. And just as they would in an actual Iberian eatery, diners often find themselves noshing, sampling, and sipping for hours. Not feeling particularly adventurous? Stick with the paella, for which Mallorca is justly famous.

Mount Washington   Map 3

Although it once housed a station on the Underground Railroad, and today houses families of turkey and deer, even to most locals Mount Washington is best known for only three things: The jaw-dropping view afforded from its Grandview Avenue, which stretches the length of its cliffside; the two inclines which traverse the side of the cliff to deliver you there; and Restaurant Row, the small collection of exceedingly romantic cafés and eateries where a plate of veal Lafayette and glass of pinot noir comes complete with one of North America's most gorgeous urban views.

Technically, Restaurant Row is located in the small neighborhood of Duquesne Heights, and if you reach Grandview Avenue by way of the Monongahela Incline, which sits directly across the street from Station Square, you'll have quite a hike if you intend to walk to a restaurant—it's approximately one mile. The Duquesne Incline, on the other hand, sits adjacent to the restaurants, but to reach it on foot from Station Square you'll need to walk past the Gateway Clipper Fleet, continue on through the parking lot, and then follow the footpath along the Monongahela River until you see the incline on your left. If you're not sure exactly where you're going, taking a taxi from your hotel would probably be your wisest bet.

It's important to note, however, that as Pittsburgh's fine-dining scene has slowly grown and improved over the years, the reputation of Mount Washington's eateries has declined. Which isn't to say that the food offered here is necessarily poor, but rather that it's significantly overpriced given its quality. In other words, if extraordinary food is what you're after, you can do much better elsewhere. Yet if it's the view and the experience you want, by all means, come and enjoy yourself. But don't come expecting anything modern: The vibe and the decor along the row are both solidly stuck in the 1970s and '80s.

AMERICAN

GEORGETOWNE INN $$$

1230 Grandview Ave., 412/481-4424,
www.georgetowneinn.com

HOURS: lunch Tue.-Sat. 11 A.M.-3 P.M., dinner Mon.-Thurs. 5-11 P.M., Fri.-Sat. 5 P.M.-midnight, Sun. 4-10 P.M.

Georgetowne Inn is always a consistent draw, and for good reason. Because while the menu essentially mirrors that of Mount Washington's other food-with-a-view spots (fairly standard beef, seafood, and pasta dishes), the ambience, at least, has been raised a notch or two in the creativity department. The walls might be stucco white, for instance, but the wooden crossbeams make for a somewhat cozy but still upscale rural experience. And if you plan to arrive with a relatively large party, consider calling ahead to reserve space in the upstairs loft, where the city view is even mightier. Light eaters should try the crab cakes or club-style sandwiches.

◖ GRANDVIEW SALOON $$

1212 Grandview Ave., 412/431-1400,
www.grandviewsaloon.com

HOURS: Sun.-Thurs. 11 A.M.-10 P.M., Fri.-Sat. 11 A.M.-midnight

It's easy to understand why the Grandview Saloon's two dining levels—as well as its two outdoor patios—are consistently packed with in-the-know tourists and locals alike: The

RESTAURANTS

view afforded from either deck is just as stunning and romantic as any other you'll find along Restaurant Row, and yet the prices are much lower because the atmosphere is more casual. The Saloon, in fact, is much more of a bistro than a fine-dining spot, a fact that the menu clearly reflects. Sandwiches, wraps, chicken salads, burgers, and hoagies are all available, although USDA prime beef steaks are as well. And if you're primarily interested in drinking, head to the restaurant's lower level, where you'll find a small horseshoe-shaped bar.

LEMONT RESTAURANT $$$
1114 Grandview Ave., 412/431-3100,
www.lemontpittsburgh.com
HOURS: Mon.-Sat. 5 P.M., Sun. 4 P.M., last reservation Sun.-Thurs. 9 P.M. and Fri.-Sat. 9:30 P.M.
Existing in equal popularity with the Cliffside Restaurant is LeMont Restaurant, a five-star locale offering essentially the same amenities as its down-the-street neighbor: traditional American cuisine including seafood and old-school meat entrées. (The two house specialties, for instance, are steak Diane and chateaubriand.) And despite its hopelessly out-of-date decor, LeMont also continues to be something of a hit with wedding receptions and business meetings. Dessert selections are appropriately filling and rich, and, for men, a coat and tie are required. This is a reservation-only venue.

THE TIN ANGEL $$$
1200 Grandview Ave., 412/381-1919
HOURS: Daily 5:30-9:30 P.M.
The Tin Angel has long been a hit with tourists and locals alike, and it certainly didn't hurt business when Bill Clinton and former

Prime Minister John Major dined here in 1994. On the menu is a bevy of American and Greek cuisine, including Black Forest filet mignon and stuffed grape leaves. You can expect the food quality and the Downtown city view here to be on essentially the same level as at the row's other restaurants: Your gaze out the window is almost guaranteed to be awe-inspiring, while your meal itself will likely be decent enough, but far too expensive.

SEAFOOD

CLIFFSIDE RESTAURANT $$$
1208 Grandview Ave., 412/431-6996
HOURS: Sun.-Thurs. 5-10 P.M., Fri.-Sat. 5-11 P.M.
One of Restaurant Row's most popular places to dine is the Cliffside Restaurant, which specializes in seafood, such as lobster tails, shrimp scampi, and scallops. Steaks and veal are also much appreciated here, as is the stunning view. But at least among locals, the Cliffside is probably best known as a romantic date destination. Show up during prom season, and you might think you've mistakenly entered the city's best-dressed high school cafeteria. There's also a small and intimate bar inside, as well as a somewhat retro piano player who performs on weekends. Entrées and desserts are all traditionally American, and a coat and tie is the accepted dress for men, who should also take care to bring along their no-limit platinum card.

MONTEREY BAY FISH GROTTO $$$
1411 Grandview Ave., 412/481-4414,
www.montereybayfishgrotto.com
HOURS: Mon.-Thurs. 11 A.M.-10 P.M., Fri. 11 A.M.-midnight, Sat. 4-10 P.M., closed Sun.
Located inside a high-rise building at the

far western end of Grandview Avenue, the Monterey Bay Fish Grotto offers an award-winning selection of fresh fish, which, aside from being flown in daily, is served in a visually striking glass enclosed dining room where every table has a phenomenal view of The Point. The steaks and seafood will definitely set you back here, and many a diner has complained that the elevated prices slightly outweigh the quality of the food. But there's simply no debating the fact that your experience here is almost certain to be detailed and unique. Various private banquet spaces can fit parties as small as 20 or as large as 100 people. And for a gathering that truly impresses, a private wine room with a 24-person capacity and a four-course prix fixe fish dinner can be reserved.

North Side   Map 4

Some of the North Side's more interesting restaurants have recently closed, although the majority of tourists who come to this part of town find themselves in the so-called North Shore area surrounding PNC Park; a good number of chain restaurants and cafés serving bar food can be found there. Wander up to the commercial strip of East Ohio Street to find more restaurants, including old taverns where patrons still toss their peanut shells on the floor. And when visiting the Andy Warhol Museum, don't hesitate to grab a bite in the downstairs cafeteria; it's owned by the Big Burrito Group, which is responsible for such local eateries as Casbah, Kaya, Soba, and Eleven.

AMERICAN

OUTBACK STEAKHOUSE PNC PARK $$
109 Federal St., 412/321-9003,
www.outbacksteakhouse.com
HOURS: Mon.-Thurs. 11 A.M.-9 P.M., Fri. 11 A.M.-10:30 P.M., Sat. 4-10:30 P.M., Sun. 4-9 P.M.

Most everyone knows what to expect at an Outback Steakhouse: enormous slabs of red meat and possibly a bloomin' onion or two. But it's safe to say that the North Side's location is unlike any you've visited before. The restaurant has actually been built into the side of PNC Park, the home of the Pittsburgh Pirates. Show up here on game day with a ticket, and you'll be seated on the "field side" of the restaurant, where giant picture windows offer a wonderful left field view of the action. Showing up during games without a ticket is allowed, of course—just expect to be seated on the restaurant's "city side," and without the coveted ballpark view.

WILSON'S BAR-B-Q $$
700 N. Taylor Ave., 412/322-7427
HOURS: Mon.-Wed. noon-8 P.M. Thurs.-Sat. noon-10 P.M.

Tucked into the deepest recesses of the Mexican War Streets, Wilson's Bar-B-Q has long been lauded as absolutely top-notch Southern pit barbeque. "Genuine" is probably the best word to describe the place: Most everyone takes the award-winning chicken and pork ribs to go, and the shop itself is utilitarian at best. But no matter, as the delectable meat at Wilson's simply melts off the bone—the result of a wood-fired grill and a family secret sauce handed down from ex-slave ancestors, according to employees.

GOURMET DELIVERY

If you're feeling like ordering in but can't stand the idea of yet another pepperoni pizza, consider using the convenient services of **Wheel Deliver** (412/421-9346, www.wheeldeliver.net), a company that home-delivers food from any of nearly three dozen area restaurants, many of the ethnic or upscale variety.

There are only a few reasonable catches: You're required to spend a minimum of $10 at each restaurant from which you order, and you'll need to spend at least $25 total if you'd like to have your order delivered to Downtown, South Side, or Mount Washington. Prices are exactly what you'd pay in each respective restaurant, plus a 15 percent service charge.

Eateries that work with Wheel Deliver include Thai, Indian, Mexican, Chinese, American, Italian, and even Ethiopian spots. Menus frequently appear in the *Pittsburgh City Paper;* you can also download menus from the company's website.

GERMAN

PENN BREWERY $$

800 Vinial St., 412/237-9402,
www.pennbrew.com

HOURS: Mon.-Sat. 11 A.M.-midnight

The Penn Brewery isn't your average brewpub. The interior is designed to resemble a Deutschland mead hall, and if you time your visit right, you might catch a lederhosen-clad German band entertaining on the outdoor patio. And although it's plenty comfortable to belly up to the bar here and order a Penn Weizen, Penn Brewery is also a fantastic place to dine. Dinners are heavy, authentic, and artery clogging; imagine steak drenched in dark beer sauce or tender beef sirloin rolls stuffed with bacon, and you'll start to get the idea. The lunch menu here is also especially popular and features all manner of *leberwursts* and *burgerneisters*. A small selection of vegetarian entrées and sandwiches are available.

Shadyside   Map 5

This upscale shopping neighborhood has two main drags—Walnut Street and Ellsworth Avenue—and both are home to a wonderful mixture of pubs, cafés, high-end eateries, and ethnic restaurants. Strolling the length of either street doesn't take long, although we've saved you some of the trouble by listing some of the better options below.

Nearby, East Liberty is a predominantly African American neighborhood that is slowly but surely becoming gentrified, although very few recommendable restaurants exist. There is a Caribbean fast food market, although soul food and Jamaican eateries seem to be found only in Garfield.

AMERICAN

BUFFALO BLUES $$

216 S. Highland Ave., 412/362-5837

HOURS: Sun.-Thurs. 11 A.M.-midnight, Fri.-Sat. 11 A.M.-1 A.M.

Buffalo Blues is the best sort of sports bar:

HIDDEN FAVORITES

Naturally, not all of Pittsburgh's best restaurants are located within the city limits. And although the majority of these out-of-the-way gems can be tough to reach via public transportation, do make an effort to visit at least one. Not only will you have experienced yet another slice of Pittsburgh's culinary eminence, you'll also have seen a part of Pittsburgh that most visitors miss.

Vincent's of Greentree (333 Mansfield Ave., 412/921-8811) is the sort of Italian restaurant you've always wanted to go to, but have somehow never succeeded in finding: The food and atmosphere are sincerely authentic, the owner frequently makes the restaurant's rounds to greet his patrons, and the pizza here is said to be of absolutely top quality.

Azul Bar y Cantina (122 Broad St., Leetsdale, 724/266-6362, Mon.-Sat. 11 A.M.-11 P.M., closed Sun.) is one of the very few truly authentic Mexican restaurants in the Greater Pittsburgh area. It was opened by a couple from San Diego who were frustrated by the lack of quality Mexican fare here, and the restaurant's chef, Jose Lemus, is a native of Mexico City.

Consistently packed with satisfied customers, **Vivo** (565 Lincoln Ave., Bellevue, 412/761-9500) serves pricey but phenomenal haute cuisine and offers truly attentive service. The menu, which may include escargot, veal chops, or blood orange cake, changes daily.

A longtime Pittsburgh favorite, **Franco's Ristorante** (1101 Freeport Rd., Fox Chapel, 412/782-5255, Mon.-Thurs. 11:30 A.M.-10 P.M., Fri.-Sat. 11:30 A.M.-11 P.M., Sun. 3-9 P.M.) serves Northern Italian cuisine for some of the city's most well-to-do food fanatics. The wine list here is especially well edited.

Like most Indian eateries in town, **Taj Mahal** (5904 Bryant St., Highland Park, 412/365-0300, lunch buffet daily 11:30 A.M.-2:30 P.M., buffet dinner Mon. 5-10 P.M., dinner Sun. and Tue.-Thurs. 2:30-10 P.M., Fri.-Sat. 2:30-10:30 P.M.) offers a massive lunch buffet for a reasonable price. The husband and wife team who run the restaurant, however, are a gastroenterologist and an attorney, respectively; their aim is to serve particularly healthy Indian cuisine. Just around the corner is **Tazza D'Oro** (1125 N. Highland Ave., 412/362-3676, www .tazzadoro.net), a lovely European-style coffee shop.

It isn't too terribly agro, but has enough oversized television sets to keep even the most voracious ESPN junkie on edge. This is also where you'll find one of the most creative selections of chicken wings in town; order yours with mustard sauce, garlic, or any combination of hot and spicy sauces. Not feeling the wings? Burgers are also big here, not to mention jambalaya and ribs, and the chicken salads are stupendous.

Make sure you do like the locals and order yours with something unhealthy on top, like barbeque sauce.

HARRIS GRILL $$
5747 Ellsworth Ave., 412/362-5273, www.harrisgrill.com

HOURS: Daily 4 P.M.-1 A.M.

Something of a contemporary American lounge with a sense of humor, Harris Grill manages to play different roles for different diners. The second floor is elegant, and even romantic, with dim lighting and a subtle Mediterranean theme. But take a look at the menu: Goat in a Boat (feta with pita wedges), Chicks with Sticks (marinated chicken breasts), and the infamous Wrongest Dessert Ever, which comes with a deep-fried Twinkie. A great icebreaker atmosphere for first dates, but it's also fun with a big group of friends.

PITTSBURGH DELI COMPANY $

728 Copeland St., 412/682-3354,
www.pghdeli.com

Definitely more interesting than the name suggests, the 16 specialty sandwiches at Pittsburgh Deli Company are among the most carefully crafted in town. Four are built specifically for vegetarians; the rest combine a selection of quality meats and cheeses, such as the Tally Ho (spicy ham and buffalo mozzarella on focaccia bread), or the That's Amore! (chicken breast and marinara on a kaiser roll). Don't miss the barrel of free pickles, and if you're around at night, visit the second-floor bar, which often hosts hip-hop and electronic music events.

ASIAN

SOBA $$$

5847 Ellsworth Ave., 412/362-5656,
www.bigburrito.com/soba

HOURS: Sun.-Thurs. 5 P.M.-10 P.M., Fri.-Sat. 5 P.M.-11 P.M.

For exquisitely crafted pan-Asian cuisine and a moderately formal ambience, look no further. Soba consists of two full floors, with a dining room and a well-tended bar on each; half of Soba's patrons on any given night are there for the dry martinis and the

schmoozing. Starry-eyed lovers and local pseudo-celebrities can be seen digging into Chef Jamie Achmoody's vegetable samosas and lemongrass strip steak. Wander up to the third floor and you'll find Umi, a Japanese restaurant also affiliated with the Big Burrito Group.

SUSHI TOO $$

5432 Walnut St., 412/687-8744,
www.sushi2-too.com

HOURS: Mon.-Thurs. 11:30 A.M.-3 P.M. and 5-10 P.M., Fri. 11:30 A.M.-3 P.M. and 5-11 P.M., Sat. 11:30 A.M.-11 P.M., Sun. 1-9 P.M.

Not to be confused with its sister restaurant, Sushi Two, which is located on the South Side, it seems as if Sushi Too has been serving up Japanese delicacies in Pittsburgh since time immemorial. A fair warning, however: This isn't the place to come if you're looking to impress a date or business associate; the decor is dated and the aesthetic presentation is minimal. But for a night out with friends, it can't be beat. Prices are reasonable, non-fish options abound, and the menu is a blast for adventurous eaters. In other words, this is a sushi restaurant for those interested only in the eating itself.

THAI PLACE CAFÉ $$

5528 Walnut St., 412/687-8586,
www.thaiplacepgh.com

HOURS: Mon.-Fri. 11 A.M.-10 P.M., Sat. 11 A.M.-11 P.M., Sun. 11 A.M.-9:30 P.M.

Lauded as one of the country's top Thai restaurants, Thai Place is conveniently situated in the heart of Shadyside's shopping district. That isn't to suggest that its ambience is anything special, which it most definitely is not. But for a flawless meal after a Saturday or Sunday of serious pavement pounding, it hits the spot perfectly. Pad thai, of course, is popular here, but the more adventurous should consider the deep-fried squid, or even the boneless crispy duck. Thai curries are also especially mouthwatering. Thai Place's Oakland location is at 311 South Craig Street, 412/622-0133. Other locations can be found in Wexford and Fox Chapel.

TYPHOON $$

242 S. Highland Ave., 412/362-2005

HOURS: lunch Mon.-Fri. 11:30 A.M.-2:30 P.M., dinner Sun.-Thurs. 5-10 P.M., Fri.-Sat. 5-11 P.M.

Pittsburgh's most recent addition to the pan-Asian scene, Typhoon refers to itself as "new-style Thai," an adage that'll make perfect sense once you walk in the front door. Opened by the former proprietor of a popular Squirrel Hill Thai restaurant and a locally based filmmaker, the entrées and small dishes here are a far stretch from those you'd find on the streets of Bangkok. Instead, expect inventive veggie and seafood dishes with a twist—ginger calamari with avocado sauce, say, or grilled halibut with salsa. The decor is equally inviting: Mahogany and bamboo paneling, earth tones, and contemporary art and sculpture complete the experience smartly.

UMI $$$

5849 Ellsworth Ave., 412/362-6198, www.bigburrito.com/umi

HOURS: Tue.-Thurs. 5-10 P.M., Fri.-Sat. 5-11 P.M., closed Sun.-Mon.

Located on Soba's top floor but with its own separate entrance, Umi is probably Pittsburgh's most style-conscious Japanese eatery. Sushi and sashimi here, prepared with high precision by a true *shokunin* (a master sushi chef), will set you back around $3 a piece.

Not a terrible price to pay, considering that executive chef Mr. Shu (winner of *Pittsburgh* magazine's recent "Chef of the Year" award) is one of the city's top sushi celebrities. (The other is Chaya's Fumio Yasuzawa.) Fish-free dishes include teriyaki, miso soups, and even an octopus salad.

CAFÉS

COFFEE TREE ROASTERS $

5524 Walnut St., 412/621-6880

HOURS: Sun.-Thurs. 6 A.M.-midnight, Fri.-Sat. 6 A.M.-1 A.M.

A caffeinating force in Pittsburgh for more than a decade now, the baristas at Coffee Tree Roasters are so serious about fresh beans that anything older than eight days gets tossed. It's no wonder the Arabica brewed here is so rich and flavorful; it's also no wonder Coffee Tree was the first United States roaster named a Cup of Excellence lifetime member. Grad students in particular seem to appreciate the wide-open space at Coffee Tree; you'll see an abundance of laptops and textbooks on any given afternoon. A quiet room in the back is reserved for particularly studious types.

CRAZY MOCHA $

5830 Ellsworth Ave., 412/441-9344, www.crazymocha.com

HOURS: Mon.-Thurs. 7:30 A.M.-midnight, Fri. 7:30 A.M-1 A.M., Sat. 8 A.M.-1 A.M., Sun. 9 A.M.-midnight

Another branch of the quickly growing Crazy Mocha chain, this café retains a slightly rarified air, and something of a neighborhood feel as well, due to its choice location on Ellsworth Avenue. Menu items are just what you'd expect: A full range of coffee and espresso drinks, with sandwiches and cheesecakes behind the counter. But even regular ol' coffee drinkers get their orders delivered straight to the table here—an interesting concept in the too-often discourteous world of independent cafés.

CONTEMPORARY AND NEW AMERICAN

CAFE ZINHO $$

238 Spahr St., 412/363-1500

HOURS: Mon.-Thurs. 5:30-10 P.M., Fri.-Sat. 5:30-11 P.M., Sun. 5:30-9 P.M.

The same crew responsible for the legendary but recently shuttered Baum Vivant operates this bistro-style eatery—an actual garage in a residential neighborhood that's been transformed into something of a culinary hipster's haven. The decor at Cafe Zinho is strictly thrift-store chic, complete with mismatched furniture and ironically bad art. But entrées and even desserts are strictly first-class, and artfully built: Think gourmet dishes complete with lamb, mussels, and even wild game. The veggie rice bowls and remarkably constructed salads regularly earn approving clucks from discriminating foodies as well.

ETHIOPIAN

ABAY ETHIOPIAN CUISINE $$

130 S. Highland Ave., 412/661-9736, www.abayrestaurant.com

HOURS: Tue.-Sat. 11:30 A.M.-2:30 P.M. and 5-10 P.M., Sun. 11:30 A.M.-2:30 P.M. and 5-9 P.M., closed Mon.

It's often said by many fans of fine dining that a major American city simply doesn't rank on the sophistication scale unless it can claim at least one Ethiopian restaurant. So imagine the joy of Pittsburgh's foodie community when Abay Ethiopian Cuisine appeared not long ago in the quickly gentrifying East Liberty district. Thankfully, the food here has more than lived up to everyone's expectations: The menu is an exotic combination of spices, oils, and vegetables. And as is the custom when eating Ethiopian-style, no utensils are used. Instead, the beans, rice, and vegetables—served communally on one large plate—are dutifully sopped up with a piece of tortilla-like bread known as *injera*. In other words, Abay is adventure and education mixed with sustenance.

ITALIAN

GIRASOLE $$

733 Copeland St., 412/682-2130

HOURS: Tue.-Thurs. 11:30 A.M.-10 P.M., Fri.-Sat. 11:30 A.M.-11 P.M., Sun. 4-9 P.M., www.733copeland.com

What was previously one of Pittsburgh's very first independent coffee shops is now Girasole, a much-loved Italian spot where simple but lovingly cooked homemade pasta dishes are drawing customers—the young and moneyed especially—away from the aging Italian standbys of Bloomfield. Diners can choose to eat on a shaded outdoor patio, and for lunch, lighter Italian offerings, such as *panini* and wonderfully airy tiramisu, are offered. Especially popular here is the ravioli, not to mention the very welcoming atmosphere in which every customer is treated like royalty.

MEDITERRANEAN

CASBAH $$$

229 S. Highland Ave., 412/661-5656, www.bigburrito.com/casbah

HOURS: lunch Mon.-Fri. 11:30 A.M.-2:30 P.M., brunch Sun. 11 A.M.-2 P.M., dinner Mon.-Thurs. 5-10 P.M., Fri.-Sat. 5-11 P.M., Sun. 5-9 P.M.

Certainly one of the city's most satisfying culinary adventures, Casbah is tough to miss: It's the tan stucco block built to resemble a Moroccan mosque. Expect a wide spread of Mediterranean and North African cuisine that's simply unmatchable elsewhere in Pittsburgh, and be prepared to expand your version of the exotic while dining; a typical menu might offer Elysian Fields lamb with red wine jus, roasted duck broth soup, and Prince Edward Island mussels. The menu, which changes daily, is seasonally based and features fresh food from area farms. Wine lovers as well will find themselves pleased; the cellar here is considered one of Shadyside's most selective.

MEXICAN

COZUMEL $$

5505 Walnut St., 412/621-5100

HOURS: Mon.-Thurs. 11 A.M.-10 P.M., Fri.-Sat. 11 A.M.-10:30 P.M., Sun. noon-9 P.M.

Featuring a fairly simplistic style of Mexican cuisine that might be called California-style, Cozumel seems designed for family dining. Burritos, enchiladas, chimichangas, and "super quesadillas" are what you'll find here; nothing too complicated or new, in other words. Cozumel also hosts occasional live entertainment evenings; free Latin dance lessons (salsa, merengue, cha cha) take place during the majority of those nights (call to confirm).

PERUVIAN

LA FERIA $$$

5527 Walnut St., 2nd Fl., 412/682-4501

HOURS: Mon.-Sat. 11 A.M.-10 P.M.

As befits its fairly obscure culinary status (a Peruvian restaurant in *Pittsburgh?*), La Feria isn't the easiest eatery to find. First, walk into the lobby of Pamela's Diner; then head up the stairs. You'll find yourself in a Latin craft shop, but an interesting selection of Peruvian sandwiches, salads, and entrées can be ordered at the counter; a small number of tables are available for in-house dining. Specials change daily; regular standbys include empanadas (stuffed pastries), *pudin de pan* (traditional bread pudding dessert), and Peruvian coffee.

SNACKS AND DESSERTS

THE CHOCOLATE MOOSE $

732 Filbert St., 412/688-8800, www.thechocolatemoose.com

HOURS: Mon.-Tue. and Thurs.-Sat. 10 A.M.-5:30 P.M., Wed. 10 A.M.-8 P.M., Sun. noon-4 P.M.

Packed nearly from top to bottom with imported and domestic chocolates, candies, and confections of all stripes, The Chocolate Moose is Shadyside's upscale answer to the old-style penny candy shop. (For a genuine retro experience, try Candy-Rama in Downtown.) More than 250 varieties of bulk candy are also on offer here, including gourmet nuts and kosher candies. Custom chocolate can also be ordered (complete with your company's logo, for instance), as well as a wide assortment of confectionary gift baskets with prices starting as low as $15.

PRANTL'S BAKERY $

5525 Walnut St., 412/621-2092

HOURS: Tue.-Sat. 7:30 A.M.-6 P.M.

Burnt almond torte may in fact be the bakery's claim to local fame, but don't be fooled—the vast majority of the pastries at Prantl's are as affordable and unpretentious as can be. The shop is strictly take-out only, but you'll need to arrive with the early birds to get first pick at the donuts, cookies, breads, and cakes that seem to be half gone by midday.

RESTAURANTS

Squirrel Hill and Point Breeze   Map 5

One of the largest Jewish neighborhoods on the East Coast, Squirrel Hill is home to a number of kosher eateries. But walk the length of the neighborhood's perpendicular main drags, Murray and Forbes Avenues, and you'll discover just about everything else, from a Korean bubble tea shop to one of the tastiest bagel bakeries in Pittsburgh.

Point Breeze is largely a residential area where very few restaurants are located. Self-caterers interested in healthy eating—but not interested in patronizing Whole Foods—should check out the neighborhood's **East End Food Co-op** (7516 Meade St., 412/242-3598, www.eastendfoodcoop.com).

Located on the opposite side of Frick Park from Squirrel Hill, Regent Square's main drag exists along South Braddock Avenue, which can be covered from one end to the other on foot in about five minutes. There isn't much here, although it's pretty tough to go wrong wherever you end up. There's a decent coffee shop and an independent movie theater on South Braddock Avenue as well.

AMERICAN

◖ D'S SIX-PAX AND DOGS $$
1118 S. Braddock Ave., 412/241-4666,
www.regentsquare.net/ds6pax.html
HOURS: Mon.-Wed. 11 A.M.-11 P.M., Thurs.-Sat.
11 A.M.-midnight, Sun. 11 A.M.-10 P.M.

A perennial Regent Square favorite, D's Six-Pax and Dogs has possibly the biggest and most diverse selection of imported and micro-brewed beer for sale in the city (more than 900 brands). Particularly amusing is the walk-in cooler, where customers can browse the selection and pick their very own out-of-town six-pack. Hot dogs are exceedingly delicious here

as well—they aren't quite gourmet but they're close, and the list of free toppings is seemingly endless. A perfect choice when you're not up for greasy bar food, but not hungry enough for a full meal. Veggie dogs are available.

GULLIFTY'S $$
1922 Murray Ave., 412/521-8222,
www.gulliftysrestaurant.com
HOURS: Mon.-Thurs. 11 A.M.-midnight, Fri.-Sat.
11 A.M.-1 A.M., Sun. 10 A.M.-midnight

Gullifty's is something of a local anomaly: With its massive dining room lit by sunlight and proceeded over by balcony seating and ceiling fans, just relaxing with a cup of coffee and one of the restaurant's legendary desserts (voted the best in Pittsburgh for more than 20 years) is an experience worth seeking out. The American bistro-style menu, however, is filled to overflowing with all the regulars: sandwiches, entrées, pizza, pasta, burgers, Tex-Mex dishes, and generously portioned salads. Stopping by before catching a movie down the street? Take care to give yourself ample time, as service can sometimes be slow.

KAZANSKY'S DELICATESSEN $
2201 Murray Ave., 412/521-4555,
www.kazanskysdeli.com
HOURS: Daily 8 A.M.-11 P.M.

Simple, old school, New York–style deli food is the name of the game here: Think chicken soup, matzo balls, corned beef, and black coffee. Fittingly, the setting's nothing fancy—just a few tables tucked into the back room of a deli that does a brisk business in candy bars and take-away beer. The menu boasts 125 separate items; favorites include the Double Yoy sandwich (corned beef, turkey, and liver

MARKETS AND GROCERY STORES

Pittsburgh's most popular grocery store chain – by a long shot – is the locally headquartered Giant Eagle. More than 200 stores are located throughout Western Pennsylvania, West Virginia, Ohio, and Maryland, and just about every neighborhood in the city seems to have its own store. Some of the bigger locations even boast in-store cafés, video rental outlets, banks, and daycare centers. Other major area chains include **Shop 'n Save** (www.shopnsavefood.com) and **Foodland** (www.foodlandstores.com). Recently, a number of Foodland stores have been bought out by **Shur Save** (www.shursavemarkets.com).

old-school Italian food mart in Bloomfield

You'll find the city's solitary **Whole Foods Market** (5880 Centre Ave., 412/441-7960, www.wholefoodsmarket.com) in East Liberty, just east of the newly reconstructed Shadyside **Giant Eagle** (5550 Centre Ave., 412/681-1500, www.gianteagle.com), which seems to be going head to head with Whole Foods in the battle for upscale customers. If organic food and healthy eating is your thing but corporations aren't, head to the **East End Food Co-op** (7516 Meade St., 412/242-3598) in Point Breeze. The Co-op has a wonderful in-store café, a fantastic organic produce selection, and probably the best bulk section in town.

The Strip District is home to a number of unique grocery stores. Topping the list is **Wholey's Market** (1501 Penn Ave., 412/391-3737, www.wholey.com), a store so legendary in Pittsburgh that it often does double duty as a tourist attraction. Shoppers come here for the wide selection of fish and meats, while out-of-towners come to gawk at the plush farm animals in the dairy section who play musical instruments at the push of

a button. (And by the way, the proper pronunciation isn't "whole-eze," it's "wool-eze.") Don't miss the sushi bar at the store's entrance.

Also check out the **Pennsylvania Macaroni Company** (2010 Penn Ave., 412/471- 8330, www.pennmac.com); call it "Penn Mac" if you want to sound like a local. Here you'll find an overwhelming selection of Italian pastas and sauces, and possibly the city's finest cheese counter.

Lotus Food Co. (1649 Penn Ave., 412/281-3050) is by far the most popular Asian grocery store in the Strip. It carries a multitude of food items imported from North and South Asia, including durian fruit!

And if you're an especially frugal or health-conscious grocery shopper, you'll surely want to wield a cart throughout the aisles of **Trader Joe's,** (6343 Penn Ave., East Liberty, 412/363-5748, www.traderjoes.com, daily 9 A.M.-9 P.M.). The store sells organic, vegan, and whole foods at relatively low prices.

RESTAURANTS

on rye) and a slew of Jewish specialties (blintzes, kugels, and knishes, for instance). Fun fact: Although now known only as Kazansky's, the deli has changed its name five times over the past 75 years.

THE MAP ROOM $$
1126 S. Braddock Ave., 412/371-1955
HOURS: Sun.-Sat. 4-11 P.M.

Operated by a British expat who has chosen to cover the walls of her cozy and smallish tavern with antique maps of the Old World, The Map Room is essentially an upscale pub where the bar food is decidedly more adventurous and of a slightly higher quality than you're likely to come across in most Pittsburgh pubs. Grilled chicken entrées, chowder soup, mussels, and bread pudding are the sorts of delights you'll find here. In other words, comfort food of a sort that perfectly accompanies a pint or two of Guinness, or maybe a cup of hot tea during yet another drizzly Steel City day.

THE SQUARE CAFÉ $
1137 S. Braddock Ave., 412/244-8002,
www.square-cafe.com
HOURS: breakfast and lunch Tue.-Sun. 7 A.M.-3 P.M., dinner Fri.-Sat. 5-10 P.M.

One of the neighborhood's most curious eateries, The Square Café acts as a fairly standard neighborhood diner during its daily breakfast and lunch service and then transforms itself elegantly on Friday and Saturday nights into something of an upscale white-tablecloth restaurant. Breakfast fare is of the standard "nuevo diner" variety—tofu scrambles, breakfast quesadillas, french toast with challah bread, and granola—while dinner service is standard American fare (meat and pasta dishes mostly) with a light fusion twist.

ASIAN

CHAYA JAPANESE CUISINE $$
2104 Murray Ave., 412/422-2082,
www.chayausa.com
HOURS: Mon.-Sat. 5-10 P.M.

As a general culinary rule of thumb, a Chinese restaurant filled with actual Chinese diners is usually a sign that you've found the real deal. Chaya, which boasts one of Pittsburgh's two best sushi chefs (Fumio Yasuzawa), operates under a similar assumption: Apparently, this is where the city's Japanese congregate when they're feeling homesick. So what's all the fuss about? For starters, no one else in town makes their own in-house wasabi. And what's more, fresh fish for sushi and sashimi is flown in chilled—not frozen—from Japan or New York. The remainder of the menu is worth writing home about as well and features a baffling assortment of traditional seafood goodies that aren't easily found on American shores.

HUNAN KITCHEN $$
5882 Forbes Ave., 412/422-7188,
www.hunankitchen.us
HOURS: Mon.-Thurs. 11 A.M.-10 P.M., Fri.-Sat. 11 A.M.-11 P.M., Sun. noon-9:30 P.M.

Formerly an all-vegetarian restaurant known as the Zen Garden, Hunan Kitchen is essentially the exact same space, but with a new name and a menu broadened slightly with meat-based dishes. That's good news for the vegetarians and vegans who flocked here en masse during the old days, but even carnivores have cause to rejoice in the restaurant's offerings of fresh, organic, and natural ingredients. Members of all culinary persuasions seem to agree that the wheat gluten and the soy protein—both persuasively meat-like in their presentation and taste—are easily Hunan's two best dishes.

SWEET BASIL & LA FILIPINIANA $$

2022 Murray Ave., 412/422-8950,
www.mysweetbasil.com

HOURS: Tue.-Fri. 11:30 A.M.-3 P.M. and 5-10 P.M.,
Sat.-Sun. noon-10 P.M.

After a long and successful run in a somewhat hidden nook of Lawrenceville, Sweet Basil has opened this second East End location; thankfully, all the ambience and uniqueness of the original seem to have made the move without much damage. Management refers to the restaurant's style as upscale casual dining, and it's true that the presentation of dishes and the quality of the traditional Thai and Filipino food approaches a level of detail that most other Southeast Asian eateries in Pittsburgh simply don't achieve. For the full experience, share the Taste of La Filipiniana combo dish with a friend. It comes complete with chicken adobo, beef *caldereta,* shrimp curry, and all the requisite trimmings.

CAFÉS

COFFEE TREE ROASTERS $

5840 Forbes Ave., 412/422-4427

HOURS: Sun.-Thurs. 6 A.M.-midnight, Fri.-Sat. 6 A.M.-1 A.M.

Appealing to a slightly older and more moneyed crowd than 61C Café, Coffee Tree Roasters is a locally based chain with multiple branches throughout the city and suburbs. The atmosphere at the Squirrel Hill branch is nonetheless intimate and decidedly cozy, though, thanks in no small part to the shop's quaintly diminutive size. Drip coffee and espresso drinks are top-notch too, with different brews offered daily.

61C CAFÉ $

1839 Murray Ave., 412/521-6161

HOURS: Mon.-Thurs. 7 A.M.-11 P.M., Fri. 7 A.M.-midnight, Sat. 8 A.M.-midnight, Sun. 8 A.M.-11 P.M.

Looking for Squirrel Hill's hipster contingent? Chances are good that at least half of them are lounging at the 61C Café this very moment, hunched over laptops or people-watching on the outdoor patio. To reach the café from Oakland or Downtown, just hop on its namesake bus. And once you're here, feel free to indulge your most obscure espresso drink desire; the majority of the 61C baristas are proud professionals. A wide pastry and tea selection is also on offer, and the wireless access is free to all.

TANGO CAFÉ $

5806 Forward Ave., 412/421-1390,
www.tangocafepgh.com

HOURS: Mon.-Fri. 9:30 A.M.-10 P.M., Sat.-Sun. 10:30 A.M.-11 P.M.

Certainly Squirrel Hill's most exotic coffee shop, Tango Café is tucked into one of the furthest reaches of the neighborhood, just down the street from the Squirrel Hill Theatre. To truly get into the swing of things, order the Tango Submarino (steamed milk with a chocolate bar dropped in), or a Mate Cocido, which is a stress-reducing herbal beverage that's particularly popular in Buenos Aires. Pastries, light sandwiches, and empanadas are also available here, and all are comparable to the offerings you'd come across in an actual Argentine café. Tango Café can be full of surprises, too: Argentine folk musicians can sometimes be found strumming away in a corner, and both tango and Spanish language lessons are occasionally offered as well.

RESTAURANTS

CONTEMPORARY AND NEW AMERICAN

◖ POINT BRUGGE CAFÉ $$
401 Hastings St. at Reynolds St., 412/441-3334, www.pointbrugge.com
HOURS: Tue.-Thurs. 11 A.M.-10 P.M., Fri.-Sat. 11 A.M.-11 P.M., Sun. noon-9 P.M., closed Mon.

Located in the same spot as the city's historic Point Restaurant, Point Brugge Café was designed by Michael Walsh of Pittsburgh's 3 Design Group to specifically feel and operate like a familiar neighborhood gathering spot. The atmosphere itself is something of a pleasant cross between traditional European sophistication and the laid back vibe of the West Coast, while the dishes—Asian fusion and contemporary American, mostly—manage to live in that difficult-to-achieve space between comfort food and modern decadence. As an added bonus, Belgian beers can often be found on tap. Reservations are recommended.

ITALIAN

MINEO'S $
2128 Murray Ave., 412/521-9864, www.mineospizza.com
HOURS: Sun.-Thurs. 11 A.M.-1 P.M., Fri.-Sat. 11 A.M.-2 A.M.

Claiming to be any city's best pizza joint can be a controversial undertaking, but the family-owned Mineo's has the awards to prove it—dozens of them, from nearly every Pittsburgh publication—lining the walls of their no-frills cafeteria-style shop. It's tough to put a finger on exactly why the pies and slices are so delectable. It could be the generous piling on of cheese. Or maybe be the always-fresh ingredients. Might be the sauces and toppings, both of which Mineo's steadfastly refuses to skimp on. And if you absolutely

can't stop by during your time here, they'll happily overnight a pie anywhere in the United States.

KOSHER

MILKY WAY $
2120 Murray Ave., 412/421-3121
HOURS: Sun.-Thurs. 11 A.M.-10 P.M., Fri. 11 A.M.-4 P.M.

Only in the ultra-liberal Jewish enclave of Squirrel Hill could an eatery like Milky Way exist: Everything here is 100 percent kosher and made completely from scratch, including the falafel, the pizzas—even the calzones. Naturally though, there's no need to be of any particular religious persuasion to enjoy an evening nosh here; gentiles might enjoy the vegetarian meatball hoagie, for instance, or the veggie lasagna, which is piled high with generous servings of extra cheese. Oy vey!

MEDITERRANEAN

ALADDIN'S EATERY $$
5878 Forbes Ave., 412/421-5100, www.aladdinspittsburgh.com
HOURS: Mon.-Fri. 11 A.M.-10:30 P.M., Sat.-Sun. 11 A.M.-11:30 P.M.

Yet another ethnic restaurant in Squirrel Hill with a focus on healthy, natural foods, Aladdin's Eatery is now a chain with more than a dozen locations throughout Pennsylvania, Ohio, and Illinois. The vibe couldn't possibly be more independent and homegrown, however: The wait staff is consistently friendly and helpful, the dining room is strictly smoke-free, and the owners even donate a bit of the profits to local charities. So, how about the food? Even better. The Middle Eastern and Mediterranean dishes here can be made vegetarian or with meat; house specialties include a phenomenal

Hummus Shawarma Plate with pita and a Mujadara Plate (steamed lentils and rice with toasted onions).

SNACKS AND DESSERTS

ROSE TEA CAFÉ $
58741/2 Forbes Ave., 412/421-2238
HOURS: Daily noon-midnight
One of the few places in Pittsburgh serving bubble tea, which is a flavored green or black tea drink with gummy tapioca balls inside (also try Lulu's Noodles on Craig Street in North Oakland), Rose Tea Café began life strictly as a snack shop, but now serves meals as well. Regulars claim that the food is strikingly similar to authentic Taiwanese cooking; dishes are mostly meat-based concoctions, such as pork and beef stew, ladled over a bed of rice.

Bloomfield and Lawrenceville   Map 6

Mention to a local that you're going out for a bite in Bloomfield, and they'll probably assume you're going to an Italian restaurant (or going to Tessaro's). But the neighborhood known as Pittsburgh's "Little Italy," in fact, is plentiful with many ethnic eateries, including Indian, Thai, and Polish. Which isn't to suggest that decades-old Italian restaurants don't abound. Bloomfield is full of them, and every Pittsburgher seems to have his or her favorite.

Formerly something of a run-down industrial wasteland, Lawrenceville has in the past few years seen an influx of creative and artistic new residents. Here you'll find two good coffee shops, a good number of fairly high-quality restaurants, and even a good ethnic eatery or two.

AMERICAN

RAY'S MARLIN
BEACH BAR & GRILL $$
5121 Butler St., 412/781-6771,
www.raysmarlinbeach.com
HOURS: Daily 11:30 A.M.-2 A.M.
A kitschy South Florida–themed bar and restaurant located in the furthest stretches of gritty Lawrenceville, Ray's means very different things to very different people. Some come here for the food, a fairly finger-licking combination of sandwiches, grilled fish, key lime pie, and passable Cuban dishes. And although not explicitly a queer bar, evenings at Ray's can often be quite a scene for same-sex couples and gay and lesbian singles, especially on weekends. This is also a perfect spot for hosting dinner parties—two separate rooms on the second floor often see large groups gathering for late-night food and drinks.

TESSARO'S $$
4601 Liberty Ave., 412/682-6809
HOURS: Mon.-Sat. 11 A.M.-midnight, closed Sun.
Red meat fanatics—and burger lovers especially—should by no means miss out on a trip to one of the city's most mouth-watering locales. Tessaro's regularly wins awards locally for serving the 'Burgh's best burgers, which weigh in as heavy as a half pound. The secret, some say, are the bits of steak and filet mixed with the meat. If the idea of a gourmet burger isn't grabbing you, try a char-grilled steak or chop instead, or just kick back at the bar and watch the cooks work their magic through the kitchen's viewing window.

RESTAURANTS

ASIAN

THAI CUISINE $$

4625 Liberty Ave., 412/688-9661

HOURS: Mon.-Thurs. 11 A.M.-2:30 P.M. and 5-10 P.M., Fri. 11 A.M.-2:30 P.M. and 5-11 P.M., Sat. noon-11 P.M., Sun. noon-9 P.M.

Of the two Thai restaurants to choose from in Bloomfield, Thai Cuisine is by far the more popular, and for good reason: The pad thai is some of the best in the city, the waitstaff are extremely good-natured and attentive, and the lunch menu is an absolute bargain. This is also a perfect choice for a first date, and with more than 100 items on the menu, even the non-adventurous stand a decent chance of finding something to like. (More than two-dozen meatless dishes are also offered.) Particularly popular is the *tom ka gai* (chicken coconut soup), which goes wonderfully with any entrée.

TRAM'S KITCHEN $$

4050 Penn Ave., 412/682-2688

HOURS: Tue.-Sun. 10 A.M.-10 P.M.

Easily one of Pittsburgh's most popular Vietnamese restaurants, even Tram's most loyal customers often feel compelled to describe the ambience with a qualifier, which I'll second here: It's a hole in the wall. But sit down with a steaming bowl of *pho* (Vietnamese soup) and order a round of spring rolls, and you likely won't care; the food at Tram's is always fresh and bursting with flavor, especially the vermicelli topped with meat or vegetables. Tram's is also a great choice for vegetarian diners.

CAFÉS

◖ COCA CAFÉ $$

3811 Butler St., 412/621-3171

HOURS: Tue.-Fri. 7 A.M.-3 P.M., Sat. 8 A.M.-4 P.M., Sun. 10 A.M.-3 P.M.

Easily one of Pittsburgh's best coffeehouses

MILLVALE'S PARISIAN PARADISE

A somewhat depressing, post-industrial village that sits across the Allegheny River from Lawrenceville in Pittsburgh's East End, Millvale is one of the last neighborhoods in town where one might expect to encounter anything approaching artistry or divine inspiration in food. But lo and behold, right there in the middle of North Avenue is the locally worshipped **Jean-Marc Chatellier** (213 North Ave., 412/821-8533, Tue.-Fri. 7 A.M.-5 P.M., Sat. 7 A.M.-2 P.M. www.jeanmarcchatellier.com), a French bakery so delectable and authentic that some Pittsburghers have claimed its offerings to be superior even to that of any bakery they've patronized in France itself.

The key ingredient, of course, is owner Jean-Marc, a third-generation baker from Brittany who apprenticed for four years with a master pastry chef in France before finding work in Cape Cod and Los Angeles. His hugely popular Millvale store, where specialties include wedding cakes, Hungarian nut rolls, and classic French pastries, has been open for almost 15 years. During a recent U.S. tour, musician David Byrne even stopped by for a bite; you can read his testimonial, as well as the glowing testimonials of dozens of other customers, at Jean-Marc's website.

in both food and drink quality as well as interior decoration, the arty COCA Café displays a regularly rotating display of locally produced sculptures and multimedia work on the shelves and walls of its front room. In its back room, retro diner booths have been chopped up and refitted into attractive works of art, and even on steaming summer days the small back patio is shaded and pleasant. Grilled sandwiches and other finger foods are available, La Prima coffee is served, and Sunday brunch here (smoked salmon omelets, vanilla-orange yogurt with granola) is of the particularly pleasing and high-end variety.

◖ CRAZY MOCHA $

4525 Liberty Ave., 412/681-5225,
www.crazymocha.com
HOURS: Tue.-Sun. 10 A.M.-10 P.M.

Still the only independent coffee shop on Bloomfield's Liberty Avenue, Crazy Mocha sets itself apart from the competition with a simple strategy: It serves truly fantastic coffee and espresso drinks. (In other words, no burned beans here.) And while Crazy Mocha is now a rapidly growing chain in the Pittsburgh area—there's even a mini-shop in the Oakland branch of the Carnegie Library—the Bloomfield location still feels something like a neighborhood secret. Generally filled with an even mixture of laptop-toting grad students and area hipsters, there's even a DVD rental shop in the back corner with a well-edited library of independent and foreign features. Even better: Wireless Internet access is free here.

THE QUIET STORM $

5430 Penn Ave., 412/661-9355,
www.quietstormcoffee.com

A vegetarian- and vegan-friendly café with ambience that might best be described as thrift-store chic. Think mismatched furniture, five-year-old copies of *Maximumrocknroll,* and baristas who pretend not to notice anyone not sporting dreadlocks or a septum piercing. Snotty attitudes aside, however, discovering an unknown entreé at the Quiet Storm can be a rather pleasant way to pass an evening. Most tables are far enough from each other to allow for private conversations, and the BYOB policy tends to keep the social interactions sufficiently lubricated.

CONTEMPORARY AND NEW AMERICAN

RIVER MOON CAFÉ $$$

108 43rd St., 412/683-4004,
www.rivermooncafe.com
HOURS: Tue.-Sat. 5-9:30 P.M., Sun. 5-8:30 P.M., Sun. brunch 11:30 A.M.-2:30 P.M.

It's no wonder that a dining experience at River Moon Café, one of Lawrenceville's most

© DAN ELDRIDGE

Liberty Avenue in Bloomfield, Pittsburgh's Little Italy

creative eateries, is both pleasingly diverse and artistically explosive. After all, Josephine LaRussa-Impola, the owner and head chef, has an astounding 42 years of restaurant experience. All those decades of food preparation seem to come together quite successfully at River Moon, where all manner of Asian, Mexican, and Mediterranean dishes are served, everything is fresh and made from scratch, and literally dozens of teas you've never heard of are on the menu. And while most entrées here are of the pasta or chicken variety, there's always more than enough—think pineapple pepper shrimp or pork-chop loin coated in raspberry chipotle sauce—to satisfy even the most eclectic of contemporary foodies.

INDIAN

PEOPLE'S INDIAN RESTAURANT $
5147 Penn Ave., 412/661-3160
HOURS: Mon.-Sat. 11:30 A.M.-10 P.M.

Its exterior may not be the most welcoming, but show up for the weekday all-you-can-eat lunch buffet and you'll immediately understand why Garfield's best-kept culinary secret probably won't be much of a secret for long. Featuring spicy cuisine from the northern Indian state of Punjab, People's Indian Restaurant has a menu extensive enough for vegetarians and meat-eaters alike. Smoky tandoor dishes are especially smart picks, as is the chewy and puffy Punjabi nan (Indian bread). Ten dollars will buy you the buffet plus tip with a bit left over. Evening entrées (chicken korma, vindaloo) are equally affordable.

TASTE OF INDIA $
4320 Penn Ave., 412/681-7700
HOURS: Mon.-Thurs. 11:30 A.M.-10 P.M., Fri.-Sat. 11:30 A.M.-2:30 P.M. and 5-11 P.M., Sun. 5-10 P.M.
Don't be put off if you visit Taste of India

around dinnertime and find the dining room nearly deserted—the crowd tends to thin here after the midday all-you-can-eat buffet, a Pittsburgh trend that's repeated in nearly every area Indian restaurant. Nonetheless, the offerings at Taste of India unquestionably represent North Indian food at its finest, and the affordable portions are surprisingly generous to boot. It's tough to go wrong with any of the entrée choices here, but do consider ordering one of the fantastic *lassis* (a yogurt shake) with your meal.

ITALIAN

DEL'S BAR & RISTORANTE DELPIZZO $$
4428 Liberty Ave., 412/683-1448,
www.delsrest.com
HOURS: Mon.-Thurs. 11 A.M.-11 P.M., Fri.-Sat. 11:30 A.M.-midnight, Sun. 1-10 P.M.

An always-packed and much-loved local standby, Del's is the place to go in Bloomfield if you want your Italian done *really* right. Hip and picturesque, however, it most certainly is not—the vibe here is definitely much more along the lines of grandma's kitchen than, say, chic eatery. That probably has much to do with the fact that Del's has long been a family-owned and -operated business; the main emphasis here is clearly on classic Italian cooking, not to mention good value. Bring your visiting parents or out-of-town guests to Del's, and try something standard, like lasagna or a Parmesan dish.

PIZZA ITALIA $
4512 Liberty Ave., 412/621-8960
HOURS: Mon.-Thurs. 11 A.M.-10:30 P.M., Fri.-Sat. 11 A.M.-11:30 P.M., Sun. 1-8:30 P.M.
If you've ever heard Pittsburgh referred to as

"The College City," you likely won't be surprised to learn that the town's East End, where most of its ivory towers are located, is also filled-to-overflowing with pizza shops. So, how to choose? If you're anywhere near Bloomfield, it's Pizza Italia—no question about it. Not only are the pies here made chewy on a perfectly crispy crust, and not only is the cheese piled high whether the pie is ordered plain or with toppings, but it's also particularly easy on the purse strings—expect to pay around $6 for a large, although prices to seem to slowly creep higher every few months.

POLISH

BLOOMFIELD BRIDGE TAVERN $

4412 Liberty Ave., 412/682-8611

HOURS: Mon.-Sat. 11 A.M.-1 A.M., closed Sun.

Although its days as one of the city's most progressive live-music venues are now little more than a memory, the BBT is still Pittsburgh's premiere locale for Polish food. To truly get into the spirit, order the massive Polish Platter, which includes *haluski* and *golumpski* (different varieties of cabbage) along with the requisite pierogi (fried dumplings) and kielbasa (sausage). Those expecting particularly attentive service or even a particularly ethnic experience might walk away disappointed, but come for the food and you'll leave with a very satisfied stomach every time. Showing up early is also a good idea, as the BBT's bar atmosphere generally prevails by early evening.

SNACKS AND DESSERTS

GRASSO ROBERTO $

4709 Liberty Ave., 412/687-2014

HOURS: Mon.-Sat. 8 A.M.-11 P.M., closed Sun.

Slick, modern, and with a slight air of exclusivity, Grasso Roberto is a welcome neighborhood addition, especially for the sort of Bloomfielder who might otherwise be more inclined to seek out a café in, say, Shadyside. Along with its authentic Italian ambience, all the expected café fare can be had here, such as panini, salads, and espresso drinks. During the summer months, the shop fills with teenagers and window shoppers in search of mouthwatering gelato and sorbetto. Both are frozen confections that are similar in taste to ice cream and that are most commonly served in a cone.

PADDY CAKE BAKERY $

4763 Liberty Ave., 412/621-4477

HOURS: Mon.-Sat. 6 A.M.-6 P.M.

A decades-old Bloomfield tradition, Paddy Cake has long been the neighborhood's premiere destination for all manner of sugared confections—donuts, cinnamon and nut rolls, wedding cakes, and practically anything else you'd expect at a no-frills bakery. Stepping into Paddy Cake, in fact, feels a bit like stepping into Pittsburgh past: Nothing fancy or pretentious here, just a wide selection of deliciously good pastries and artery-clogging cakes. Be prepared to take a number and wait in line, especially if you show up early on a weekend morning.

RESTAURANTS

ARTS AND ENTERTAINMENT

The writer and poet Charles Bukowski once remarked that great art is equal to cheap rent, which may be one reason why the music and art scenes in Pittsburgh today are so healthy and vibrant. (A recent cost-of-living survey ranked our town as one of the most affordable cities in the United States.)

And while it's true that a decade has passed since the jam band Rusted Root officially put Steel City music on the international map, punk and indie-rock outfits like the hugely famous Anti-Flag and the quickly rising Modey Lemon continue to form (and break up) at an almost awe-inspiring pace.

A slew of contemporary dance troupes and ballet companies are introducing new shows in East End studios every season. Ultra-independent art galleries are continuing to pop up throughout Downtown and along the Penn Avenue Corridor. Theater is especially prominent; Broadway-quality performances are always on offer in the Cultural District's historical American music halls, while indie fare and university shows happen all across the city. And possibly because of Pittsburgh's rich literary tradition, readings are particularly popular here. Museums, too, are in abundance; art lovers worldwide regularly travel to Pittsburgh specifically to see the internationally

© DAN ELDRIDGE

HIGHLIGHTS

LOOK FOR ◖ TO FIND RECOMMENDED ARTS AND ENTERTAINMENT.

◖ **Best Live-Music Venue:** Easily the most intimate live music experience in the city, **Club Café** is the place to catch up-and-coming singer-songwriters just before they break into the mainstream. A host of jazz, blues, and folk legends perform regularly as well (page 109).

◖ **Best Dive Bar:** Bearded hipsters and mulleted locals adore its cheap swill with equal fervor: It's **Gooski's,** of course, Pittsburgh's most authentic house of late-night debauchery (page 115).

◖ **Best Lounge:** With four levels, two dance floors, a wine bar, and a sushi bar, it's no wonder celebrities are often found drinking the night away at **Dejavu Lounge,** the most contemporary hot spot in the Strip District (page 119).

◖ **Best Installation Museum:** Although most Pittsburghers couldn't find it on a city map, the **Mattress Factory** is known throughout the contemporary art world (page 126).

◖ **Best Fine Art Gallery:** Probably the most important gallery in Pittsburgh, **James Gallery** features sculpture, photography, fiber arts, and more. The artists themselves range from relatively unknown locals to international superstars (page 128).

◖ **Best Small Gallery:** From bizarre installation art to photography to contemporary video, the exhibitions at **Wood Street Galleries** consistently amaze (page 131).

◖ **Best Theater:** Popularly known as Pittsburgh's most forward-thinking theater, the South Side's adventurous

City Theatre stages new works, spoken word, and the occasional world premiere (page 132).

◖ **Best Art-House Cinema:** Take a journey back to the Golden Age of cinema at **Oaks Theater,** a recently restored art deco theater built in 1941 (page 138).

◖ **Best Festival:** With two full weeks of contemporary art, live music, crafts, dance performances, and more, the annual **Three Rivers Arts Festival** is an absolute must-do summer experience (page 144).

© FRANK WALSH; COURTESY OF THREE RIVERS ARTS FESTIVAL

Dance Alloy Theater performs at the Three Rivers Arts Festival.

ARTS AND ENTERTAINMENT

acclaimed Mattress Factory and the Andy Warhol Museum. And, as anyone who knows anything about life in Pittsburgh can tell you, this town most certainly does not want for lack of nightlife.

As is the case in most American cities, summer is the best time to catch Pittsburgh at its most creative—that's when the majority of events and festivals take place, including the two-week-long Three Rivers Arts Festival and the ever-popular Three Rivers Regatta. Summers here are perfect for a mishmash of other activities, too: Free outdoor movies in Schenley Park, for

instance. Or retro arena rock concerts at Chevy Amphitheatre and Post-Gazette Pavilion. And ever popular here are the sidewalk dining and people-watching scenes in Oakland and Shadyside.

But no matter what time of year you arrive, you're practically guaranteed to find something unusual going on. Just do as the locals do: Wander around, pick up a paper, talk to strangers. And if you're so inclined, go ahead and investigate that cheap apartment rental—you may just discover a lifetime of great art and entertainment in your future.

Nightlife

LIVE MUSIC

BRILLOBOX   Map 6
4104 Penn Ave., 412/621-4900,
www.brillobox.net

Pittsburgh's newest see-and-be-seen spot for the bedhead crowd, Brillobox is run by a husband-and-wife team who relocated here after establishing themselves in New York City's contemporary art world. The ground floor is strictly a drinking establishment where Cat Power and M.I.A. records serenade the city's hipster glitterati; the owners' tastefully displayed paintings and sculptures decorate the walls and shelves. Live music takes place on the second floor, which conveniently has its own bar tucked into the back corner. Local pop and indie-rock bands perform here about as often as do national touring acts; other popular happenings include deejay nights and the occasional multimedia art show or literary event.

This Bloomfield-area pub and clubhouse is popular with Pittsburgh's artsy types.

◖ CLUB CAFÉ Map 3

56 S. 12th St., 412/431-4950,
www.clubcafelive.com

No other live music experience in Pittsburgh comes anywhere near to that at Club Café, which likes to call itself the city's premiere "wired" nightclub. (Most shows are filmed live; an *Austin City Limits*–style TV program and a DVD series have already been produced.) The room here is so small, and the seating so close to the stage, it's practically possible to reach out and touch the performers midsong. Music is generally of the singer-songwriter variety; past artists include Jill Sobule and Citizen Cope. Blues and indie-pop bands also show up with some regularity; the crowd generally consists of well-behaved young professionals.

CLUB ZOO Map 1

1700 Penn Ave., 412/201-1100, www.clubzoo.net
After a long and successful run as Metropol, an industrial music dance club that doubled as one of the most popular live music venues in the city, the converted warehouse at 1700 Penn Avenue in the Strip has been reborn as Club Zoo. Technically, Club Zoo is an under-21 spot where high schoolers can congregate in an alcohol-free environment. But much like Metropol, live music is also a big seller; marquee-level alternative and hip-hop acts can easily draw thousands of fans here. With its post-apocalyptic warehouse vibe, Club Zoo is a particularly amenable place to catch guitar-heavy rock.

DOWE'S ON 9TH Map 1

121 9th St., 412/281-9225, www.doweson9th.com
Featuring a massive dance floor and a decidedly classy interior design, Dowe's on 9th currently holds the title as Pittsburgh's premiere locale for jazz, big band, blues, salsa, and swing performances. Locally loved crooners such as Etta Cox and Jessica Lee show up regularly; legendary jazz and soul artists also stop by, but with a bit less frequency. Soul food is also celebrated with passion at Dowe's. Cornbread, collard greens, fried chicken, and "yardbird wings" (chicken wings) can be had before shows.

GARFIELD ARTWORKS Map 6

4931 Penn Ave., 412/361-2262,
www.garfieldartworks.com
Although technically a visual arts gallery, Garfield Artworks is also one of the most prolific live-music venues in town, booking an almost nightly schedule of underground rock bands, avant-jazz artists, goth and industrial outfits, and the occasional electroclash spectacle. This is thanks in no small part to the locally infamous Manny Theiner, a longtime music promoter who has been bringing indie bands to Pittsburgh for two decades. The digs here aren't much to look at—Garfart is nothing more than a big open box, sometimes with a plastic tub of free beer stashed in a far corner. No matter, though—the disaffected and mostly teenage indie-rockers tend to provide more than enough visual stimulation.

MODERNFORMATIONS GALLERY Map 6

4919 Penn Ave., 412/362-0274,
www.modernformations.com
Much like its down-the-street neighbor Garfield Artworks, ModernFormations is also first and foremost an art venue, yet it hosts a wonderfully cutting-edge calendar of indie- and art-rock groups. When particularly popular acts pass through, MoFo can find itself packed from wall to wall, so take

PITTSBURGH'S HOLIEST HOUSES OF SIN

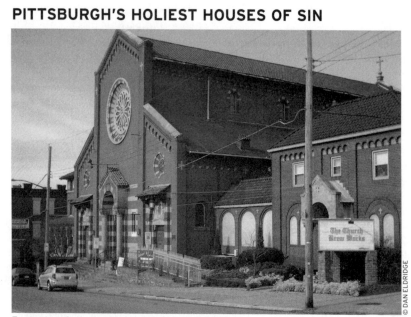

Formerly a Catholic church, The Church Brew Works creates its craft beer right upon the original altar.

Consider for a moment one of Pittsburgh's oddest development trends: Over the past 10 years or so, plucky entrepreneurs have been transforming old and abandoned churches into bars, cafés, and nightclubs. Is it a testament to the industrious nature of the Steel City, or just plain ol' blasphemy? You be the judge.

A restaurant and brewpub that serves some of the tastiest gourmet pizzas in town, **The Church Brew Works** (3525 Liberty Ave., Lawrenceville, 412/688-8200) opened just over a decade ago in the shuttered St. John the Baptist chapel. Sure to be especially offensive to the ultra-devout are the brewpub's steel and copper tanks, which occupy the place of honor upon the altar. Mother Mary pray for us.

Located in the industrial burgh of Millvale, St. Ann's became the site of Pittsburgh's most radical church transformation when a recording studio by the name of **Mr. Smalls** (400 Lincoln Ave., Millvale, 412/821-4447) moved in. Small's has since grown to become one of the city's most popular concert halls, and now serves up an almost nightly mix of punk, reggae, and hip-hop.

Once a Presbyterian church servicing Ukranian immigrants, **Charlie Murdoch's Piano Bar** (1005 E. Carson St., South

Side, 412/431-4256, www.halocafepgh. com) is now one of the only two dueling piano bars in the city. Even better than the elegant double staircase and the massive rectangle bar are the stained-glass windows, which features classic Catholic imagery. Makes you feel a bit guilty by your fourth or fifth Yuengling, but what the hell?

Should you find yourself in the depths of South Oakland with a hankering for a bit of the ol' hubble bubble, stop by **Sphinx Cafe,** an Egyptian-themed hookah bar where wide-eyed college freshmen inhale hits of apple tobacco in between sips of herbal tea and mango smoothies. Sphinx is housed within a disused church of indiscernible denomination. A faux-Rastafarian employee, however, has informed us that the structure was clearly of the Presbyterian persuasion, on account of the stained-glass windows and stuff.

One of Pittsburgh's most recent sinful transformations took place in (where else?) the Strip District, where **Altar Bar** (1602 Penn Ave., 412/263-2877, www .altarbar.com) can now be found. A purportedly naughty nightclub offering "three levels of tantalizing pleasures" along with a sound and light show, deejays, and drink specials, we're not entirely convinced that the Father, the Son, or the Holy Ghost would green light this particular project. Then again, it doesn't look like anyone's asking.

Assuming you're game for a trip to the suburbs, and assuming you're the type who considers a zoot suit and a Big Bad Voodoo Daddy CD appropriate accessories for the weekend, you may indeed find your own private Idaho at **Cefalo's Restaurant & Nightclub** (428 Washington Ave., Carnegie, 412/276-6600, www .clubcefalo.com). A lounge and restaurant where the spirit of the Rat Pack is celebrated within the bricks and mortar of the structure formerly known as the First Presbyterian Church of Carnegie, Cefalo's boasts frequent live music and a cozy and professional dining atmosphere.

Finally, there's **The Union Project** (801 N. Negley Ave., Highland Park, 412/363-4550, www.unionproject.org), a multipurpose space located inside the former Union Baptist Church. Quite unlike the aforementioned locales, The Union Project is the sort of place where good deeds are done on a regular basis; visual artists work here, community organizers organize here, and inner-city youth gain valuable skills and knowledge here, such as the importance of cultural diversity. The Union Project also has its very own café, the Union Station, so feel free to stop by if you're interested in simply poking around. To make a financial donation to The Union Project, call or visit the organization's website.

And, by the way, if you're planning on patronizing some of the aforementioned businesses but still haven't settled on accommodations, consider bunking down for a night at **The Priory** (614 Pressley St., 412/231-3338 or 866/377-4679, www.thepriory.com), a charming B&B on the North Side that was once a Benedictine monastery. It's within easy walking distance of Downtown, breakfast is served inside the old refectory, and wireless Internet access is available in all rooms and throughout the premises.

ARTS AND ENTERTAINMENT

© DAN ELDRIDGE

ModernFormations, a gallery and concert venue in Garfield

care to arrive early when the next Skin Graft or Dischord band stops by. Insider's tip: If you're feeling hunger pains between bands, grab an order of fresh spring rolls from Pho Minh, the Vietnamese place next door.

MOONDOG'S   Map 7

378 Freeport Rd., 412/828-2040

Moondog's isn't particularly easy to get to without your own method of transportation—it sits way north of the city in a blue-collar burgh along the Allegheny River—but if authentic local and national blues music is your bag, it's more than worth the trip. When live music isn't happening, Moondog's acts as a cozy neighborhood pub. But on most weekends, local R&B acts and singer-songwriters like Norm Nardini take the stage. Sometimes true blues legends show up; over the past decade and a half, Moondog's has hosted the likes of Keb Mo, Koko Taylor, and A. J. Croce.

MR. ROBOTO PROJECT   Map 7

722 Wood St., 412/247-9639,
www.therobotoproject.org

The Mr. Roboto Project is essentially Pittsburgh's version of New York City's ABC No Rio or Berkeley's 924 Gilman Street—a politically active punk club and collective run by a board where card-carrying members receive discounts to hardcore and punk shows. As the main room is a relatively small storefront, don't show up expecting out-of-control moshpits or, for that matter, drunken or drugged-out behavior; the neo-anarchists who frequent Roboto are generally well behaved. In true DIY fashion, a zine library is located on the premises.

MR. SMALL'S THEATRE   Map 6

400 Lincoln Ave., 412/821-4447,
www.mrsmalls.com

Cleverly located inside the nave of the former St. Ann's Catholic church, Mr. Small's is a midsize venue with near-perfect acoustics. Performers here run the gamut—everyone from Ziggy Marley to Michael Franti to Gwar have graced the stage; They Might Be Giants even recorded a venerable song about Small's. The management also runs its own record label and maintains two professional-grade studios on-site. An affiliated skatepark is located nearby, and for aspiring rock stars, Small's offers occasional workshops and music camps.

REX THEATRE   Map 3

1602 E. Carson St., 412/381-6811, www.rextheatre.com

Formerly a movie theater with a fantastic art deco facade, The Rex has since transformed itself into a midsize concert venue without actually, well, transforming much. The reclining theater seats were never removed, for instance, so even during big-name punk shows, the energy level can feel rather lackluster. The popcorn and candy counter in the front lobby remains as well; it's now a bar. The occasional alternative burlesque performance or independent film screening also takes place here. Better still, the theater's original art deco signage can still be seen.

31ST STREET PUB   Map 1

3101 Penn Ave., 412/391-8334, www.31stpub.com

Owned and operated by a bearded and heavily tattooed Harley-Davidson enthusiast, the 31st Street Pub is the Steel City's official headquarters for gritty garage rock, punk, and all other subgenres generally associated with black leather and power chords. The crowd here tends to be equally underworldly; depending on which band

is on the bill you might spot aging junkie punks, skinheads, heavy metal fans, or smartly coifed hipsters. If you're looking to get soused, you've come to the right place. Domestic beer, served in plastic cups, is exceedingly cheap, and Jägermeister is available on tap. Party on, Garth!

DANCE CLUBS

BASH   Map 1

1900 Smallman St., 412/325-0499

It can't be anything but a bad sign when a Strip District club attempts to draw in partiers by offering free admission, right? Well, maybe not. Bash certainly isn't a whole lot to look at, but late weekend nights here are legendarily rowdy; you know you've happened upon a hardcore party spot when bartenders regularly roam the dance floor with liquor bottles, looking to pour shots straight into the gaping maws of scantily clad college girls. The elevated deejay booth is a nice touch as well, as are the garage doors that open wide during warm weather months.

MATRIX   Map 3

7 E. Station Square Dr., 412/261-2220, www.matrixpgh.com

Pittsburgh's only four-in-one dance club, Matrix will appeal especially to the noncommittal partier. Mall rats and fraternity and sorority types seem to flock here in the greatest numbers, but the truth is that there's something for everyone: Club Exit for industrial and alt-rock fans; Club Liquid for club kids and the electronica crowd; Club Velvet for salsa and a Latin vibe, and the especially popular Club Goddess, where Top 40 pop and much grinding on the dance floor can be found. Most impressive is Matrix's acoustically sound layout; even though the four rooms sit next to one another in a circle, the various ear-shattering sound systems somehow never seem to bleed.

SADDLE RIDGE   Map 3

4 E. Station Square Dr., 412/434-6858,
www.saddleridgepittsburgh.com

Pittsburgh's first (and indeed, its only) country-and-western saloon, Saddle Ridge isn't exactly tops in the authenticity department. No sawdust floors, for instance, or well-worn swinging doors leading to the men's room. But as a slightly Disney-fied theme bar, Saddle Ridge serves the Achy Breaky set with aplomb. Only the newest and most popular C&W hits are spun by top-of-their-game deejays, mechanical bull rides keep the alpha males occupied, and the female servers get into the act with dangerously tailored Wild West wear. Line-dancing instruction even takes place on occasional weekends; call for updated schedules.

BARS

BAR 11   Map 3

1101 Braddish St., 412/381-0899

With an atmosphere that much more closely resembles a house party than an actual bar, it's perhaps surprising that the unmarked Bar 11 has stayed such a well-kept secret for so long. No need to mince words, however: Bar 11 is a tried-and-true dive; it's the even-tempered waitstaff and the creative party-favor shtick that keeps things exciting. The room is perpetually lit by black lights and covered in aluminum foil, and patrons are encouraged to draw on each other with highlighter pens.

BLOOMFIELD BRIDGE TAVERN   Map 6

4412 Liberty Ave., 412/682-8611

Although popularly known as Pittsburgh's best choice for authentic Polish dining, the BBT, as it's known locally, is also a popular neighborhood bar and live-music destination. There isn't anything too terribly exciting on tap here, although the bar's parking lot and its front porch always fill with bike messengers and activist types during the weekly Thursday Dollar Night, when import and craft-brewed bottles past their expiration date are hawked for a buck each. Drum and bass events, which often feature legendary deejays, are staged here once or twice a month, and the Calliope folk music society holds its open mike nights here.

DEE'S CAFÉ   Map 3

1316 E. Carson St., 412/431-1314,
www.deescafe.com

Less of a dive bar than a home away from home for some of the South Side's most ambitious imbibers, Dee's is dirty, dank, and perpetually clouded in smoke. Best of all, it's cheap and probably the most fun you'll have in any of Pittsburgh's shot-and-a-beer bars, especially if you hang around long enough to get to know the locals. What does the crowd look like? Picture a Nine Inch Nails concert, circa 1994: combat boots, trench coats, Manic Panic hair, etc. The crowd at the upstairs bar, where pint glasses are strictly verboten, is a touch older and more upscale. Action around the billiards tables on both levels is always in full effect.

DOC'S PLACE   Map 5

5442 Walnut St., 412/681-3713,
www.docsplacepittsburgh.com

After 20 straight years at the corner of Walnut and Bellefonte Streets in Shadyside, it's easy to understand how Doc's Place has be-

Dee's Café is South Side's only pub with the official Charles Bukowski seal of approval.

come an East End institution: It's got a great location, a nonsmoking martini bar, and satellite TV screening almost nonstop sports. But even draught-only drinkers who couldn't care less about the playoffs have another perfectly good reason to show up—namely, the massive rooftop patio, which, incidentally, is one of the city's most pleasant places to doff a pitcher of Yuengling when the weather's balmy. Generally, the crowd here is college-age and of the fraternity and sorority persuasions. (In other words, a great choice for well-dressed singles on the prowl.)

GOOSKI'S   Map 1
3117 Brereton St., 412/681-1658

Call it a dive, call it a hipster hangout, or call it Pittsburgh's most legendary neighborhood watering hole—just make sure that before leaving town you spend at least one weekend night at Gooski's, preferably with a pitcher of cheap beer in front of you. Long known as one of the hardscrabble Steel City's most

representative hangouts, the true beauty of Gooski's lies in its diametrically opposed clientele: Saddle up to the bar, and you'll soon find yourself in conversation with an unemployed steel miner, or maybe a tough-talking motorcycle maven. Area hipsters—many who aren't from the area at all, but who've driven for miles just to make the scene—fill the bar's booths and the billiards room. Expect to pay a $3 cover on Saturday nights, when local garage rock bands perform.

JACK'S BAR   Map 3
1121 E. Carson St., 412/431-3644

Take our word for it: No one goes to Jack's Bar, which probably has greater name recognition than any other watering hole along the South Side strip, for its beverage selection. Nor do they go for the atmosphere, the ambience, or the music. That's because Jack's is the city's meat market *par excellence,* plain and simple. Being that this is Pittsburgh, that generally means an overabundance of

© FABIAN BAUTISTA

thick-necked men in white ball caps and coeds with teased hair and high heels. It also means an almost nightly procession of fistfights, so do hang on tight to your Iron City should you find yourself packed into a far corner. In true Steel City style, Jack's never closes its doors, except when forced by Pennsylvania law.

KELLY'S BAR Map 6
6012 Penn Circle S., 412/363-6012

One of Pittsburgh's newest nightlife successes, the lovingly refurbished Kelly's is practically synonymous with style and sophistication, but in a slightly retro and ironic sort of sense. With its art deco design, Wurlitzer jukebox, and tiki-themed back deck, it's no surprise that Kelly's has played such an important role in the recent revitalization of East Liberty. The bad news is the too-cool-for-school waitstaff, some of who are infamous for their inattentiveness. You'll soon forget about all that, however, after getting your hands on one of the bar's expertly mixed cocktails or a jerk-chicken burger from the surprisingly competent kitchen.

LAVA LOUNGE Map 3
2204 E. Carson St., 412/431-5282

One of two South Side bars operated by the owners of the Beehive coffee shop, Lava Lounge looks a lot like it sounds. Picture a tavern where, say, the Flintstones might pass an evening, and you'll start to get the idea: Tables, booths, and high-backed chairs are all designed to resemble a liquid molten lava flow. Even the interior design is creatively cave-like. Do be aware that draft beer isn't available; wine, pricey imports, and cocktails are what you'll be drinking here. Unknown rock bands—some from out of town, but

mostly local—play in the back room periodically. Deejays spin retro '80s records and other hipster miscellanea most nights.

MULLANEY'S HARP & FIDDLE Map 1
2329 Penn Ave., 412/642-6622,
www.harpandfiddle.com

Mullaney's certainly isn't the only Irish pub in the city, although it is unquestionably one of the best designed and most inviting. And because it sits relatively far from the majority of the Strip's meat-market bar district (but still within walking distance), Mullaney's doesn't get a ton of walk-in traffic. Revelers here are generally well-intentioned regulars, or maybe folk music fans who've come for the live music and jig dancing. Traditional Irish entrées (Shepard's Pie, Corned Beef and Cabbage) can be ordered in between rounds of Guinness.

PETER'S PUB Map 2
116 Oakland Ave., 412/681-7465

Only at Peter's Pub can one experience all the raucousness and debauchery of a Pitt frat party without actually having been invited. University athletes and the type of undergrads who obsessively follow the NCAA playoffs are whom you can expect here; also count on ridiculously affordable daily beer specials ($1 Miller Light drafts aren't uncommon). On the second floor is a separate bar, as well as a dance floor that quickly grows sweaty and crowded on weekend nights.

PIPER'S PUB Map 3
1828 E. Carson St., 412/381-3977,
www.piperspub.com

A drinking and dining Mecca for the city's British expat community, Piper's Pub has all the charm of an authentic English pub. At

© FABIAN BAUTISTA

Piper's Pub, a Scottish-Irish bar in the heart of South Side

the bar, selections on draft include Strongbow, Old Speckled Hen, Smithwicks, and Boddingtons; the single malt scotch menu is literally dozens of names long, and bottled beers are available from all across the British Isles and beyond. A large dining room fills the majority of the bar, which is perfectly fitting, considering how unusually tasteful the pub grub is; try the Ploughman's Platter (a cheese plate with apple slices and gherkins) or the Guinness Stew. Traditional Irish bands perform most weekend nights, and live footie matches are even beamed in via satellite.

REDBEARD'S   Map 3
201 Shiloh St., 412/431-3730
Located just steps from the lobby of the Monongahela Incline and the overlook decks of Grandview Avenue, Redbeard's is probably

the only Mount Washington bar that doesn't come complete with an intimidating, locals-only feel. Of course, the majority of the folks who line the bar here and fill the back booths *are* locals, but Duquesne University students in particular flock here for Redbeard's many discount beer and wing nights. Because of its generous size, Redbeard's can accommodate quite a crowd on warm summer evenings, which is also when the umbrella-covered patio seating fills up especially fast.

THE SHARP EDGE   Map 6
302 S. St. Clair St., 412/661-3537,
www.sharpedgebeer.com
Respected by beers snobs locally, and even countrywide, The Sharp Edge is perhaps best known for its extensive selection of obscure Belgian drafts. But with more than 300 internationally crafted and brewed beers available, there's almost something for everyone here, no matter which European or developing nation you'd like to explore in pint or bottle form. Few of the imported selections come cheap, of course; try the $3 mystery brew if you're drinking on a budget. Burgers, sandwiches, pizzas, and other assorted American finger foods are also a big draw; grab a table in the back room if you'd prefer your dinner party quiet.

SILKY'S SPORTS BAR & GRILL   Map 5
1731 Murray Ave., 412/421-9222
If Squirrel Hill's venerable hipster havens aren't exactly your idea of a good time, consider Silky's, a welcoming sports bar with a friendly, nonexclusionary vibe. During particularly important sporting contests—or any time the Steelers are playing—Silky's can get a bit overrun with rowdy and often overzealous fans. But any other day of the

ARTS AND ENTERTAINMENT

week, it's a perfectly anonymous place to unwind with an Iron City, a burger, and a side of fries. And although it appears small from the outside, Silky's two floors and upper balcony are actually quite roomy, making it a smart choice for large groups.

THE SMILING MOOSE   Map 3
1306 E. Carson St., 412/431-4668,
www.smiling-moose.com

Something of an unofficial headquarters for the city's tattooed and thick-necked skinhead contingent, The Smiling Moose also packs in a colorful assortment of vampish Goth girls, old-school punk rockers, and Vespa-driving mods. Perhaps not surprisingly, fistfights aren't uncommon here. Obscure speed metal and punk bands play free shows in the back of the bar most weekends; if the noise gets to be a bit much, simply slip up to the new second-floor bar, where conversation and a game of billiards can be more easily accomplished.

SMOKIN' JOE'S   Map 3
2001 E. Carson St., 412/431-6757,
www.smokin-joes.com

The success of Smokin' Joe's, which from the outside appears to be simply yet another in an endless procession of bars, is based on a relatively simple philosophy: Stock a larger variety of beer than the guy next door. *Way* larger. We're talking hundreds and hundreds, some on draft, some in the massive cooler just inside the front door. In a nutshell, that's why serious drinkers come to Joe's. The interior is rather cramped and plain, and although budget wing nights are a draw for some, the pub grub here really isn't much to write home about (try Fat Heads next door if you're really hungry). Insider's tip: Don't pass up Joe's just because the bar

is packed to overflowing; there's often ample seating on the second floor balcony.

SQUIRREL HILL CAFÉ   Map 5
5802 Forbes Ave., 412/521-3327

Don't bother calling it the Squirrel Hill Café, as it's fairly unlikely that anyone will know what you're talking about. It's known locally as "The Cage," a relatively unimposing room filled only with cafeteria-style booths, two TV sets tuned to sports, and a small balcony that opens only on busy nights. But don't be fooled: The Cage has long been one of the city's most popular scenester bars, largely because of Squirrel Hill's former popularity with musicians and artists. But even though rents have risen here, the vibe at The Cage remains. Grad students from CMU and Pitt have long populated the bar's booths as well; show up during the afternoon to spot English teachers grading term papers while sipping pints of Guinness or Penn pilsner.

THUNDERBIRD CAFÉ   Map 6
4023 Butler St., 412/682-0177

If you're looking for an authentic dive bar in the East End—in other words, one that hasn't long ago been gentrified by college students—the Thunderbird Café might just be your place. And what's more, although the Thunderbird was previously known as little more than a cheap spot to get good and sloshed, it's now known as a cheap spot to get good and sloshed while taking in live music, often of the indie-rock or alt-country variety. It's also not a bad place in which to wind down after knocking down the bowling pins at Arsenal Lanes, which is located just down the street on the corner of Butler and 44th Streets.

© FABIAN BAUTISTA

Get your Mai Tai on at Tiki Lounge, the South Side's Polynesian paradise.

TIKI LOUNGE   Map 3

2004 E. Carson St., 412/381-8454,
www.tikilounge.biz

It ain't Trader Vic's, but it comes mighty close. Tiki Lounge is the city's solitary Polynesian-themed bar, a fact that's made all too clear even to the casual passerby—just keep your eyes peeled for the massive Tiki god in the front window. (You'll have to pass through his massive mouth before gaining entry to the lounge.) Inside, it's something of a South Pacific paradise, with wooden masks, bamboo stalks, and all manner of Hawaiian island paraphernalia lining the walls, including an indoor waterfall. The cocktail menu is equally exotic: Choose from such wonders as a Headhunter, a Fu Manchu, and a Coconut Kiss. Deejays light up the relatively small dance floor with pop and house music on weekends.

LOUNGES
CLUB HAVANA   Map 5

5744 Ellsworth Ave., 412/661-2025

Among the city's after-hours and nightclubbing circles, Club Havana is probably best known for its weekend dance parties, which for years have consistently attracted some of the best house and hip-hop deejay talent in the city. But this is also a solid place to simply kick back and relax with a glass of whiskey or beer and a plate of finger foods. With its pseudo art deco design and sunny South Beach-meets-Cuba interior, the club easily succeeds in taking most anyone miles away from the reality of yet another drizzly day in the 'Burgh.

◖ DEJAVU LOUNGE   Map 1

2106 Penn Ave., 412/434-1144,
www.dejavuloungepa.com

One of the few destination spots in Pittsburgh swank enough to draw regular visits from area sports celebrities (Steelers QB Ben Roethlisberger has been spotted, among others), Dejavu Lounge boasts two separate levels, a glass-enclosed dance floor, copious couches for chatting up friends new or old, and even a wine bar and a sushi cart. You'll want to dress smartly if you're planning an evening here; you'll also want to make sure you're packing plastic—the martinis and specialty cocktails don't come cheap.

FIREHOUSE LOUNGE   Map 1
2216 Penn Ave., 412/434-1230,
www.firehouse-lounge.com

Although something of an overambitious meat market on the weekends, middle-of-the-week evenings find the Firehouse Lounge at its relaxing and intimate best. The vibe is casual but eclectically upscale; a smallish dance floor sits at one end of the room, a spacious bar in the center, and a conversation and mingling area—complete with boudoir-style couches—on the other. The Firehouse is indeed a perfect place to meet friends for an after-work winddown.

RED ROOM   Map 6
134 S. Highland Ave., 412/362-5800

A fairly recent addition to the gentrified corner of East Liberty that also houses Kelly's Bar and Abay Ethiopian Cuisine, the Red Room has done a wonderful job of filling the upscale martini-and-wine bar void. It's easy to feel important here—the leather couches are suitably luxurious, the crowd is frequently well dressed, and the waitstaff is always ready with a cocktail suggestion or two. The Red Room also has a fairly innovative Contemporary American dinner menu; food can be ordered in the main dining room or the lounge area.

SHADOW LOUNGE   Map 6
5972 Baum Blvd., 412/363-8277,
www.shadowlounge.net

Hip-hop dance parties, spoken-word battles, and live music are what you'll generally find on the calendar at the community-oriented Shadow Lounge, although both the vibe and the crowd seem to morph considerably as the day stretches on. Show up during early afternoon and you'll find yourself in an East Village-esque tea and coffee shop, complete with thrift-store furniture and jazz on the sound system. The party goes off almost every night, and that may mean a deep-house deejay, a documentary film screening, a live-rock show, or drinks and conversation in the newly constructed back room.

Z LOUNGE   Map 3
2108 E. Carson St., 412/716-3920

Formerly known as Zythos Lounge, the newly christened Z Lounge still retains its former glory as a hotspot for flavor-of-the-month deejays and the trainspotting crowd. Which isn't to say that this isn't also a decent place for simply sitting and enjoying a beer; the lounge is small, dark, and intimate enough to create a fairly successful romantic atmosphere. Two or three small tables are often set up on the sidewalk outside during the summer, and live bands occasionally perform in the bar's second lounge on the top floor.

QUEER NIGHTLIFE
DONNIE'S PLACE   Map 1
1226 Herron Ave., 412/682-9869

Essentially the city's only lesbian bar, Donnie's Place sits behind Lawrenceville's Iron City Brewery, just past the end of the bridge leading to Polish Hill. Don't show up expecting anything classy or chic, however; Donnie's is an old-school Pittsburgh pub through and through: It's perpetually smoke-filled, it could use a good scrubbing, and no one dresses up for a night out here. Drinks are cheap, though.

5801 VIDEO LOUNGE & CAFÉ   Map 5
5801 Ellsworth Ave., 412/661-5600

Long known as New York, New York, this established Shadyside lounge hasn't changed much more than its name. 5801 Video Lounge & Café now sports a few new plasma television sets that constantly loop retro pop videos, but the laid-back queer crowd—most in their late-twenties to midthirties—has stayed essentially the same. Happy hours are particularly popular, especially during dry-weather days when the spacious wooden patio fills with the after-work crowd and college kids.

PEGASUS   Map 1
818 Liberty Ave., 412/281-2131

The undisputed granddaddy of Pittsburgh's queer nightclub scene, Pegasus has long been favored by a much younger demographic than that found at the majority of the city's other queer bars. Romance is most definitely not in the air here and the decor is somewhat post-apocalyptic.

PITTSBURGH EAGLE   Map 7
1740 Eckert St., 412/766-7222,
www.pitteagle.com

Although not located in one of the city's safest neighborhoods (you absolutely need a car to get here, and even some cabbies might have trouble finding the place), the Pittsburgh Eagle consistently draws swarms of loyal club goers every weekend night. Without a doubt, the Eagle exists within Pittsburgh's hidden-gem category; the deejays do an outstanding job of getting the crowd on the dance floor, yet with four separate levels, there's always another nook and cranny to explore when it's time to take a rest. At the top level of the club, drag queens often perform with willing accompaniment from the crowd.

SIDE KICKS   Map 1
931 Liberty Ave., 412/642-4435

Although the general ambience certainly isn't the most sophisticated of the city's gay and lesbian havens, Side Kicks nonetheless draws a consistently sophisticated crowd; most seem to be age-old friends, or at least convivial drinking buddies. Patrons here also tend to be a bit more reserved than at your typical dance club. This isn't a pick-up joint so much as an inviting locale in which to enjoy the company of likeminded friends, or even the occasional stranger.

ARTS AND ENTERTAINMENT

The Arts

Here's an idea for a potentially explosive experiment: Once you arrive in Pittsburgh, ask a local musician, and then a visual artist, a journalist, a photographer, a dancer, and an actor what each one has to say about the state of the arts here. If history is anything to go by, you'll want to duck soon to avoid the flying hyperbole.

Which isn't to say that the members of Pittsburgh's creative class have particularly bad attitudes, or that they don't approve of the music and art being created here. On the contrary, the general consensus among the town's right-brained types today seems to be that when it comes to competing in the arts on an international scale, our community simply isn't living up to its potential. And because Pittsburgh is such a big city that feels so much like a small town, and because the living is so cheap and easy in Southwestern Pennsylvania, potential is probably the one word you'll keep humming to yourself if you spend enough time here.

Naturally though, more than a few creative types have taken full advantage of the town's growing opportunities. In years past, for instance, the East End neighborhood of Garfield has seen the once-bedraggled Penn Avenue Corridor transformed into a collection of contemporary galleries. Recently, scores of locally grown conferences and lecture series have continued to draw crowds, including the 54th Carnegie International (a contemporary arts biggie), the bookish Second Annual Creative Nonfiction Festival, and even the second annual Handmade Arcade, a DIY crafts fair that drew vendors from all across the country.

Of course, as is to be expected in any midsize urban area with limited resources, artists tend to pick up and leave with alarming frequency; the city's economic and cultural gatekeepers have long been scratching their heads and hoping for a solution to the apparent brain-drain. Grassroots arts organizations like Ground Zero and community groups like the Sprout Fund have been doing their part, spending copious amounts of time and money in an attempt to make Pittsburgh a more attractive and a more exciting place to play.

So what exactly does the future of creative expression look like in the Steel City? Certainly, some things are expected to improve, such as the family of Carnegie Museums, which in mid-2005 acquired a new director, David Hillenbrand. Losses will continue on in Pittsburgh as well, such as the loss of Pulitzer Prize–winning playwright August Wilson, an area native who passed away in the fall of 2005. In the meantime, the Pittsburgh arts population—potentially explosive as it may well be—will no doubt continue to soldier on.

MUSEUMS

When you consider the ever-shrinking size of the city of Pittsburgh—we've gone from a peak of 677,000 residents in 1950 to around 330,000 today—it's perhaps surprising that two major museums have opened during the past two decades. And the contemporary gallery scene here continues to rattle and hum.

One of those new museums, the **Andy Warhol Museum** (see the *Sights* chapter for more information), still manages to occa-

PENN AVENUE CORRIDOR

It starts at the corner of Penn Avenue and Main Street in Bloomfield, and then winds through the neighborhoods of Garfield and Friendship before finally reaching East Liberty. The **Penn Avenue Corridor,** as it's known by the music and art fans who flock there on weekend nights, is easily Pittsburgh's most explicit example of gentrification in motion.

Still somewhat rough around the edges, the stretch has long been regarded as something of a dangerous no-go zone. But an ever-growing collection of eclectic art galleries and live music venues have altered the mood considerably.

One of the best ways to explore Penn Avenue is by joining the **Unblurred** gallery crawl, which is free to the public; the event happens from 6 to 11 P.M. during the first Friday of each month. Pamphlets featuring neighborhood maps and gallery schedules can be found at some of the more popular stops along the route, or simply visit www.pennavenuearts.org to plan your trip in advance.

Two of the most-visited Penn Avenue galleries include **ModernFormations,** which displays contemporary visual art by mostly local and unknown artists, and **Garfield Artworks,** which offers occasional shows of textile and installation art along with photography, painting and other visual arts, also by locals. Both venues also host a regular rotation of indie-rock concerts; the locally infamous curator of Garfield Artworks, Manny Theiner, has been booking underground rock and jazz shows throughout Pittsburgh for nearly two decades.

Also worth a look is the nonprofit **Pittsburgh Glass Center,** where all manner of flame-working and glass artistry takes place.

If you're looking for an artistic way to take a break during your exploration of Penn Avenue, try the **The Quiet Storm,** a café that acts as something of an unofficial clubhouse for the city's creative class. Offering an inspired menu of mostly vegetarian- and vegan-friendly foods, The Quiet Storm is also home to a reading library and occasional visual art shows. Also well worth your time is the café's weekly Sunday brunch, which has quickly become the stuff of local legend.

ARTS AND ENTERTAINMENT

sionally sprout with controversy. One of Warhol's most popular exhibitions, in fact, featured a booth where porn films were screened. Especially shocking to some—even more so than the porn itself—was the fact that a box of tissues had been provided. It's certainly fair to say that back in the 1950s, when the Steel City was nothing less than an economic powerhouse, museum-going was nothing at all like this. But considering the sort of city that Pittsburgh is, it shouldn't come as a surprise to learn that for every boundary-pushing museum and gallery, there is an equal and opposite arts venue with exhibitions that are positively child-friendly. The Smithsonian-affiliated **Pittsburgh Regional History Center** (see the *Sights* chapter for more information) has a permanent collection that celebrates Southwestern Pennsylvania with an uplifting, rah-rah enthusiasm, while its special exhibits are generally historical and quite often of regional importance, yet rarely challenging or disagreeable.

Both of these museums reflect the myriad art and museum experiences available throughout the city itself.

BAYERNHOF MUSIC MUSEUM

Map 7

225 St. Charles Pl., O'Hara Township, 412/782-4231, www.bayernhofmuseum.com

HOURS: Tours given by appointment only

COST: $10

A gorgeous stone house overlooking the Highland Park lock and dam on the Allegheny River, Bayernhof was built by the late Charles B. Brown III, the founder and former CEO of Gas-Lite Manufacturing. Toward the end of Brown's life, he discovered the rather unique hobby of collecting rare automatic music machines. Before long, Brown got a bit carried away with his new obsession, and today, rare and antique machines can be found in every single one of Bayernhof's rooms. Thankfully, Brown had the foresight to add an amendment to his living will stating that upon his death, the instruments should be properly restored, and the house should be opened to the public as a museum. Brown passed away in 1999, and now all visitors to Pittsburgh can view the Bayernhof Music Museum.

Some of the machines you'll see here include a massive Seeburg Pipe Organ orchestra, a Wurlitzer "Style A" Automatic Harp, an Encore Automatic Banjo, a Wurlitzer 125 Military Band Organ, and a combination phonograph and music box known as a Reginaphone Music Box. It's also worth mentioning that completely aside from the music machines, Bayernhof itself is a wonderfully unique house, if a bit on the unconventional side. A hidden passageway takes visitors to a cave, for instance, which winds past small waterfalls and pools. And the entire south side of the house is glass-lined, affording beautiful views of Highland Park, Oakland, and Downtown.

CHILDREN'S MUSEUM OF PITTSBURGH

Map 4

10 Children's Way, Allegheny Square, 412/322-5058, www.pittsburghkids.org

HOURS: Mon.-Sat. 10 A.M.-5 P.M., Sun. noon-5 P.M.

COST: $8 adult, $7 child and senior

After a recent expansion project transformed the Children's Museum of Pittsburgh from a relatively insignificant structure into something of a youth-oriented educational town square, Pittsburgh now has bragging rights to one of the most pioneering and novel museums for kids in the country. Even better is the building's environmentally friendly focus: Designed and constructed with sustainable materials, the museum is soon to become an officially LEED-certified "green building." Now four times as large as the previous museum, with part of the building located in a disused U.S. Post Office and part in the former Buhl Planetarium, there are nine permanent exhibits in total, including a replica of the television world seen on PBS's *Mister Rogers' Neighborhood* and a room known as the Nursery, which is a uniquely creative space for infants, toddlers, and their parents.

For the remainder of the museum's intended demographic, there is an excellent collection of interactive exhibits built around a philosophy quite similar to that of the Carnegie Science Museum: The house's official mantra is "Play with Real Stuff," and it means that by playing and experimenting, as opposed to simply looking and listening, kids will be more excited to learn about the world that surrounds them. For instance, the museum includes an art studio featuring printmaking, papermaking, and painting. There's a garage where machinery and engines can be tinkered with. And definitely don't miss the Attic, with its oddly tilted Gravity Room.

FORT PITT MUSEUM   Map 1

101 Commonwealth Pl., Point State Park, 412/281-9284, www.fortpittmuseum.com
HOURS: Wed.-Sun. 9 A.M.-5 P.M.
COST: $5 adult, $2 child (ages 6-17), $4 senior

It's certainly fitting that the Fort Pitt Museum is located within stone-throwing distance of the confluence of Pittsburgh's three rivers. As the site of the French and Indian War, the Point, as the confluence is known, is also where the history of Pittsburgh itself first began being written. The museum uses dioramas and historical artifacts to tell the story of the war, the outcome of which was much more important than even most Americans realize. (If Fort Pitt had ultimately fallen to the French, guess what language this guide would probably be written in?) Next door is an authentic blockhouse; it's the city's oldest building.

FRICK ART AND   Map 5
HISTORICAL CENTER

7227 Reynolds St., 412/371-0600, www.frickart.org
HOURS: Tue.-Sun. 10 A.M.-5 P.M.

A complex of historical museums and buildings located on the eastern stretch of **Frick Park,** the Frick Art and Historical Center is bookended by its two most important structures. The **Frick Art Museum** displays a portion of the artworks collected by legendary Pittsburgh industrialist Henry Clay Frick, including paintings by Peter Paul Rubens (the majority of Frick's art investments can be found at the Frick Collection Museum in New York City). On the opposite end of the center is **Clayton** (guided tours $12 adult, $10 student and senior, reservations recommended), the industrialist's 23-room chateau-style mansion; it underwent a $6 million renovation in 1990 and can be explored on a guided tour.

Writing in *Architectural Digest,* the journalist Susan Mary enthused that Clayton is "a triumph of restoration." Indeed, when the Fricks left for New York City in 1905, they had spent 22 years in Pittsburgh, and Clayton, of course, was a well-lived-in house. Much to the delight of modern-day visitors and historians, the Fricks failed to bring the majority of their belongings with them to New York; 93 percent of the house's artifacts are originals. Visitors can view children's toys in the nursery, bedroom furniture, and even the study.

Clayton was purchased for $25,000 in 1882, but at the time it boasted "only" 11 rooms. Less than a decade later, the architect Frederick J. Osterling was hired to spice up the building; he masterfully transformed it into the same 23-room mansion seen today.

Also located on the grounds is the popular **Car and Carriage Museum** where visitors can ogle 20 vintage automobiles, including Frick's 1914 Rolls Royce Silver Ghost and Howard Heinz's 1898 Panhard, which some say was Pittsburgh's first car.

Admission is free for The Frick Art and Historical Center grounds, the Frick Art Museum, Car and Carriage Museum, and the Greenhouse. Other tours and programs are subject to various admission fees.

ARTS AND ENTERTAINMENT

THE GEORGE WESTINGHOUSE MUSEUM
Map 7

325 Commerce St., Wilmerding, 412/823-0500, www.georgewestinghouse.com

HOURS: Mon.-Fri. 10 A.M.-4 P.M., Sat. 11 A.M.-3 P.M.

COST: Free

Located in the Wilmerding section of Pittsburgh, the building known as "The Castle" once acted as the general offices of the Westinghouse Air Brake Company. Today however, The Castle houses the George Westinghouse Museum, a dedication to the life and work of a man who was one of the most productive inventors of all time and whose work was largely responsible for the perpetuation of the Industrial Revolution.

The museum houses four permanent exhibits: The Family Room houses a collection of artifacts and curios; each one has some sort of connection to the Westinghouse family. Included is the actual flatware and glassware used during dinner parties at Solitude, the Point Breeze estate of the Westinghouse family that archaeologists have since attempted to excavate. (The land is now known as Westinghouse Park.)

The museum's Inventions Room is packed with artifacts and other documents relating to Westinghouse's many inventions, including his hundreds upon hundreds of patents. Here you'll see a medal inducting Westinghouse into the National Inventors Hall of Fame and a number of historic and original drawings.

As the museum's largest room, the Room of Achievement is filled with memorabilia documenting the many important social developments that have resulted from the various companies Westinghouse founded. Of particular interest is a historic recording of the first-ever radio broadcast—it took place on Westinghouse's KDKA station, which continues to operate in Pittsburgh today.

Finally, there's the Appliance Room, containing historical Westinghouse refrigerators, sewing machines, toasters, and more.

◖ MATTRESS FACTORY
Map 4

500 Sampsonia Way, 412/231-3169, www.mattress.org

COST: $9 adult, $6 student, $7 senior

Not only is the Mattress Factory an internationally recognized organization that focuses singularly on installation art, it also hosts a truly unique residency program. Over the past three decades, more than 250 artists have lived at the museum while creating new work. And while any given year sees a regular rotation of such new (and temporary) installations, the museum owns many permanent pieces as well. Some of the most stunning are James Turrell's odd and unsettling works of neon and light. Don't miss *Pleiades,* an entirely dark room where a presence of light may or may not appear. Another can't-miss is Yayoi Kusama's *Infinity Dots Mirrored Room;* entering it may just change your perspective on reality itself.

Admission is free for children under 6 and CMU students. University of Pittsburgh students can get in free during the fall and spring semesters. Every Thursday the museum offers half off the admission price (with the exception of group tours).

PENNSYLVANIA TROLLEY MUSEUM
Map 7

1 Museum Rd., Washington, 724/228-9256, www.pa-trolley.org

HOURS: Memorial Day-Labor Day Mon.-Fri. 10 A.M.-4 P.M., Sat.-Sun. 11 A.M.-5 P.M., after Labor Day Fri. 10 A.M.-4 P.M., Sat.-Sun. 11 A.M.-5 P.M.

COST: $7 adult, $6 senior, $4 child

Consisting of a historic trolley car house and a visitor education center, the Pennsylvania Trolley Museum is a documentation of the state's streetcars and of the era during which they were regularly traversing the Keystone State's urban areas.

The museum opened its doors in 1963, although the concept first dawned on the PTM founders in the early 1940s, when it seemed as if the cars—a truly quaint and important chapter of U.S. public transport history—were quickly disappearing from American cities. Today, a gift shop and a trolley car restoration site are a part of the facilities as well.

Admission includes a guided tour of the trolley car barn, which takes approximately 90 minutes to complete, as well as all the trolley rides you can handle along the museum's four-mile-long train track. Pictoral exhibits are always on display in the education center, and for an additional $2 charge ($1 children), visitors can tour the Trolley Display Building, a 28,000-square-foot site where 30 restored cars from the tri-state area are stored.

PHOTO ANTIQUITIES MUSEUM   Map 4

531 E. Ohio St., 412/231-7881,
www.photoantiquities.com
HOURS: Mon., Wed.-Fri. 10 A.M.-4 P.M., Sat. 10 A.M.-3 P.M.
COST: $6.50 adult, $3 child, $5 senior

A 2,500-square-foot museum dedicated to the preservation of historical photography, the Photo Antiquities Museum is decorated with a quaint Victorian interior and boasts an archive of more than 100,000 negatives and prints. Beginning with the very earliest days of photography, the collection spans not only images, of which roughly 3,000 are always on display, but also cameras and other photo-graphic accessories. The era of the earliest Daguerreotype (roughly 1839) is documented, as is every important photographic era including the digital cameras of the 21st century. The relatively small museum has literally hundreds of historical photographs on display, and at the on-site gift shop, visitors can purchase reproductions—from 8 by 10 to mural-sized—of any of the museum's images. Lectures and tours are occasionally given by volunteers; call for upcoming schedules. At the time of writing, the museum was considering a move to another location; it might be wise to call before visiting.

TOUR-ED MINE AND MUSEUM   Map 7

748 Bull Creek Rd., Tarentum, 724/244-4720,
www.tour-edmine.com
HOURS: Memorial Day-Labor Day daily 10 A.M.-4 P.M., closed Tue.
COST: $7 adult, $5 child

With a collection of more than 9,000 authentic mining artifacts dating as far back as the 1850s, the Tour-Ed Mine and Museum wonderfully documents both the deep-mining and strip-mining histories of Southwestern Pennsylvania.

Schoolchildren especially enjoy the immersion experience of entering the Tour-Ed Mine, which was first mined for coal sometime around 1850 and eventually had its named changed to Avenue Mine. Since 1970, more than one million tours have been given at the site, each one led by experienced former miners. Tour groups will have a chance to examine mining tools and actual mining methods up close, and although the tour focuses partly on historical mining methods, modern advanced methods are also demonstrated and explained. Hydraulic machines are used to mine coal today, for instance, although in the mid-1800s it was largely dug by hand. Light jackets are recommended, as the mine's temperature remains steady at around 55°F year-round.

To ensure that every visitor has a chance to clearly view the demonstrations, tours never consist of more than 25 people. Visitors will also have a chance to view a working sawmill, as well as a reproduction of a 1900-era mine village, complete with a general store and a barbershop.

Just more than three miles away, you'll find the **Galleria at Pittsburgh Mills** (590 Pittsburgh Mills Circle, 724/904-9000, Mon.–Sat. 10 A.M.–9:30 P.M., Sun. 11 A.M.–6 P.M., www.pittsburghmills.com), an indoor and outdoor shopping center with a bowling alley, a movie theater, and numerous retailers, including H&M, Forever 21, and Borders Books & Music.

GALLERIES

BOX HEART   Map 6
4523 Liberty Ave., 412/687-8858
Much like the emerging artists who live in the neighborhood, Box Heart gallery is a grassroots sort of place where handmade jewelry, handmade soaps, and other crafts can be found among paintings and other items of visual art by local up-and-comers.

BREW HOUSE SPACE 101   Map 3
2100 Mary St., 412/381-7767
Formerly home of the Duquesne Brewery, the Brew House Space has since been converted into a series of loft-like spaces that double as working studios for around a dozen of the city's most prolific visual artists. The building's residents also act as a nonprofit collective; it was one of the collective's regular meetings that led to the creation of Space 101, where critically acclaimed group shows regularly take place. With high, warehouse-like ceilings and nearly a city block's worth of space, the gallery is ideal for installation art and giant sculpture. Theater performances and rock shows often take place in the attached Industrial Arts Co-op room.

FUTURE TENANT   Map 1
801 Liberty Ave., 412/325-7037,
www.futuretenant.org
The Pittsburgh Cultural Trust hosts this project of Carnegie Mellon University, an ever-changing art space where exhibitions might take the place of amateur installations, literary events, video art presentations, or pretty much anything else the creative mind can conceive. Given the truly experimental nature of Future Tenant, shows can understandably be somewhat hit or miss. And although use of the space isn't technically limited to artists from the CMU community, the work of the school's students and faculty are certainly represented with frequency. MFA exhibitions take place at the end of each school semester.

◖ JAMES GALLERY   Map 7
413 S. Main St., 412/922-9800,
www.jamesgallery.net
One of the city's most respected houses of contemporary, modern, and older works, James Gallery exhibits work not only by Pittsburgh's top artists, but also by national and international artists of note. Work here is created in all manner of media, including sculpture, photography, and fiber arts, and many of the artists represented by the gallery are available for site-specific commissions.

LAWRENCEVILLE'S 16:62 DESIGN ZONE

Previously occupied almost entirely by lower-income and working-class families, the East End neighborhood of Lawrenceville has lately experienced something of an artistic rebirth. The city's gay and lesbian community became responsible for much of the area's turnaround after some snapped up cheap row houses along the main commercial thoroughfare of Butler Street and then proceeded to transform them into antique shops and quirky boutiques. Wisely, a number of area business owners choose to take advantage of the changes by creating the 16:62 Design Zone, a district stretching from the 16th Street Bridge in the Strip District to the 62nd Street Bridge in Lawrenceville. Here, more than 100 galleries, unique interior design vendors, and professional creative firms can be found.

Keep in mind that while the Strip District has long been packed with curiosities, the Lawrenceville stretch of the Design Zone is still a relatively young creation. In other words, don't expect to find galleries or boutiques of great interest on every last block. Your best bet is to start somewhere around 35th and Butler Streets and to then slowly wander east (away from Downtown and the Strip District). **Scavengers Antiques and Collectibles** (3533 Butler St., 412/682-6781) is one of Lawrenceville's older retail spaces; here you'll find a rambling collection of kitschy toys and assorted Americana treasures. The next few blocks east are home to newer shops, such as **Sugar Boutique** (3703 Butler St., 412/681-5100, www.sugarboutique.com), which stocks designer women's clothing and accessories; and **Pavement Shoes** (3629 Butler St., 412/621-6400, www.pavementshoes.com), where distinctively unique women's footwear can be found. Galleries worth your while include **Fe Gallery** (4102 Butler St., 412/860-6028), an especially forward-thinking space known for its sometimes shocking contemporary art shows; and **Digging Pitt Gallery** (4419 Butler St., 412/605-0459, www.diggingpitt.com), whose shows tend to lean toward lowbrow, pop culture, or politically influenced work. Also, don't miss **Who Knew?** (5156 Butler St., 412/781-0588), a self-described "retro-mod" home furnishings store with rare designer goods from the 1950s, '60s, and '70s.

Once you've gotten your fill of shopping and gallery-going, or if you simply need to refuel, stop in at one of the Design Zone's better cafés or eateries. **Coca Cafe** (3811 Butler St., 412/621-3171) does a decent breakfast and Sunday brunch while serving up the usual assortment of espresso drinks and pastries in a hipster-friendly environment, while **Piccolo Forno** (3801 Butler St., 412/622-0111) offers Tuscan-style wood-fired pizzas covered with ingredients imported from Italy.

Handy 16:62 Design Zone guidebooks are available free of charge at many district locations; you can also visit www.1662designzone.com and request to have a guide mailed directly to your home.

ARTS AND ENTERTAINMENT

MANCHESTER CRAFTSMEN'S GUILD

Map 7

1815 Metropolitan St., 412/322-1773,
www.manchesterguild.org

Something of a cross between an educational music and arts facility, a gallery, and a concert space with an on-site recording studio, Manchester Craftsmen's Guild is one of the local scene's most intriguing and culturally philanthropic arts institutions. Located in out-of-the-way Manchester, not far from some of the city's roughest North Side neighborhoods, it's appropriate that the guild offers arts and photography classes to disadvantaged high schoolers. Grown-ups can take courses as well, although many folks who flock here do so for the notable jazz concert series. Anyone is free to wander into the main lobby, however, which doubles as the guild's ever-changing, multimedia art gallery.

MENDELSON

Map 5

5874 Ellsworth Ave., 412/361-8664

Particularly interesting and worth a visit not only for its extensive collection of impressive modern selections (work by Keith Haring and Robert Mapplethorpe has been displayed in the past), but also for the fact that Steve Mendelson's East End gallery, Mendelson, is also his home.

PITTSBURGH CENTER FOR THE ARTS

Map 5

6300 5th Ave., 412/361-0873,
www.pittsburgharts.org

A self-described "non-profit community arts campus," the Pittsburgh Center for the Arts is one of the region's most unique resource centers for visual artists. Artists-in-training can sign up for one of the center's ever-popular studio classes, while working professionals can apply to the residency program that takes place at various sites throughout the city. The work displayed in the gallery here is produced largely by southwestern Pennsylvanians with various skill levels. You'll find works by well-established artists displayed alongside pieces by newcomers.

PITTSBURGH GLASS CENTER

Map 6

5472 Penn Ave., 412/365-2145,
www.pittsburghglasscenter.org

Not content to exist simply as a static gallery, the nonprofit and architecturally stunning Pittsburgh Glass Center is also an education hub. Wannabe glass blowers can attend a slew of classes here, including flameworking, casting, and hot glass workshops. Show up during an evening exhibition and you'll find staff members and student glass blowers alike demonstrating their skills and often selling their wares; glass jewelry is an especially popular medium. Or simply peruse the current exhibition at the Hodge Gallery—stunning creative glass art and mixed media shows happen here regularly.

SILVER EYE CENTER FOR PHOTOGRAPHY

Map 3

1015 E. Carson St., 412/431-1810,
www.silvereye.org

Aside from the occasional student shows that take place at Pittsburgh Filmmakers' Melwood Photography Gallery, the Silver Eye Center is the city's solitary locale dedicated exclusively to the photographic arts. And what a gallery it is. Comprising two small but inviting rooms, there's almost nothing in the space that intrudes on whatever contemporary or archival show is currently taking place. And although shows featuring Pittsburgh-based artists are commonplace, so too are exhibitions featuring work from around the world. Independent films are occasionally screening at Silver Eye as well.

SOCIETY FOR CONTEMPORARY CRAFT   Map 1

2100 Smallman St., 412/261-7003,
www.contemporarycraft.org

Located in an industrial warehouse space, the Society for Contemporary Craft has been presenting exhibitions both duly conservative and wildly eccentric for more than 30 years. The permanent collection includes blown glass by Dale Chihuly and rare chairs by the likes Frank Gehry and Mr. Imagination; clay, metal, and fiber crafts are also on display. Temporary exhibitions might feature anything from decoupage collages by inner-city high school kids, to outsider art from the Deep South, to utilitarian crafts by self-taught Native Americans. Should you find yourself at the Steel Plaza "T" station Downtown, be sure to check out the society's satellite gallery, located inside the One Mellon Bank Center building.

SPACE   Map 1

812 Liberty Ave., 412/325-7723,
www.spacepittsburgh.org

Curated by a former *Pittsburgh City Paper* arts editor, SPACE is perhaps the city's most contemporary-minded arts emporium. And with deejays, live music, and hordes of the city's prettiest young things showing up *en masse* for nearly every event, openings tend to more closely resemble house parties than the stale wine-and-cheese happenings found at your average gallery. Special attention is paid to local artists whose work is generally ignored or overlooked, especially those photographers,

visual artists, or installation builders who consistently push the envelope of oddity.

WOOD STREET GALLERIES   Map 1

601 Wood St., 412/471-5605,
www.woodstreetgalleries.org

Certainly one of Pittsburgh's most ambitious contemporary galleries, Wood Street, which is publicly funded by the Pittsburgh Cultural Trust, is so-named because of its location above the Downtown Wood Street "T" station. Exhibitions here are decidedly hit or miss but almost always worth at least a cursory look. Multidisciplinary artists from Pittsburgh and, indeed, around the world, have shown here; the curators seem to have especially weak spots for industrial-themed installation art and wildly contemporary video art. Conceptual photography projects show up occasionally, as do local arts experts who participate in the galleries' eye-opening noontime lecture series.

THEATER

BENEDUM CENTER   Map 1

719 Liberty Ave., 412/456-6666,
www.pgharts.org/venues/benedun.aspx

Formerly known as the Stanley Theater, the Benedum Center is another of Pittsburgh's Downtown Cultural District cornerstones. The Pittsburgh Opera, the Civic Light Opera, and the Pittsburgh Ballet Theater all use the building as a home base, so patrons here are often seasonal subscribers of the fur-draped and jewel-encrusted variety. This is also where mainstream Broadway fare (*Cats, Phantom of the Opera*) can be consumed. And as for the simply stunning $43 million restoration? Let's just say that it's no wonder the Benedum is now on the National Register of Historic Places.

SHAKING UP THE BOARDS

Looking for theater that's a touch more progressive than the standard Cultural District fare? Consider tracking down a performance by one of the following progressive companies:

Don't expect complicated stage sets during a **barebones productions** (www.barebonesproductions.com) play. As the name implies, this company aims to use only the "bare essentials" during its emotionally intense character-driven plays. Robert Altman would approve.

Quantum Theatre (412/697-2929, www.quantumtheatre.com) Company Director Karla Boos is known locally for staging bizarre theater productions in equally bizarre locales. Past plays have taken place at the Pittsburgh Zoo, inside a Downtown parking garage, and at the Allegheny Cemetery.

A mixture of surrealist theater and junkyard folk music, the **Squonk Opera** (412/372-4264, www.squonkopera.com) puts on one of the most entertaining and unsettling multimedia shows in town. The players are often on the road; they recently starred in a Broadway production.

BYHAM THEATER   Map 1

101 6th St., 412/456-1350, www.pgharts.org/venues/byham.aspx

At just more than 200 years old, the Byham Theater (originally known as the Gayety Theater, and then as the Fulton) remains one of the most important cornerstones of the city's Cultural District theater scene. And although the Gayety was largely a vaudeville house and the Fulton a movie theater, today the main stage presents a mixture of dance, ballet, theater, and even live music. The fully restored, 1,500-seat interior is classic American music hall and apparently no detail was spared. Imagine a luxurious lobby, a full balcony, and friendly ushers who escort latecomers to their seats with a flashlight. The Byham is a true American classic.

CHARITY RANDALL THEATRE   Map 2

Forbes Ave. at Bigelow Blvd., 412/624-7529, www.pitt.edu/~play/facilities.htm

One of the three performance spaces used by the University of Pittsburgh's Theatre Department (the other two are the Henry Heymann Theatre, located just downstairs, and the Cathedral of Learning's Studio Theatre), the Charity Randall Theatre is an intimate, 478-seat auditorium. This is where the vast majority of student-run performances take place; Shakespeare is particularly popular, and years past have seen a similar glut of student-friendly fare (George Bernard Shaw, Andrew Lloyd Webber). Artists-in-residence working at Pitt can often be seen performing alongside the student actors.

◖ CITY THEATRE   Map 3

1300 Bingham St., 412/431-2489, www.citytheatrecompany.org

Known as one of the city's most experimental and adventurous companies, City Theatre is tucked away in a cozy redbrick building just a block from the corner of East Carson and 13th Streets. The 270-seat main studio has something of an industrial warehouse feel, a vibe that works especially well when the performance is particularly edgy. Artistic Director Tracy Brigden has been lead-

© FABIAN BAUTISTA

Heinz Hall, the Pittsburgh Symphony Orchestra's home base

ing the company since 2001 and has since produced monologues, a number of world premieres, and even an oddly avant-garde live music experience with Pittsburgh's own Squonk Opera.

HEINZ HALL   Map 1

600 Penn Ave., 412/392-4900,
www.pittsburghsymphony.org

Anyone interested in taking in a performance by the Pittsburgh Symphony Orchestra will need to settle in at Heinz Hall, which is the ensemble's Downtown home base. And although not currently at the very top of its game—as it was during conductor Lorin Maazel's tenure—the PSO has consistently been recognized by experts around the world as one of the country's greatest orchestras. The hall itself is a splendidly restored former hotel and boasts such features as an adjustable orchestra pit and an outdoor gar-

den plaza with a waterfall. Guided tours are available to groups of eight or more.

KELLY-STRAYHORN COMMUNITY   Map 6
PERFORMING ARTS CENTER

5941 Penn Ave., 412/363-3000,
www.kelly-strayhorn.org

As its name implies, the Kelly-Strayhorn doesn't support a home theater company, but rather opens its doors to a widely diverse range of events and performances. Located in the heart of East Liberty's still relatively blighted business district, the center is named in honor of two East Libbers who made it big: Stage man Gene Kelly and jazz great Billy Strayhorn. Past events have included area high school dance companies, traditional dancers from India and Brazil, and even film screenings. Care to lease the center for a performance of your own? It can be had during a weekday for as little as $450.

ZANY UMBRELLA CIRCUS

Founded by the largely self-taught circus aerialist, juggler, and funnyman Ben Sota, Pittsburgh's Zany Umbrella Circus (412/390-4054, www.zanyumbrella.com) is something of a poor man's Cirque du Soleil. Imagine a ragtag gang of grown-up punk-rockers and activist types performing daredevil stage stunts, and you'll start to get the idea.

Zany Umbrella hasn't been around for long; the company was founded in early 2004 after being awarded a $10,000 grant from the Sprout Fund, a community arts organization. After its coming-out party at that year's Three Rivers Arts Festival, Sota and his troupe's popularity exploded in Pittsburgh, and for months they could be seen performing their unique mixture of drama, music, and old-style carny stunts at just about every important arts function in town.

Zany's astounding skills have lately taken them on the road; they recently entertained children displaced by the Hurricane Katrina tragedy in Louisiana, and have also taken a good-will show to the children of Afghanistan.

O'REILLY THEATER   Map 1
(PITTSBURGH PUBLIC THEATER)
621 Penn Ave., 412/316-1600,
www.pgharts.org/venues/oreilly.aspx

Unbeknownst to even most locals, the O'Reilly Theater was designed by superstar architect Michael Graves, a name you might recognize if you've lately perused the kitchen utensils aisle at Target (Graves is also a product designer). The 650-seat theater opened in late 1999, and it was built specifically with acoustic excellence in mind. It's also the only theater space Downtown featuring a "thrust" stage, meaning that the audience surrounds the stage floor on three sides in a "U" shape. Performances here are suitably eccentric while still maintaining mainstream appeal; successful Off-Broadway and comedy shows seem to do well.

PITTSBURGH PLAYHOUSE   Map 2
22 Craft Ave., 412/621-4445,
www.pointpark.edu

Situated in a somewhat obscure stretch of South Oakland (if you can find Magee-Women's Hospital, you're close), the Pittsburgh Playhouse is home to a professional company known as The Rep, as well as three student companies based at the nearby Point Park University: A children's theater company, a dance company, and a standard theater company. In other words, there's a *lot* going on at the playhouse during any given month—indeed, there are 235 performances annually—so there's a good chance that no matter your specific arts preference, you'll be able to find something here that grabs your interest.

CONCERT VENUES
A. J. PALUMBO CENTER   Map 1
600 Forbes Ave., 412/396-6058

Although technically the home of the Duquesne University Dukes and Lady Dukes basketball teams, the A. J. Palumbo Center frequently transforms into a pop and rock concert hall after dark. Only the biggest artists at the top of their game perform here; years past have seen Public Enemy, Jane's

Addiction, Green Day, and the Counting Crows take the stage. Other entertainment and sporting events happen occasionally, such as wrestling and boxing. Insider's tip: To avoid being crushed on the floor during a rock show, arrive early and grab a seat in the general admission bleachers nearest the stage.

CARNEGIE MUSIC HALL   Map 2
4400 Forbes Ave., 412/323-1919

Tucked into the same building as the Carnegie Museums of Art and Natural History, the beautifully restored and antique Carnegie Music Hall is a 1,928-seat venue often described as "acoustically perfect." That's good news for the patrons of the Pittsburgh Chamber Music Society, who perform here regularly; folk concerts organized by the Calliope Music Society take place here as well. And the Carnegie Lecture Series brings to the music hall an always-impressive rotation of literary celebs.

CHEVROLET AMPHITHEATRE   Map 3
1 Station Square, 412/232-6200,
www.chevroletamphitheatre.com

As far as outdoor stadiums go, Chevy Amphitheatre has an enviously unbeatable view. Situated just across the Monongahela River from Downtown, the vista grows more picturesque with each passing minute as the sun begins to fall and the lights of Pittsburgh's skyline illuminate. And since the venue itself isn't much more than an open-ended tarp with a stage on one end, it's also possible to watch the procession of passing trains on the nearby hillside. Bands and artists performing

FLASH DANCERS

You may find yourself somewhat surprised to learn that Pittsburgh has a fairly progressive modern dance scene, but, after all, this is the city where the Adrian Lyne film *Flashdance* was based.

Attack Theatre (412/441-8444, www.attacktheatre.com) is currently one of the area's most intriguing troupes; comprising mainly of cofounders Michele de la Reza and Peter Kope, the gorgeously sophisticated duo were described by the *Pittsburgh Post-Gazette* as "the Fred and Ginger of the '90s where Ginger does most of the lifting." Internationally acclaimed cellist Dave Eggar frequently performs with the two.

The phenomenally talented **Dance Alloy** (412/363-4321, www.dancealloy.org) is a somewhat more traditional modern troupe that tours both nationally and around the world. It performs both original and commissioned works. Visit the troupe online for a schedule of Pittsburgh performances and for information about the Dance Alloy School, where professional instructors teach standard classes and intensive workshops.

Also worth exploring is the **Nego Gato** (412/201-4564, www.negogato.org) organization. The troupe explores Afro-Brazilian culture through a combination of music, dance, and a Brazilian martial art known as capoeira. (Adult and youth capoeira classes are offered frequently.)

The **UMOJA African Arts Company** (412/471-1121, www.umojacompany.com) is a nonprofit organization whose mission is to raise awareness of African culture and heritage. Performances combine dance, drumming, and storytelling.

here are generally of the Top 40 variety; pop-punk, country, and jam band acts are particularly popular. The amphitheater is closed during the snowy winter months.

MELLON ARENA   Map 1
66 Mario Lemiuex Pl., 412/642-1800,
www.mellonarena.com

Although previously known as the Civic Arena, the massive silver dome that sits on the outskirts of Downtown is more popularly known as "The Igloo," in part because this is where the Pittsburgh Penguins hockey club competes locally. But when pro sports or wrestling matches aren't happening, the Igloo hosts pop and rock concerts of the light-and-stage-show variety; think Rolling Stones, Britney Spears, Madonna. Scenes from two movies have also been filmed here: 1979's *The Fish That Saved Pittsburgh* and 1995's *Sudden Death*.

PEPSI-COLA ROADHOUSE   Map 7
565 Rte. 18, 724/947-1900,
www.pepsiroadhouse.com

Imagine going to a dinner theater way out in the sticks, but instead of a murder-mystery taking place on stage, you're being entertained by a classic-era country-and-western act. That's the scene at the Pepsi-Cola Roadhouse, where hundreds of show-goers squeeze in around tables to nosh on barbeque ribs and nod their heads to Kenny Rogers or Dwight Yoakam. A number of video projection screens and a state-of-the-art sound system fill the roadhouse, so even if you don't happen to be right up against the stage, every show here is practically guaranteed to be an unequivocally intimate experience.

PETERSEN EVENTS CENTER   Map 2
3719 Terrace St., 412/323-1919,
www.pittsburghpanthers.com

Constructed by the University of Pittsburgh in 2002 as a home for the Pitt Panthers basketball team, the main stadium at Petersen Events Center can seat roughly 10,000 fans, and that's not including club and luxury seats. Sports and fitness isn't the only game here, however; top-selling pop and hip-hop acts like Outkast and the Counting Crows perform frequently. In fact, Downtown's Mellon Arena is the only large-capacity venue in town with more seating. Alcohol isn't available at this venue.

POST-GAZETTE PAVILION   Map 7
Rte. 18 at Rte. 22, 412/323-1919,
www.starlakeamp.com

As Western Pennsylvania's largest concert venue, Post-Gazette Pavilion is essentially Pittsburgh's version of Denver's Red Rocks Amphitheater, or the Gorge in the Pacific Northwest. In other words, this is where the touring summer festivals stop on their way through the tri-state area; Lollapalooza and the Lilith Fair have both showed up in years past, as have a slew of big-name jam bands, such as Phish and the Grateful Dead. Tickets can be purchased for the seating area near the stage, which is in fact covered by a pavilion. Most show-goers prefer the cheaper general admission tickets, however, which will earn you a seat somewhere on the grass. Keep in mind that the Pavilion is roughly a 45-minute drive from Downtown Pittsburgh.

CINEMA
ANDY WARHOL MUSEUM   Map 4
117 Sandusky St., 412/237-8300,
www.warhol.org

Although certainly not a standard movie theater in the conventional sense of the term, the cinema room at the Andy Warhol Museum nonetheless boasts a professional-level projector and sound system, as well as especially comfortable seating. Admission is included free with a museum ticket, and the theater maintains a daily, rotating schedule of films by or about Warhol and his long guest list of superstars and protégés. Factory Diaries, featuring interviews with celebrities like David Bowie and Lou Reed, are frequently screened, as is the occasional rare and arty film with little apparent relation to Warhol or the Factory crew.

CARNEGIE SCIENCE CENTER   Map 4
OMNIMAX THEATER
1 Allegheny Ave., 412/237-3400,
www.carnegiesciencecenter.org

Leave it to the smart folks at the Carnegie Science Center to improve ever so slightly on the already fascinating IMAX theater experience, a high-quality, large-screen film format where the picture is usually three stories high, or roughly 50 feet. The Carnegie's screen, however, is four stories high. It's also concaved, so that the on-screen action takes place not just in front of you, but also on both sides. Thankfully, the seats recline, so there's no need to worry about painful neck strain. And although most IMAX films are relatively brief, every screening here is proceeded by a showing of *Pittsburgh's Big Picture,* a short documentary about life in the Steel City.

HARRIS THEATER   Map 1
809 Liberty Ave., 412/471-9700,
www.pghfilmmakers.org/harris.html

As a member of the Pittsburgh Filmmakers family of art house cinemas, Harris Theater is one of the most progressive places to watch movies in town. And aside from a few adult bookstore video booths, it's the only theater in the Downtown area. Independent and foreign films are what you'll find here, although since many movies screen only for a limited time, you'll want to move quickly if something grabs your interest. If you're in town specifically for the annual Three Rivers Film Festival, you'll be spending a lot of time at the Harris, which will quite likely be the closest theater to your Downtown hotel.

MANOR THEATER   Map 5
1729 Murray Ave., 412/422-7729

One of only two movie houses in Squirrel Hill, the Manor Theater typically screens so-called big-budget indie films; in other words, movies that are on a somewhat limited release but that generally aren't too terribly left of center. Family fare and children's pictures also screen regularly here, which makes sense given the abundance of youngsters in this family-friendly neighborhood. With a total of four screens, there's bound to be something that appeals. And if not, head down the hill to the more mainstream Squirrel Hill Theatre on Forward Avenue. Insider's tip: The nearby Gullifty's (1922 Murray Ave.) is a perfect spot for post-movie coffee and dessert.

MCCONOMY AUDITORIUM   Map 2
Carnegie Mellon University, 5032 Forbes Ave., First Floor, 412/268-8704

Located inside CMU's student union building—the University Center—McConomy Auditorium does triple duty as a lecture hall, a popular location for touring events (Dr. Ruth spoke here recently), and a movie

ARTS AND ENTERTAINMENT

theater. Since the cost of the films is supported by CMU's student activities fee, CMU students with proper I.D. can attend any screening without paying. Nonstudents are welcome as well, although most films will set you back anywhere from $3–5. McConomy shows a fairly even mixture of second-run blockbusters, cult films from the 1970s and '80s, documentaries, and foreign films.

MELWOOD SCREENING ROOM   Map 2

477 Melwood Ave., 412/682-4111,
www.pghfilmmakers.org/melwood.html
Located on the second floor of Pittsburgh Filmmakers, a film, video, and photography production center and training facility in North Oakland, Melwood Screening Room is the city's premiere locale for ultra-unusual indie films. When Matthew Barney's Cremaster Cycle came to town, for instance, the Melwood was the no-brainer choice to host. Student films play in this 130-seat venue as well, as does the local phenomenon known as Film Kitchen, a monthly independent film and video series featuring a selection of mostly local-made shorts.

🄲 OAKS THEATER   Map 7

310 Allegheny River Blvd., Oakmont, 412/828-6311,
www.theoakstheater.com
It's no wonder the Oaks Theater was named Best Independent Movie Theater by the readers of *Pittsburgh City Paper;* as a 65-year-old Pittsburgh area institution, it's one of the very few movie houses in town that genuinely evokes the Golden Age of cinema. Even better, seating is most definitely

not limited—430 film fanatics can gather together at the Oaks, which, yes, is still a one-screen operation. And while independent and foreign films are shown throughout the week, a regular series of midnight cult classics (*Rocky Horror,* plus films by David Lynch, George Romero, et al.) takes place regularly as well.

REGENT SQUARE THEATER   Map 7

1035 S. Braddock Ave., 412/682-4811,
www.pghfilmmakers.org/regent.html
A 300-seat, single-screen art house cinema, Regent Square Theater is located on the opposite side of Frick Park from Squirrel Hill. Regent Square, like Oakland's Melwood Screening Room and Downtown's Harris Theater, is also a member of the Pittsburgh Filmmakers family; that means that eclectic films both domestic and foreign are the order of the day.

SQUIRREL HILL THEATRE   Map 5

5824 Forward Ave., 412/421-7900
Unfortunately, the Squirrel Hill Theatre doesn't have a whole lot going for it other than its convenient location. There are six screens, but most are decidedly on the small side. Nonetheless, if you're in the East End and in the mood for a mainstream Hollywood flick—and if you don't feel like making the journey all the way to the Waterfront in Homestead—the Squirrel Hill is really your only option. Which isn't to say that the theater is dirty or unpleasant. Suffice it to say that if you've ever been to a suburban shopping mall theater, you'll know what to expect.

Festivals and Events

Perhaps because so many pockets of Pittsburgh still preserve a proud small-town vibe, it's not unusual to see even the most plebian of neighborhood parades, block parties, and ethnic-themed gatherings packed full of families, teenagers, or anyone else who happens to wander by. And should you choose to show up at one of Pittsburgh's annual citywide fests, you might wonder if maybe the entire town hasn't arrived. In particular, the Three Rivers Arts Festival, First Night Pittsburgh, and Light Up Night are absolute can't-miss events for any true local, or for that matter, any visitor interested in understanding what it means to live in the Steel City in the 21st century.

In other words, most festivals here are true community events, and not just excuses to swill cheap beer out of plastic cups (although if that's what you're looking for, you won't likely be disappointed).

The weeks between Memorial Day and Labor Day are a particularly active time for outdoor gatherings and organized events.

WINTER

FIRST NIGHT PITTSBURGH   Map 1

Pittsburgh Cultural Trust, 803 Liberty Ave., 412/471-6070,

www.firstnightpgh.com, www.pgharts.org

Yeah, we know: December 31 is actually the *last* night of the year, not the first. But hey, this is Pittsburgh; we're not exactly known for sweating the small stuff. Not that First Night is ever anything small. On the contrary, this is one of the most popular and

the Sprout Fund's annual Hothouse party

© MARA RAGO

ARTS AND ENTERTAINMENT

packed events of the entire year, regardless of the fact that it's usually freezing cold outside. The party takes place in and around the Market Square and Cultural District areas of Downtown, and the celebration, naturally, is all about ringing in the New Year. The twist is that this party is family-friendly and alcohol-free. Entertainment changes a bit from year to year, but generally involves onstage music and dance, a street parade, copious food booths, and, at the end of the night, a spectacular fireworks display.

LIGHT UP NIGHT   Map 1
Pittsburgh Downtown Partnership, 412/566-4190, www.downtownpittsburgh.com

For Pittsburghers, Light Up Night signals the official start of the holiday season each November. Tens of thousands of people stream into Downtown for the occasion, which literally consists of lighting up the night; major department stores and small businesses alike line their facades with blinking holiday lights, and the city suddenly becomes a mini–Winter Wonderland. A few special exhibits are erected as well, including a massive Christmas tree near the Market Square fountain, which becomes an outdoor ice skating rink during this time of year. Also festively lit up and worth a look is Station Square, which can easily be reached on foot by traversing the Smithfield Street Bridge.

PITT NATIONALITY   Map 2
ROOMS HOLIDAY TOURS
Cathedral of Learning, University of Pittsburgh, corner of 5th Ave. and Bigelow Blvd., 412/624-6000, www.pitt.edu/~natrooms

What better time to tour the Nationality Rooms at Pitt's Cathedral of Learning than the holiday season (November–January), when every room is fully decked out in each country's respective holiday style? Even if you've already toured the rooms, which are a series of fully functional classrooms designed and decorated to resemble classrooms from 26 separate nations, the holiday tour is still worth considering, especially if you're traveling with youngsters who might benefit from learning something about the historical culture of Christmas.

SPRING
PEDAL PITTSBURGH   Map 3
Station Square at Carson St. at the Smithfield Street Bridge, 412/232-3545, www.pedalpittsburgh.org

Pittsburgh may not be well known as a popular city for cyclists, but what with its hills, valleys, bridges, waterways, and, yes, miles of bike trails, it's a simple fact that one of the best ways to experience the unique sights and landscape of the city is atop two wheels. And that's exactly why Pedal Pittsburgh, which, by the way, is a recreational ride and not a race, is so popular. More than 2,000 cyclists show up every year in May at the Chevy Amphitheatre in Station Square, where the ride begins and ends; the six separate courses range from six miles to 60 miles, so whether you're a hardcore cyclist or you're leading a family of small children, you'll be able to fully participate at a comfortable pace. Departures take place in the early morning; lunch and live entertainment is scheduled during the middle of the day.

PITTSBURGH FOLK FESTIVAL   Map 1
1000 Fort Duquesne Blvd., David L. Lawrence Convention Center, 412/565-6000 (center), 412/278-1267 (office), www.pghfolkfest.org

Now in its fifth decade, the Pittsburgh Folk

Festival, which takes place in May, presents an ideal opportunity to explore the cultural intricacies of more than two dozen nationalities, all without leaving Downtown. Ethnic food and entertainment is offered throughout the day, and visitors have the chance to practice ethnic dances or to simply shop for souvenirs in the international bazaar. Participating nationalities vary from year to year; participants in 2006 included nationals from Pakistan, Germany, India, Ireland, Poland, Scandinavia, Croatia, and many more.

PITTSBURGH INTERNATIONAL CHILDREN'S FESTIVAL   Map 4

West Park, 412/321-5520,
www.pghkids.org/festival.htm

For parents who aim to be educationally responsible, but who can't possibly bear to suffer through another brain-numbing performance of *Barney on Ice,* the Pittsburgh International Children's Festival may be just the thing. A weeklong showcase in May of pro theater companies from around the world, this is entertainment you can feel proud exposing your kids to. England, Germany, China, West Africa, and even Pittsburgh were represented in last year's festival; performances run the gamut from acrobatics to music and dance to comedy and drama.

ST. PATRICK'S DAY PARADE   Map 1

www.pittsburghirish.org/parade

Get this: Pittsburghers are so nuts about St. Paddy's Day that, depending on which day the holiday actually falls on, it's sometimes celebrated *twice.* It works like this: The St. Patrick's Day Parade always takes place on a Saturday in March, so if St. Paddy's Day falls on a weekday, the parade will happen the Saturday *before* the actual holiday. Con-

fused yet? Just remember this: In Pittsburgh, that means two excuses to party. And what a party it is. The parade, which, begins as early as 10 A.M. and snakes throughout Downtown, is a fete of almost unbelievable proportions. Think floats, marching bands, and a very inebriated crowd. And no, you don't have to be Irish (or a connoisseur of green beer) to join in.

SUMMER

E-FEST   Map 6

Corner of Highland and Penn Aves.

A community-oriented arts festival held on the streets of East Liberty in July, E-Fest draws around 5,000 people annually to this quickly changing inner-city neighborhood. Area high school students help organize the festival and work closely with artists and vendors. The fest presents a decent mix of music and dance performances; some artists are contemporary and experimental, while others, such as the East Liberty Presbyterian Church's Bach Choir, are more conservative. Games and a plethora of food and crafts vendors round out the event, much of the proceeds of which are given away to charity.

FOURTH OF JULY   Map 1

Point State Park

Pittsburgh's celebration of Independence Day probably won't come across as anything other than business as usual for anyone who was born and raised somewhere between sea and shining sea. Pittsburgh's celebration takes place at Point State Park; arrive early to secure a seat near the rivers. Blankets are suggested if you'll be staying awhile, and entertainment is generally provided by massive public address–style speakers blasting patriotic rock 'n' roll.

ARTS AND ENTERTAINMENT

COURTESY OF VISITPITTSBURGH

The crowds come out en masse for the annual Three Rivers Regatta in Point State Park.

HOTHOUSE

www.sproutfund.org/hothouse

COST: $40 general admission

Organized annually in June to benefit the Sprout Fund, an organization working to keep Pittsburgh a fun and artistic place to live and play, Hothouse is one of the most important events of the year for the city's see-and-be-seen crowd. The location tends to change each year, as do the performers and art installations, but if you'd like to know who is on the roster before laying out cash for a ticket, simply log onto the Sprout Fund's website and look for the list of artists who've won cash grants over the past year. Past award recipients include an artist who makes puppets out of drier lint and a Pittsburgh-affiliated group that organized a sidewalk-chalk mural competition. However, the majority of Hothouse exhibits are relatively sophisticated and meant to be taken seriously. Dress to impress.

PENNSYLVANIA MICROBREWERS FEST   Map 4

800 Vinial St., 412/237-9402, www.pennbrew.com

Craft brewers from all across Pennsylvania and beyond gather annually in June for this celebration of obscure and creatively brewed beer. The event, which has been going strong since 1995, conveniently takes place at the North Side's Penn Brewery. Attendees are welcome to sample nearly unlimited quantities of roughly 100 different beers, from Belgian Ales to India Pale Ales to organic beers. A meal is included with the price of admission, which should run about $32.

PITTSBURGH BLUES FESTIVAL

412/460-2583, www.pghblues.com

Not content to simply celebrate the blues, the Pittsburgh Blues Festival, which takes place in July, is also a highly successful food drive that has raised $600,000 for the Greater Pittsburgh Community Food Bank during its 12 years of existence. Of course, most folks do come primarily for the music and no wonder: Nationally and internationally acclaimed artists perform throughout the weekend, and especially big-name acts take the stage every evening. The location of the festival changes every year, so be sure to call or visit the festival's website well in advance. The setup is always the same, however: Food vendors offer Southern-themed eats, a Kids' Zone tent keeps the little ones amused, and hours upon hours of good ol' American blues fill the ears.

PITTSBURGH THREE RIVERS REGATTA
Map 1

Point State Park, 412/875-4841,
www.pghregatta.com

One of the city's most beloved summer events, the four-day-long Three Rivers Regatta pays tribute to one of Pittsburgh's most valuable resources: its winding waterways. The festival takes place in July inside Downtown's Point State Park, and, naturally, many of the best events take place in the drink. Families can enjoy Grand Prix Powerboat races, personal watercraft stunt shows, bass fishing, and even a boat demonstration by the U.S. Navy from the stadium-style seating that lines the Allegheny River. But fun stuff happens on land and in the air, too: hot air balloon rides, a dog Frisbee show, a U.S. Navy parachute team exhibition. There's even a concert series featuring marquee-level acts.

PITTSBURGH TRIATHLON AND ADVENTURE RACE
Map 4

33 Terminal Way, Friends of the Riverfront,

412/488-0212, www.friendsoftheriverfront.org, www.pittsburghtriathlon.com

The Pittsburgh Triathlon, a serious physical endurance test involving water, cycle, and foot races, will undoubtedly be your only opportunity to swim in the fairly polluted Allegheny River without being considered completely out of your mind. But this isn't a contest to be taken lightly; the event, which takes place in August, begins with a 1.5K swim from the North Shore to the Roberto Clemente Bridge and back, and then a rigorous 40K bike ride along I-279, and finally a 10K run along the Allegheny River. In other words, don't bother entering unless you're in absolutely top physical shape. Observing the race is an event in itself, however, and there's always the Adventure Race—a light two-mile canoe paddle followed by a 3.2-mile run that takes place at the same time as the Pittsburgh Triathlon. This is a good option for people who are not physically fit enough to participate in the triathlon.

PITTSBURGH VINTAGE GRAND PRIX
Map 2

Schenley Park, 412/687-1800,
www.pittsburghvintagegrandprix.com

A 10-day festival of races, car shows, and motorsports events, the Pittsburgh Vintage Grand Prix features one of the finest vintage car shows of its kind in the country. A bevy of classic car enthusiasts—all amateur drivers—motor throughout the streets of leafy Schenley Park for 10 days each July. Motorists arrive in what will almost certainly be the most unusual assortment of vehicles you've ever seen in one setting; expect mint-condition antique and exotic vehicles from all over the world. Proceeds benefit Pittsburghers with disabilities, although all events are free for spectators.

ARTS AND ENTERTAINMENT

◖ THREE RIVERS   Map 1
ARTS FESTIVAL
412/281-8723, www.artsfestival.net
Pittsburgh simply wouldn't be the same without the much-loved Three Rivers Arts Festival, a two-week-long celebration in June of live music, crafts, dance, performance, visual and contemporary art, and even a touch of carnival culture. Founded more than 35 years ago by a committee affiliated with the Carnegie Museum of Art, portions of the festival take place at various locations throughout Downtown, although the bulk of the activity happens in and around Point State Park. Keep your eyes peeled for festival schedules, which include maps and free concert listings. You'll need to stroll the length of Downtown's Penn and Liberty Avenues to explore all the participating galleries, while vendors who arrive from around the country to hawk handicrafts cluster near the Hilton, just across the street from Point State Park and the never-ending row of food carts. Installations and a rotating schedule of performance art take place just inside the park.

FALL

BLACK SHEEP   Map 3
PUPPET FESTIVAL
2100 Mary St., 412/381-7767,
www.blacksheeppuppet.com
A celebration of puppetry as an art form? True, it doesn't sound like much of a party. But the Black Sheep Puppet Festival, held every October at the Brew House artists' collective, is legendary among Pittsburgh's creative community. Performances, exhibitions, and museum shows take place for nearly the entire month of October at locations all over town, although the main event—an eclectically programmed schedule of puppet theater shows—takes place over two days at the Brew House. And no, these shows aren't just for kids; performances tend to tackle such serious business as depression and existential philosophy.

MEXICAN WAR STREETS   Map 4
HOUSE AND GARDEN TOUR
412/323-9030, www.mexicanwarstreets.org
Neighborhood renovation is the theme of the decidedly upscale Mexican War Streets House Tour during September, when owners of gorgeously restored homes in Pittsburgh's Victorian-era district open their doors and allow complete strangers to tramp through their living rooms. Many homes you'll see along the tour are listed in the National Register of Historic Places; even swankier is the black-tie pretour gala; it takes place in a different location each year. The tour is given in the Mexican War Streets neighborhood of the North Side. You will need to visit the website or call 412/323-9030 for ticket and location information.

OKTOBERFEST   Map 4
412/237-9400, www.pennbrew.com
Although smaller and less popular Oktoberfest celebrations take place at a handful of brewpubs throughout Southwestern Pennsylvania every September, Pittsburghers on the hunt for the biggest and best party always head to the outdoor patio at **Penn Brewery.** The event takes place over the length of two weekends, and the festivities follow the same schedule as Oktoberfest in Munich. And just like in Germany, the party is all about food, drink, music, and dance. Traditional German bands perform in both the outdoor tent

and the restaurant. All manner of schnitzels and wursts are available, as is the brewery's special-edition Oktoberfest brew. For *serious* Oktoberfest fans willing to take a bit of a drive, the free-to-the-public Pennsylvania Bavarian Oktoberfest in Canonsburg (about a 30-minute drive from Downtown) is known as one of the biggest celebrations of its type in the country. Call 724/745-1812 for more information.

PITTSBURGH DRAGON BOAT FESTIVAL
Map 3

Riverfront Park, 724/348-4836,
www.pittsburghdragonboatfestival.org

Something of a cross between a rowing competition and a celebration of pan-Asian culture, the Pittsburgh Dragon Boat Festival has been growing in popularity for five years now. For the uninitiated, a dragon boat is a long canoe-like vessel constructed to resemble (what else?) a dragon; the boats and races are a 2,400-year-old Chinese phenomenon. In Pittsburgh, the festivities take place near the boat launch at the South Side's Riverfront Park. Each boat fits 20 paddlers as well as one captain, known as a steersperson, and a drummer who pounds from the back of the boat. Non-racers will have more than enough to keep them busy as well; activities include martial arts, tai chi, and origami demonstrations.

PITTSBURGH IRISH FESTIVAL
Map 3

1 W. Station Square Dr., Chevrolet Amphitheatre,
www.pghirishfest.org

Station Square's open-air Chevy Amphitheatre is the site of the city's annual weekend celebration of the Emerald Isle, the Pittsburgh Irish Festival. Taking place in September, many activities revolve around the main stage, where both traditional and contemporary Irish musicians perform daily. Celtic dancing, traditional instrument demonstrations, traditional Irish eats, and activities aimed specifically at children round out the long weekend. But do be aware that although the festival is advertised as family friendly, a good number of attendees here tend to get pretty inebriated. So if you're sensitive about exposing your kids to this kind of behavior, you might consider hiring a sitter.

PITTSBURGH NEW WORKS FESTIVAL
Map 1

111 9th St., CAPA, 412/881-6888,
www.pittsburghnewworks.org

For thespians and theater buffs in the Steel City, no event compares with the New Works Festival, an annual showcase in September and October of one-act plays that stretches over four weeks. As is the case with most new-works festivals, an even mixture of comedy, drama, and highly experimental work is presented, and although a number of performances are the work of Southwestern Pennsylvania–based playwrights, playwrights from across the country are represented as well. Shows take place at a variety of locations around town. The main location of the festival is at Pittsburgh's Creative and Performing Arts High School in Downtown. Some of the events may happen at various other locations.

RICHARD S. CALIGUIRI CITY OF PITTSBURGH GREAT RACE
Map 5

Starts at Frick Park, 412/255-2493,
www.rungreatrace.com

Now that the Pittsburgh Marathon has been permanently cancelled due to citywide financial troubles, the annual Great

ARTS AND ENTERTAINMENT

Race in September is now Pittsburgh's sole opportunity for competitive foot racing. The contest consists of a 5K run and walk (about eight miles), as well as a 10K run (about 16 miles). The run, which begins at Squirrel Hill's Frick Park and ends at Point State Park, Downtown, generally draws as many as 10,000 participants. But unless you're at the absolute height of your competitive game, don't count on coming home with a prize; Kenyan athletes almost always take top honors.

THREE RIVERS FILM FESTIVAL

412/681-5449, www.3rff.com

An annual presentation of the Pittsburgh Filmmakers family, the Three Rivers Film Festival is now a quarter of a century old. Documentaries, foreign films, locally produced shorts, and a wide and varied schedule of films that would otherwise never be screened in a market as small as Pittsburgh's play during the festival at three separate locations: the **Regent Square Theater** (1035 S. Braddock Ave., Edgewood), **Harris Theater** (809 Liberty Ave., Downtown), and **Melwood Screening Room** (477 Melwood Ave., Oakland). The festival takes place in November and special events vary from year to year. Past festivals have featured Pere Ubu playing live to a Roger Corman film, and a screening of nickelodeon films from the 1900s.

SHOPPING

The average tourist or visitor arriving in Pittsburgh for a short-term stay may be here to take in a pro sporting event, attend a corporate conference, or to study at a local university, but it's rather unlikely, however, that they've arrived with an Amex Black Card in tow and a heart-pounding anticipation to hit the shops.

And yes, we'll admit it: It's certainly true that Pittsburgh has a limited number of districts where dozens of boutiques and eateries all sit within easy walking distance of each other. Yet as it turns out, the Steel City is actually home to a veritable gold mine of shopping opportunities if you know where to look.

Assuming you arrived via airplane, you've already gotten a sneak preview of the shopping bliss this city has to offer. I'm referring to Pittsburgh International's AirMall, of course, which has more going for it than many suburban malls. And inside the city itself, especially in the shopping havens of Shadyside, Oakland, and Squirrel Hill, you'll find the owners and staff to be surprisingly friendly and down to earth, even in the most elegant and expensive boutiques. Most of the local stores take pride in customer service and will go out of their way to make shoppers happy.

Perhaps surprisingly, nearly every major designer clothing label can be found in

© DAN ELDRIDGE

HIGHLIGHTS

LOOK FOR ◖ TO FIND RECOMMENDED SHOPS.

◖ **Best Bookstore for Browsing:** In a city not known for its bookstore selection, **Joseph-Beth Booksellers** is a literal godsend. It's also bigger in square footage than the biggest of chains, which means more room for readings, obscure magazines, and just about everything else (page 153).

◖ **Best Place to Find Rare Grooves:** There's a perfectly good reason why serious crate-diggers show up at **720 Records** in droves: Not only does the shop offer bins of downtempo, rare groove, classic hip-hop, and battle records – they also push magazines, T-shirts, DVDs, deejay accessories, and more (page 153).

◖ **Best Place to Try on Things You Can't Afford: Emphatics** carries the latest couture and ready-to-wear lines from Stella McCartney, Prada, and more. And although you probably won't find anything under $400, the staff treats every last customer like a queen (or king), making this shop the city's ultimate fantasy boutique (page 156).

◖ **Easiest Place to Find a Betsey Johnson Dress on Sale:** Although it's one of the smallest boutiques in Shadyside, **MaxAlto** still manages to somehow be one of the most eclectic and funky. Prices are standard, yet thankfully, so are sales (page 156).

◖ **Best Men's Clothing Store: Charles Spiegel for Men/The Garage** carries more stylish and European brands for men than you're likely to find anywhere else in town (page 158).

◖ **Best Gift Shop:** A cross between a novelty store, a gag shop, and a classy gift boutique, **Kards Unlimited** is a perfect one-stop shop when you need to pick up a present for Grandma, your kid brother, or, of course, yourself (page 160).

◖ **Best Place to Pamper Yourself Silly:** Although its services are considerably high-end and upscale, the pros at **Sewickley Spa** are known for always making their guests feel 100 percent comfortable. First-timers unfamiliar with the routine can expect VIP treatment (page 162).

◖ **Best Outdoor Shopping Center:** Home to a wide diversity of big chains, little boutiques, and everything in between, **SouthSide Works** has something for everyone (page 165).

◖ **Best Place to Score an Eames Chair for Cheap: Thriftique** stocks modern furniture worth thousands of dollars for mere hundreds. You know Taschen's *1000 Chairs* book? This is where those pieces sometimes live (page 166).

© DAN ELDRIDGE

Pittsburgh. The city is also known for its very active arts and crafts community; shops in many neighborhoods feature affordable pieces by local artisans.

And as the population in Pittsburgh continues to age, the resale shops have become prime hunting grounds for vintage and antique finds.

Arts and Crafts

B & B STUDIO   Map 5
5417 Walnut St., 412/621-1140
HOURS: Tue. and Thurs.-Sun. 11 A.M.-5 P.M., Wed. 11 A.M.-7 P.M.

Not unlike the popular shops where kids can create their own ceramic plates, B & B Studio lets its customers design their very own purses. It's a near-to-genius idea for the woman who absolutely *must* have an entirely unique bag. Of course, if you aren't the artistic type, the studio will gladly sell you an off-the-rack bag, or one of the shop's employees will design a bag specifically for you and the look you're after. The art here isn't cheap, however: Expect to pay between $200–500.

THE BEAD MINE   Map 3
1703 E. Carson St., 412/381-8822, www.beadmine.net
HOURS: Tue.-Sat. 11 A.M.-7 P.M., Sun.-Mon. noon-5 P.M.

The name pretty much says it all: The boxes at the all-encompassing Bead Mine contain more or less every last type of bead made today. That includes Swarovski crystal, wood, and metal, as well as very rare and imported beads. Understandably, some of what you'll find here can be prohibitively expensive, but if it's the cheaper stuff you're after, you'll have no trouble finding it. The Bead Mine also regularly holds classes, and the shop can be rented for parties of any sort.

IRISH DESIGN CENTER   Map 2
303 S. Craig St., 412/682-6125, www.irishdesigncenter.com
HOURS: Mon.-Sat. 10 A.M.-5:30 P.M.

An Irish import shop with all the standard tchotchkes (rings, books, etc.), the real gems at the Irish Design Center are the authentic sweaters. All are hand-knit, and all are absolutely the real deal (in other words, none are mass produced). What's more, the knits carried here—whether blankets, throws, pullovers, or shawls—are all very uniquely styled.

KNIT ONE   Map 5
2721 Murray Ave., 412/421-6666, www.knitone.biz
HOURS: Tue. and Thurs. 10 A.M.-8 P.M., Wed., Fri., and Sat. 10 A.M.-5 P.M., Sun. noon-4 P.M.

A large, open, and brightly painted store decorated with woven area rugs, Knit One also offers the largest amount and widest variety of knitting classes in the city. Classes run the gamut from the relatively simplistic (Introduction to Lace Knitting) to the advanced (Modular Knitting; Intarsia Method). Even the inventory itself is artistic here, displayed as it is in modular boxed shelving that is cleverly attached to the shop's walls. Private lessons are also available, and knitting enthusiasts can even rent the space for bridal showers, baby showers, and birthdays.

SHOPPING

EXPLORING THE SHOPS OF SEWICKLEY

Located about 25 minutes by car from Downtown, the neighborhood of Sewickley is one of the Greater Pittsburgh area's most enjoyable places to shop. With the quaint look and feel of a small town or even a village, simply wandering between the various bookstores, boutiques, and cafés is one of the most pleasant and relaxing ways to spend an afternoon here. Which isn't to say that Sewickley is countrified or old-timey. On the contrary, the nearby residential areas are home to some of the city's most expensive real estate. A good number of professional sports figures, judges, and politicians live nearby, in fact, so it makes perfect sense that most of the retail outlets are decidedly upmarket. The local Chamber of Commerce probably says it best. It likes referring to Sewickley as a small-town village with a sense of 21st-century sophistication.

The area is known for holding generous sidewalk sales, and it's practically common knowledge that a good number of retailers keep last season's discounted merchandise tucked away in the back of the store. Don't be shy about asking. One other important detail to keep in mind when shopping is that retailers tend to close early here, usually between 5 and 7 P.M. so do plan accordingly.

What else makes Sewickley such a great place to play? For starters, many of the women's clothiers are the only stores in the Pittsburgh area carrying certain lines by certain high-end designers. Visit **Bailey & Bailey** (page 154) and **perfect.** (page 156) if the urban-casual look is what you're after. The town also has a rather lively café culture. Try the **Sewickley Hotel** (509 Beaver St., 412/741-5804) or **The Sewickley Cafe** (409 Beaver St., 412/749-0300) for a fantastic dining experience, and if the weather's nice, grab a table in the back garden and under the tent.

If shopping really isn't your thing, consider checking out the **Sweetwater Center for the Arts** (200 Broad St., 412/741-4405, www.sweetwaterartcenter.org), where lectures, film screenings, and performances take place alongside a schedule of arts classes. Fitness enthusiasts should keep in mind the **Sewickley Valley YMCA** (625 Blackburn Rd., 412/741-9622, www.sewickleyymca.org); it's probably the nicest YMCA facility you've ever seen. Dog lovers, too, are in abundance here, and it often seems as if every other family is taking an extended stroll with a happy pup in tow. But should your extended stroll – or even your extended shopping – have you dragging your feet by day's end, drop into the **Sewickley Spa** (page 162), where the pampering is deliciously and absolutely top-notch.

For more detailed information about Sewickley, visit www.clicksewickley.com.

PITTSBURGH CENTER FOR THE ARTS

Map 5

6300 5th Ave., 412/361-0873, www.pittsburgharts.org

HOURS: Tue.-Sat. 10 A.M.-5 P.M., Sun. noon-5 P.M.

In addition to the gallery here, which displays a rotating schedule of visual work and installations by both emerging and established artists, Pittsburgh Center for the Arts maintains a wonderful gift shop with a large variety of pieces, all of them created by locals. More than 150 artists are currently represented—expect to find works of fiber, print, ceramic, and glass, among much more.

And as the end of the year draws near, a special holiday shop sale takes place; it's always worth at least a cursory look.

THE STORE AT THE SOCIETY FOR CONTEMPORARY CRAFT

Map 1

2100 Smallman St., 412/261-7003, www.contemporarycraft.org
HOURS: Tue.-Sat. 10 A.M.-5 P.M.

The relatively small gift shop area of this folk art museum usually carries handmade purses, scarves, and stationery, as well as decorative items made of glass and wood. Known simply as The Store, you'll also find a small selection of home furnishings here, such as lamps, tables, and chairs. Jewelry, toys, and other small gift items are popular and generally well stocked.

Books and Music

THE BIG IDEA INFOSHOP

Map 6

504 Millvale Ave., 412/687-4323, www.thebigideapgh.org
HOURS: Wed., Fri., and Sat. noon-7 P.M., Thurs. noon-10 P.M., Sun. noon-5 P.M.

An all-volunteer-run bookshop specializing in Leftist politics, queer issues, and other radical and alternative cultures, The Big Idea Infoshop originally existed only as a small corner of a small room inside Wilkinsburg's Mr. Roboto Project. Along with the standard collection of neo-anarchist lit, the Big Idea also stocks a good selection of zines and other independent publications. Volunteers are always needed, and educational classes and workshops occasionally take place at the store.

CALIBAN BOOKSHOP

Map 2

410 S. Craig St., 412/681-9111, www.calibanbooks.com
HOURS: Mon.-Sat. 11 A.M.-5:30 P.M., Sun. 1-5:30 P.M.

Specializing in rare first editions, leather-bound books, and fine arts and philosophy tomes, Caliban Bookshop carries the sort of printed curiosities you simply aren't going to stumble across at the neighborhood Barnes &

Noble. New treasures seem to show up almost daily, and if you're looking to sell something rare and counterculture-esque, Caliban may very well be looking to buy. Just about every last item from the *McSweeney's* catalog is stocked here as well, and a tiny CD store, **Desolation Row,** can be found in the back corner.

EIDE'S ENTERTAINMENT

Map 1

1121 Penn Ave., 412/261-0900, www.eides.com
HOURS: Mon.-Thurs. 9:30 A.M.-7 P.M., Fri. 9:30 A.M.-9 P.M., Sat. 9:30 A.M.-6:30 P.M., Sun. 10 A.M.-5:30 P.M.

Although Eide's isn't as popular among the city's punk- and alternative-music-buying masses as it was, say, a decade ago, this triple-tiered pop culture emporium continues to do a smashing business because of the variety—not to mention the sheer mass—of its inventory. These days, music for sale at Eide's is generally of the gangster rap or death metal variety. Yet comic books and collectible toys are still available on the basement floor, the magazine section continues to stock obscure titles, and the books and videos upstairs, which document everything from tattoo culture to vintage porn, remain

SHOPPING

© DAN ELDRIDGE

Jerry's Records, a vinyl geek's fantasy come to life

as odd as ever. Used CDs, non-sport cards, and collectible 45s are also available.

THE EXCHANGE   Map 3
1709 E. Carson St., 412/488-7001
HOURS: Mon.-Sat. 10 A.M.-10 P.M., Sun. noon-7 P.M.

With locations now dotting the city and suburbs, it's clear The Exchange must be doing something right, especially considering the sorry economic state of the independent record store in the early 21st century. The drill here is fairly simple, if also a bit cold and void of personality: Customers sell used CDs for cash or trade, and to examine a disc for sale, it's necessary to track down an employee who will unlock the glass case of your choice with an often undignified grunt. The good news is that The Exchange is legendary for buying just about every disc you can throw at them, and there's often a decent selection of

never-been-opened CDs at both discounted and regular rates.

JAY'S BOOKSTALL   Map 2
3604 5th Ave., 412/683-2644
HOURS: Mon.-Fri. 9:30 A.M.-5:45 P.M., Sat. 9:30 A.M.-4:30 P.M.

A tiny and staunchly independent bookstore located in the heart of Oakland and just steps from the University of Pittsburgh campus, Jay's Bookstall is one of the very few truly noncorporate booksellers left within the city limits. Jay himself has become something of a legend within the local literary community, and even Michael Chabon, the author of *Wonder Boys* and *The Mysteries of Pittsburgh,* worked the Jay's Bookstall register while studying at Pitt.

JERRY'S RECORDS   Map 5
2136 Murray Ave., 412/421-4533,
www.jerrysrecords.com
HOURS: Mon.-Tue. 10 A.M.-5 P.M., Wed.-Fri. 10 A.M.-8 P.M., Sat. 10 A.M.-6 P.M., Sun. noon-5 P.M.

One of the most legendary vinyl shops on the entire East Coast, record enthusiasts have been known to travel from as far away as Japan just to spend endless hours digging through the crates at Jerry's. There's no other way to explain it: The almost ridiculously large selection here simply boggles the mind, and there seems to be a separate section devoted to just about every genre of music on earth, including many you never knew existed. Turntables and accessories are also sold, and prices on all but the rarest of finds are surprisingly fair. According to a Jerry's employee, the recent rumors of the shop's demise have been greatly exaggerated, and while the collection will continue to be downsized, the store itself—fingers crossed—should remain open well into the future.

JOSEPH-BETH BOOKSELLERS Map 3

2705 E. Carson St., SouthSide Works,
412/381-3600, www.josephbeth.com

HOURS: Mon.-Fri. 10 A.M.-10 P.M., Sat. 9 A.M.-
10 P.M., Sun. 10 A.M.-8 P.M.

Although technically an independent shop, Joseph-Beth now has five locations in North America, and the company's stores are more massive and carry a wider selection than your average Borders and Barnes & Noble put together. The Pittsburgh location is an absolute dream for book lovers: Readings take place here regularly, and along with gifts and reading accessories of all sorts, there's a CD selection on-site and probably the best periodicals department in all of Western Pennsylvania.

PAUL'S CDS Map 6

4526 Liberty Ave., 412/621-3256,
members.aol.com/paulsstore

HOURS: Mon.-Sat. 10 A.M.-7 P.M., Sun. noon-5 P.M.

Something of a local headquarters for indie- and art-rock aficionados, Paul's CDs is tiny little box of a store, yet its supremely well-edited collection is consistently top-notch. You'll find the best of the best here in traditional blues and jazz, world music, hip-hop, electronic, and all manner of experimental sounds. DVDs and a small music magazine section are also popular, as is the used CD bin in the front of the store. Local pop music icon Karl Hendricks can often be spotted here; he works as the store's manager.

RECORD VILLAGE Map 5

5519 Walnut St., 412/682-1984

HOURS: Mon.-Tue. and Thurs.-Fri. 10 A.M.-7 P.M., Wed. 10 A.M.-9 P.M., Sat. 10 A.M.-6 P.M., Sun. noon-5 P.M.

Help yourself to a small bit of window shopping along Walnut Street, and you'll find it

window-shopping on Walnut Street, Shadyside

almost impossible to avoid stumbling upon Record Village. In large part, that's because the store cranks a mix of international music from its outdoor stereo speakers on busy shopping days. Peruvian pan flutes, West African *djembe* drums, the latest club obsessions from Ibiza—if it's entrancing music and it's made outside the lower 48, you'll hear it on Walnut Street, and you'll find it for sale in the bins upstairs. (Popular American CDs are available as well.) Staffers are quite knowledgeable and most seem to enjoy helping new customers discover new sounds.

720 RECORDS Map 6

5943 Penn Ave., 412/661-7330,
www.720records.com

HOURS: Mon.-Sat. 11 A.M.-7 P.M., Sun. noon-5 P.M.

Primarily a hip-hop and urban music store, 720 Records specializes in rare and hard-to-find vinyl. Rare jazz, funk,

SHOPPING

© DAN ELDRIDGE

and downtempo can also be found in the bins, and if you're looking for something local or unique, the shop sells CDs and mix tapes from local groups and deejays. (Hip-hop heads in particular should ask for local recommendations; although virtually unknown outside the city limits, Pittsburgh's underground rap scene is surprisingly accomplished.) Like most still-successful record stores, 720 does the bulk of its business these days online, which means that clerks are always happy to fill special orders in the store.

UNIVERSITY OF PITTSBURGH BOOK CENTER
Map 2

4000 5th Ave., 412/648-1455,
www.pitt.edu/~bookctr/contact/index.htm
HOURS: Mon.-Thurs. 8:30 A.M.-8 P.M., Fri.-Sat. 9 A.M.-5 P.M.

Not content to exist solely as a locale for new Pitt students to purchase textbooks and school supplies, the massive Pitt Book Center has such a well-stocked selection of fiction and nonfiction, as well as gifts and accessories, that you'll barely need to stop by Borders or Barnes & Noble during your four

years here. Of course, non-students fill the Book Center as well, which boasts a particularly well-stocked regional section. Be prepared to leave all your belongings in a locker at the store's entrance.

SHOPPING LATE?

Thanks to an interesting idea conjured up by various neighborhood Chambers of Commerce, a number of shopping districts in Pittsburgh have chosen one specific day of the week during which most retailers stay open for business later than usual. In Shadyside, Wednesday's the late night – you'll find most Walnut Street stores keeping their doors propped open until as late as 8 or 9 P.M. On Thursday, head to Lawrenceville, where boutiques, cafés, and galleries on and around Butler Street keep the lights on until 8 P.M., with some staying open even later. To find participating Lawrenceville businesses, just look for a "Late Night Thursdays" sign in the window.

Clothing and Accessories for Women

BAILEY & BAILEY
Map 7

425 Walnut St., 412/741-0700
HOURS: Mon.-Tue. and Thurs.-Fri. 10 A.M.-6 P.M., Wed. 10 A.M.-8 P.M., Sat. 10 A.M.-5:30 P.M.

At Bailey & Bailey, absolutely one of the area's top spots for tracking down new and unique designer names, customers can always expect to come across recent lines from favorites such as Cynthia Vincent, Parameter, and Anna Sui. Ultimately, this is a great place to find

trendy fashions with a classic, ageless appeal. Expect also to find chic T-shirts in the softest of knits, as well as wonderfully silky camisole dresses with perfect detailing. But since the store is a bit outside the city, we recommend calling ahead, assuming you're looking for a specific piece by a specific designer. Employees at Bailey & Bailey are especially kind and honest, and even if what you're looking for isn't in stock, you'll probably find they're quite talented at steering customers toward other appropriate pieces.

BOMBSHELL BOUTIQUE   Map 5
204 S. Highland Ave., 412/365-2133
HOURS: Mon.-Sat. noon-7 P.M.

The only genuine urban boutique in Pittsburgh catering to women, the especially edgy Bombshell specializes in rare and hard-to-find lines like Lynn, 2bFree, Sophomore, Bartack, Joomi Joolz, and Cheeky. Fittingly, the inside decor is stylishly minimalist—just a bit of simple track lighting with hardwood floors, color-blocked fixtures, and stainless steel accents. And Bombshell's owners are always around and are known locally for being exceptionally nice. If it's young, casual, spunky, and attitude-rich you're looking for, this is it.

CAESARS   Map 5
5417 Walnut St., 412/621-0345
HOURS: Mon.-Tue. and Thurs.-Sat. 11 A.M.-5:30 P.M., Wed. 11 A.M.-6:30 P.M.

Possibly the hottest shop featuring original jewelry designs in the city, Caesars is nonetheless a relatively small boutique at which the owner—Caesar—is always on-site. His designs feature a very simple yet bold style with sometimes oversized fine gemstones, and in fact there's even an entire collection here dedicated to oversized pieces. And since Caesar is the designer, he also does custom work in the studio. Prices start just under $1,000 and go skyward from there.

CHERYL W   Map 5
5817 Forbes Ave., 412/422-9099
HOURS: Mon., Wed., Fri., Sat., 10 A.M.-5:30 P.M., Tue. and Thurs. 10 A.M.-7:30 P.M.

Probably because of its amazing selection of both costume jewelry and fine gem jewelry, not to mention its great accessories, Cheryl W seems to attract the thrifty and single college gal just as much as it does the moneyed and middle-aged Squirrel Hill professional. Come for the handbags and the hair clips, or simply while away a few minutes by poking through the decent-sized selection of affordable and unique handmade jewelry.

CHOICES   Map 5
5416 Walnut St., 412/687-7600
HOURS: Mon.-Tue. and Thurs.-Sat. 10 A.M.-5:30 P.M., Wed. 10 A.M.-8 P.M.

Known as one of the most elite shops in the city, Choices is also known for being one of the only places in Pittsburgh carrying Jimmy Choo, not to mention plenty of Prada and Manolo Blahnik. The space is wide open and very minimalist—think hardwood floors and off-white gallery walls. As for inventory, just about every new Prada line is carried, as well as a few in-season pieces from other A-list designers. Keep in mind, however, that this is not off-the-rack shopping; the racks contain only one or two of each item for viewing, and if you find something you're fond of, a salesperson will bring the piece to your fitting room. (Conveniently enough, everything is tailored in-house.)

EB PEPPER   Map 5
5411 Walnut St., 412/683-3815
HOURS: Tue. and Thurs.-Sat. 10 A.M.-5:30 P.M., Mon. 10 A.M.-5 P.M., Wed. 10 A.M.-8 P.M., Sun. noon-5 P.M.

An absolute must for those who care to count themselves among the city's best dressed, the lower level at eb Pepper consists mainly of career and formal attire, while the top floor is not-to-be-missed for chic casualwear. You'll

SHOPPING

find suiting here by Milly, casual clothing by Nikka, as well as all the standards in premium denim, such as 7 and Paper. The store is best known, however, for its mascot: Ms. Pepper's pet pug, Chloe, who practically lives at the store and who incidentally struts her own style with custom fashions by **Spoiled Pets** (412/422-2116), a local hand-tailored dog clothier.

◖ EMPHATICS   Map 1

1 Oxford Centre, 412/471-4773

HOURS: Mon.-Fri. 10 A.M.-6 P.M., Sat. 10 A.M.-5 P.M.

Without a doubt, Emphatics is the absolute best high-end designer shopping in Pittsburgh for both men and women. With its very sleek and sophisticated atmosphere and sales team, labels carried include Prada, Jean-Paul Gaultier, Chloe, Rochas, Issey Miyake, Stella McCartney, and Alexander McQueen. And despite the sometimes shockingly high price tags, you can expect to be treated like royalty from the moment you walk in the door—the service here is incredibly warm and friendly. You'll be assisted even when trying on garments—for women, the store carries appropriate bras, shoes, and even try-on costume jewelry that enables customers to see exactly how their new clothes will look, fit, and feel. And if your budget is a touch tight, feel free to ask if the store has anything off-season still tucked away in the back. This store also offers the same high-quality service and the same high-end designers for men.

◖ MAXALTO   Map 5

5426 Walnut St., 412/683-0508

HOURS: Mon.-Tue. and Thurs.-Sat. 10 A.M.-5 P.M., Wed. 10 A.M.-7 P.M.

A funky and fun little boutique where customers sit on plush velvet couches while deciding what to purchase, MaxAlto carries lines by Betsey Johnson, Anna Sui, LAMB (by Gwen Stefani), Miss Sixty, and others of similar ilk. The decor here is unique and spunky: Antique hatboxes used as shoe displays, fitting rooms with long velvet curtains. Extra plusses: The owner is particularly nice, and wonderful sale items can almost always be found in the back of the shop.

PERFECT.   Map 7

503 Broad St., 412/749-5801, www.perfectboutique.com

HOURS: Tue.-Fri. 10 A.M.-5 P.M., Sat. 10 A.M.-4 P.M.

Yet another classic Sewickley boutique, perfect. is a bit more budget-friendly than most of the neighborhood's other women's apparel shops. Brands you'll spot here include Earl Jeans, Blue Tattoo, Triple 5 Soul, and Joil—in other words, the average perfect. shopper is younger, more urban, and probably a bit more trendy than most of the folks you'll find strolling Sewickley's sidewalks. And true to form, the vibe inside the store is especially casual, friendly, and fun.

PITTSBURGH JEANS COMPANY   Map 3

2222 E. Carson St., 412/381-5326, www.pittsburghjeanscompamy.com

HOURS: Mon.-Sat. 11 A.M.-7 P.M., Sun. 11 A.M.-6 P.M.

Aside from Pittsburgh Jeans Company being the only place in town to pick up Rock & Republic denim, it also carries lines by Paper, 7, and True Religion, to name but a few. The store also boasts fitting specialists, in-house tailoring, and special-order shipping. There's even a curious back story: The first shop on this site, founded in the 1920s, was designed specifically to address the clothing needs of area steel workers. The store you see today?

More than 40 brands of women's designer denim can be found at Pittsburgh Jeans Company.

It was revamped just a few years ago by the grandson of the original owner.

PURSUITS   **Map 5**

740 Filbert St., 412/688-8822

HOURS: Mon.-Tue. and Thurs.-Sat. 10:30 A.M.-5:30 P.M., Wed. 10:30 A.M.-7:30 P.M., Sun. noon-4 P.M.

A bit more bohemian and New Agey than your average women's clothing store in Shadyside, Pursuits is a wonderfully funky boutique that carries way too many brands to mention here. Don't expect top-of-the-line designer gear but, rather, relaxed fashions and dresses. In other words, this is the outfitter to visit if you're aiming to achieve the bohemian look that has lately been particularly popular. Candles and other accessories are also available.

SHOPPING

Clothing and Accessories for Men

◖ CHARLES SPIEGEL FOR MEN/THE GARAGE
Map 5

5841 Forbes Ave., 412/421-9311

HOURS: Mon., Wed., Fri., Sat. 10 A.M.–6 P.M., Tue. and Thurs. 10 A.M.–9 P.M., Sun. noon–5 P.M.

Certainly one of the best spots in Pittsburgh for unique designer clothing, this location is technically two stores in one. Charles Spiegel for Men claims a wide swath of the space, and it's on these racks that you'll find a great mix of suiting, including pieces by Vestimenta, Etro, and J Keydge. The Garage offers much more casual and trendy gear, perfect whether you're at the club or simply at the café. The selection of button-downs, outerwear, T-shirts, and pants include lines by Mavi, Diesel, and Chip & Pepper. The atmosphere is very warm and friendly—it's also a great place to take your boyfriend if he needs to kick it up a notch in the style department.

MODA
Map 5

5401 Walnut St., 412/681-8640

HOURS: Mon.-Tue. and Thurs.-Fri. 11 A.M.-7 P.M., Wed. 11 A.M.-9 P.M., Sat. noon-6 P.M., Sun. noon-5 P.M.

Carrying Dolce & Gabbana, Paul Smith, and others, Moda is one of the city's trendiest clothing stores for men, complete with a decent shoe collection, plush black carpet, and a somewhat snooty staff. While the store does carry a small selection of suiting, its focus is largely centered around casualwear, such as designer denim and graphic T-shirts.

TIME BOMB
Map 5

200 S. Highland Ave., 412/661-2233

HOURS: Mon.-Sat. noon-8 P.M.

Something of an unofficial headquarters for Steel City hip-hop heads—as well as the rap industry celebs who occasionally pass through town—Time Bomb is the only non-chain hip-hop gear spot in the 'Burgh. Well stocked in labels like Triple 5 Soul and LRG, the store also stocks nontextiled gear for the hip-hop enthusiast, including magazines, mix tapes, and DVDs. Owned and operated by local legend Brian Brick, Time Bomb has proven so popular lately that even members of the Pittsburgh Steelers have gear specially ordered from the shop. (Heinz Ward is said to be a loyal customer.) Skateboarding equipment can also be found.

Furniture and Home Decor

HOT HAUTE HOT
Map 1

2124 Penn Ave., 412/338-2323, www.hothautehot.com

HOURS: Mon.-Wed. 10 A.M. 4 P.M., Thurs.-Fri. 10 A.M.-7 P.M., Sat. 9 A.M.-5 P.M.

Specializing in eclectic and truly one-of-a-kind furniture pieces, the artists at Hot Haute Hot select used, vintage, or antique furniture items and customize each with a truly unique touch of creativity. In other words, this is the perfect showroom for anyone on the hunt for a piece that no one else will ever have. To put it simply, Hot Haute Hot is the polar opposite of your run-of-the-mill, standard contemporary furniture shop.

PERLORA

Map 3

2220 E. Carson St., 412/431-2220 or 800/611-8590, www.perlora.com

HOURS: Mon.-Tue. and Thurs.-Sat. 10 A.M.-6 P.M., Wed. 10 A.M.-8 P.M., Sun. noon-5 P.M.

Offering trendy contemporary furniture, Perlora is located in a retrofitted building that is now a loft-style showroom. Interestingly, quite a few interior designers are on staff here, which makes sense given the ultramodern and traditional designs for sale, not to mention the ergonomic chairs and mattresses available. And while it's true that Perlora's furniture is anything but affordable, many of the originals are quite striking and not easily available elsewhere in the city.

WEISS HOUSE

Map 5

324 S. Highland Ave., 412/441-8888, www.weisshouse.com

HOURS: Mon.-Tue. and Thurs.-Fri. 10 A.M.-6 P.M., Wed. 10 A.M.-8 P.M., Sat. 10 A.M.-5 P.M.

Carrying high-end furniture lines like B&B Italia, Cassini, and Ligne Roset, Weiss House also has a highly educated crew of interior designers on staff who specialize in custom work, contemporary kitchen design, and renovation. The store has a large selection of carpeting, as well as exotic wood flooring materials. Recently added items include Asian antiques—all of them hand selected and one of a kind.

WHO NEW?

Map 6

5156 Butler St., 412/781-0588, www.who-new.com

HOURS: Wed.-Sat. noon-6 P.M., usually open on Sun.

This is easily the best place in the city to track down midcentury decor. Owned and

Perlora, one of Pittsburgh's most unusual furniture stores

© DAN ELDRIDGE

SHOPPING

operated by two men who might best be described as "20th-century design encyclopedias," Who New? carries a wide-ranging selection of retro home furnishings, the majority originating from the 1950s through the 1970s. Along with original pieces by Eames, Sascha Brastoff, Russell Wright, and Paul McCobb, you'll find an incredible selection of vintage barware and kitchen items. The owners are more than willing to bargain, and curiously enough, one is even a professionally trained circus clown. A small selection of new novelties (baby onesies, greeting cards) is also available.

Gifts

CULTURE SHOP   Map 3

1602 E. Carson St., 412/481-8284

HOURS: Mon.-Fri. noon-9 P.M., Sat. 11 A.M.-9 P.M., Sun. noon-5 P.M.

A wonderfully unique import shop offering clothing, accessories, and gifts from (mostly) India and the Far East, the Culture Shop feels something like a cross between a Haight-Ashbury head shop and a magic store straight out of a *Harry Potter* novel. All the usual hippie accoutrements are here: incense, peasant dresses, silver rings, and statues bearing the likeness of Ganesha. But many come specifically for the striking jewelry, as should you, assuming you're looking for something expressly unique. Can't spare the cash? There's always Nag Champa!

E HOUSE   Map 3

1511 E. Carson St., 412/488-7455, www.ehousecompany.com

HOURS: Mon.-Thurs. 10 A.M.-7 P.M., Sat. 10 A.M.-8 P.M., Sun. noon-5 P.M.

Self-described as the most eco-friendly store in Western Pennsylvania, E House deals exclusively in products that tread lightly upon the earth. You'll find organic household products, as well as a wide selection of all-natural clothing and accessories. Looking for a journal or a purse made out of an old license plate? Or maybe a belt designed from an actual automobile seat belt, and decorated with bottle caps? This is your spot, then. Insider's tip: The Burt's Bees collection here is possibly one of the city's most extensive.

⬤ KARDS UNLIMITED   Map 5

5522 Walnut St., 412/622-0500

HOURS: Mon.-Sat. 9:30 A.M.-9 P.M., Sun. noon-5 P.M.

Hardly your average card store, Kards Unlimited is more of a well-edited novelty shop that also carries a good selection of books, posters, candles, T-shirts, wrapping papers, and unusual jewelry items, such as cigarette cases and lighters. Anyone looking for Blue Q products (magnets, creams, and balms) or Yankee candles would do well to take a look here, as the selections are huge. Need a unique gift for a hard-to-shop-for friend? You're more than likely to find something amusing among the stuffed shelves.

A PLEASANT PRESENT   Map 5

2301 Murray Ave., 412/421-7104 or 877/421-7104, www.apleasantpresent.com

HOURS: Mon.-Thurs. 10 A.M.-8 P.M., Fri.-Sat. 10 A.M.-6 P.M.

A queer-themed gift and novelty shop with a great selection of gift baskets for just about any occasion imaginable, A Pleasant Present also sells party supplies, cards, gag gifts, and the like. In other words, this is a one-stop shop for anyone needing a present or party favor—whether serious or not so serious—for a coworker, a family member, a lover… or even yourself.

TEN THOUSAND VILLAGES   Map 5
5824 Forbes Ave., 412/421-2160,
www.tenthousandvillages.com
HOURS: Mon.-Wed. and Fri.-Sat. 10 A.M.-6 P.M., Thurs. 10 A.M.-8 P.M.

A founding member of the International Fair Trade Association, Ten Thousand Villages has been in business at various locales across North America since 1946. The shops all sell arts and crafts from artisans living in Africa, Asia, Latin America and the Middle East. The ultimate goal? That craftspeople from developing nations might one day be able to earn a living wage. Pieces on sale at the Pittsburgh store include jewelry, blankets, ceramics, clothing, and even musical instruments and home decor.

WATERMELON BLUES   Map 2
311 S. Craig St., 412/681-8451
HOURS: Mon.-Sat. 10 A.M.-5 P.M.

It certainly isn't easy to navigate your way through the tight aisles at Watermelon Blues, a cozy North Oakland gift shop where you'll find novelties that simply don't exist at other like-minded area stores. Aside from stocking one of the East End's best card selections, you'll also find cookbooks, specialty candy and toys, unique stationery supplies, and loads of other good stuff you never knew you needed… until now.

Health and Beauty

COSMETIQUE DESTEFINO'S   Map 5
5533 Walnut St., 412/681-4632
HOURS: Mon. 10 A.M.-5 P.M., Tue., Thurs., and Fri. 10 A.M.-7 P.M., Wed. 10 A.M.-9 P.M., Sat. 10 A.M.-6 P.M., Sun. noon-5 P.M.

The Shadyside location of Cosmetique DeStefino's sells products on its first floor and maintains a salon—complete with lots of open space and lots of windows—on its upper floor. Definitely pretentious and with a smartly well-dressed staff, DeStefino's very much has the feel of a big city salon. The store itself has an amazing selection of hair care products, including items by Pureology, Bumble & Bumble, Tigi, Redken, and Matrix. You'll also find fun costume jewelry here, such as long beaded necklaces, flat and round brushes, and unique handbags.

DEAN OF SHADYSIDE   Map 5
5404 Centre Ave., 412/621-7900
HOURS: Mon. noon-8 P.M., Tue.-Thurs. 9 A.M.-8 P.M., Fri. 9 A.M.-5 P.M., Sat. 8 A.M.-4 P.M.

With locations on Centre Avenue, in the Hillman Cancer Center, and at UPMC Montefiore and the Oxford Athletic Club in Wexford, it's no wonder Dean of Shadyside is such a well-loved Pittsburgh salon. In fact, this was one of the city's first salons to offer great-length hair extensions à la Paris Hilton. Today, Dean's is the only area salon specializing in hair for cancer patients, including extensions and thickening treatments (wig specialists are on staff). And while the Wexford location (Rte. 19 at Wallace Rd., 724/933-1911) is also a full-service spa, the main locations all offer hair cutting,

SHOPPING

coloring, and style services, including manicures, pedicures, and waxing.

ESSENSIA DAY SPA Map 5

5884 Ellsworth Ave., 412/361-0604,
www.essensiadayspa.com

HOURS: Tue.-Thurs. 11 A.M.-7 P.M., Fri. 11 A.M.-6 P.M., Sat. 11 A.M.-4 P.M., closed Sun.-Mon. (by appointment only)

An exclusive and private spa that operates only by appointment, Essensia Day Spa offers all manner of massages, facials and skin care, and full body and facial waxing. And because the spa only does individual bookings, a very personalized and attentive experience is practically guaranteed. Even better: The staff here is known for being laid-back and decidedly nonpretentious. Only one person is scheduled at a time, which means no groups are allowed.

MCN SALON Map 1

1108 Smallman St., 412/201-5151,
www.mcnsalon.com

HOURS: Tue.-Wed. 10 A.M.-8 P.M., Thurs. 10 A.M.-6 P.M., Fri. 10 A.M.-4 P.M., Sat. 8 A.M.-4 P.M.

Located in a completely renovated loft space, MCN Salon is especially popular with the city's most style-conscious and forward-thinking fashionistas. Specializing in color and also offering hair cuts, textures, waxing, manicures, and pedicures, among other services, MCN is also beautiful to look at: Imagine hardwood floors, big windows, and fresh-cut flowers. Don't forget to say hello to the salon's mascot, Josie—the owner's pet dog. Making appointments in advance is recommended.

◖ SEWICKLEY SPA Map 7

337 Beaver St., 412/741-4240

HOURS: Daily 8:30 A.M.-6:30 P.M.

Very high-end but not the least bit pretentious, Sewickley Spa is the absolute epitome of relaxation and peacefulness; a good number of local spa enthusiasts claim it to be the Greater Pittsburgh area's very best spa, hands down. The atmosphere here is more or less in tune with what you'd expect at any high-quality spa, yet with touches and details that complete the picture perfectly, such as waterfalls, comfy plush chairs, and changing rooms with trays of fruit and pastries. If that's not convincing enough, consider that a total of 112 ultimate spa treatments are offered. There's a good reason women and men both can be spotted here: There's literally something for everyone.

SHOPPING

Kids' Stores

BABYLAND Map 6

5542 Penn Ave., 412/362-1222 or 888/316-8952,
www.babylandpa.com

HOURS: Mon. and Fri. 9:30 A.M.-8 P.M., Tue.-Thurs. and Sat. 9:30 A.M.-5:30 P.M., Sun. 1-5 P.M.

The largest baby and infant retailer in Western Pennsylvania, Babyland carries just about any accessory you could possibly imagine that an infant or its parents might desire: cribs, strollers, highchairs, breast pumps, toys, diaper bags—even Pittsburgh Steelers apparel for the littlest football fan in your family. Admittedly, Babyland hardly has the world's greatest atmosphere, and it's certainly not located in the most pleasant corner of town. Nonetheless, the prices are great, the selection is huge, gift ideas are everywhere, and there's even a kids' section featuring furniture, bedding, and more, which means you can continue shopping here even after your baby has grown a bit older.

TOTS & TWEEDS   Map 5
809 Ivy St., 412/661-6500
HOURS: Mon.-Sat. 9:30 A.M.-5 P.M.
If it's unique kids clothing you need, Tots &

Tweeds may soon become your favorite Pittsburgh store; some of the clothing and accessories carried here simply can't be found anywhere else in town. If you're the sort of discriminating young parent who considers your baby's uniquely upscale look just as important as your own, this is the spot you're looking for. Children's wedding attire and clothing and accessories for infants are also carried.

Pet Supplies and Grooming

BOW WOW DOGGIE DAYCARE   Map 1
2726 Penn Ave., 412/566-1083,
www.bowwowdoggiedaycare.com
Offering a wonderful service for busy dog owners who don't like the idea of leaving their pets at home alone, Bow Wow Doggie Daycare takes pains to make sure your favorite hound stays happy, healthy, and socialized—with people as well as other dogs—throughout the day. Bow Wow's founder, Teri Miller, who is fully accredited by the ABKA, left her corporate accountancy career to start the business; she also owns two rescued greyhounds who act as "official greeters" at Bow Wow. In other words, your furry friend will be in extremely safe and caring hands here.

GOLDEN BONE PET RESORT   Map 6
6890 5th Ave., 412/661-7001,
www.goldenbonepetresort.com
Located not far from the East End neighborhood of Shadyside, Golden Bone Pet Resort seems to be the favored kennel among discerning dog owners in the city. Decent kennels are never cheap, of course, but Golden Bone is an excellent value, and it also does double duty as a grooming spot—you'll find bathing and other grooming rates to be

a much better value here than at the chain stores. But assuming you are leaving Spot for an overnight stay, you'll be pleased to learn of the in-house amenities, which include air conditioning, in-floor heat, two large outdoor exercise areas, and around-the-clock care and security. Nervous pet owners interested in touring the facilities may do so Monday–Saturday 1–3 P.M.

SMILEY'S   Map 5
215 S. Highland Ave., 412/362-7556
HOURS: Mon., Wed., and Fri. 10 A.M.-7 P.M., Tue. and Thurs. 10 A.M.-6 P.M., Sat. 10 A.M.-5:30 P.M., Sun. noon-5 P.M.
One of the best independently owned pet supply stores in town, Smiley's carries just about everything imaginable for cats, dogs, and other small animals. You'll find nearly every line of pet food on the market here, from all-natural brands to the vet-recommended Eukanuba and Science Diet lines. Smiley's also stocks handmade toys and collars for both dogs and cats, not to mention a great selection of fleece bedding. There are always a few sweaters and T-shirts on hand for the fashionable pup, and if the store doesn't have something in stock, a customer can always request a special order.

SHOPPING

Shoes

FOOTLOOSE   Map 5

736 Bellefonte St., 412/687-3663

HOURS: Mon.-Tue. and Thurs.-Sat. 10 A.M.-
5:30 P.M., Wed. 10 A.M.-9 P.M.

Footloose is a relatively small boutique specializing almost entirely in high-end women's
designer lines from Italy, Spain, and France.
You'll find a very well-chosen collection of
pumps, stilettos, and strappy sandals here,
although you'll also need a healthy budget—
not much of the inventory here is cheap. That
said, anyone with a fascination for heels will
likely find themselves in metaphorical footwear heaven. For a better selection of walking
and sporting shoes, try Footloose's location
in Mount Lebanon's Galleria Mall (412/531-
9663, www.galleriapgh.com).

LITTLES   Map 5

5850 Forbes Ave., 412/521-3848 or
800/646-7463, www.littlesshoes.com

HOURS: Mon.-Sat. 9:30 A.M.-9 P.M., Sun.
noon-5 P.M.

Little's is one of the very few nonchain and
non-department stores in the city carrying
men's shoes. The shop is quite large and
seemingly always overstaffed, and on the
many racks and shelves here you'll find everything from sneakers to formal styles. Brands
include Kenneth Cole, Clarks, Birkenstock,
Diesel, Cole Haan, Puma, and Steve Madden. In the women's section, which is significantly larger than the men's section and
offers much trendier choices, you'll also find
handbags and accessories. Try to avoid showing up on busy Saturdays.

TEN TOES   Map 5

5502 Walnut St., 412/683-2082

HOURS: Mon.-Tue. and Thurs.-Fri. 10 A.M.-7 P.M.,
Wed. 10 A.M.-9 P.M., Sat. 9:30 A.M.-6 P.M., Sun.
11:30 A.M.-5 P.M.

Although the selection of women's shoes at
the tiny Ten Toes is rather limited, the collection itself is nonetheless very smartly edited. Lines you'll come across here include
BCBG and Steve Madden, as well as a good
number of other midrange lines; most shoes
are somewhere in the $50–150 range. Be
forewarned that the good stuff goes especially quick, but when the two male owners
get to know your buying habits, they'll happily set shoes aside for you as soon as appropriate pairs arrive. Insider's tip: Always dig
around in the back of the store, where great
bargains can often be found.

Shopping Centers and Chain Retailers

THE GALLERIA   Map 7

1500 Washington Rd., 412/561-4000,
www.galleriapgh.com

HOURS: Mon.-Sat. 10 A.M.-9 P.M., Sun. noon-5 P.M.

An upscale if slightly small indoor shopping
mall located deep in the South Hills, The
Galleria is home to a number of treasured retailers who have no other locations elsewhere
in the city. To name just a few, you'll find An-
thropologie, Nicole Miller, and Restoration
Hardware stores, as well as a movie theater
and small food court. And possibly because
of its ever-present high price tags, the Galleria
almost never grows too terribly crowded.

VERONA'S ANTIQUE MALL

For some of the very best one-stop antique shopping in the area, it's well worth the drive to visit Verona's locally famous **Miller's Antique Mall** (615 E. Railroad Ave., 412/828-3288, Tue.-Sat. 10:30 A.M.-5 P.M., Sun. noon-5 P.M.). With a full three stories of antiques packed tight onto every shelf and in every corner, you're almost guaranteed to find some sort of age-old treasure, assuming, of course, that you're willing to put in at least a somewhat serious effort.

So, what can a collector – or even a casual shopper – expect to find here? Tons of furniture, for starters. There's also California pottery, all conceivable manner of art, and various household and furniture items. The antique mall is also a perfect spot to hit if you'd like to decorate an apartment cheaply but with style. And since everything is divided into separate categories and sections, it isn't terribly tough to discern the wheat from the chaff.

Also worth a visit is **Trader Jack's** (Rte. 50/Washington St., 412/257-8980, Sat.-Sun. 7 A.M.-3 P.M.), a year-round flea market located in Bridgeville where literally hundreds of vendors hawk antiques, random junk, and plenty of other surprises.

◖ SOUTHSIDE WORKS   Map 3

445 S. 27th St., 412/481-8800,
www.southsideworks.com

An outdoor shopping center complete with exclusive boutiques, big box chains, cafés and restaurants, a movie theater, and even high-end apartment buildings, it didn't take long for SouthSide Works to earn its reputation as one of the city's most successful recent retail projects. Clothiers here include Urban Outfitters, Benetton, BCBG, Kenneth Cole, Puma, Forever 21, REI, American Eagle, and H&M. You'll also find a Sharper Image store, a Joseph-Beth Bookstore, two coffee shops, an Irish bar, a luggage store, and a dentist (whew!). Insider's tip: If you plan to dine at the Cheesecake Factory on a Friday or Saturday evening, make reservations way, *way* in advance.

For more information, visit the **Guest Services kiosk** (412-481-8800 or 877/977-8800, Mon.–Thurs. 11 A.M.–9 P.M., Fri.–Sun. 11 A.M.–9:30 P.M.) located outside the Cheesecake Factory at the corner of 27th and Sidney Streets. Free wheelchairs can be rented here, and gift cards can be purchased. At the time of writing, a stroller rental service was being planned.

To reach SouthSide Works on foot, simply head east on East Carson Street (the Monongahela River will be on your left). The 51-A bus, which travels south on Smithfield Street in Downtown, also passes the center. During summer months, the free **South Side Shuttle** (www.thesouthsider.net) runs between Station Square, the South Side Flats, and SouthSide Works on Thursday and Friday 5 P.M.–2:30 A.M., on Saturday noon–2:30 A.M., and on Sunday noon–7 P.M.

THE WATERFRONT   Map 7

300 Waterfront Dr., Homestead, 800/366-0093,
www.waterfronttowncenter.com

Perched along the Monongahela River in between Squirrel Hill and Homestead, The Waterfront is a massive outdoor

SHOPPING

shopping center located on the former site of the Homestead Steel Mill. Try to arrive at the Waterfront by traveling through Squirrel Hill and then crossing the Homestead High Level Bridge, also known as the Homestead Grays Bridge, as the view of the river and of Homestead beyond is spectacular. Also look out for the line of preserved smoke stacks off to the right. You'll find just about everything you'd expect in a traditional mall here, in addition to a cinema with stadium seating, dozens of eateries in all budget ranges, a grocery store, a hardware store, a Target, and much, much more.

Vintage and Antiques

AVALON Map 2
115 Atwood St., 412/621-1211

HOURS: Mon.-Sat. 11 A.M.-8 P.M., Sun. noon-6 P.M.

Hugely popular with the area's college undergrads, Avalon is a favored outfitter for the rebellious teen and twentysomething. Originally an all-vintage clothing shop, Avalon now carries some new lines (Triple 5 Soul, Ecko), yet retro style remains especially popular. Bags, hats, wigs, designer shoes, and other accessories are also available, making Avalon something of a one-stop shop for the aspiring club kid or punk rocker with an Amex card.

EONS Map 5
5850 Ellsworth Ave., 412/361-3368

HOURS: Mon.-Fri. noon-5 P.M., Sat. 11 A.M.-5 P.M., Sun. noon-5 P.M.

A great spot for both men's and women's fashions from the 1920s through the 1970s, Eons is possibly best known for its sidewalk mannequin that gets dressed daily by the store's eclectic owner. The best finds here are definitely dresses, costume jewelry, and hats, although there are also loads of very feminine pieces and some wonderful pants and shirts for guys. Being that Eons is a very tiny store with a ton of clothing and accessories stuffed into all its various nooks and

Eons, a Shadyside vintage-clothing boutique

© DAN ELDRIDGE

crannies, browsing here can sometimes be a slight bit frustrating.

◖ THRIFTIQUE Map 7
7400 Church St., Swissvale, 412/271-0544

HOURS: Call for store hours

A little-known spot filled with hidden gems of all sorts, sizes, and shapes, Thriftique is the perfect vintage spot to dig through if you're looking to spend under $300 on an actual designer piece. The owners keep rather erratic hours, but it's honestly worth your while to check in on a regular basis, assuming you have a bit of design knowledge and know roughly what you're looking for. Pieces from the 1950s and '60s show up here with the most regularity.

RECREATION

Due to the city's ongoing success of its professional sports teams—the Steelers, the Pirates, and the Penguins—Pittsburgh has been known as "The City of Champions" since the 1970s. It's only fitting, then, that the recreational opportunities in the city and its outlying areas should provide ample opportunities for training, competing, and playing hard.

Joggers and walkers, for instance, can enjoy the miles of trails inside Schenley Park, while the mountain biking paths that run through Frick Park are said to be some of the best in the country.

Naturally, Pittsburgh's three rivers (Allegheny, Monongahela, Ohio) offer ample opportunities for water activities, such as boating, canoeing, rowing, and yachting, all of which take place throughout the warmer months. And in the winter season, skiing and snowboarding excursions aren't more than an hour away in Laurel Highlands.

For those who lack the competitive spirit, but still enjoy a bit of healthy exercise, recreational opportunities abound. Caves not far from the city can be explored with experienced spelunkers who act as guides. The state's only official lawn bowling court is located in Frick Park, and the city itself provides a plethora of tennis courts and

© MARA RAGO

HIGHLIGHTS

LOOK FOR  TO FIND RECOMMENDED ACTIVITIES.

◖ Best City Park for Serious Mountain Bikers: The challenging trails that crisscross **Frick Park** are some of the most pulse-pounding in the entire state (page 169).

◖ Best Way to Explore Allegheny River: Cruising the length of the Allegheny River in one of **Kayak Pittsburgh**'s canoes or kayaks is a wonderfully relaxing way to experience the Steel City (page 183).

◖ Best Urban Fishing Experience: Every Wednesday, from May to October, **Downtown TriAnglers/Venture Outdoors** help amateurs cast a line, right in Point State Park (page 184).

◖ Best Ice Skating Spot: Spin in circles with family members or loved ones when the outdoor fountain at the Philip Johnson-designed **PPG Place** transforms into an ice-skating rink (page 187).

◖ Best Skiing or Snowboarding Excursion: With 275 acres of powder, the most diverse range of mountains in Pennsylvania, and numerous runs for novices and old pros alike, it's no wonder *Ski Magazine* called **Seven Springs Mountain Resort** the top ski resort in the entire mid-Atlantic (page 188).

◖ Best Climbing Wall: Explore 14,000 square feet of nubby, knobby, and faux-rock surfaces at **The Climbing Wall,** an indoor playground where pros and newbies alike soar to impressive heights (page 194).

◖ Best Public Swimming Pool: Built by the wealthy industrialist Henry W. Oliver, the South Side's **Oliver Bath House** is a gorgeous spot for an afternoon dip. The pool is heated, it's located indoors, and it even boasts a splendid cathedral ceiling (page 194).

◖ Best Skatepark: The outdoor **Imperial Skatepark** in Findley Township is an absolutely unreal concrete dream and well worth the drive (page 199).

Frick Park's Reynolds Street gatehouse

© MELISSA MCMASTERS, PITTSBURGH PARKS CONSERVANCY

swimming pools. Venture deep into Schenley Park during the year's coldest season, and you'll find families ice skating inside the park's ever-popular rink.

No matter what the season, you won't need to dig deep during your time in Pittsburgh to discover just about any sort of outdoor fun.

Parks

On one hand, it's unfortunate that Pittsburgh's city planners haven't done a better job of creating a ribbon of parks along one or more of our urban waterways. Yet on the other hand, it's a breeze to explain the main benefit of the city's most popular leafy escapes, Schenley Park and Frick Park: Entering their gates is something akin to entering an entirely different world, while still remaining right within the center of town.

The city's green spaces are equally useful for relaxation and recreation, and unlike the reception you may receive in bigger towns, locals here are generally amenable to welcoming an out-of-towner into their game of Ultimate Frisbee or pickup basketball.

Interested in schmoozing with the college crowd? Head to Schenley Park's Flagstaff Hill (it's across the road from Phipps Conservatory), where CMU students play, sunbathe, and flirt whenever the weather's warm.

◖ FRICK PARK   Map 5
Corner of Forbes Ave. and S. Braddock Ave., 412/422-6550, www.pittsburghparks.org
The largest of the city's parks, Frick Park practically begs walkers, joggers, and bikers to get lost among its many trails and forested areas. But strolling the valleys and hills is hardly the only recreational option. Frick also has a number of playgrounds that are perfect for families with small children, as well as a wide-open field where dogs are allowed to run leash-free. You'll also find red clay tennis courts here and a lawn bowling green (the only public court in Pennsylvania), where competitive seniors can be found whiling away the afternoon.

HIGHLAND PARK   Map 6
Highland Ave., 412/422-6550, www.pittsburghparks.org
Located in an East End neighborhood of the same name, Highland Park sits on an overlook atop the Allegheny River, close to the Pittsburgh Zoo. Because of its enviable vista, the park is especially popular with joggers but also with walkers who enjoy circling the 0.75-mile path around the reservoir, a historic city site officially known as Reservoir No. 1. The sand volleyball courts are a popular destination in the summer, as is the swimming pool, which is the only long-course pool in Pittsburgh.

MELLON PARK   Map 5
Corner of 5th and Shady Aves., 412/255-2676
Unlike the majority of Pittsburgh's other public parks, Mellon Park is relatively tiny. If you've ever visited the Pittsburgh Center for the Arts, you've also been in Mellon Park—it's the green space that surrounds the center. The area directly behind the center is a gorgeously restful and hilly expanse—it's also one of the city's quaintest locales for an afternoon or evening picnic.

PITTSBURGH BY THE NUMBERS

Pittsburgh has long been known as a city of firsts, but maybe it should also become known as a city of the biggest, the best, or even the steepest. Take a look at some of the surprising facts below, and see if you don't agree.

- With 120 bridges located inside the city limits and 521 found throughout Allegheny County, Pittsburgh boasts more bridges than any city on Earth aside from Venice, Italy.

- The fountain located in Downtown Pittsburgh's Point State Park sprays 6,000 gallons of water every minute. It shoots its geyser an impressive 275 feet high.

- Pittsburgh is home to 712 sets of outdoor stairways, which contain a total of 44,654 steps. To explore the steps on foot or bicycle, pick up a copy of Bob Regan's *The Steps of Pittsburgh: Portrait of a City* (Local History Co.).

- The Eliza Furnace Trail, also known as the Jail Trail, totals 3.5 miles long and stretches between Downtown and North Oakland. It's ideal for walking, biking, and, in decent weather, for commuting.

- Thanks to a relentless effort by local cyclists to improve Pittsburgh's reputation as a good place to bike, the town now sports more than 130 cleverly designed "Public Art Bike Racks." Each rack can support two bikes.

- Downtown Pittsburgh is small and compact enough to be pleasantly walkable, but because its triangular shape is surrounded by rivers on two sides, it contains an impressive 38 miles of shoreline.

- Fourteen regional parks can be found within Allegheny County. In total, they contain 13,763 acres. And if you were expecting Pittsburgh to be smoggy and sooty, get this: The city has more trees per square mile than any other major metropolis in the country.

On the opposite side of bustling 5th Avenue you'll find Mellon Park's Tennis Bubble. A court with a bubble-like covering, it protects players from the biting cold throughout the winter and early spring.

SCHENLEY PARK   Map 2

Boundary St. at Schenley Dr., 412/422-6523, www.pittsburghparks.org

Donated to the city by Mary Schenley in the late 1800s and designed by William Falconer, Schenley Park is home to 456 green acres of inner-city paradise. From the Carnegie Library in Oakland, simply stroll over the Panther Hollow Bridge and toward the expanse of hills and trees; you'll likely forget you're smack-dab in the center of a city in no time.

Recreation opportunities are many and varied on the fields and greens of Schenley, which is one of the largest city-operated parks in the eastern region of the country. Along with its 13 tennis courts, swimming pool, soccer field, running track, ice skating rink, and hiking trails, there's an 18-hole golf course and a relaxing, somewhat secluded lake.

Bicycling

In 1990, Pittsburgh's cycling community received a mighty blow when *Bicycling* magazine named it one of the 10 worst biking cities in the United States. Nearly two decades later, a lot of the bad news remains. Pittsburgh motorists, for instance, still show little respect for roadside cyclists. And with the exception of Beechwood Boulevard in Squirrel Hill, bike lanes in the vast majority of neighborhoods are all but nonexistent.

Yet the biking scene here is slowly improving, thanks to grassroots organizations like Bike Pittsburgh (www.bike-pgh.org), a bicycle advocacy group, and Free Ride (www.freeridepgh.org), a DIY-style society that recycles and reuses old bikes. And while the long-talked-about trail running from Pittsburgh to Washington, D.C., has yet to materialize, the city *has* added bike lanes recently (in the West End), and the extensive Three Rivers Heritage Trail continues to evolve.

TRAILS

ELIZA FURNACE TRAIL   Map 1

Trailhead starts in Downtown and ends in Oakland, north of Schenley Park, www.friendsoftheriverfront.org

Also known as the **Jail Trail** because of the route it takes behind the Downtown Allegheny County Jail, the Eliza Furnace Trail is a 3.5-mile-long path that is technically an extension of the Three Rivers Heritage Trail. Much of the route runs right alongside a major expressway, and it would be misleading to pretend that more than a small stretch or two of the Eliza Furnace is a peaceful pathway. Its beauty, however, lies in its location; the trail starts smack-dab in the center of Downtown, and it has a convenient exit point in North Oakland, right in between the Pitt and CMU campuses. This is an obvious boon to any of the thousands of East Enders who work Downtown, as any other route into the city is fraught with unruly traffic and undue stress.

To enter the trail from Downtown, travel south on Grant Street, away from the Strip District and toward the Monongahela River. The trail literally abuts the river, so keep going and you'll eventually run into it.

THREE RIVERS   Map 7
HERITAGE TRAIL

www.friendsoftheriverfront.org

Comprising 37 miles of paved and unpaved pathways, the Three Rivers Heritage Trail is actually a system of roughly a half dozen trails that line either side of the Allegheny, Monongahela, and Ohio rivers. The trail's various links are a thing of beauty; cyclists, pedestrians, inline skaters, and moms with baby carriages enjoy cruising its paved pathways, many of which dramatically bump up right against the water.

The trail's major problem, however, has everything to do with the many "missing links" along the way. Cruise along the picturesque path that lines the north side of the Allegheny River, for instance, and you'll find the surface transforming into a mess of rocky gravel underneath the 40th Street Bridge.

To avoid this sort of disappointment during your own ride, download a PDF map of routes on the Heritage Trail's website. You'll be amazed at the views the trail affords of Pittsburgh's unusual urban and industrial landscapes.

CRITICAL MASS

Yes, the infamous bicycle revolution has a monthly ride in Pittsburgh. Established in San Francisco, **Critical Mass** is an activist-led event that takes place in dozens of cities worldwide once a month. The cyclists always time their ride with the onset of rush hour; the idea is to fill busy urban streets with bikes, thus encouraging motorists to at least contemplate the notion of cheap, nonpolluting forms of alternative transportation. Many of the cyclists at any given Critical Mass claim their ride to be a celebration of biking and not a protest, but do be aware that rides are often monitored by police. Arrests are not unusual. To join Pittsburgh's event, which takes place at 5:30 P.M. on the final Friday of every month, simply show up with a bicycle by the giant dinosaur outside the Carnegie Museum, which is located on Forbes Avenue in Oakland.

RESOURCES

DASANI BLUE BIKES PROGRAM   Map 3

33 Terminal Way, off E. Carson St., 412/488-0212

Organized by Friends of the Riverfront, the corporate-sponsored Dasani Blue Bikes Program offers the use of an absolutely free bike—a sky-blue beach cruiser—for anyone wishing to explore the length of the city's Three Rivers Heritage Trail. The bikes are stored in a locker at the start of the trail near Terminal Way on the South Side, but it's necessary to first visit the Friends of the Riverfront office, where riders will be issued a swipe card after showing a state-issued driver's license or passport. The cards are then validated for one year, and only two rules apply: Bikes must be returned before dark, and they're to be used on the Heritage Trail only. (Although we seriously doubt you'd be taken away in handcuffs if you veered off the path here and there.)

FREE RIDE   Map 5

214 N. Lexington Ave., inside Construction Junction, 412/731-4094, www.freeridepgh.org

Staffed by the sort of cycling enthusiasts you'd expect to find leading a Critical Mass rally, Free Ride is a recycle-a-bike shop where old and unloved rides are given a new lease on life. The program works like this: Bikes are donated to Free Ride in a generally sorry state of disrepair. Volunteers spend hours in the shop bringing the bikes up to code. The resulting mountain bikes, road bikes, and BMX bikes are then sold at affordable rates.

The deal is even better if you already own a beat-up ride: The mechanics at Free Ride will help out with repairs at no charge, and will even educate riders about bike maintenance along the way. But here's the rub: Anyone who receives free assistance is asked to give back by volunteering a bit of his or her time at the shop. Marxism on two wheels and a saddle seat, you might say.

Spectator Sports

With the exception of the Steelers' 2006 Super Bowl victory, local sports fanatics haven't had much of a reason to think of Pittsburgh as a City of Champions for going on a quarter-century now. The Pirates have been ranked toward the bottom of the National League for ages. The Penguins and their fans have recently been mired in frustration over owner Mario Lemieux's insistence on a new arena. The Pens' beloved TV announcer Mike Lange was fired during the summer of 2006 for reasons that remain not entirely clear. And in 2005, Steelers' radio broadcaster and local legend Myron Cope called it a career after three and a half decades.

But interest in the pros never really seems to wane in Pittsburgh. For one thing, there are the exceptionally talented University of Pittsburgh teams. The men's football and basketball squads especially are followed with something approaching religious fervor. And if all else fails, there's always next season.

BASEBALL

PITTSBURGH PIRATES   Map 4

PNC Park box office, corner of Federal and General Robinson Sts., 800/289-2827 (tickets), http://pittsburgh.pirates.mlb.com

As a ball club with a history stretching all the way back to the late 1800s, it's no surprise that the Pittsburgh Pirates are equally rich in both legend and lore. Originally known as the Pittsburgh Alleghenies, the team started out in life on a rather positive note by winning its first-ever professional game. The contest took place at the North Side's Recreation

COURTESY OF VISITPITTSBURGH

PNC Park, home of the Pittsburgh Pirates

PITTSBURGH'S AFRICAN AMERICAN BASEBALL LEGACY

Still discussed with much reverence by serious fans and baseball historians, Pittsburgh's **Homestead Grays** were indisputably one of the most eminent and respected clubs in the history of African Americans in baseball and the "Negro Leagues." The franchise was formed in 1912 by Cumberland "Cum" Posey, a business-minded innovator who would go on to become one of the team's most significant leading lights. Among his chief accomplishments in the black leagues was the popularization of paying ballers a respectable wage; he was also institutional in developing the concept of enticing players away from competing clubs.

The Grays soldiered on for 38 consecutive seasons and won nine straight Negro National League Pennants. And although the team was originally based in the steel-producing town of Homestead (most of the players were steelworkers themselves), many of its home games during the late 1930s and throughout the '40s took place at Oakland's **Forbes Field,** which at the time was also the home of the Pittsburgh Pirates. Some "home" games, though, took place at Washington, D.C.'s Griffith Stadium. In 2004, the district seriously considered renaming its newly acquired professional ball club in honor of the Grays. (The team was instead dubbed the Washington Nationals.)

Also of crucial importance in the history of African Americans in baseball were the Hill District-based **Pittsburgh Crawfords** – originally a semipro team before being bought in 1931 by the infamous **Gus Greenlee,** a taxi driver, bootlegger, and numbers runner who also owned the legendary Crawford Grill nightclub. At one point, the team's roster featured five soon-to-be Baseball Hall of Famers, including **Satchel Paige.**

Like the New York Yankees of today, the Crawfords were able to build one of the most competitive clubs in the Negro Leagues; this was due in no small part to Greenlee's mostly ill-gotten gains, although, to his credit, Greenlee was also well known as a philanthropist. With his help, scores of poor Hill District residents were able to attend schools and purchase homes.

Even the home ballpark of the Crawfords has historical relevance. Known as **Greenlee Field,** it was the first black-owned major league field in the country, and one of the very few built for use only by a Negro League team. Unfortunately the field was demolished in 1938 after the Crawfords called it quits. It was located at 2500 Bedford Avenue in the Hill District, between Chauncey and Duff Streets.

Park in 1887; it pitted the Alleghenies against the Chicago White Stockings. The Alleghenies became known as the Pirates in 1891, and soon began playing at the now long-gone Exposition Park. Incidentally, Exposition was located not far from PNC Park, where the Pirates play today.

So what about all that history-making? Well, for starters, the Pirates competed in the first ever World Series, in 1903. (Pittsburgh lost the series to the Boston Pilgrims.) In 1954, the Pirates made history of another sort as second baseman Curt Roberts became the first African American to join the squad.

The following season would become known as an even more memorable year for minority athletes in Pittsburgh: This was when the soon-to-be-legendary Roberto Clemente, a Puerto Rican player, was brought on board. Nearly 35 years after Clemente's first major league game, Pittsburgh's 6th Street Bridge was renamed in Clemente's honor. And of course there were the World Series of 1971 and 1979; Pittsburgh defeated the Baltimore Orioles during both.

But as the saying goes, all good things must come to an end, and many fans are still in resolute agreement that the beginning of bad tidings for the Pirates began sometime in 2000. That was when a referendum asking local taxpayers to foot the bill for two new sports stadiums—one for the Pirates and another for the Steelers—was severely beaten down. Regardless of the wishes of the voting public, though, the city went forward with construction. Unbelievably, Allegheny County residents were made to cough up $211.8 million of the $259.6 million cost for the Pirates' PNC Park, as well as $157.6 million for the $280.8 million Heinz Field project. Understandably, Pittsburghers remain salty about the underhanded tactic even today. In a truly painful coincidence, the Pirates Hall of Famer Willie Stargell passed away mere hours before the first pitch was tossed at PNC Park.

As if the financial fumble wasn't bad news enough, the players themselves seem to be getting worse—or at the very best remaining stagnant—with each successive season. The Pirates managed to lose 100 games during their first year in the new stadium and have posted a losing record every season since.

These days, Pirates fans are hanging the majority of their hopes and dreams on Canadian player Jason Bay, a quickly rising star who was named the National League Rookie of the Year in 2004.

So what does the future hold for the ball club that, in the 1970s, was partly responsible for Pittsburgh becoming known internationally as the City of Champions? Tough to say, with the likely exception of more impressive batting from Bay. In fact, many disgruntled fans and local sports writers are putting the blame on Pirates owner Kevin McClatchy for the team's recent poor performance. (A petition to oust the owner has even circulated online.) In the meantime, a small core of diehard fans continues to follow the team on television and, to a slightly lesser degree, at the ballpark. As one such loyal fan remarked to a *Pittsburgh Post-Gazette* reporter after watching the Buccos lose the 2006 home opener to the Dodgers, "Hope springs eternal, I guess." We couldn't have said it better ourselves.

BASKETBALL

The hardcore B-movie fanatics among you may be able to recall *The Fish that Saved Pittsburgh,* a 1979 film that portrayed a pro basketball team with skills so poor that an astrologer (Stockard Channing) was brought in to assist. But alas, the Pittsburgh Pythons were nothing more than a fictional crew, and to this day the Steel City lacks an NBA team.

DUQUESNE DUKES   Map 1
1302 Forbes Ave., 412/232-3853 (tickets), www.goduquesne.com

College basketball fans who can't score tickets to a Panthers match might instead check out the Duquesne Dukes, a much-lauded Atlantic 10 Conference crew that calls

PITTSBURGH'S SPORT CELEBRITIES

For some decades now, the gritty mill towns adjoining the Monongahela River in Western Pennsylvania have been well known as particularly rich territory among pro football scouts. Joe Montana, for one, perfected his craft in the city of Monongahela, which lies south of the city in Washington County. But much like the geography of Western Pennsylvania itself, Pittsburgh's sports legends come from backgrounds as varied as their respective pursuits. Some, like entrepreneur Mark Cuban, are wealthy beyond belief. Others lead lives that are substantially more modest. But all have one thing in common: They've played considerably significant leading roles in the illustrious story of Pittsburgh, The City of Champions.

- **Kurt Angle:** Born in the tony South Hills suburb of Mount Lebanon, Angle was the recipient of a freestyle wrestling gold medal in the 1996 Olympic Games. Angle has also performed for the World Wrestling Federation (WWF) and also the World Wrestling Entertainment organization, where he played the role of El Gran Luchadore, a masked Mexican wrestler.

- **Terry Bradshaw:** Long before the reign of Big Ben, there was the good-natured quarterback Terry Bradshaw, who led the Steelers to four Super Bowl wins. Bradshaw is an almost ubiquitous figure in sports media today: He can be seen on both the silver screen and on television, where he works as an NFL commentator and appears in the occasional commercial.

- **Roberto Clemente:** The first Latin American to be inducted into the Baseball Hall of Fame and practically a worshipped figure in Western Pennsylvania, Clemente played 18 seasons with the Pittsburgh Pirates.

- **Billy Conn:** Also known as "The Pittsburgh Kid," Billy Conn was a Light Heavyweight world champ and a true boxing legend. He grew up in East Liberty and retired to Squirrel Hill, where he lived until his passing in 1993.

- **Myron Cope:** A Pittsburgh Steelers radio broadcaster for an astounding 35 years, the beloved Myron Cope first attained local fame due to his oddly nasal voice and his penchant for creating memorable nicknames and Yiddish aphorisms (*Double yoi!*). Cope is also the inventor of the Steelers' Terrible Towel.

- **Mark Cuban:** A dot-com billionaire from Mount Lebanon, Cuban is best known for his controversial business dealings and explosive temper. He currently owns the Dallas Mavericks and remains active in various media ventures.

- **Mike Ditka:** Born in Carnegie, "Iron" Mike Ditka achieved fame as head coach for the Chicago Bears. Ditka was highly regarded as a tight end during his three seasons with the Pitt Panthers.

- **Tony Dorsett:** A running back for the Pitt Panthers, Tony Dorsett was a Heisman Trophy winner and a rushing superstar during his time with the Dallas Cowboys. Dorsett entered the Pro Football Hall of Fame in 1994.

- **Ken Griffey, Jr.:** Born in Donora, Pennsylvania (also the birthplace of Baseball Hall of Famer Stan Musial), Ken Griffey, Jr. is known as one of baseball's finest players. In 1990, Griffey made baseball history with his father, Ken Griffey, Sr., when the two became the first father and son teammates to play on the same major league team (the Seattle Mariners) at the same time.

- **Franco Harris:** As the running back responsible for one of pro football's most unforgettable plays — the Immaculate Reception — Franco Harris remains a perennial favorite among Steelers fans worldwide. He's particularly loved by Pittsburgh's Italian community, who've dubbed themselves "Franco's Italian Army."

- **Mario Lemieux:** Currently the owner of the Pittsburgh Penguins hockey team, Mario Lemieux is generally considered to be one of the most talented hockey players in the history of the game.

- **Dan Marino:** A Pittsburgh native and NFL great who quarterbacked for both the Pitt Panthers and the Miami Dolphins, Dan Marino grew up in South Oakland.

- **Joe Montana:** Born in Monongahela, Montana took the San Francisco 49ers to four Super Bowl victories; he is now regarded as one of the best quarterbacks to have played in the NFL. In 1996, the town of Ismay, Montana (population 26) renamed itself Joe, Montana in honor of the quarterback.

- **Joe Namath:** Born in Beaver Falls, Joe Namath was one of pro football's most controversial players; today he's remembered as much for his hedonistic "Broadway Joe" reputation as for his skill on the gridiron. He made frequent cameo TV appearances in the 1970s and was welcomed into the Pro Football Hall of Fame in 1985.

- **Bruno Sammartino:** A Worldwide Wrestling Federation (WWWF) legend also known as "The Italian Strongman," Sammartino continues to live in Pittsburgh, where he occasionally appears at neighborhood events.

- **Lynn Swann:** A forever-legendary Pittsburgh Steeler who has appeared intermittently in films and on television, Lynn Swann recently turned his attention to politics. His 2006 bid for the governorship of Pennsylvania, however, was unsuccessful. The democratic incumbent contender, Ed Rendell, beat Swann by a large margin.

- **Johnny Unitas:** Known as "Mr. Quarterback," Unitas played in Pittsburgh for the semipro Bloomfield Rams before moving onto a legendary career with the Baltimore Colts. The Rams' former field still stands at the corner of 40th and Butler Streets in Lawrenceville.

- **Honus Wagner:** A native of Carnegie, Honus Wagner was one of the first five players to be inducted into the Baseball Hall of Fame. Wagner's likeness appears on the most valuable baseball card of all time, which is said to be worth approximately $1.5 million. A life-size statue of Wagner can be found outside PNC Park's main entrance.

Duquesne University home. According to *U.S. News & World Report,* the Dukes have nearly as much prowess in the classroom as they do on the court: The magazine recently ranked the school's athletic program 15th in terms of graduation rates.

PITT PANTHERS   Map 2
3719 Terrace St., Petersen Events Center,
412/648-8076, www.peteseneventscenter.com
Probably the most popular b-ball squad in the city, the University of Pittsburgh's Pitt Panthers are a Big East crew frequently ranked near the top of the league. Home games are played at the recently built Petersen Events Center—it's generally agreed upon by sports journalists as being one of the county's finest college basketball arenas. Also of interest at Petersen is the **McCall Panthers Hall of Champions.** Located in the center's lobby, it displays decades worth of Pitt athletics achievements. Admission is free; the hall is open Monday–Friday, 9 A.M.–5 P.M., as well as during all men's basketball games.

PITTSBURGH XPLOSION   Map 2
3719 Terrace St., Petersen Events Center,
412/648-8076, www.peteseneventscenter.com,
www.pittsburghxplosion.com
NBA or no NBA, in late 2005 pro basketball finally did come to town in the form of the American Basketball Association's Pittsburgh Xplosion. The minor league team plays games at the University of Pittsburgh's Petersen Events Center, as well as at Mellon Arena, where the fictional Pythons attempted to shoot hoops. Yet while the Xplosion's stats are consistently more impressive than those of the Pythons, attendance at games has generally been stunted in the hundreds.

FOOTBALL
PITT PANTHERS   Map 4
100 Art Rooney Ave., Heinz Field,
800/643-7488 or 412/648-7488 (tickets),
www.pittsburghpanthers.com
The University of Pittsburgh's Pitt Panthers football squad has a particularly impressive history, with possibly an even more impressive list of famous alumni. Dan Marino, Tony Dorsett, Mike Ditka, Pop Warner, and scores of NFL players have all spent time as Panthers. Perhaps fittingly, the team now plays its home games at Heinz Field, which is also the home base of the Pittsburgh Steelers. The Panthers' most intense rivalry exists between the West Virginia University Mountaineers; the two teams meet every Thanksgiving during a game known as the Backyard Brawl. The Brawl is an experience not to be missed, although tickets are hard to come by. Pitt and the Penn State Nittany Lions also maintain a healthy rivalry.

To purchase game tickets, visit the team's website or www.peteseneventscenter.com. You can also purchase tickets at the Petersen Events Center Ticket Office (corner of Desoto and Terrace Streets in Oakland). The office is open Monday–Friday 8:30 A.M.–5 P.M.

PITTSBURGH PASSION   Map 3
930 E. Carson St., George Cupples Stadium,
724/452-9395, www.pittsburghpasssion.com
Formed in 2002, the Pittsburgh Passion is a professional, all-women's contact football team and a member of the National Women's Football Association (NWFA). Oddly, the majority of the players had very little football experience before joining the Passion. Some had barely played the game at all, and instead came from softball,

volleyball, soccer, basketball, lacrosse, or hockey backgrounds. In other words, you'll want to pack your sense of humor along with the beer coolers and binoculars.

The Passion plays home games from late April through mid June at George Cupples Stadium. Tickets are available at the gate ($12 adult, $5 child and student, $8 senior).

PITTSBURGH STEELERS   Map 4

100 Art Rooney Ave., Heinz Field, 412/323-1200, www.steelers.com

It's hard to believe that the American institution known as the Pittsburgh Steelers, whose ups and downs in many ways mirror the ups and downs of the Steel City itself, is now three quarters of a century old. Also hard to believe—but true—is that like the Pittsburgh Penguins, the Steelers were also first

known as the Pittsburgh Pirates; the moniker was meant to be a nod to the city's major league ball club. It wasn't until 1940 that owner Art Rooney bestowed the team with its current and much more sensible name, which even today continues to celebrate the region's proud steel-producing history, long after the majority of Pittsburgh's mills have dried up or moved overseas.

In 1943, however, the Steelers would see their name change again, if only temporarily. World War II, as it turned out, delivered quite a blow to the NFL when many of its best players were drafted onto the battlefield. Facing the prospect of not having a team large enough to take to the gridiron, Pittsburgh teamed up with its cross-state rivals, the Philadelphia Eagles, who were suffering from the very same problem. The combined team, known as the Phil-Pitt Steagles, lasted

Heinz Field, home of the champion Pittsburgh Steelers

just one season. In 1944, with the war still well underway, Pittsburgh joined forces with the Chicago Cardinals. The largely disappointing team, officially known as Card-Pitt, lost all of the season's 10 matches. In 1945, with the war coming to a close, the Steelers were reunited with some of their most valuable assets—including their name.

In 1955, the organization suffered from an embarrassing fumble that today remains something of an NFL legend: After selecting Pittsburgh native Johnny Unitas in a 20th-round draft pick, the Steelers never bothered to put him on the field. Unitas was subsequently let go, and was soon after signed by the Baltimore Colts, where he eventually grew into arguably the greatest quarterback of all time.

Regardless of the teams' past gaffs, however, a squad began to emerge in 1970 that the sports world would soon refer to as the "Super Steelers." Chuck Knoll had been hired on as head coach the previous season, and one of his first official acts was to bring defensive tackle "Mean" Joe Greene onto the roster. Greene would go on to become arguably the most important element of the "Steel Curtain," the defensive team that saw Pittsburgh through an unprecedented four Super Bowl wins during the decade. 1970, incidentally, was a year of firsts for the Steelers: Terry Bradshaw became quarterback, and the team played its first game in the new Three Rivers Stadium. (Pittsburgh lost to the Houston Oilers.)

The competitive energy of the Steelers began to slowly boil over throughout the next two seasons, right up until the now-legendary "Immaculate Reception" incident, which took place during a 1972 match against the Oakland Raiders. Most sports

historians agree that the maneuver—Franco Harris catching an impossible Terry Bradshaw pass to win the game with only seconds left on the clock—remains the single most important moment in Steelers history and a pivotal turning point for a club that had suffered through decades of losing seasons. The Steelers went on to win the Super Bowl in 1974, 1975, 1978, and 1979.

For the most part, the 1980s were not kind to the Steelers. The majority of the celebrity players from the '70s had retired, and toward the end of the decade, owner Art Rooney passed away at the age of 87. Ushering in a new era five years later was head coach Bill Cowher, who managed to take the team to its first Super Bowl in 16 years; Pittsburgh ceded the match to the Dallas Cowboys.

Having recently defeated the Seattle Seahawks in Super Bowl XL, however, the Steelers and its fans are once again on top of the competitive world. At the time of writing, the majority of gossip weaving its way throughout the newly invigorated Steelers Nation was revolving around Ben Roethlisberger. In early summer 2006, the 25-year-old superstar quarterback narrowly escaped death during a grisly motorcycle accident. Roethlisberger, who wasn't wearing a helmet, was launched from his bike and then onto a car's windshield, which he cracked open with his head. Now *that's* hard as steel. Could a return to the long-ago glory days of the Steel Town Tough possibly be far behind?

Steelers tickets are notoriously hard to come by. Your best bet is the scalpers who troll outside all home games, but be forewarned that scalping is technically illegal; purchase tickets (none of which are guaranteed to be authentic) at your own risk. Fans can also try calling the Steelers ticket office: 412/323-1200. Find more information at www.steelers.com.

HOCKEY

PITTSBURGH PENGUINS   Map 1

66 Mario Lemieux Pl., Mellon Arena box office

412/642 1800 (tickets), www.mellonarena.com

Curiously enough, the Steel City's first professional National Hockey League team was actually known as the Pittsburgh Pirates, which was the Pittsburgh Steelers' original moniker as well. The club played its first game in November 1925, but due to crushing debt, chose to relocate to Philadelphia five years later. The Penguins didn't arrive in Pittsburgh until 1967, when the NHL expanded by adding six clubs.

The Penguin's first two decades were fairly unremarkable. The players struggled through losing season after losing season and, in the mid-1970s, suffered from financial woes. Bankruptcy was declared, and the team was made to suffer the indignity of having its own office doors padlocked.

The tables began to turn, however, in the mid-1980s. Because of the Penguins' ranking as the worst franchise in the league during the 1983–1984 season, the team was given the opportunity to make the following year's first draft pick. Pittsburgh went with Mario Lemieux, still a teenager who had yet to become known as one of the best professional players to ever touch ice.

Nonetheless, it took another half dozen seasons before the Penguins became known as a truly unforgettable organization. It was in 1991 that the team took then rookie Jaromir Jagr under its collective wing; eerily, fans noted that the letters in Jaromir's name could be rearranged to form the anagram

"Mario Jr." So perhaps it shouldn't have come as much of a surprise when, by season's end, the Penguins had captured their first ever Stanley Cup victory. In 1992, the Penguins took the Stanley Cup for the second time in a row, despite the death of Coach Bob Johnson earlier in the season. In 1993, Pittsburgh nearly captured a third straight Stanley Cup, but in Game 7 of the championship bid, the Penguins lost to the New York Islanders in a surprising overtime upset.

Pittsburgh soldiered on through the end of the 1997 season, when Lemieux, who had been suffering from Hodgkin's disease for the better part of the decade, chose to retire. He was immediately admitted into the Hockey Hall of Fame. Two years later, Lemieux and the Penguins would face and then defeat yet another challenge when the club faced bankruptcy once again. To the surprise of the entire NHL, Lemieux himself stepped forward to rescue the team. Once the Penguins' star center, "Super Mario" was now also its owner.

Two days after Christmas at the start of the 2000 season, Lemieux made hockey history by rejoining the Penguins, and thereby becoming the first ever pro hockey player to also be his team's owner and a Hall of Famer. But from then onward, life at the Igloo, as the Mellon Arena is known, has gone largely downhill. Due to a still struggling financial situation, Jaromir Jagr was eventually traded to the Washington Capitals, a team that had once rivaled the Penguins. Next up was the disappointing 2004 season, during which the Penguins limped along until literally finishing at the bottom of the statistical heap. Due to a player strike, the following NHL season was cancelled entirely.

Today, the main debate surrounding

Lemieux and the Penguins has much less to do with the team than it does with the team's rink. To make a long and somewhat complicated story short, Lemieux has threatened to take his Penguins elsewhere if the city won't foot the bill for a new arena. The city council, in the processes of choosing which gaming corporation will be awarded a recently acquired slots gaming license, has made a rather controversial suggestion: Whichever corporation agrees to build a new stadium for the Penguins, they've said, might also win the bid to operate Pittsburgh's solitary casino. But as of the time of writing, a new tangle has emerged: Lemieux might be planning to sell. And the potential buyers? None other than Pittsburgh native and famed NFL quarterback Dan Marino, and with him Pittsburgh native Mark Cuban, the infamous and outspoken dot-com billionaire who also owns the Dallas Mavericks. Let the games begin!

For information about purchasing individual game tickets or season tickets, visit www.ticketmaster.com or stop by any authorized Ticketmaster outlet. Alternately, order by phone at 412/323-1919, or stop at Gate 1 at the Mellon Arena box office.

HORSE RACING

LADBROKE AT THE MEADOWS
Map 7

Race Track Rd., 412/563-1224 or 724/225-9300, www.themeadowsracing.com

About a half hour's drive south of Pittsburgh is Ladbroke at the Meadows, a harness facility with a year-round racing schedule; its website proclaims it as "Greater Pittsburgh's best-kept secret." That may be something of a stretch, but because of its somewhat secluded location near the town of Canonsburg, it is true that the Meadows doesn't see the sort of traffic it probably deserves. Admission and parking are both free at the Meadows, which offers both casual and fine-dining options. Check out the facility online for live racing schedules and wagering information, or call any one of the Meadows's off-track betting locations if you'd rather not visit the track: Moon Township (412/262-3100), New Castle (724/654-2221), West Mifflin (412/650-9000), Harmar Township (412/828-0610), or Greensburg (724/830-2612).

RUGBY

Although the combative sport of rugby is still a relative novelty in North America, its popularity in Pittsburgh seems to be growing. The **Pittsburgh Rugby Club,** for instance, claims more than 300 members of all ages and both sexes. Aside from simply playing, the club is also a do-good nonprofit organization that occasionally does its bit to help out with various community service projects.

If you'd simply like to see the teams rumble, however, head to www.pghrugby.com and view the upcoming schedules; most matches take place in Boyce Park.

PITTSBURGH HARLEQUINS RUGBY FOOTBALL CLUB
Map 7

Eisele Rd. at Cove Run Rd., Founders Field, Indianola, www.pittsburghharlequins.org

Especially serious are the players of the Pittsburgh Harlequins Rugby Football Club. The club was founded in 1973 and today is a member of the USA Rugby Football Union, the Mid-Atlantic Rugby Football Union, and the Potomac Rugby Union. The team plays on a green known as Founders Field, which is located about 16 miles from Downtown Pittsburgh in Indianola. Visit the team's website for an updated game schedule.

RUGGERS PUB   Map 3
40 S. 22nd St., 412/381-1330
To get a feel for the size and intensity of Pittsburgh's rugby scene yourself, show up at Ruggers Pub, which also serves as the local headquarters of the Pittsburgh Rugby Club. The players congregate and refuel here after local matches. The experience of seeing a team fill the pub after a win can be quite eye-opening, especially for Americans who know little about the, uh, ruggedness of the sport. Naturally, matches are shown on the telly here, but if you'd rather hit the field yourself, contact the area club at www .pghrugby.com. For information about joining the **South Pittsburgh Hooligans Men's Rugby Club,** call 412/734-8998 or visit www.southpittrugby.com.

Water Activities

For a city with a geographical nucleus surrounded on three sides by waterways, it's surprising that Pittsburgh's captains of industry haven't devised more ways to take advantage of perhaps the town's loveliest natural resource. But dive deep enough, and you'll find more than a thing or two to keep you busy off dry land. The local nonprofit organization **Venture Outdoors** (304 Forbes Ave., 2nd Fl., Downtown, 412/2555-0564, www.ventureoutdoors.org) is responsible for a surprisingly large percentage of the activities that take place on Pittsburgh's rivers; check its website or newsletter for a bevy of outdoorsy activities, both water and non-water related.

ROWING AND KAYAKING
◖ KAYAK PITTSBURGH   Map 4
412/969-9090, www.kayakpittsburgh.org
Kayak Pittsburgh offers what may very well be the most enjoyable and affordable way to explore Pittsburgh's waterways. The company rents flat-water kayaks that even the completely nonexperienced can easily navigate. Canoes and hydrobikes are also available. To reach the rental shack, cross the 6th Street Bridge (also known as the Roberto Clemente Bridge) from Downtown and head toward the North Side; the shack sits underneath the staircase, adjacent to PNC Park. Rental prices for solo kayaks are $14 for the first hour and $10 every subsequent hour. Tandem kayaks are $20 for the first hour, then $15 every hour after that. Canoes and hydrobikes are $15 for the first hour, $10 every hour after that. Kayak Pittsburgh is open from May to October 31. Hours are Monday–Friday 4 P.M.–dusk and Saturday–Sunday 9 A.M.–dusk.

THREE RIVERS   Map 4
ROWING ASSOCIATION
412/231-8772, www.threeriversrowing.org
Pittsburgh's Three Rivers Rowing Association is a nonprofessional group that organizes rowing and kayaking activities and events on the Allegheny River. Anyone is welcome to join in or become a member, regardless of age or experience. The TRRA has two facilities, one on Washington's Landing under the 31st Street Bridge, and another in the Millvale

FREE DOCKING IN THE CITY LIMITS

Thanks to the insistence of local lovers of the outdoors, Pittsburgh has recently gained a number of new destination spots at which it's possible to temporarily dock one's boat for free (or cheap). Andy Talento, the editor of *Anchors Aweigh*, likes to call them "destinations by boat." Probably the most popular place for boaters to dock is along the newly developed **North Shore**, during a Pirates or Steelers game. In years past, boaters wanting to enjoy a match had to mollify themselves by bobbing in the river and listening to the team on a radio. But now, even ticket holders can arrive via ship, as well as those simply interested in drinking or dining at a North Shore restaurant. Quite a concept.

Station Square is now also a boat-friendly locale. A spot in a slip here will put you back $5 an hour. Boats can dock at **Point State Park,** a particularly popular option during the annual Three Rivers Regatta. (Boaters are even allowed to dock overnight during the regatta, provided they adhere to a series of rather strict rules. Read them – and take them seriously – at www.pghregatta.com.)

Waterfront Park, underneath the 40th Street Bridge. But exploring the association's website before stopping by would be prudent; there you'll find detailed information about kayak tours, rowing classes and events, listings for sweep and sculling classes, information about joining a Dragon Boat team, and quite a bit more. Call for information about purchasing an annual membership, which provides access to all TRRA facilities and equipment. Activities generally take place between April and November.

FISHING

⬤ DOWNTOWN TRIANGLERS/   Map 1
VENTURE OUTDOORS

304 Forbes Ave., 2nd Fl., 412/255-0564, www.ventureoutdoors.org

Pittsburgh's ubiquitous Venture Outdoors group is also responsible for creating what may indeed be the city's strangest waterway activity: **Urban Fishing,** hosted by the Downtown Trianglers. Every Wednesday 11:30 A.M.–1:30 P.M. during the summer months (May–Aug.), Downtown office workers and all would-be fishers are invited to cast a reel into the drink, right in the heart of Point State Park. Rods, reels, and bait are provided for a flat $5 season fee, although fishers will need to show a Pennsylvania fish license ($21), which can be purchased at sporting goods stores such as Dick's (The Waterfront, 412/446-9940, www.dickssportinggoods.com) or online at www.fish.state.pa.us. When walking through the park toward the Point, be on the lookout for signs indicating which river you should be heading toward, as fishing spots vary from week to week. Thanks to ongoing efforts to keep the rivers clean, you can expect to snag a variety of smallmouth bass, catfish, and carp.

KEYSTONE BASS BUDDIES

www.kbass.com

The largest fishing tournament club in the state of Pennsylvania, the Keystone Bass Buddies is something of a cross between a social club and a competitive team. Members gather

GREATER PITTSBURGH AREA DOCKS AND MARINAS

Reams of information about the boating and fishing scenes in Pennsylvania can be found at the website of the **Pennsylvania Fish and Boat Commission** (www.fish.state.pa.us), including regulations regarding boating licenses and safety certificates. You'll also find a list of every marina in the state, as well as a convenient mapped list of public launches. Here are the basics:

Situated northeast of Downtown on the Allegheny River, the swanky **Fox Chapel Yacht Club** (1366 Freeport Rd., 412/967-1500) also boasts a restaurant, a swimming pool, a spa, and banquet facilities.

The city's newest dock, **Station Square Marina** (www.stationsquare.com/landing.htm), is also the region's only pay-by-the-hour marina. Expect to pay $5 an hour for each of the 47 slips.

Located in the newly developed residential district of Herr's Island, **Washington's Landing Marina** (100 Waterfront Dr., 412/321-3600) can be found directly beneath the 40th Street Bridge. A rowing center and public park are nearby; a restaurant overlooks the marina itself.

Founded in 1903, the **Oakmont Yacht Club** (11 Washington Ave., 412/828-9847, www.oakmontyachtclub.com) is the oldest inland yacht club in the country.

A family-owned operation that has been in business since 1959, the **Aspinwall Marina** (285 River Ave., 412/781-2340, www.aspinwallmarina.com) also sells, services, repairs, and stores boats. It's located on the Allegheny River.

The boat launch found at **South Side Riverfront Park** is the only public boat and canoe launch in the city. It was also a featured location in the 1993 Bruce Willis film *Striking Distance*. You'll find the entrance to the park on 18th Street, along the Monongahela River.

---

often to practice their respective angling techniques in a number of Western Pennsylvania's rivers. For more information about the group, or to download a membership application, visit the not-for-profit organization's website or email them at steve@kbass.com.

YACHTING AND BOATING FACILITIES

We know what you're thinking: Yachts, marinas, and pleasure craft in working-class *Pittsburgh?* Believe it. In fact, locals self-conscious of the town's rough-and-tumble image have long boasted of the fact that Allegheny County has more registered boats—more than 25,000—than any other county in the state. Maybe there's more blue blood than blue collar in Pittsburgh these days, after all.

Understandably, rising fuel costs have lately cleared the channels of the rivers to some degree. But for boaters to whom $3 a gallon isn't an issue, the local waterways remain indisputably picturesque locales in which to take to the drink. The Downtown skyline and city parks take on an almost majestic presence when viewed from a floating vessel. And words can barely describe the extraordinary experience of moving on water past the industrial detritus and shuttered steel mills that line the river's outer reaches.

Newcomers to the area might want to start

BOATS FOR SAIL

You can probably guess the main motive of most folks who flock *en masse* each year to the ever-popular **Pittsburgh Boat Show** (412/798-8858, www.pittsburghboatshow.com), which takes place in late January or early February at the David L. Lawrence Convention Center, Downtown. With literally acres of new and used vessels on offer, you couldn't hope for a better selection of seaworthy craft anywhere else in the tri-state area. But the boat show isn't all about buying and selling. There are also boating and fishing seminars, displays of classic and antique boats, safe boating education classes and more. Tickets are $8; children under 12 are admitted free with an adult.

their exploration of the Pittsburgh yachting scene online at the website of **Anchors Aweigh** (www.anchorsaweighmgazine.com), a journal for Western Pennsylvania's recreational boaters. The magazine's publisher also heads up the Pittsburgh chapter of the **Safe Boating Council** (www.safeboatingcouncil.org).

FOX CHAPEL MARINE   Map 7
SALES & SERVICE
1366 Old Freeport Rd., 412/967-1500,
www.foxchapelmarine.com

Particularly popular with the area's biggest-spending boaters, Fox Chapel Marine Sales & Service claims to have the largest selection of both new and used craft in the tri-state

area. Financing is available here, and the dealership often runs specials on pre-owned boats and new boats alike.

P&L BOAT SALES   Map 7
1401 Preble Ave., Manchester, 412/323-1010,
www.pandlboatsales.com

Once it's time to start laying out cash, a trip to P&L Boat Sales might be in order. The pleasure craft retailer is located right next to the West End Bridge in Manchester on the North Side, and has not only a knowledgeable staff but also a wide selection of boats on display in its showroom.

WATER PARK

SANDCASTLE   Map 7
100 Sandcastle Dr., Homestead, 412/462-6666,
www.sandcastlewaterpark.com

Sandcastle is one of the Pittsburgh area's premiere amusement parks, second in popularity only to Kennywood. The park is located in Homestead next to the Waterfront shopping complex and boats 14 water slides, a wave pool, hot tubs, and a children's area. Special events include "Dive in Movies," during which family-friendly films are projected above a pool, and the "Waves Under 18 Party," a dance party that, yes, takes place in a wave pool. After dark, the over-21s head to Sandbar, an on-site outdoor nightclub. The park is open June–August; adult admission is $22.95, or $16.95 after 3 P.M. Seniors are $16.95, kids 46 inches and under are $10.95. If you're feeling particularly energetic, consider picking up a Sandcastle/Kennywood Same Day Combo Pass for $28.95.

Winter Recreation

ICE SKATING

If you've never before had the pleasure of skating on ice, be aware that it's a much more difficult endeavor than inline skating. In Pittsburgh, a good place to learn the basics is the **Airport Ice Arena** (330 Hookstown Grade Rd., Parkway West, Moon Township, 412/264-2222, www.airporticearena.com), where future hockey players and figure skaters also train.

ICE CASTLE ARENA   Map 7

990 Castle Shannon Blvd., Castle Shannon, 412/561-9090, www.icecastlearena.com

HOURS: Call for hours of operation

COST: $6 adult, $5 child (5-12 years)

The indoor Ice Castle Arena in Castle Shannon is open year-round; public skating takes places on two NHL regulation-size rinks. Beginning adult skaters and children can take lessons at the Ice Castle, which is also a perfect location to host a child's birthday party.

◖ THE RINK AT PPG PLACE   Map 1

PPG Place, 412/394-3641, www.ppgplace.com/rink.shtml

COST: $6 adult, $5 child and senior, skate rental $3

The Rink at PPG Place is Downtown Pittsburgh's version of the winter skating experience at Manhattan's Rockefeller Center (although PPG is actually 2,000 square feet larger). Located directly south of Market Square in the shadow of Philip Johnson's dramatic PPG Place building, the rink opens for business every year on Light Up Night in November and closes in early March. The experience of circling the rink's lighted Christmas tree, especially after dark, is absolutely unforgettable.

SCHENLEY PARK   Map 2
SKATING RINK

Overlook Dr., 412/422-6523

The Schenley Park Skating Rink, located near the park's tennis courts and baseball fields, is open from November through March. Inline skaters and roller hockey players often fill the rink during the summer months. And since students from nearby Pitt and CMU flock here on weekend nights, the rink can be a decent place to take a first date—or to find a first date. Should your coupling turn into something more serious, consider returning on February 14 for the annual "Valentine's on Ice" event.

SKIING, SNOWBOARDING, AND SNOWMOBILING

The ski and snowboarding season in Western Pennsylvania generally runs from mid-December through mid-March, weather conditions permitting. But even when the powder isn't falling, it's usually still possible to hit the slopes, as the area's better resorts cover their mountains in artificial snow when Mother Nature fails to provide.

Snowmobile hobbyists might want to visit the website of the **Pennsylvania State Snowmobile Association** (www.pasnow .org, 888/411-7772), which works to maintain trails and a high level of snowmobiling safety throughout the state.

For more information about ski areas and resorts statewide, consult the Pennsylvania Ski Area Association at www.skipa.com.

BOYCE PARK   Map 7

675 Frankstown Rd., Monroeville, 724/733-4665

The ski slopes at Boyce Park won't be of

RECREATION

much interest to the advanced skier, but they're ideal for beginners and the generally timid. And because Boyce Park is located in nearby Monroeville, this is the perfect choice for a day trip. Snowboarders here have access to two quarter pipes and one of the longest half pipes in Pennsylvania. Adult slope fees are a reasonable $9 a day.

HIDDEN VALLEY FOUR SEASON RESORT
Map 7

1 Craighead Dr., Hidden Valley, 814/443-8000, www.hiddenvalleyresort.com

Hidden Valley Four Season Resort is located in the picturesque Laurel Highlands, about 60 miles east of the city. Although it started life more than 50 years ago as a family-run bed-and-breakfast, it now offers a year-round schedule of activities, including downhill and cross-country skiing, hiking, biking, and golfing. The ever-popular Seven Springs Resort is nearby, as is the white-water rafting destination of Ohiopyle. The 12 lifts at Hidden Valley run 9 A.M.–10 P.M.; call 866/443-7544 for snow reports. Adult lift tickets are $30 on weekends, $24 on weekdays. Adult season passes are $425.

NEMACOLIN WOODLANDS RESORT
Map 7

1001 LaFayette Dr., Farmington, 800/422-2736, www.nwlr.com

This is a truly luxurious vacation spot offering all manner of recreation possibilities, including adventure sports (off-road driving, fly-fishing), culinary classes, and the occasional wine tasting. Skiers and snowboard-ers can take advantage of 10 separate slopes and a half pipe atop the 2,030-foot Mystic Mountain. Snow tubing is also big here. Nemacolin is located in Fayette County, about 60 miles southeast of the city. Daily adult passes are $33 ($20 for cross-country skiing or snowshoeing); adult season passes are $179.

◀ SEVEN SPRINGS MOUNTAIN RESORT
Map 7

777 Waterwheel Dr., Champion, 800/452-2223, www.7springs.com

The peak at Seven Springs Mountain Resort has an elevation of nearly 3,000 feet with a vertical drop of 750 feet; it boasts 14 slopes and 17 trails. Its longest trail is 1.25 miles long. No wonder Seven Springs is one of the area's most popular ski resorts. (*Ski Magazine* rated it the number-one resort in the mid-Atlantic.) The expert-level snowboard park is 400 feet wide and 500 feet long. Lift ticket and season pass rates vary; call for detailed information.

SNOZONE
Map 7

On Rte. 88 in Finleyville, near South Park, 724/348-7399, www.snozone.net

Not up for a ski trip, but still want to have fun in the snow? Check out the tubing scene at SnoZone. Three lifts take tubers to the top of one of the longest runs in the area. Rates are $10 Wednesday–Friday for adults and children. On weekends and holidays, adults pay $14.50; kids nine and under pay $11.50. The same rates apply at SnoZone's snowboarding park. Season passes are $75.

Gyms and Health Clubs

If you're looking to get in a good workout while in Pittsburgh, you're in luck, no matter what your income level or, for that matter, your current physical condition. Because just like fitness fanatics themselves, exercise facilities here come in nearly every shape and size. There are state-of-the-art clubs filled with steam rooms and beautiful people. There are no-frills iron pumping gyms that might befit a Rocky Balboa in training. And thankfully, there's just about everything else in between (with the glaring exception, I'm sorry to report, of a 24-Hour Fitness franchise).

The equipment is relatively run-of-the-mill, and some of it is slightly outdated, but there seems to be more than enough of almost everything, and lines rarely form around even the most popular pieces of equipment. And while you won't find a pool or sauna, there is a tanning bed and a steady stream of eardrum-shattering house music blasting from the sound system. The clientele is generally friendly, accommodating, and college-aged. (A second location recently opened in a former roller skating rink in Forest Hills.)

CLUB ONE   Map 6
6325 Penn Ave., 412/362-4608

With memberships currently running at about $80 per month, this is certainly one of the pricier fitness facilities in town. But Club One isn't just a gym, it's a full-fledged health club complete with a heated swimming pool overseen by a lifeguard, a basketball court, a complete schedule of yoga and aerobics classes that take place in an upstairs studio, and a racquetball court. And the clean and spacious locker rooms, complete with complimentary toiletries, are a thing of true beauty.

FITNESS FACTORY   Map 5
212 S. Highland Ave., 412/362-6306,
www.fitnessfactorypgh.com

There's much to recommend about Shadyside's Fitness Factory, which sits right on the border of the newly gentrified corner of East Liberty. For starters, you simply can't beat the membership rates. In fact, if cost is your top factor when choosing a gym, don't even bother comparing rates elsewhere.

SOUTH SIDE ATHLETIC CLUB   Map 3
2026 E. Carson St., 412/488-1120

A fairly cut-and-dried exercise room with a convenient location, the facilities at the South Side Athletic Club are about as simple as they come: One cardio room and one free-weight and nautilus room, with a reception desk separating the two. It might not sound like much, but the gym pickins' are exceedingly slim on the South Side; your only other option here is the somewhat frightening Southside Ironworks, which is located in an out-of-the-way spot near the Birmingham Bridge.

VYGOR FITNESS AND NUTRITION   Map 6
4614 Liberty Ave., 412/681-4605,
www.vygorfitness.com

Located on the second and third floors of a former row house on Bloomfield's main drag, Vygor offers little more than a convenient location and fairly competitive membership rates. But unfortunately, for anyone residing in Bloomfield, Lawrenceville, or North Oakland, there isn't much of an alternative aside from a handful of roughneck workout rooms scattered here and there.

So what *does* Vygor offer? Basically, one floor of free weights and the usual machines, one floor of cardio equipment with a convenient row of TVs, and, to be fair, a truly friendly and accommodating staff. Vygor also maintains a slightly more appealing second location at 3390 Saxonburg Boulevard in Fox Chapel (412/767-5240). Members of the Bloomfield gym are welcome at the Fox Chapel location, and vice versa.

X SHADYSIDE   Map 5
5608 Walnut St., 412/363-9999,
www.xshadyside.com

Although X Shadyside claims to be the city's only 24-hour health and fitness club, it's actually not—the gym closes at 6 P.M. on Saturday and Sunday nights. Still, this is the closest you'll get to 'round-the-clock workout access in Pittsburgh, and the facilities, by the way, are top notch. Free weights are plentiful and seemingly brand new, but the machines, which work the body's muscles with an almost uncanny precision, are even better; you simply won't find a better (or newer) selection in town.

X Shadyside has no swimming pool or steam room, but it does boast its own room of cardio equipment and a roomy studio where yoga and aerobics classes take place (all classes are included in the price of a gym membership, which is roughly $50 a month, not including an initiation fee).

The average exerciser here tends to be the same sort of person you'd see shopping along Shadyside's streets: gorgeously styled young women and men. Need more convincing? X Shadyside was recently voted the "Best gym for spotting hotties" by the readers of *Pittsburgh City Paper*.

YMCA   Map 1
330 Blvd. of the Allies, 412/227-6457,
www.ymcaofpittsburgh.org

If you're searching for a gym that's convenient to your Downtown office, consider skipping Bally's and take a tour of the YMCA instead, which is located close to the Art Institute. If you haven't been in a YMCA for a while, you're likely to find yourself pleasantly surprised; this is the largest gym in the city by a long stretch, complete with a massive lap pool, a jogging track, a spinning room, and all the free weights and Nautilus equipment a mind could muster. There are also step aerobics and stress-management classes, yoga programs, personal nutrition counseling—you name it. The bad news is that membership doesn't come cheap. Expect to pay between $60 and $85 per month, not including a one-time initiation fee of $100.

Guided and Walking Tours

Much like San Francisco, a town to which Pittsburgh is occasionally compared, you'll find that a good number of neighborhoods here are hilly, rough-hewn, and generally best explored on foot (or at the very least, atop a bicycle). The guided walking tours organized by the Pittsburgh History and Landmarks Foundation are a good place to start—they're packed with intriguing historical and architectural trivia, and most are only an hour long. But once you get your footing, try striking out on your own—dig through a neighborhood you haven't passed through before, or maybe even one you've never heard of before.

The Greater Pittsburgh area is filled with rarely visited but historically curious pockets; to enjoy the city's more obscure reaches on your own, head to the Pennsylvania section of the Carnegie Library or any local bookstore and look for locally published guides and maps, many of which aren't widely distributed outside the area. *Seeing Pittsburgh* by Barringer Fifield (University of Pittsburgh Press) includes both walking and driving architectural tours; *60 Hikes Within 60 Miles: Pittsburgh* by Donna Ruff (Menasha Ridge Press) offers diverse hiking suggestions in the city and beyond; *The Steps of Pittsburgh* by Bob Regan (Local History Co.) is a fascinating guide to the city's 712 sets of outdoor steps. And when you're ready to get out of town, pick up *Quick Escapes Pittsburgh* by Michelle Pilecki (Globe Pequot), which offers 25 mini-vacations in mostly tranquil settings.

JUST DUCKY TOURS Map 3

125 W. Station Square Dr., 412/402-3825, www.justduckytours.com

Nearly every decent-sized American town with river real estate now has an amphibious vehicle city tour. Pittsburgh's version, headquartered at Station Square, is Just Ducky Tours. The tour, which passes through Downtown, parts of the North Shore, and the Monongahela and Ohio Rivers, takes place in a vintage World War II amphibious vehicle, able to traverse both land and sea. Tours are roughly an hour long; expect to be pelted with miscellaneous Pittsburgh trivia and bad jokes. Adult tickets are $19, students and seniors $18, children 3–12 $15, and kids 2 and under are free. Just Ducky operates April 10 through October and weekends only in November.

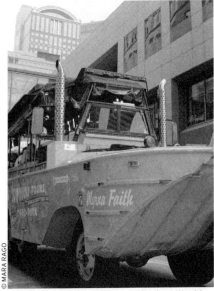

© MARA RAGO

tourists exploring the Steel City in a World War II amphibious vehicle

MOLLY'S TROLLEYS   Map 1

3046 Penn Ave., 412/281-2085,
www.mollystrolleys.com

If you're looking for a relatively standard city bus tour, Molly's Trolleys is without a doubt the most creative, amusing, and professionally run game in town. Yet as the company's name suggests, tours take place not inside a bus, but rather a replica of a 1920s-era trolley—albeit one with four street-legal tires.

Molly's offers a number of one- and two-hour sightseeing tours that explore Downtown, Mount Washington, and other popular neighborhoods. Specialized package tours and wedding tours are also popular. Do be aware, however, that the trolleys don't run on any sort of a regular schedule and can only be rented by groups with a minimum of 20 people.

PITTSBURGH HISTORY   Map 3
AND LANDMARKS
FOUNDATION TOURS

100 West Station Square Dr., Ste. 450,
412/471-5808, www.phlf.org

The Pittsburgh History and Landmarks Foundation is a nonprofit preservation group whose members work to save the city's most important structures from demolition or misuse. In an effort to educate the public about certain buildings and parts of the city they may have otherwise passed by without so much as a single thought, the group has organized a number of wonderfully educational guided walking tours.

The tours are a smart place to start for anyone interested in learning about the historical relevance of the city, packed as they are with intriguing well-researched trivia. Most tours are roughly an hour long, and although donations are encouraged, all tours are free.

Some of the more popular excursions include an architectural tour of the South Side, a look at the Old Allegheny County Jail, and a stroll through Downtown's historical 5th and Forbes Corridor.

PITTSBURGH   Map 7
NEIGHBORHOOD TOURS

412/481-0561, ext. 17,
www.pittsburghneighborhoodtours.com

Partly conceived and created by the city's own tourism bureau, the wonderfully educational Pittsburgh Neighborhood Tours were designed not only for tourists and other out-of-towners, but also for longtime locals who may not have taken the time to explore some of the city's most unique and culture-rich areas.

To participate, simply point your Internet browser to the Neighborhood Tours website and start clicking. You'll find reams of insider information about neighborhoods like Bloomfield, Mount Washington, the Strip District, and the South Side. A handful of detailed and self-guided tour suggestions are available for each of the featured neighborhoods.

PITTSBURGH WALKING   Map 7

412/362-8451, www.pittsburghwalking.com

You might call it a walking tour for the sort of person who doesn't normally enjoy taking tours: Pittsburgh Walking is a solitary organization led by Steel City history buff Donald Gibbon, who leads highly personalized tours of Downtown and its environs. But unlike the experience you'd probably have inside, say, a double-decker Redline tour bus, the Pittsburgh Walking experience is whatever you choose to make it. In other words, if given a bit of advance warning, Gibbon will research and plan tours in other city neighborhoods tailored to an individual or group's specific interest.

Gibbon is also happy to meet tour-goers at their Downtown hotel, or in Oakland, or on the North Side... or pretty much wherever. And as Gibbon's website says, his tours, which differ slightly each time he gives them, can be as long or short as the customer desires. Tours are $50 minimum for one hour; $100 minimum for three hours.

PNC PARK TOURS   Map 4
115 Federal St., 412/325-4700,
http://pittsburgh.pirates.mlb.com/NASApp/
mlb/pit/ballpark/tours.jsp

You don't necessarily need to be a Pirates fan to enjoy a tour of the ball club's newest North Side stadium. In fact, given that PNC Park is considered by many baseball insiders to be one of the country's finest parks, this is an experience that even a non-sports fan might find worthwhile.

Naturally, tour participants will have a chance to view sections of the park not open to fans during game time. Some of the experiences include a trip down to the field itself and an up-close-and-personal view of the batting cages and even the press box, which is generally considered the best seat in the house.

RIVERS OF STEEL   Map 7
HERITAGE TOURS
338 E. 9th Ave., Homestead, 412/464-5119,
www.riversofsteel.com

Comprising 3,000 square miles throughout seven counties of Southwestern Pennsylvania, the Rivers of Steel Heritage Area was created by Congress in 1996. The purpose was to honor the culture and the American way of life that existed hand-in-hand with the industry of Big Steel—an industry that no longer exists in this part of the county.

In Pittsburgh's Homestead neighborhood, however, it's now possible to tour the areas where steel production took place. Tours and their themes occasionally change, so it's best to call or check the organization's website before planning a trip. Past tours, however, have explored the infamous site of the Homestead Steel Strike of 1892 and the remains of the Carrie Furnace. Personal cassette recorders with headphones can also be rented; a narrated tape allows listeners to take a self-guided tour of the immediate area. For most tours, expect to pay around $20.

SEGWAY IN PARADISE   Map 7
724/625-3521, www.segwayinparadise.com

It's a fairly safe bet to assume that the majority of the people reading this book don't own a Segway and have never ridden one but have always wanted to try. If that's you, and if you're in Pittsburgh, you're in luck. A local sightseeing organization now offers two-hour tours aboard the battery-powered, self-propelled scooters for the cost of $49 per person. Appropriately enough, Segway in Paradise pioneers begin their exploration at the Carnegie Science Center on the North Side before heading over the Allegheny River to Point State Park, through Downtown, and then over the Monongahela River to Station Square before looping back.

RECREATION

Other Recreation

ADVENTURE SPORTS

THE CLIMBING WALL   Map 5

7501 Penn Ave., 412/247-7334,
www.theclimbingwall.com

An intense full-body workout, a sometimes terrifying experience, a serious mental test, and an absolute blast: That pretty much sums up the sport of indoor rock climbing, which can be practiced safely and affordably at the recently expanded The Climbing Wall at The Factory in Point Breeze. An introductory class will run you only $30; private advanced lessons and kids' lessons are also available. Can't make it to Point Breeze? Make the scene instead at the SouthSide Works' **REI** (412 S. 27th St., 412/488-9410, www.rei.com), where shoppers can ramble up an indoor wall before picking up a new pair of discounted Merrells.

THE PITTSBURGH GROTTO   Map 2

412/682-8654, www.karst.org/pgrotto

The Pittsburgh Grotto is a local organization of spelunking enthusiasts; members meet on the fourth Wednesday of every month (with the exceptions of May and December) to talk shop. You'll find them in room 203 of Thaw Hall on the University of Pittsburgh campus.

PUBLIC SWIMMING POOLS

Because of the area's troubling financial woes, the city has had a tough time over the past few summers paying the employees of its 31 outdoor public pools. One recent season even saw every single pool close early—well before the cool weather of fall had set in. But things are apparently looking up: After receiving more than $600,000 in donations from cor-

porations and foundations, the city reopened a little more than half its pools in 2006.

Pool tags are required for season-long admission; a family of four pays $60; adults 16 years and older pay $30 each; children 3–15 years old are charged $15 each. Not a city resident? Not a problem, although you'll be expected to hand over a whopping $45 for the season. Daily admission is available for those not interested in purchasing a season pass. The cost is $4 for adults 16 years and up and $3 for children 3–15. For info about pool locations or tag purchases, call 412/323-7928, or visit www.city.pittsburgh. pa.us/parks/html/swimming_pools.html.

Pittsburghers are rather fond of the city's three **wave pools,** all of which are wheelchair accessible and open every day from June through September (with some exceptions). Adult admission is $4; kids 6–12 and adults over 60 pay $3; kids 5 and under pay $1. The pool in **Boyce Park** (675 Frankstown Rd., 724/325-4677) is the most conveniently located if you're staying in the city; there's a snack bar and plenty of sunbathing space on the premises. **Settler's Cabin Park** in Oakdale (1225 Greer Rd., 412/787-2667) boasts trails, log cabins, a diving pool, and a wave pool. **South Park** (Buffalo Dr., 412/831-0810) also has a wave pool, as well as 9- and 18-hole golf courses, an ice skating rink, 33 lighted tennis courts, and a model airplane field.

Some of the most convenient and popular city pool locations include Schenley Park Pool and Ormsby Pool.

OLIVER BATH HOUSE   Map 3

38 S. 10th St., 412/488-8380

Possibly the most interesting of all the public pools is also the only one located indoors, and it's open year-round. The Oliver Bath House was built by Oliver Iron and Steel in 1910. The corporation's owner, a successful industrialist by the name of Henry W. Oliver, had it constructed specifically for his employees who had nowhere else to bathe. Five years later, Oliver presented the structure as a gift to the city. With its cathedral ceiling and blue-tiled, well-heated pool (the water is usually around 80°F), the bathhouse is the absolute picture of peace and serenity (especially during adult swim).

ORMSBY POOL   Map 3

79 S. 22nd St., 412/488-8377

If there were a competition for the most conspicuous and oddly located public pool, Ormsby would win it, hands down. Yet on the flip side, you won't have any trouble finding the place: Simply drive or walk across the Birmingham Bridge toward the South Side, and once you reach East Carson Street, there it is, right on the corner of one of the city's busiest intersections. Which isn't necessarily a bad thing, although if you don't like the idea of the world at large being able to see you in your bathing suit, you'd probably be better off swimming elsewhere. Then again, its convenience is exactly what makes Ormsby such a popular place: Where else can you perform a cannonball splash one minute, and then be gulping down a cold pint of I.C. Light the next? And aside from the many pubs on the Carson Street Strip, the pool also sits right next door to a public library, just down the street from the South-Side Works shopping center, and an easy walk to dozens of popular neighborhood cafés and boutiques.

SCHENLEY PARK POOL   Map 2

1 Overlook Dr., Schenley Park, 412/422-4266

As one of the most popular public swimming spots in the city, the Schenley pool on scorching summer days can feel just as crowded as a Florida beach during Spring Break. Undoubtedly, that has much to do with its convenient location near Central and South Oakland, neighborhoods with a lot of concrete, a lot of young people, and very few private swimming pools.

The facility itself is fair, but not outstanding. There isn't much shade to speak of, although the pool is appropriately large. Young children (as well as young children at heart) will appreciate the fact that Schenley Park's ubiquitous ice cream truck passes by dozens of times a day.

TENNIS

Tennis players in Pittsburgh are rather, uh, well served when it comes to choosing a court, whether public or private. An indispensable website is **Court Matters** (www.johnlaplante.com/tennis), which attempts to describe and map every court in Allegheny County. So far 224 courts have been documented, including indoor courts, courts with unusual surfaces, and even apartment complexes with courts.

For practical information about area news and events, including info about clinics, tournaments, and leagues, visit **Tennis in the Burgh** (www.pghtennis.com), which also maintains a Pittsburgh-specific tennis blog.

Citiparks maintains regional tennis courts in Frick Park, Highland Park, McKinley Park, Mellon Park, Schenley Park, and West Park, as well as in 50 smaller neighborhood parks. For locations and addresses, call 412/244-4188. The **Citiparks Tennis**

FITNESS AND RECREATION FOR THE ANTI-JOCK

In a town where the act of consuming a 16-ounce can of Iron City Beer is often spoken of as a metaphor for exercise (locals like to talk of "pumping a pint of Iron"), it's only fitting that sundry sports and recreational activities should abound for the beer-bellied, the uncoordinated, the noncompetitive, and the otherwise altogether out-of-shape. Which isn't to say that Pittsburgh's myriad and offbeat outdoor pursuits aren't physically demanding. Consider the local chapter of the Hash House Harriers, for instance: A motley crew of men and women who jog for miles upon miles throughout the city's backstreets, they stop only occasionally to raise their spirits, you might say, at a neighborhood tavern.

But whatever your current level of physical vigor, you're almost certain to find some sport or activity of interest in Pittsburgh. In other words, welcome to the City of Champions, where even a 255-pound running back named after a mass-transit vehicle (The Pittsburgh Steelers' Jerome Bettis, a.k.a. "The Bus") can become an honest-to-goodness American hero.

BILLIARDS

If you're truly serious about your pool game, **Shootz Cafe & Billiards** (2305 E. Carson St., 412/488-3820, www.shootz cafe.com) is the sort of place that'll have you gasping in admiration. Located near the Birmingham Bridge in the South Side's pub district, Shootz is the polar opposite of the clichéd down-and-dirty pool hall. Unlike other bars on East Carson Street, its 18 tables are always kept in impeccable condition. And while the crowd varies between professional types and ball cap–wearing college kids, the atmosphere is always upscale, thanks to the fireplaces and luxurious couches scattered about. Even pop superstar Prince once held an after-party event in a private VIP room here.

HASH HOUSE HARRIERS

A self-described "drinking club with a running problem," the Hash House Harriers were formed in the 1930s by a group of British soldiers stationed in Malaysia. Looking for a creative way to combine exercise with social activity, they modified the English game of hares and hounds into something of a drinking contest. Today, Hash House Harriers clubs, known as kennels, exist in just about every major city on Earth – Pittsburgh included. To put it simply, a hash is a combination of a long-distance jog, a scavenger hunt, and a keg party. Anyone is welcome to join in; call the Pittsburgh Hash Hotline for details at 412/381-6709, or go online at www.pgh-h3.com.

LAWN BOWLING

Perfect for players young and old, physically fit, or weak and frail, lawn bowling is an ancient Roman game that was first introduced to America by the English. Unlike the variety of bowling that takes place in an alley, lawn bowlers compete against one another in each game; part of the strategy involves knocking an opponent's ball out of play. The bowling green in Point Breeze's Frick Park – not far from the Henry Clay Frick estate – is the only such court in the region. Open bowling takes place on Thursdays and

the legendary pinball room at South Side's Beehive

Fridays at 7 P.M. and on Saturdays and Sundays at 1 P.M. For more information, call 412/782-0848, or visit the website of the **Frick Park Lawn Bowls Club** at http://members.tripod.com/~fplbc.

PINBALL

If you know much at all about pinball, you'll no doubt be impressed to learn that Pittsburgh is home to the **World Pinball Championships,** an annual series organized by PAPA (www.papa.org), the Professional Amateur Pinball Association. The championship games take place in suburban Scott Township. Do be aware, however, that the majority of the flipper fanatics here will be adults, not children. More than $33,000 in prize money changes hands during the tournament; the winner takes home $10,000.

For more information about the local pinball scene, visit www.pinburgh.com.

ROCK & BOWL

Looking for an unusual way to spend a Monday evening that involves ugly shoes, indie rock, and cheap beer in plastic cups? We thought so. You might try paying a visit to **Rock & Bowl at Arsenal Lanes** (212 44th St., 412/683-5992, www.arsenalbowl.com) in Lawrenceville. It's a once-a-week event where hipster types and college kids bowl to the accompaniment of a local rock band. The night will set you back $8, which includes all the frames you can squeeze in between 9 P.M. and the stroke of midnight. And no need to feel self-conscious about your nonexistent bowling skills; while some of Pittsburgh's best bowlers frequently congregate at Arsenal Lanes, they tend to steer clear of this event. Can't imagine why.

ULTIMATE FRISBEE

A noncontact team sport that combines elements of soccer, basketball, and American football, Ultimate Frisbee was created in 1960 by college students who originally tossed around pie dishes. Today the sport is played internationally, and more than 50 countries hold tournaments. Contrary to popular belief, however, UF players must be in top physical shape to perform well. The local organization known as **Pittsburgh Ultimate** (www.pittsburgh-ultimate.org) is home to a number of seasonal leagues, as well as college teams, a women's league, and a junior league. Visit the organization's website to find contact information for the various team representatives.

Program offers lessons for children, adults, and seniors. Tennis camps sponsored by Citiparks for children 5–17 years old take place every June and July. Call 412/665-4017 for information, or visit Citiparks online at www.city.pittsburgh.pa.us/parks.

One of the city's best racquet sports specialty shops is **Tennis Village** (5419 Walnut St., 412/621-2399). Located in Shadyside for the past two decades, it stocks shoes, clothing, accessories and supplies for tennis, racquetball, and squash players.

MELLON PARK TENNIS CENTER   Map 5

6425 5th Ave. at Beechwood Blvd., 412/665-4017

Ever driven past a structure on 5th Avenue near Penn Avenue that resembles a giant inflatable dome and wondered what went on there? Now you know: It's nothing less than an indoor, year-round tennis court. Known locally as the Tennis Bubble, the dome itself measures an impressive 118 feet wide by 265 feet long. Most enthusiasts will be pleased to learn that the playing surface is a Premiere Court (a slightly cushioned hard court), and that when the dome is removed during the summer months, use of the courts are free to the public. (Inexplicably, the bubble isn't removed every summer.) Players should call ahead to reserve one of the bubble's five courts which cost between $20–30 per hour, depending on the time of the day and the day of the week. The bubble, which maintains a pleasant temperature of 65°F, is open 7 A.M.–11 P.M. every day of the week.

SCHENLEY PARK   Map 2
TENNIS COURTS

Overlook Rd., Schenley Park,
www.pittsburghparks.org

It's easy to understand why the courts in Oakland's Schenley Park are so popular with Pittsburgh's racket enthusiasts. For starters, the park features an impressive 13 courts that sport hard, Plexipave surfaces. And with so many courts to choose from, players are almost certain to find at least a few spaces open on any given day of the week, even though the area quite often hums with activity. What's more, the area is well lit, and all courts are in wonderful condition—which is saying something, given that the city-sponsored facilities are free and open to the public. Do be aware that the courts, which sit next to Schenley Park's soccer and softball fields, are often in use Saturday mornings and weekday evenings by city-sponsored tennis clinics or tournaments.

WASHINGTON'S LANDING   Map 7
TENNIS COURTS

Washinton's Landing

A 42-acre island formerly known as Herr's Island, and located about two miles east of Downtown on the Allegheny River, the formerly blighted area referred to as Washington's Landing is today a collection of expensive townhomes, a marina, a rowing center, and one of the most gorgeously situated public tennis courts in all of Pittsburgh. With an unbelievably beautiful riverside setting, it almost wouldn't matter if the courts here were uneven and cracked. And while three of the five courts are in fact in poor condition, two are perfectly usable. That less-than-perfect situation doesn't often create a problem, because due to its somewhat obscure location, the courts usually see very little action, even on perfect weather days.

The playing surface here is hard, and

there are no lighting or restroom facilities. To find the courts, drive north along the 31st Street Bridge (from the Strip District toward Route 28), then take a left onto the downward-sloping ramp, which sits mere feet from the end of the bridge. Take a left at the bottom of the ramp and follow that road until it dead-ends into the tennis courts' parking lot.

SKATEBOARDING

As is the case in most cities, skateboarding parks in Pittsburgh come in two distinct classes: There are city-sponsored public parks, which are free, and there are private parks, all of which require skaters to cough up an admission fee. The Polish Hill Bowl at the West Penn Recreation Center and McKinley are the only free parks located within the city limits.

For more info about area parks, visit www.skateboardpark.com. And should you care to stay abreast of Pittsburgh's skateboarding news and gossip, log on to www.pittskate.com.

B-CUBED SKATEPARK   Map 7
330 Hookstown Grade Rd., Moon Township, 412/264-2222, www.bcubedskatepark.com
This pay park is located at the Airport Ice Arena in Moon Township, not far from Pittsburgh International Airport. One of Pittsburgh's better parks, B-Cubed is the sort of wooden, indoor facility often seen in skateboarding videos; it sports a massive bowl as well as a bevy of pipes, ramps, rails, and street obstacles. At the time of writing, the park, which also attracts its fair share of BMX riders and inline skaters, was planning a complete redesign.

◖ IMPERIAL   Map 7
SKATEPARK
800 Rte. 30, Findlay Township's Clinton Community Park, www.findlay.pa.us
Generally agreed upon as the best and most challenging skate park in the Greater Pittsburgh area, Imperial Skatepark is nothing less than a concrete dream. Here you'll find a beautifully constructed concrete snake run, a kidney-shaped pool, and small ramps scattered throughout. There's also a standard street area with rails, as well as a half pipe. The park is well lit and open late, and BMX riders are welcome.

MCKINLEY SKATEPARK   Map 7
Bausman St., Beltzhoover, 412/488-9119
Located in Beltzhoover's McKinley Park, this skate park is often empty during the day. Offering a four-foot metal half pipe and a decent collection of street obstacles, the park can be accessed by taking the Liberty Tunnel out of the city and then turning left onto Route 51 South. From there, hang another left onto Bausman Street; you'll soon see the park on your left. Thrift store connoisseurs should take care not to miss the nearby **Red White & Blue Thrift Store** (935 Ohio River Blvd., 412/766-6098).

MR. SMALLS SKATEPARK   Map 6
40 Riverfront Dr., 412/821-8188, www.mrsmalls.com
Situated not far from the East End is the extremely popular Mr. Smalls Skatepark which you'll find underneath the 40th Street Bridge on the Millvale side of the Allegheny River. Along with a large street course and a huge vert ramp that was used in the 2001 X Games, Mr. Smalls offers private and group lessons for beginning skaters and has an on-site skate shop.

THE POLISH HILL BOWL   Map 1

450 30th St., 412/622-7353

The Polish Hill Bowl is the easiest to reach if you don't have a car. It's also not far from Gooski's—convenient should you care to do a bit of pre- or post-session drinking. The 77A and 77B buses pass by the park, as does just about every other 54C, but be sure to ask the driver if his or her route passes through Polish Hill. True to its name, the park doesn't offer much more than a bowl, albeit a relatively nice one. Some street skating facilities are also on-site.

YOGA AND MEDITATION

BREATHE YOGA STUDIO   Map 3

1113 E. Carson St., 3rd Fl., 412/481-9642, www.pittsburghyoga.com

Located in a 1,400-square-foot studio in the heart of the South Side Flats, Breathe Yoga offers beginning and intermediate Hatha classes, including Iyengar classes, and a Yoga Basics class, which focuses on simple breathing and posture techniques. That doesn't begin to describe the school's full schedule, however. Breathe has also managed to somehow squeeze in Middle Eastern dance classes, capoeira instruction, and modern dance classes taught by instructors from the local Laboratory Company.

KEARNS SPIRITUALITY CENTER   Map 7

9000 Babcock Blvd., Allison Park, 412/366-1124, www.falundafa-pgh.org

Falun Gong, also known as Falun Dafa, is an ancient Chinese meditation technique closely related to *qigong*, in which the mind and body are refined and improved through various low-impact exercises and meditative techniques. What makes Falun Gong slightly different is that its practitioners also focus on the improve-

ment of moral character. Despite (or maybe because of) the persecution and numerous arrests of Falun Gong groups in China, English-speaking organizations have popped up in cities all over the world during the past decade or so. In Pittsburgh, you can join in every Saturday morning 8:30–10 A.M. on the lawn outside the Frick Fine Arts Building, which is located on the Pitt campus in between the Carnegie and Hillman libraries. A Falun Gong informational class takes place every Monday 10–11:30 A.M. at the Kearns Spirituality Center in Allison Park. Classes and meditation sessions are always free of charge.

SCHOOLHOUSE YOGA   Map 1

2401 Smallman St., 412/401-4444, www.schoolhouseyoga.com

Yoga studios in Pittsburgh seem to arrive and then disappear with frequency, which makes it all the more heartening to witness the success of Schoolhouse Yoga, an organization that did, in fact, start out in a disused Lawrenceville schoolhouse. Today, Schoolhouse operates two increasing popular locations, and both shops offer a wide variety of classes at all skill levels. Ashtanga, Hatha, and Kundalini yoga classes are all available. Other varieties include Gentle Yoga, for students recovering from an injury or illness, Prenatal Yoga, and even Plus-Size Yoga for Men & Women, which is specially designed to fit the needs of overweight students. There is a second location at 2010 Murray Avenue in Squirrel Hill.

STILL MOUNTAIN   Map 7
TAI CHI AND CHI KUNG

Mount Lebanon, 412/480-9177, www.stillmountaintaichi.com

Because Pittsburgh doesn't have much of an

immigrant Chinese community to speak of, you won't find the martial art of tai chi practiced in public parks here as it is in, say, San Francisco's Washington Square. But the ancient form of Chinese exercise is taught at a number of Kung Fu and martial arts studios around town, including Still Mountain Tai Chi and Chi Kung.

The practice at Still Mountain leans toward Chinese Buddhism and involves a combination of martial arts, spiritual development, and health. A wide variety of classes and workshops take place at the Still Mountain studio, including classes that involve weapons, self-defense, and meditation workshops.

ACCOMMODATIONS

When it comes time to find a place to stay in Pittsburgh, the good news is that this city has more than enough hotel rooms to house just about any guest for about any length of time. Visit during a large convention, or during the holidays, or even at the beginning or end of a school year, and you're practically assured of finding some sort of vacancy somewhere. Yet it's an unfortunate fact that the variety of accommodation options leaves quite a bit to be desired. What you'll find in abundance here are mostly corporate-style and chain hotels, most of them pricey. Hotels and guesthouses in Pittsburgh also tend to be clustered together in only a handful of neighborhoods, which means you're somewhat limited in terms of where in the city you'll stay.

The backpackers and budget travelers among you will no doubt be disheartened to learn that Pittsburgh's solitary youth hostel, a lovely Hostelling International–sponsored building that was located atop a hill in Allentown, permanently closed its doors in 2003.

But don't trade in your air ticket for a round-trip to Cleveland just yet; there *is* good news in the Steel City lodging scene, most of it revolving around the town's especially quaint bed-and-breakfasts. Visit just

© FABIAN BAUTISTA

HIGHLIGHTS

LOOK FOR ☾ TO FIND RECOMMENDED ACCOMMODATIONS.

☾ **Most Elegant Hotel:** With its gorgeous grand lobby and truly dignified sleeping quarters, it's no wonder upper-crusters such as John F. Kennedy and Lawrence Welk have been landing at the **Omni William Penn** since 1916 (page 204).

☾ **Best Room with a View:** Ask for a room on one of the top two floors of Downtown's **Renaissance Pittsburgh Hotel,** and you'll be able to take in a ball game from the comfort of your queen-size mattress. The top floor is the best, and make sure your room faces the Allegheny River (page 206).

☾ **Best Queer-Friendly Bed-and-Breakfast:** Owned and operated by a wonderfully accommodating couple, Jeff and Karl, **The Inn on the Mexican War Streets** is Pittsburgh's most gloriously decorated residence (page 211).

☾ **Best Themed Accommodation:** A uniquely Caribbean-themed bed-and-breakfast situated close to Heinz Field, **The Parador** is a gorgeously restored Victorian house run by a Pittsburgher who conceived of the idea while residing in Florida (page 211).

☾ **Most Historic Hotel:** Built in 1886 and now a historical landmark, the renovated **Sunnyledge Boutique Hotel** was originally the home of Dr. James McClelland. He's best known locally as being the founder of the nearby Shadyside Hospital (page 214).

© MARA RAGO

about any bed-and-breakfast in the city, in fact, and chances are you'll be pleasantly surprised to find such refined and sophisticated interiors in a town most popularly known for its grittiness and blue-collar community. Do keep in mind, however, that since most bed-and-breakfasts have a very small number of rooms, advance reservations are highly recommended, even in the off-season.

CHOOSING AN ACCOMMODATION

For any of the Pittsburgh visitors who've come to study or work at a college or area hospital, the university district of Oakland is the obvious choice. Not only does it have a decent number of hotels, but also a fair amount of variety. Two Oakland hotels, for instance, offer full suites, and one offers a substantial discount to students.

Just a bit farther east is Shadyside, a relaxed and leafy neighborhood where both the homes and the commercial district are upscale. Here you'll find a number of bed-and-breakfasts; there's also a newly built hotel directly across the street from Shadyside Hospital.

It's in Downtown Pittsburgh, however, where the majority of the town's tourists and business travelers call it a night. As is the case in most midsize downtowns, pricey chain hotels are the order of the day here. Many Downtown hotels, however, offer a decent mix of telecommuting accessories and on-site eateries, making a weekend in the Golden Triangle as professional and productive as it is entertaining, unusual, and unique.

Most guidebooks to the region encourage the shoestring traveler to investigate the many chain hotel options near the airport, and while that advice is certainly useful in theory, it does little good for anyone arriving by bus or by train, not to mention anyone without the use of a private vehicle. Those *truly* drained of funds might consider the North Side's **Allegheny YMCA** (600 West North Ave., 412/321-8594, www.ymcaof pittsburgh.org), which largely houses street people and the unemployed, yet is considerably cheaper than even a Motel 6.

If you'd prefer to stay a bit outside the city, visit www.pittsburghbnb.com, which contains a list of inns and bed-and-breakfasts throughout the Greater Pittsburgh area and its surrounding countryside.

For a more comprehensive listing of hotels and motels, cabins, campgrounds, bed-and-breakfasts, and resorts, visit the very useful www.visitpa.com. Also useful for accommodation listings—as well as information about regional events—is www.visitpittsburgh.com.

The rates in this chapter are based on double occupancy in the high season (summer).

Downtown   Map 1

Downtown Pittsburgh is small enough that its entire distance can easily be covered on foot, so when choosing a hotel, there's really not much of a need to consider *where* in Downtown it's located. You can rest assured that shopping, theaters, and restaurants will always be just a brief walk or taxi ride away.

$100-150

HILTON PITTSBURGH

600 Commonwealth Pl., 412/391-4600,
www.hilton.com

Located directly across the street from the entrance to Point State Park, the Hilton Pittsburgh ($119–274) is one of the largest hotels in the city. All 713 rooms boast a phenomenal city view; some gaze out over the park and the three rivers. The Hilton frequently plays host to small or midsize conferences, and with 40,000 square feet of meeting space, a business room is almost always available. Guests planning to catch up on office work will be pleased to learn that all rooms come with ergonomically designed work areas. There's also a 24-hour fitness center and a decent restaurant on-site. Pets are welcome.

◖ OMNI WILLIAM PENN

530 William Penn Pl., 412/281-7100,
www.omnihotels.com

Known as Pittsburgh's premiere luxury

hotel, the Omni William Penn ($119–345) has been welcoming well-heeled guests (including Lawrence Welk and John F. Kennedy) since 1916. Luckily, it's possible to experience the grandeur of the place even if you're not a registered guest: Simply sink into one of the massive lobby's deep couches and gaze upon the many chandeliers and the baby grand. Or, wander into the attached Starbucks, the Tap Room (an English-style ale house), or the Palm Court, a restaurant known for its exquisite cocktails. Lodgings are absolutely top-notch, too, and come complete with all the modern conveniences, including cherrywood furniture, plush bathrobes, and personalized voicemail.

PITTSBURGH MARRIOTT CITY CENTER

112 Washington Pl., 412/471-4000 or 888/456-6600, http://marriott.com/ property/propertypage/pitdt

Although not necessarily the most conveniently located hotel for those doing daily business anywhere in the heart of Downtown, the Pittsburgh Marriott City Center ($119–139) is especially well located for anyone who's come to town specifically to attend an event at Mellon Arena (a.k.a. Civic Arena); it literally sits directly across the street. Celebrity obsessives staying here may even get the chance to spy their favorite star; band members and other performers appearing at Mellon Arena often bunk here because of its obvious convenience. Guest rooms here are meticulously decorated, from the carpets to the curtains to the artwork on the walls. And all rooms come equipped with a work desk suitable for the business traveler. Right downstairs is the Steelhead Brasserie and Wine Bar, a popular contemporary American eatery.

WESTIN CONVENTION CENTER PITTSBURGH

1000 Penn Ave., 412/281-3700, www.starwoodhotels.com/westin

As the name cleverly suggests, the Westin Convention Center Pittsburgh ($119–169) is an ideal lodging choice for any out-of-towner planning to attend the recently remodeled David L. Lawrence Convention Center. In fact, an enclosed skywalk connects the two buildings. The Westin is also home to The Original Fish Market, a fantastic seafood eatery with one of the city's best sushi bars. There's an 8,000-sqaure-foot fitness center as well, complete with a sauna and a lap pool. Rooms here are some of the Downtown area's largest; each one has a view of the central business district. Complimentary transportation to the Warhol Museum and PNC Park is offered. Pets are welcome.

$150-250

COURTYARD MARRIOTT DOWNTOWN

945 Penn Ave., 412/434-5551, http://marriott .com/property/propertypage/pitcy

As Downtown Pittsburgh's newest hotel, the Courtyard Marriott ($169–289) sits uniquely inside four side-by-side historical buildings. By contrast, Downtown's other lodging options are all stand-alone structures, most of them enormously large. What that equates to is that even though the buildings have been thoroughly renovated, some interesting architectural details remain, such as the 12- or 14-foot vaulted ceilings found in each room. The fitness room here stays open around the clock, and right next door is the especially popular Sonoma Grille, a contemporary American restaurant with a fantastic wine list. On-site parking is available for $22 a day, and the David L. Lawrence Convention Center is little more than a stone's throw away.

DOUBLETREE HOTEL
PITTSBURGH CITY CENTER

1 Bigelow Sq., 412/281-5800 or 800/222-8733, http://doubletree.hilton.com

Located literally in the heart of the Golden Triangle, the Doubletree Hotel ($199–249) sits just steps from the U.S. Steel Tower, the David L. Lawrence Convention Center, and Mellon Bank Headquarters, making it a convenient choice for the busy business traveler. Guests are also welcome to access the hotel's 24-hour business center, which offers free printing, faxing, copying, and high-speed Internet access. The spacious yet not especially modern rooms all come with work desks, ergonomic chairs, and flat-screen TVs. Also complimentary is access to the adjacent Downtown Athletic Club, a fitness center with an indoor pool and tanning bed.

◖ RENAISSANCE PITTSBURGH HOTEL

107 6th St., 412/562-1200, http://marriott.com/property/propertypage/PITBR

Although owned by the Marriott organization, the Renaissance Pittsburgh Hotel ($149–299) is designed to look and feel like

Renaissance Pittsburgh Hotel, Downtown

© FABIAN BAUTISTA

a stylish and creatively detailed boutique hotel. With its old-world, European theme, it's also the only choice in Downtown for anyone interested in lodging that lacks the cookie-cutter, corporate feel. Guest rooms, although outfitted with all the conveniences one would find in any Marriott, are smartly decorated as well, and the on-site restaurant, Opus, is a locally celebrated and gorgeously designed Mediterranean spot with an impressive wine list. Baseball fans should request a room with a PNC Park view.

LONG-TERM STAYS

Staying for a week, a month, or longer? Consider a smart and fantastic alternative to the faceless hotel, the **Shadyside Inn & Suites** (5405 5th Ave., 412/441-4444 or 800/767-8483, www.shadysideinn.com). This hotel is actually a collection of fully furnished apartments, all of which contain the same amenities of a luxury hotel. And while it's certainly possible to stay here for just one night, the majority of Shadyside Inn guests are long-term and are particularly interested in something of a home-away-from-home environment.

During Pittsburgh's brief flirtation with Hollywood, for instance, a number of actors and actresses in town for film shoots lodged here, including Sharon Stone, Bruce Willis, Sally Field, and Julianne Moore. Astronaut Buzz Aldrin has stayed a number of times, and Jodie Foster bunked at the Shadyside Inn for three full months.

Conveniently enough, rates here are generally lower than what you'd encounter at an equivalent hotel ($625 weekly or $2,095 monthly for a studio suite; $725 weekly or $2,395 monthly for a one-bedroom suite), and all room rates include free off-street parking. All suites also come with free high-speed Internet access, a TV and VCR, and a fully equipped kitchen. To see floor plans and color photos of the suites, visit the Shadyside Inn website.

Oakland   Map 2

Oakland is the city's university district, and as such it's naturally home to a number of chain hotels which do a booming business at the beginning and end of every school year. (I recommend booking well in advance if you'll be staying in this neighborhood during the end of August, the beginning of September, the end of April, or the start of May.) Oakland is also a good alternative to Downtown—you'll be surrounded by all the urban amenities here, and Downtown is always reachable by a quick taxi or bus ride.

$100-150

HAMPTON INN UNIVERSITY CENTER

3315 Hamlet St., 412/681-1000 or 800/426-7866, www.pittsburghhamptoninn.com

Although South Oakland's Hampton Inn ($119–129) is perfectly located for anyone visiting Magee-Womens Hospital, Carlow College, or the Pittsburgh Playhouse, it should be noted that because of its slightly hidden location in a somewhat confusing part of the city, out-of-towners arriving in their own vehicles will likely find themselves turned around unless they've been given very detailed directions. Conveniently enough, directions can be downloaded from the hotel's website; look for the "hotel fact sheet" PDF link. On the bright side, the Hampton Inn quite often has rooms available when the rest of Oakland is booked solid (at the beginning and end of college semesters, for instance). And although rooms are relatively plain, a daily hot breakfast and a complimentary shuttle service are included. A fitness center and business center are on-site.

QUALITY INN UNIVERSITY CENTER

3401 Boulevard of the Allies, 412/683-6100 or 800/245-4444, www.choicehotels.com

It's perhaps a bit ironic that with a name like Quality Inn ($99–129), most travelers staying the night here wouldn't necessarily expect to experience much quality at all. Yet all things considered, this particular location is actually rather nice. It's no boutique hotel, of course, but the rooms and beds are fairly large, and most come complete with small balconies. (Perfect for smokers who've checked into a nonsmoking room.) The hotel's real benefit, though, is its location: The Quality Inn is located deeper in South Oakland than any other hotel, so parents visiting college students who live in the neighborhood will be well positioned, even if they've arrived without a car. Extra bonus points: Parking is free, and there's a Panera Bread on the ground floor.

$150-250

FORBES AVENUE SUITES

3401 Forbes Ave., 412/325-3900 or 877/335-3900, www.forbesavesuites.net

Offering suites with one, two, or three rooms, Forbes Avenue Suites ($139–215 daily, $700–1,291 weekly, $1,950–3,872 monthly) sits smack-dab in the center of the university district and, according to management, serves mainly two types of clientele: folks affiliated with the surrounding universities (grad students, guest lecturers) or those doing business with the surrounding hospitals (residents, patients' families). The digs here, however, are decidedly grim and with nary a single piece of designer furniture in sight. Yet considering the fact that full-size stoves, ovens, refrigerators, microwaves, dishwashers, and TVs are included, it does serve an important purpose: Should you find yourself in town for a week, a

FAMILY HOUSE

In late 1983, a small group of doctors and influential community leaders in Pittsburgh took notice of a troubling trend taking place in the waiting rooms and hallways of the city's many hospitals: Out-of-town family members of patients undergoing long-term treatment for serious illnesses were sleeping in corridors and plastic chairs for days on end. Sometimes weeks on end. Determined to do something about it, the group formed a nonprofit organization and eventually raised enough money to refurbish an old mansion near the city's main hospital complex. Families of patients with life-threatening illnesses, and in some cases the patients themselves, were welcomed to temporarily move into the mansion at a very reasonable cost. A communal kitchen was built to cut down on the prohibitive expense of eating every single meal at a restaurant.

The popularity of **Family House** (412/647-7777, www.familyhouse .org), as the group called its accommodation, soon outgrew the confines of that first mansion. Today the organization has rooms and suites in three separate locales: 514 N. Neville Street in North Oakland, 233 McKee Place in South Oakland, and 5245 Centre Avenue in Shadyside. All houses offer free shuttles to West Penn Hospital and most UPMC hospitals, as well as libraries, fitness rooms, on-site laundry facilities, TV lounges, cable TV in each room, private phone lines and voice mail in each room, 24-hour security, and most important of all, a warm and caring family environment at very affordable rates. For more information or to request a room, call or visit the Family House website.

month, or longer, you'll have all the amenities of home without the hassle of a sublet-apartment search. Parking is $10 extra per night, and students receive a 20 percent discount.

HOLIDAY INN SELECT AT UNIVERSITY CENTER

100 Lytton Ave., 412/682-6200, www.hiselect.com
If you need to stay in Oakland but would prefer not to be polluted by the noise of the urban jungle, the Holiday Inn Select at University Center ($160–190) would be a wise choice. Located almost across the street from the Cathedral of Learning, the hotel sits a few buildings in from busy 5th Avenue. Rooms are more or less what you'd expect: clean, but with no exciting amenities. There is an indoor pool, however, as well as a restaurant and a small gift shop.

RESIDENCE INN MARRIOTT

3896 Bigelow Blvd., 412/621-2200 or 800/513-8766, http://marriott.com/property/propertypage/PITRO
Located in a rather odd stretch of North Oakland, the Residence Inn Marriott ($189–259) may seem like an impossibly inconvenient place to stay for visitors who've arrived without private vehicles. But the truth is that as the only hotel in the neighborhood, it's perfectly positioned for anyone visiting North Oakland–based friends or family, and a shuttle service to and from central Oakland is complimentary for guests. As for the digs themselves, this is Oakland's only all-suite hotel, and, as such, rooms come complete with a refrigerator, microwave, toaster, dishwasher, and a full stove and oven. There's also a basketball court, indoor pool, and exercise room on-site, as well as a special area for pet-walking.

WYNDHAM GARDEN HOTEL

3454 Forbes Ave., 412/683-2040, www.wyndham.com/hotels/PITUP/main.wnt
A 198-room, eight-floor hotel in South Oakland, the Wyndham Garden Hotel ($170–229) is a relatively standard spot close to Carlow College, Magee-Womens Hospital, UPMC Presbyterian, and Children's Hospital. On-site you'll find a restaurant, a fitness center, and a complimentary shuttle that will drop off or pick up anywhere within three miles of the hotel. Pets are welcome for an additional $10 charge per day, and six rooms are available for guests using wheelchairs.

South Side   Map 3

Most Pittsburghers think of the South Side as one of our town's most sinful and eclectic neighborhoods. Bars and clubs are everywhere, so if you've come to Pittsburgh primarily to play, sleeping on the South Side makes good sense. But aside from a six-room bed-and-breakfast, there are only two options in the entire area, so booking in advance is recommended. For additional good advice about what to see, do, and eat in the area, visit www.southsidepgh.org.

$150-250

HOLIDAY INN EXPRESS HOTEL & SUITES

20 S. 10th St., 412/488-1130, www.hiexpress.com
The Holiday Inn Express Hotel & Suites ($160–190) is frequently booked full. Which isn't to say that it's a particularly unique or

special place, although it is wonderfully located: It sits at the base of the 10th Street Bridge, making a walk into Downtown quite possible. And it's just blocks from the heart of the South Side Flats. Guest rooms are certainly comfortable and clean enough, but if a South Side location isn't important to you, save a few dollars and bunk elsewhere.

MORNING GLORY INN

2119 Sarah St., 412/431-1707, www.gloryinn.com

A bed-and-breakfast so subtly concealed on a residential street that even most locals don't realize it's there, you might say that the peacefully relaxing Morning Glory Inn ($150–350) is the absolute antithesis of the hard-partying neighborhood it calls home. A lovingly restored 1862 Victorian, this is the South Side's only independent lodging. And trimmed as it is with antiques, period fireplaces, a cozy two-level "Attic Suite," and a wildly popular back garden area where wedding receptions are held most weekends, it's also one of Pittsburgh's better bed-and-breakfasts. Do bear in mind, however, that neither Downtown nor Oakland are within walking distance, regardless of the claims made on Morning Glory's website.

OVER $250

SHERATON HOTEL STATION SQUARE

300 W. Station Square Dr., 412/261-2932, www.sheraton.com

Should you find yourself booked into the

Morning Glory Inn, an intimate South Side bed-and-breakfast

Sheraton Hotel Station Square ($279–289), you may feel somewhat isolated from town. But assuming the weather is nice, reaching the business district is actually quite pleasant—just take a five-minute walk across the Smithfield Street Bridge. The Monongahela Incline leading to Mount Washington is also nearby. And unlike most chain hotels in the city, this one is smartly designed and boasts a beautifully modern lobby. The guest rooms are nicely understated, and there's a fitness room, a pool, and a wonderful steak restaurant—Pittsburgh Rare—on-site.

North Side   Map 4

The North Side certainly isn't rich in hotels, although with all the recent development around the North Shore area, it's quite possible that something new will open before this guide sees its second edition. When it comes to bed-and-breakfasts, however, the story is radically different. There are scores of bed-and-breakfasts in the area, and every last one is creatively decorated and overflowing with character. Crossing one of the bridges to Downtown on foot is simple, not to mention a perfect way to get a great view of the city skyline. Yet with all there is to do on the North Side, you could easily spend a long weekend without ever needing to leave the neighborhood.

$100-150
⟨ THE INN ON THE
MEXICAN WAR STREETS
604 W. North Ave., 412/231-6544,
www.innonthemexicanwarstreets.com
Without a doubt, this inn ($139–189) is the city's best all-around bed-and-breakfast. Boasting eight individually and uniquely decorated suites, a front porch shaded by stone arches and columns, a gorgeous lobby complete with a baby grand piano, and off-street parking, you just couldn't ask for a lovelier locale. This bed-and-breakfast is gay-owned, gay-friendly, and is patronized largely by gay men and lesbians. Heterosexuals are more than welcome, of course. At the time of writing, plans for an on-site French restaurant and a martini bar were in the works.

⟨ THE PARADOR
939 Western Ave., 412/231-4800 or
888/540-1443, www.theparadorinn.com
Owned and operated by a Pittsburgher who was transferred to Florida and subsequently influenced by that state's tropical flavor, The Parador ($150) is a Caribbean-themed bed-and-breakfast situated in the unlikely locale of Allegheny West, just up the hill from the Carnegie Science Center. Previously known as the 8,000-square-foot Rhodes Mansion, which was built in 1870, The Parador's many suites and common areas seem to stretch on forever. Each room is decorated and detailed to suggest a different tropical flower, and the lavish 2,000-square-foot ballroom, with its incredibly ornate back bar mirror, must be seen to be believed. At the time of writing, plans for a full beach-themed garden were well under way.

$150-250
MARRIOTT SPRINGHILL SUITES
223 Federal St., 412/323-9005, http://marriott
.com/property/propertypage/PITNS
Because of its location next door to the Pittsburgh Pirate's PNC Park, the recently constructed Marriott Springhill Suites ($189–219) seems to have been built for the express purpose of housing pro sports fans. Yet it's also true that every tourist locale on the North Side is within walking distance, as is Downtown. Parking is available for $17 a day, and a complimentary shuttle will drop you off and pick you up anywhere within a three-mile radius of the hotel. All suites are equipped with a sofa and a small pantry area. A spa, a heated pool, and a fitness center are also on-site.

THE PRIORY

614 Pressley St., 412/231-3338,
www.thepriory.com

A 24-room European-style boutique hotel located within walking distance of all the North Side's major attractions, The Priory ($149–190) is a restored 19th-century Benedictine rectory that has been welcoming and harboring guests for just over two decades. In fact, you might say that The Priory is Pittsburgh's most famous hotel. Dozens of local and national publications have sung its praises over the years, which shouldn't come as much of a surprise considering its timeless Victorian charm, its truly friendly and personalized service, and its lovely outdoor courtyard, which has been many a wedding planner's reception location of choice. Don't forget to poke your head into the adjacent Grand Hall—formerly St. Mary's German Catholic Church—that today is used to host elegant large events. (Single-person rooms at The Priory, by the way, can be had for as little as $79 a night.)

Shadyside   Map 5

The bed-and-breakfasts in Shadyside are all located within walking distance of Walnut Street and Ellsworth Avenue, which is where the vast majority of the neighborhood's shopping, dining, and entertainment options can be found. If you're in town to visit one of the colleges or universities, walking is certainly an option, although you might prefer using a rental car or taxi to get there and back.

$50-100

HOUSE OF ZEN GUEST HOUSE

5820 Howe St., 412/361-6321 or 412/721-7520,
www.thehouseofzen.com

Regardless of its fairly exotic-sounding name, spending the night at the House of Zen ($50, two rooms $80, three rooms $100) is probably quite similar to spending the night at someone's house. Why's that? Well, it *is* someone's house. A lovely Victorian with a peaceful backyard garden, it's also beautifully designed and decorated. Asian artwork lines the walls, and a meditation pit that can easily fit a dozen Zen masters fills the entirety of the living room. (*Sati* meditation sessions take place regularly.) Three of the upstairs bedrooms are used as guest rooms: One has a double bed, another sports a fold-out couch, and the last has something of double-platform setup; guests sleep on bare mattresses, minimalist-style. All rooms come with cable TV and wireless Internet access, although the solitary bathroom is shared. The rates are probably the lowest in the entire city, although guests are required to stay for at least a week or two.

$150-250

THE APPLETREE INN

703 S. Negley Ave., 412/661-0631,
www.theinnsonnegley.com

Located almost directly across the street from its sister B&B, the Inn at 714 Negley, The Appletree Inn ($180–235) is a remarkably similar structure: Both houses were built in the late 1800s, both have their original wood flooring, and both are luxuriously decorated. The Appletree Inn, however, is certainly the more stately of the two; with its Victorian ambience and lack of almost any modern details, lodging here almost feels like a trip back in time. The first-floor Braeburn Apple Room, which includes a king-size canopy bed and fireplace, is wheelchair accessible.

COURTYARD MARRIOTT

5308 Liberty Ave., 412/683-3113,
http://marriott.com/property/propertypage/PITOK

Unlike the bed-and-breakfasts listed earlier in this section, the Courtyard Marriott ($159–219) sits right on the Shadyside/Bloomfield border, and it's the best choice for anyone visiting patients at the nearby Shadyside Hospital or the UPMC Hillman Cancer Center. It's also conveniently located for anyone visiting family or friends in Bloomfield or Friendship, and it isn't terribly far from North Oakland or East Liberty. The guest rooms, while clean and comfortable enough, aren't much to write home about, although there is a small indoor swimming pool and a Starbucks onsite. A parking lot open only to guests is another bonus, although you'll be charged $19.50 a day for the privilege.

THE INN AT 714 NEGLEY

714 S. Negley Ave., 412/661-0631,
www.theinnsonnegley.com

A restored period home built in the latter part of the 19th century, The Inn at 714 Negley ($180–235) is a wonderfully quaint bed-and-breakfast tucked away in an upscale residential neighborhood. Individual rooms, as well as the inn itself, are professionally decorated with antiques and period furniture; the overall style is a nicely done mixture of country charm and European sophistication. Each room

© DAN ELDRIDGE

The Inn at 714 Negley, a European country-style bed-and-breakfast comes with an imported down comforter and either a jetted shower system or whirlpool tub in the bathroom.

◖ SUNNYLEDGE BOUTIQUE HOTEL

5124 5th Ave., 412/683-5014,
www.sunnyledge.com

A historic landmark built in 1886, the Sunnyledge Boutique Hotel ($189–275) is one of the East End's most gorgeous bed-and-breakfast choices. Original oak paneling and fixtures are found throughout, and each of the eight guest rooms is decorated in its own unique and truly elegant Victorian style. Rooms come complete with whirlpool tub, minibar, and cable TV, and a library, exercise room, and 24-hour concierge are all on-site. Sunnyledge also features a five-star restaurant, known as the Tea Room, as well as a martini bar.

Greater Pittsburgh   Map 7

Assuming you've arrived in Pittsburgh with your own vehicle, staying in Oakmont is a smart compromise between small-town living and the big city. Downtown Pittsburgh is less than a half-hour drive away, yet you'll still feel somewhat secluded from the urban bustle and energy here.

and corporate conferences can also be accommodated, and, what's more, management operates a free shuttle service from the nearby Pittsburgh International Airport. Vacationing couples should consider reserving the creatively designed whirlpool tub suite ($200).

$50-100

THE SEWICKLEY COUNTRY INN

801 Ohio River Blvd., Sewickley, 412/741-4300
or 800/835-6072, www.sewickleyinn.com

With 147 truly restful rooms, this abidingly popular hotel is found in a whisper-quiet, residential section of Sewickley, one of the Greater Pittsburgh area's most upscale neighborhoods. And although the Sewickley Country Inn ($80) is quite clearly a staff-run hotel—rooms come complete with cable and HBO, after all, and a restaurant and lounge can both be found on-site—the intimate ambience of a secluded bed-and-breakfast seems to reside here as well. The hotel's 250-seat banquet room is a popular wedding, bridal shower, and baby shower spot; the space includes a 1,100-square-foot dance floor. Family reunions

$100-150

ARBORS BED & BREAKFAST

745 Maginn Ave., 412/231-4643,
www.arborsbnb.com

A 19th-century farmhouse nestled into a wooded and relatively obscure corner of the North Side, Arbors Bed & Breakfast ($115–145) is just minutes from the North Side's commercial district by car. Two rooms and one suite are available; all three are decked out in a fairly traditional "county inn" style, and all come with cable TV and a VCR. Just off the small downstairs kitchen is the Arbors' sunroom; with its in-floor radiant heat and hot tub, it's undoubtedly the B&B's best feature. The management is particularly friendly and quick to offer sightseeing, nightlife, and dining recommendations.

HYATT REGENCY PITTSBURGH INTERNATIONAL AIRPORT

1111 Airport Blvd., 724/899-1234,
http://pittsburghairport.hyatt.com

Every decent-size airport in the United States is surrounded by hotels that serve the sort of traveler who, for whatever reason, doesn't need to actually enter the urban center of the city he or she's just flown into. But in Pittsburgh, the Hyatt Regency ($129–209) has introduced a concept you may not have seen before: Because an enclosed walkway attaches the hotel to the airport, lodgers can go from baggage claim to check-in without ever leaving the building. The interior, too, is impressive. Designed to resemble a modern boutique hotel, you'll find detailed and tasteful touches almost everywhere, from the warmly accented lobby to the fitness center. Rooms come with a large desk, dual phone lines, and a dataport.

THE INN AT OAKMONT

300 Rte. 909, 412/828-0410,
www.theinnatoakmont.com

With eight guest rooms, all of them equipped with a "sleep machine" programmed with, say, tropical noises or ambient sounds, The Inn at Oakmont ($130–150) is your smartest bed-and-breakfast option if you'd like to be far from an urban neighborhood, but still relatively close to Downtown Pittsburgh via car. A public golf course sits just across the street from the B&B, and, as an added bonus, the charming town of Oakmont is ideal for an afternoon or evening stroll and a bit of window-shopping.

ACCOMMODATIONS

EXCURSIONS FROM PITTSBURGH

As any serious gridhopper would most likely admit, sometimes the best part about visiting a city is waving goodbye. After all, in order to gain a proper perspective on a place, first you've got to leave. And even those with an unending love of the concrete jungle occasionally need to escape its reach.

Even if you're only planning on being in Pittsburgh for a week or two, I'd still encourage you to consider at least a brief day trip, if not a slightly longer weekend adventure. And while it's probably something of a widespread assumption that the further reaches of Western Pennsylvania don't have much to offer the average traveler, the exact opposite, in fact, is true.

Globetrotters the world over have long been visiting the state's Laurel Highlands, and for good reason: Not only does world-famous architecture coexist with the quiet beauty of wooded nature here, but regular ol' fun can be had as well, especially along the banks of the almost-unpronounceable Youghiogheny (pronounced yaw-ki-GAY-nee) River, where some of Pennsylvania's wildest tubing and rafting takes place.

And while art, history, and railroad museums seem to exist in every last nook and cranny of this corner of the world, it's quite

HIGHLIGHTS

LOOK FOR ◖ TO FIND RECOMMENDED SIGHTS, ACTIVITIES, DINING, AND LODGING.

◖ **Best Residential Architecture:** Still regarded by critics and professionals alike as one of the finest examples of American residential architecture, **Fallingwater** is quite possibly the most gorgeous – and the most photogenic – of Frank Lloyd Wright's uniquely constructed works of utilitarian art (page 219).

◖ **Best River-Rafting:** Whether you're looking to master some of the country's most vicious Class V white-water rapids, or if you'd simply prefer to float lazily along a slow river in a giant inner tube, you'll find scores of outfitters along the banks of the Youghiogheny in **Ohiopyle State Park** happy to help you do just that (page 223).

◖ **Best Landmark:** A must-see sight for rail fans the world over, **Horseshoe Curve National Historic Landmark,** a 220-degree curve, is still considered an absolutely masterful feat of modern engineering (page 227).

◖ **Best State Park:** With its Old Mill and its covered bridge, the forested **McConnell's Mill State Park** is as beautifully picturesque as it is welcoming to adventurists (page 232).

◖ **Best Blast from the Past:** Just a short drive from Downtown Pittsburgh, **Old Economy Village** is the former home of the somewhat bizarre yet fiscally ingenious Harmony Society. The village, located in Ambridge, gives some of the best clues as to how the society lived and worked (page 232).

COURTESY OF LAUREL HIGHLANDS VISITORS BUREAU

EXCURSIONS

likely that you'll learn much more in locales with less institutional flavor. In a booth at a backwoods diner, for instance, where the apple pie and the eccentric locals remind you more of *Twin Peaks* than "America the Beautiful." Or maybe in front of the shelves at an out-of-the-way thrift store, where a stack of ultra-rare vinyl records are waiting for you in a wooden bin and priced at $0.50 each.

But ultimately, it doesn't much matter which way you explore the outer reaches of Pittsburgh, nor how you decide to have fun. What matters is that you've simply gotten out there. You've explored. You've tried something new. And when the novelty of the rural areas and the tiny little towns begins to wear thin, you know what to do, right? (Hint: Sometimes the best part about visiting the country is waving goodbye.)

EXCURSIONS

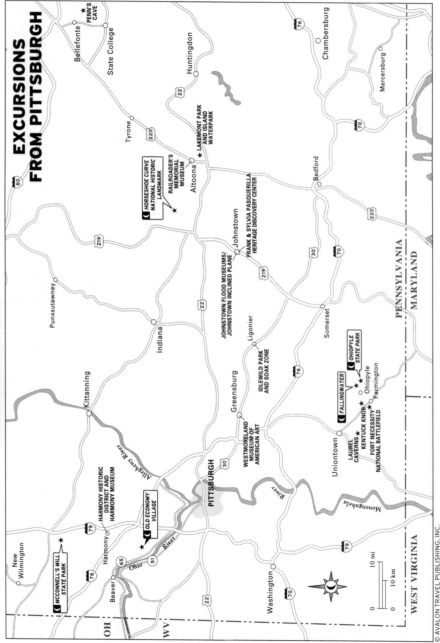

EXCURSIONS FROM PITTSBURGH

PENN'S CAVE

Bellefonte

State College

Chambersburg

Mercersburg

Huntingdon

Tyrone

◀ HORSESHOE CURVE NATIONAL HISTORIC LANDMARK

RAILROADER'S MEMORIAL MUSEUM

LAKEMONT PARK AND ISLAND WATERPARK

Altoona

Bedford

FRANK & SYLVIA PASQUERILLA HERITAGE DISCOVERY CENTER

Johnstown

Punxsutawney

JOHNSTOWN FLOOD MUSEUMS/ JOHNSTOWN INCLINED PLANE

Indiana

Ligonier

Somerset

IDLEWILD PARK AND SOAK ZONE

Kittanning

◀ OHIOPYLE STATE PARK

Ohiopyle

Greensburg

◀ FALLINGWATER

Allegheny River

Farmington

WESTMORELAND MUSEUM OF AMERICAN ART

HARMONY HISTORIC DISTRICT AND HARMONY MUSEUM

LAUREL CAVERNS

KENTUCK KNOB

FORT NECESSITY NATIONAL BATTLEFIELD

Uniontown

◀ OLD ECONOMY VILLAGE

PITTSBURGH

Harmony

New Wilmington

◀ MCCONNELL'S MILL STATE PARK

Beaver

Ohio River

Monongahela River

PENNSYLVANIA

MARYLAND

Washington

WEST VIRGINIA

OH

WV

10 mi

10 km

© AVALON TRAVEL PUBLISHING, INC.

PLANNING YOUR TIME

Because Pennsylvania is such a large and sprawling state, it's naturally wise to consult a decent map before simply heading out on the highway. The Keystone State is literally packed with quaint rural areas, small towns that modern time seems to have forgotten, and still-pristine wilderness areas. But it's also heavy with industrial detritus and drab, four-lane highways. So do yourself a favor and take the time to sit down with a friendly guesthouse or B&B owner, or a decent state guidebook, before setting out. For comprehensive state and day-trip info, I recommend *Moon Pennsylvania* by Joanne Miller and *Quick Escapes Pittsburgh* by Michelle Pilecki.

Visitors with not a lot of time to spare would probably do best to consider heading toward the nearby Laurel Highlands. Not only can the area be reached quickly by car from Pittsburgh (about an hour's drive), it also offers a wide variety of popular activities, from protected wilderness areas to amusement parks to world-famous works of architecture.

Those with a bit more time on their hands might also consider heading north to the Lake Erie area. Aside from the grandeur of the Great Lake itself, Erie is home to the seven-mile-long peninsula known as Presque Isle State Park. Along the way, there are a number of interesting little towns and unique shopping opportunities located not far off I-79.

Laurel Highlands

Luckily for visitors to Pittsburgh, not only is the Laurel Highlands region relatively nearby, it also contains a wealth of diverse activities. A family of four with differing interests may need to visit four separate sites to keep everyone happy, but for what it's worth, you'll probably find all four of them here. The area's most popular tourist attraction is Frank Lloyd Wright's Fallingwater, but if you're planning to visit the house during a quick day trip, consider leaving a little earlier and mixing in a few side activities along the way.

A massive archive of area activities can be found on the website of the Laurel Highlands Visitors Bureau (120 E. Main St., 724/238-5661 or 800/333-5661, www.laurelhighlands.org).

SIGHTS
◖ Fallingwater

Declared by architects and critics worldwide as one of the most stunning private struc-

tures ever built in the United States, Frank Lloyd Wright's Fallingwater (Rte. 381, Mill Run, 724/329-8501, www.fallingwater.org, Tue.–Sun. 10 A.M.–4 P.M., admission $16 adult, $10 child) is an absolute must-see for anyone visiting Pittsburgh who also has access to a car. Considering that a mere 90-minute drive from Downtown will get you there, this makes for a fantastic day trip no matter what the season.

Designed in 1935 for the Kaufmann family, who at the time owned one of Pittsburgh's most profitable department store companies, Fallingwater is quite possibly the finest example of Wright's praiseworthy architectural philosophy, which he referred to as "organic architecture": Wright was a staunch believer in the concept that art and nature could coexist peacefully, so when Edgar J. Kaufmann asked for his house to be built next to a favorite waterfall in Mill Run, Wright instead

HAROLD CORSINI PHOTO COURTESY OF THE WESTERN PENNSYLVANIA CONSERVANCY

Frank Lloyd Wright's masterful Fallingwater is built directly into the hills of the Laurel Highlands.

designed it to rest *above* the falls. To see the house from its left or right sides is equally stunning; Wright cleverly built the boxy sandstone shapes and cantilevered levels directly into the sloping earth.

After serving its initial purpose for 26 years (the house was used as a weekend getaway), Fallingwater opened to the public in 1963. Notably, it remains the only important Wright structure open to the public with both its furniture and artwork intact. (Wright was legendary for wishing to control the interior look and layout of the homes he designed.)

Along with regular and in-depth tours, visitors may choose a "Sunset Tour" ($80) or a "Land of Fallingwater Nature Hike" ($55). Adjacent to the Fallingwater grounds is the 5,000-acre **Bear Run Nature Reserve**—great for hiking and bird-watching. And Frank Lloyd Wright's **Kentuck Knob** (www

.kentuckknob.com)—another oddly designed residence—is only seven miles away.

Fort Necessity National Battlefield

If you've already visited the Fort Pitt Museum in Pittsburgh's Point State Park, you may be encouraged to stop by Fort Necessity National Battlefield (1 Washington Pkwy., Farmington, 724/329-5512, www .nps.gov/fone, daily 9 A.M.–5 P.M., admission $5 adult, children 15 and under are free), where the French and Indian War of 1754 first rang out. To start, stop by the battlefield's **Visitor Center** for a current schedule of activities and to screen a short film, *Road to Necessity*, which summarizes the bloody events that took place here. Interactive museum exhibits briefly explain the war as well.

Next, follow a short path to an area known as **Great Meadow.** Nestled into the shadow

THE JIMMY STEWART MUSEUM

The city of Indiana is a pretty good distance to travel for just one museum, but for hardcore Jimmy Stewart fans, the pilgrimage will be more than worth your while. The now-deceased star of the silver screen grew up in Indiana, and the town boasts a statue of his likeness as well as the **Jimmy Stewart Museum** (845 Philadelphia St., 3rd floor, 724/349-6112 or 800/835-4669, www.jimmy.org, Mon.-Sat. 10 A.M.-5 P.M., Sun. noon-5 P.M., admission $5 adult, $3 child, $4 senior), which can be found inside the Indiana library and next to city hall.

The museum contains all manner of movie memorabilia pertaining to Stewart's life, including posters and film clips. There's also a decent gift shop. Don't miss the separate room dedicated to the Stewart family history in Western Pennsylvania – Jimmy Stewart's kin, apparently, have lived in and around the Indiana area since the time of the Civil War.

While at the museum, ask for directions to Jimmy's boyhood home, which remains a private residence. Also ask for directions to the former location of J.M. Stewart & Sons Hardware, where Jimmy worked as a boy and which his father owned.

Indiana is roughly a 75-minute drive from Downtown Pittsburgh. To reach the museum by car, take I-376 east, to Route 22 east, to Route 119 north. After merging onto Wayne Avenue, take a left onto South 7th Street, and then another left onto Philadelphia Street. Greyhound buses depart from the Downtown Pittsburgh depot en route to Indiana at 5 A.M. and 3:40 P.M. daily. Expect to pay about $16 each way.

of the Allegheny Mountains, this is a site of serious historical proportions, as the fighting itself actually began here. Visitors feeling a bit restless may want to explore the five miles of hiking trails that surround the site, while history buffs might prefer the seven-mile side trip to **Jumonville Glen** (open daily 9 A.M.–4 P.M.), where George Washington met the French face to face for the very first time.

Ohiopyle State Park, Fallingwater, and Laurel Caverns are all located nearby.

Idlewild Park and Soak Zone

Originally constructed in 1878, Idlewild Park (Rte. 30 East, Ligionier, 724/238-3666, www.idlewild.com, June–Aug. daily 10 A.M.–8 P.M., admission $23.95 adult, $15.95 senior) was during its salad days not much more than a recreational campground with picnic tables and an artificially constructed lake. As the mid-20th century approached, however, Idlewild began attempting to transform itself into an honest-to-goodness amusement park. That plan didn't fully come to fruition until 1983, when the Kennywood Park Corporation bought the company out.

Today, the park consists of seven theme areas, including Olde Idlewild, where the Ferris wheel, the merry-go-round, and other similarly quaint attractions are located, and Soak Zone, a water park with various slides and pools. The five remaining areas, including Mister Rogers' Neighborhood of Make-Believe and Story Book Forest, are considerably tame, and clearly aimed more

EXCURSIONS

toward younger guests than teenaged coaster fans or anyone seeking thrill rides.

Kentuck Knob

Although it's certainly less visited than Fall-ingwater, Frank Lloyd Wright's more famous residential cousin that sits only seven miles away, Kentuck Knob (640 Ohiopyle Chalk Hill Rd., Fayette County, 724/329-1640, www.kentuckknob.com, March–Dec. daily 9 A.M.–4 P.M., Jan.–Feb. daily 11 A.M.–3 P.M., admission $15 adult, $8 child) is nonetheless a fascinating and truly unique work of art; exploring both structures during a day trip from Pittsburgh is certainly possible.

Wright was 86-years-old when he designed Kentuck Knob for a family—the Hagans—who had visited Fallingwater a number of times and greatly admired it. Alternately known as "Hagan House" and "The Child of Fallingwater," the house was constructed according to the specifications of a style Wright referred to as "Usonian," which had no attics or basements and was intended to keep building and utility costs low. Derived partly from Wright's prairie-style homes, the Usonians were relatively small, one-story structures with flat roofs. Kentuck fits that descriptor well, although it also features a number of surprising 60-degree angles; the house was built on a hex-agonal grid. (Pay attention while wandering around the house, as the hexagonal theme is repeated throughout.)

Laurel Caverns

Located 50 miles south of Pittsburgh near Uniontown, the 435-acre Laurel Caverns Geological Park (2 Skyline Dr., Farming-ton, 724/438-3003 or 800/515-4150, www

COURTESY OF LAUREL HIGHLANDS VISITORS BUREAU

Laurel Caverns is the largest cave in the state of Pennsylvania.

.laurelcaverns.com, May–Oct. daily 9 A.M.–5 P.M., March, April, and Nov. Sat.–Sun. 9A.M.–5 P.M., tours $10 adult, $9 senior) offers a wealth of family-style activities, including 55-minute guided tours of the sandstone caverns, as well as much more strenuous caving exploration tours lasting as long as three hours. Before or after taking a tour of the caverns, visitors can pay $45 to rappel three times off a 45-foot high cliff. And for a mere $5 there's Kavenputt, an 18-hole miniature golf course inside a 10,000-square-foot artificial cave.

Originally called Laurel Hill Cave, and then Dulaney's Cave, Laurel Caverns is the largest cave in the state of Pennsylvania. It's also the 16th-longest developed cave in the United States; there are a total of 2.8 miles of passages here for visitors to safely explore. According to local

EXCURSIONS

historians and anthropologists, the caverns have been explored since the late 1700s and were once used by Native Americans as protection from enemies as well as the natural elements.

Because the temperature inside the caverns remains steady at about 55°F year-round, visitors are encouraged to bring sweaters or light jackets even on warm summer days.

◖ Ohiopyle State Park

Encompassing just more than 19,000 forested acres, Ohiopyle (724/329-8591, www .dcnr.state.pa.us/stateparks/parks/ohiopyle. aspx) provides any number of standard state park activities: Biking, trekking, horseback riding, fishing, and even hunting. But without a doubt, the vast majority of Pittsburghers who come here have something else in mind: A white-water boating or white-water rafting trip on the ever-popular Youghiogheny River.

There are all sorts of reasons why Pennsylvanians love the Yough (pronounced yock), but the diversity of the river is certainly at the top of the list. Beginners can easily float down the Lower Yough's Class II rapids, while at the same time, some of the country's most experienced rafters can challenge themselves in the Class IV and V rapids of the Upper Yough, where some of the finest white-water rafting on the entire East Coast takes place. Numerous outfitters in the area rent equipment and offer tours for all levels.

Camping at Ohiopyle is a possibility— visit the park's website for detailed information and a campground map. Wooden camping cottages that sleep five people are also available.

What's more, Ohiopyle doesn't empty out during the winter months. Snowmobiling, cross-country skiing, and sledding all take place here.

Westmoreland Museum of American Art

One of only three museums in the state that focuses exclusively on American art, the Westmoreland Museum of American Art (221 N. Main St., Greensburg, 724/834-1500, www .wmuseumaa.org, Wed.–Sun. 11 A.M.–5 P.M., Thurs. 11 A.M.–9 P.M., admission $3 adult suggested donation, free child) has been welcoming visitors to Greensburg ever since 1959. Especially in its first two decades, the curatorial team managed to build a rather impressive collection of work by American masters, including paintings by Winslow Homer, Mary Cassatt, and John Singer Sargent. Artists based in Southwestern Pennsylvania have frequently been featured as well.

Along with various paintings and portraiture, items kept in the permanent collection include sculpture, toys, works on paper (such as lithographs and etchings), and decorative arts, which include jugs, cupboards, and other largely utilitarian pieces.

Families visiting the museum might enjoy spending time at KidSpace, a hands-on, interactive room where children can make their own creations while being surrounded by pieces from the museum's folk art collection.

RESTAURANTS

Located in downtown Ligonier, the **Ligonier Tavern** (137 W. Main St., Ligonier, 724/238-4831, www.ligoniertavern .com, Mon.–Thurs. 11:30 A.M.–9 P.M., Fri.– Sat. 11:30 A.M.–10 P.M., Sun. noon–8 P.M.) has three separately designed dining rooms inside a beautifully detailed turn-of-the-20th-century Victorian house. Cuisine here is fairly casual and leans toward American and seafood. Sandwiches, salads, pasta, and chicken entrées are all popular. If the weather is nice, diners can choose to sit outside on the house's second-floor patio. There's also a bakery on-site offering a wide selection of fantastic cakes.

Should you find yourself jonesing for Chinese takeout after a long and hard day of serious sightseeing, hit the **Main Moon Restaurant** (113 N. Center St., Somerset, 814/445-3674, daily 10:30 A.M.–9:30 P.M.) in Somerset. As is the case with the very best of Chinese joints, the prices are more than affordable, the menu list is pleasingly long, and the food is fantastic. Main Moon is particularly popular with locals.

With a name like **Ruthie's Diner** (Hwy. 30, Ligonier, 724/238-6030, daily 6 A.M.–9 P.M.), you can probably guess the sort of food that's on offer here: burgers, sandwiches, and cups of black coffee, for the most part. This is the perfect place to make a pit stop if you're in the midst of road-tripping and searching for the heart of America, or some such romantic notion. And as any local will surely tell you, Ruthie's also serves one of the finest breakfasts in town. Not terribly healthy, of course, but delicious and protein-packed just the same.

ACCOMMODATIONS

Roughly a 20-minute drive from Fallingwater is **The Lodge at Chalk Hill** (Rte. 40 East, Chalk Hill, 724/438-8880 or 800/833-4283, www.thelodgeatchalkhill.com, $79 s, $84 d), a lakeside lodge and mountain retreat situated on 37 acres of land. Visitors to Ohiopyle, Fort Necessity, Laurel Caverns,

and the Christian Klay Winery will all find their destinations within an easy drive of the lodge. Rooms here are a bit dated and could certainly use a 21st-century makeover, although it's worth noting that the location itself—the lodge grounds as well as the nearby attractions—are what you come here for. Groups and bus tours are welcome here, and there's also an on-site banquet room that can accommodate bridal showers, graduation parties, and the like.

Located along Route 40 in Farmington, the **Stone House Inn** (3023 National Pike, Farmington, 800/274-7138, www.stone houseinn.com) sits a mere two miles from the Fort Necessity Battlefield. Fallingwater, Kentuck Knob, and Ohiopyle are also close.

One of the first inns to open along the National Road, Stone House Inn has been lodging and feeding travelers since 1822. There are seven Victorian-style bed-and-breakfast suites on-site, as well as six modern rooms in the New Zeigler Wing that come complete with whirlpool tub, contemporary furnishings, and other modern conveniences. Bed-and-breakfast rooms are $89 a night, while modern rooms go for $149 a night.

A four-star luxury resort, **C Nemacolin Woodlands** (1001 LaFayette Dr., Farmington, 800/422-2736, www.nemacolin.com, $200–570) is so lovely that you may decide not to leave the grounds at all. Visitors and guests can indulge in golfing, luxurious spa packages, casual or fine dining, and a wide variety of adventure- or cultural-recreation activities. Lodgers have the option of choosing among six different destinations, including a boutique hotel, a classic European-style hotel, a lodge, and a townhouse. Accommodation costs are steep, but well worth it for the unique experiences offered here.

PRACTICALITIES
Tourist Office
The Laurel Highlands Visitor Bureau is located at 120 East Main Street in Ligonier; office hours are Monday–Friday 9 A.M.– 5 P.M. For directions, call 724/238-5661 or toll-free at 800/333-5661. Information for Fayette, Somerset, and Westmoreland Counties can be collected at the bureau, or you can simply gather the info online at www.laurelhighlands.org.

Media
The region's largest newspaper is Greensburg's right-leaning *Tribune-Review* (www .pittsburghlive.com/x/tribunereview), a daily that also publishes a Pittsburgh-specific edition. The affiliated *Daily Courier* (www.daily courier.com) covers the Connellsville area, while the weekly *Mount Pleasant Journal,* the flagship paper of the Greater Mount Pleasant Area, has been in business since 1873.

Getting There
The majority of the Laurel Highlands' major attractions can be accessed by heading east of the city on U.S. Route 30. Yet since the region is so large, drivers will probably want to have an updated road atlas on hand. Rand McNally's oversized *The Road Atlas* is prob-ably the country's most popular; it can be purchased at most major bookstores, and also includes driving maps of Canada and Mexico. For travelers who only need driving directions to one or two specific addresses, the MapQuest website (www.mapquest.com) can be an invaluable resource.

Greyhound buses regularly travel to a number of cities within the Laurel Highlands region. For more information, call 800/231-2222 or visit www.greyhound.com.

A one-way Amtrak train ride from Pittsburgh to Greensburg will set you back $8.

The Arnold Palmer Regional Airport (www.palmerairport.com) serves the Greater Greensburg area.

Getting Around
For the most part, visitors to Laurel Highlands would be well advised to arrive with a car or other private vehicle. Contact information for a number of travel and transportation options can be found on the website of the Laurel Highlands Visitors Bureau (www .laurelhighlands.org), including companies that offer organized tours of the area.

Visitors to Greensburg can visit the website of the Westmoreland County Transit Authority (www.westmorelandtransit.com) for schedule and fare information.

Altoona, State College, and Johnstown

Even if you're a longtime Pittsburgh resident who knows the Steel City inside and out, if you haven't yet explored much of Johnstown, you may very well find yourself surprised at the fairly large number of activities and sights of interest the town offers. And Johnstown's a simple drive, too: If you're headed east toward the Westmoreland Museum of Art or Idlewild, you're halfway there.

Not much farther to the northeast is Altoona, which is something of an international meeting point for rail fans. (The Railroaders Memorial Museum and the Horseshoe Curve Historic Landmark are both there.)

EXCURSIONS

Keep on until State College, the home of Penn State University. It's a perfectly quaint college town and also home to a number of small museums as well as interesting cave sites, many of which can be explored during guided tours.

For detailed information about Johnstown and Cambria County, visit or write to the Convention and Visitor Bureau at 416 Main Street, Suite 100, Johnstown, PA 15901. Alternately, call 814/536-7993 or 800/237-8590, or visit www.visitjohnstownpa.com. The State College tourism board has an online presence at www.statecollege.com/tourism; the Altoona board's site is at www.altoona.com/tourism.

SIGHTS
Frank & Sylvia Pasquerilla Heritage Discovery Center

Included with the price of admission to the **Johnstown Flood Museum** is admission to the Frank & Sylvia Pasquerilla Heritage Discovery Center (201 6th Ave., Johnston, 814/539-1889 or 888/222-1889, www.jaha.org/DiscoveryCenter/virtualtour.html, daily 10 A.M.–5 P.M., admission $6 adult, $4 student, $5 senior). It tells the stories of the thousands of Southern and Eastern European immigrants who flocked to Johnstown during the last two decades of the 1800s and the first decade of the 1900s.

The museum's main exhibit, *America: Through Immigrant Eyes,* uses a wide selection of interactive media to explain exactly how the immigrants passed their days in Pennsylvania. You'll learn what life was like in Johnstown for a Slovakian butcher, a Russian shopkeeper, and a Hungarian goose farmer, to name just a few. Through an interactive video display, visitors will also view the experience of immigrants being questioned at Ellis Island, and they'll learn about the conditions in Europe that led many to seek a new life elsewhere in the first place.

Other exhibits at the museum show what

JOHNSTOWN FOLKFEST

Should you happen to find yourself in the Pittsburgh area over Labor Day weekend, and should you happen to be a fan of Americana music – blues, zydeco, folk, jazz, and R&B, for instance – you're in luck. That's when the Johnstown FolkFest (www.jaha.org/FolkFest) takes place at the city's Festival Park (90 Johns St., Johnstown), which can be found just across the river from Point Stadium and beside the Cambria Iron National Historic Landmark.

Throughout the three days of the festival, concertgoers can expect to hear roughly 70 hours of live music by bands both world-famous and nearly unknown. Past performers have included Sleepy LaBeef, Balkan Beat Box, Sharon Jones and the Dap-Kings, Brave Combo, Red Elvises, Big Sandy & His Fly-Rite Boys, Robbie Fulks, Southern Culture on the Skids, Buckwheat Zydeco, and R. L. Burnside. And here's the best news of all: The entire thing is free of charge. Check the FolkFest's webpage for information about accommodations and driving directions. Free parking is generally available – signs will be posted – and free shuttle buses frequently travel back and forth between parking lots and the festival grounds.

life was like in the steel mills where many immigrants toiled, while the Generations Theater exhibition includes interviews with both the children and grandchildren of the immigrants. Temporary exhibits can be found on the museum's second floor.

◖ Horseshoe Curve National Historic Landmark

A longtime favorite of hardcore rail fans who journey to Altoona to visit the Railroaders Memorial Museum is the Horseshoe Curve National Historic Landmark (Visitor's Center at 40th St. and Burgoon Rd., Altoona, 814/941-7960, www.railroad city.com/hc/index.php, Mon.–Sat. 10 A.M.– 6 P.M., Sun. noon–6 P.M., admission $5 or free with admission to Railroaders Memorial Museum). A legendary railroad curve located about six miles west of Altoona at the Kittanning Gap, the rail's extreme bend is in fact shaped like a horseshoe. Its 220-degree arc was designed by J. Edgar Thomson; it opened to trains in 1854 as a way to significantly reduce the travel time from one end of Pennsylvania to the other. The arc was necessary because of the summit of the Allegheny Mountains, which the track was designed to skirt.

Designated as a National Historic Landmark in 1966, the curve has been a successful tourist attraction for decades. It's wise to stop by the visitors center first, where a number of displays illustrate the construction of the curve. The center also features a gift shop packed with items of interest to the rail fan. From there, guests can ride a funicular railway up to the actual train tracks, or they can choose to hike up the stairway instead.

It's interesting to note that because of the curve's economic importance to the country, a Nazi plan to explode it was in place during WWII.

Johnstown Flood Museum

After the recent tragedy in New Orleans, visitors to Southwestern Pennsylvania may find the Johnstown Flood Museum (304 Washington St., Johnstown, 814/539-1889 or 888/222-1889, www.jaha.org/Flood Museum/oklahoma.html, daily 10 A.M.– 5 P.M., admission $6 adult, $4 student, $5 senior) particularly relevant. It documents a massive flooding catastrophe that took place in that city on May 31, 1889, in which 2,209 people perished. Curiously enough, the causes of the disaster were a neglected dam and massive storm.

Visitors to this especially well-done museum will have the chance to view a number of artifacts and documents relating to the greatest tragedy ever to befall the city of Johnstown, including a 26-minute Academy Award–winning documentary film that recreates the flood by using archival photos. Also on-site is a relief-map model that uses lights and sound effects to illustrate the flood's path through the Conemaugh Valley. Particularly moving—even disturbing—is the museum's collection of personal artifacts that were recovered after the flood, including a set of keys belonging to a telegraph operator who warned of the dam's impending danger. And also part of the permanent exhibit is an original, renovated "Oklahoma" House. Although they were originally designed for Oklahoma Territory homesteaders, the prefab houses, which measured either 10-by-20 feet or 16-by-24 feet, were also used to house Johnstown residents made homeless by the flood.

Visitors can also request information

about a downtown Johnstown walking tour, during which many historic buildings that survived the flood can be seen. A self-guided tour and a map of the downtown area can both be found on the museum's website.

Johnstown Inclined Plane

Known as the world's steepest vehicular inclined plane, the cable cars of the Johnstown Incline (711 Edgehill Dr., Johnstown, 814/536-1816, www.inclinedplane.com, May 1–Sept. 30 daily 9 A.M.–11 P.M., Oct. 1–April 30 daily 11 A.M.–11 P.M., tickets $2.25 one way, $4 round-trip) travel a distance of 896.5 feet up the side of Yoder Hill—which has a grade of 70.9 percent—to reach an elevation of 1,693.5 feet. Built by the Cambria Iron Company in 1890 and '91, the incline was designed specifically so that residents of the hilltop community known as Westmont could easily transport their horses and wagons from ground level to home and back again.

However on March 1, 1936, the incline served a distinctly different role when, once again, the city was flooded. Nearly 4,000 area residents were lifted to dry, higher ground via the incline. This happened a second time, on June 20, 1977, during the city's most recent flood.

Visitors to the incline, which was built by Samuel Diescher, the engineer also responsible for building Pittsburgh's Duquesne and Monongahela Inclines, can walk out onto an extended observation deck that offers a rather lovely view of the Johnstown area. A visitors center displays archival photographs of the city and its numerous floods, and from the center's lobby it's possible to view the massive machinery of the incline in action. The James Wolfe Sculpture Trail can be found directly behind the incline.

Lakemont Park & Island Waterpark

Although it first welcomed visitors in 1894 as a trolley park, and then in 1899 as a full-fledged amusement park, Lakemont Park (700 Park Ave., Altoona, 800/434-8006, www.lakemontparkfun.com, call for hours, admission $7.95) isn't a particularly large attraction. There are just a scattering of rides here, including two roller coasters and a go-kart track. Also located on-site and included with the cost of admission is Island Waterpark, complete with slides and pools. Visitors are welcome to enjoy the park's 18-hole miniature golf course and its arcade.

Historically speaking, Lakemont holds two particularly interesting claims to fame: Not only is it the eighth-oldest amusement park in the country, it's also home to the historic Leap-The-Dips coaster, a wooden ride built in 1902 that is known by roller coaster enthusiasts everywhere as the world's oldest. The figure-eight style coaster makes for a fairly slow and gentle ride and was given its due respects in 1996 when it was awarded national landmark status.

Penn's Cave

Known as the country's only all-water cavern, Penn's Cave (222 Penns Cave Rd., Centre Hall, 814/364-1664, www.pennscave.com, call or visit website for hours, cavern tours $12 adult, $5.75 child, $11 senior, wildlife tours $17.95 adult, $9.75 child, $16.95 senior) is a particularly unique local site. Because the caverns are literally flooded, guided one-hour tours take place inside a motorboat. Along the way, visitors will see a wide selection of stalagmites, stalactites, and limestone corridors, as well as trout fish that can often be seen jumping high above the water. (Look out for the stalagmite that bears a striking resemblance to the Statue of Liberty.)

Interestingly, Penn's Cave also offers a 90-minute wildlife tour, during which safari buses shuttle visitors throughout the area's 1,500 acres of preserved forests and fields. Mountain lions, wolves, bison, black bears, and wild mustangs are just some of the animals you may encounter.

Railroaders Memorial Museum

One of Western Pennsylvania's most popular railroading attractions, the Railroaders Memorial Museum (1300 9th Ave., Altoona, 814/946-0834, www.railroadcity.com, April–Oct. Mon.–Sat. 9 A.M.–5 P.M., Sun. 11 A.M.–5 P.M., Nov.–Dec. Sat. 9 A.M.–5 P.M., Sun. 11 A.M.–5 P.M., admission $7.50 adult, $5 child, $6 senior) was designed specifically to honor the American railroaders who have contributed significantly to the country's culture and industry. And it makes good sense that the site is located in Altoona: Not only has the city long been known as an important epicenter of rail activity, but the Horseshoe Curve National Historic Site and the Staple Bend Tunnel, which was the country's first railroad tunnel, are both located nearby.

Built in 1998, the museum uses a mixture of interactive monitors, video presentations and exhibits to tell the cultural and social story of those who worked in the industry. In other words, the major emphasis here is not on the wheels, gears and tracks that moved the industry forward, but rather on the people who worked on and alongside the rails throughout the 1920s. And because the light-and-sound exhibits are fairly advanced, the museum feels much more like a place to play than simply a place to drearily read placards and gaze at dusty models.

RESTAURANTS

Conveniently located in Somerset, **The Summit Diner** (791 N. Center Ave., Somerset, 814/445-7154) is a 24-hour greasy spoon with surprisingly decent food. You'll find it open for business literally every day of the year. The menu is filled with American standards, and the hotcakes here are a local favorite. Assuming this sort of thing is important to you, all the meat is both cut and served right in the restaurant's kitchen.

A third-generation family-owned and -operated establishment, **Mel's Restaurant and Bar** (127 W. Patriot St., Somerset, 814/445-9841, www.somersetcounty.com/mels, daily 9 A.M.–2 A.M.) is the sort of honky-tonk café where one might expect to find a preponderance of gentlemen sporting cowboy hats and chewing tobacco. The menu is an ultra-budget selection of cheeseburgers, hot dogs, and sloppy joes, and don't be surprised if yours is served on a paper plate. Mel's also boats a 240-square-foot dance floor, live music on the weekend, and a pool table. This is Middle America at its finest, folks.

ACCOMMODATIONS

Just south of Altoona, the **Majestic World Lodge and Retreat** (RD 2, Box 301A, Memory Lane, Poratage, 814/693-0189 or 877/365-6972, www.majesticworldlodge .com) is a family-owned and -operated lodge situated 3,000 feet up in the Alleghenies—one of the highest elevations in the state. The lodge itself is actually a converted, historic barn where guests can gaze out at an elk herd from the comfort of a covered wooden deck. The grounds are absolutely gorgeous, and, incidentally, the snowy winter season is a particularly picturesque time of the year to visit. In spring, the grounds are covered with a carpet of lovely wildflowers.

All rooms are differently designed; hunters and other rustic types will feel especially at home with patchwork quilts covering the beds and incredibly creative headboards made out of antler horns and cedar logs. Rates begin at $85 a night.

The Flight 93 Memorial Site is close to the lodge in Somerset. Other nearby attractions include the historic Bedford Village and the numerous sights and museums of Johnstown. The home field of the Altoona Curve, a minor league baseball club, is roughly a 35-minute drive.

One of the most gorgeous and unusual places to spend the night in Somerset County, the **Stone Ridge Bed & Breakfast** (2825 Carpenters Park Rd., Davidsville, 814/288-3931, http://members.aol.com/stoneridgebb) is essentially an A-frame lodge that guests have all to themselves. The grounds couldn't be more romantic—especially during winter. The A-frame comes complete with a stone fireplace, two bedrooms, and two decks, one with a grill. A hot tub is available for use year-round, and the especially rustic surroundings are home to a number of animals, including wild turkey and deer. Rates are $150 for double occupancy.

Blue Knob, Seven Springs, and Hidden Valley are all relatively close, and downtown Johnstown is only seven miles away.

Located in the East Hills area of Johnstown, the **Homestead Retreat and Guesthouse** (1077 Crest Ave., 814/539-2273, http://home .earthlink.net/~nrsmall/thehomesteadjohn-stownpa) is a turn-of-the-20th-century farmhouse available for nightly stays or weekly and short-term rentals. Following an extensive remodeling, the Homestead resembles nothing more than an actual home. Fans of intimate B&Bs will feel right at home with an eat-in kitchen, a TV room, and a grill and campfire area. Smoking is prohibited at the Homestead, although pets are welcomed. Rates are $75 a night, $350 a week, and $800 a month.

PRACTICALITIES
Tourist Office
The Central Pennsylvania Convention & Visitors Bureau services State College; its office is at 800 E. Park Avenue in State College and is open Monday–Friday 8 A.M.–6 P.M. and weekends 9 A.M.–6 P.M. To reach an agent on the phone, dial 814/231-1400 or toll-free at 800/358-5466. The bureau maintains a website at www.centralpacvb.org.

Anyone heading to Altoona would be wise to stop by the Allegheny Mountains Convention and Visitors Bureau, located at 1 Convention Center Drive in Altoona. Contact the bureau by dialing 814/943-4183 or 800/842-5866, or by visiting www.alleghneymountains.com.

Those headed to Johnstown should check out www.visitjohnsonpa.com, or the Johnstown and Cambria County Convention & Visitors Bureau office at 416 Main Street, Suite 100, in Johnstown. Dialing 814/536-7993 or 800/237-8590 will take you there as well.

Media
The daily *Tribune-Democrat* (www.tribune-democrat.com) is the best-known newspaper covering the Johnstown area, while *Johnstown Magazine* (www.johnstownmag .com) digs deeper into the culture and lifestyles of the region. Pick up a copy of the *Centre Daily* newspaper (www.centredaily .com) for daily news about the Central PA area. *State College Magazine* (www.state

collegemagazine.com) celebrates the region in all its glossy, four-color glory. The daily *Altoona Mirror* (www.altoonamirror.com) covers both Altoona and State College.

Getting There

From Pittsburgh, a drive to either Altoona, State College, or Johnstown will require a trip on U.S. Route 22. Those headed to Johnstown will eventually go south on Route 219, while explorers venturing up to Altoona or State College will use Route 220.

Greyhound buses leave the Downtown Pittsburgh depot multiple times a day for State College; the one-way fare is $21.50. Buses leave twice a day each for Johnstown ($15 one way) and Altoona ($27 one way).

Amtrak trains service Johnstown ($12 one way) and Altoona ($16 one way).

University Park Airport (www.statecollege airport.org) is located right in State College and is served by a handful of major airlines.

Getting Around

Public transport in the State College area is handled by CATA, the Centre Area Transportation Authority. Visit www.catabus .com for schedules and a downloadable PDF of the most recent Ride Guide. To order a taxi in the area, call AA Taxi at 814/231-8294.

The Cambria County Transit Authority (www.camtranbus.com) is responsible for public transportation in Johnstown; when in Altoona use AMTRAN (www.amtran.org). For 24-hour taxi service in either Cambria or Somerset Counties, call 814/535-4584 or 814/539-1584.

Beaver County and Butler County

The counties of Beaver and Butler sit just north of the city of Pittsburgh and are quite often considered a part of Pittsburgh, especially by the counties' own residents. Old Economy Village and the Harmony Historic District are the big tourism draws—at both sites you can observe the unique and alternative way of living practiced by the now nonexistent Harmony Society.

For more extensive information, spend some time on the counties' official tourism sites: www.visitbeavercounty.com and www .visitbutlercounty.com.

SIGHTS
Harmony Historic District and Harmony Museum

Founded in 1804 and now a National Land-

mark District, the Harmony Historic District is a relatively small but engaging area where examples of both Harmonist and Mennonite lifestyles can be seen and studied. This walkable area is where the Harmony Museum (218 Mercer St., Harmony, 888/821-4822, www.harmonymuseum .org, daily 1–4 P.M., admission $5 adult, $2 child, $4 senior) can be found. At the museum you'll see an example of a communal Harmonist room; also on-site is a Harmonist's wine cellar, accessible by way of a stonecut staircase. The museum also owns a small collection of Native American artifacts that were discovered in the area.

Other structures of interest in the district include the **Wagner-Bentel House,** which is a brick duplex that was constructed by the

Harmonists for two sisters and their families, and the reconstructed **Henry Denis Ziegler log house,** which sits directly across the street from the museum and is made of hand-hewn oak logs.

McConnell's Mill State Park

Encompassing 2,546 acres of the Slippery Rock Creek Gorge, McConnell's Mill State Park (via I-79 near the intersection of PA 19 and U.S. 422, Portersville, 724/368-8811, www.visitpaparks.com, open daily sunrise–sunset, free) is named after a logging mill built to channel the creek's water, as well as the water's power. The park has long been a favorite day trip of teenagers living in Pittsburgh's northern suburbs, but considering that it's less than 40 miles from Downtown, it also makes for a worthwhile day trip if you're staying in the city and need a quick wilderness break.

There are any number of activities to keep you occupied once inside the park. You're almost certain to see rock climbers here, especially if you venture toward Rim Road's climbing area, which sits on the other side of the creek from the Old Mill, where an emergency phone is also located. Head to the intersection of Breakneck Bridge Road and Cheeseman Road to discover the advanced climbing area. White-water rafting and kayaking is also big here, and with seven miles of trails, it would be simple to pass half a day simply exploring the pristine, forested splendor of McConnell's Mill.

The McConnell's Mill Heritage Festival takes place during the third or fourth weekend of September. The operational era of the Old Mill (1852–1928) is celebrated during the festival, and visitors can enjoy activities such as corn grinding demonstrations, mill tours, and old-time musical entertainment.

To reach the park from Downtown, take I-79 to U.S. 19 (Exit 28). Look for signs pointing toward McConnell's Mill Road, where you'll find the park sitting roughly 1,000 feet north of the PA 19 and U.S. 422 intersection.

Old Economy Village

Formerly the home of the 19th-century communal Christian group known as the Harmony Society, the village of Economy, known in its current restored form as Old Economy Village (corner of 14th and Church Sts., Ambridge, 724/266-4500, www.oldeconomyvillage.org, Tue.–Sat. 9 A.M.–5 P.M., Sun. noon–5 P.M., admission $7 adult, $5 child, $6 senior), was in its day widely recognized as a God-fearing and stoically hard-working place.

The Harmonists fled Germany in the late 1700s due to persecutions from the Lutheran Church and went on to purchase 3,000 acres of land in Pennsylvania's Butler County. After moving to Indiana and then returning to Pennsylvania, they settled here and continued the working of their curious sect, which today is regarded as one of the country's most successful experiments in economics and alternative living. Completely regardless of gender, the Harmonists shared all manner of village tasks; they also produced everything needed for survival within the confines of the village. And although the society lasted for more than a century, no Harmonists remain today. Why not? The society's members were all unmarried, and none believed in the concept of procreation. Oops.

Nonetheless, the Harmony Society and

the Old Economy Village site both make for fascinating studies. Village visitors will have the opportunity to see the society's community kitchen, its cabinet shop and blacksmith shop, a granary, the Economy Post Office, and more.

Prime Outlets

Located in Grove City and about an hour away by car from Downtown Pittsburgh, Prime Outlets (intersection of I-79 and Route 208, Grove City, 888/545-7221, www.primeoutlets.com, Mon.–Sat. 10 A.M.– 9 P.M., Sun. 10 A.M.–7 P.M.) is an almost ridiculously large outlet mall—it covers so much ground, in fact, you may have to return for a second visit in order to see it all. There are more than 140 brand name outlet stores here, including Brooks Brothers, Coach, Old Navy, Polo, Ralph Lauren, Adidas, Gap, Nike, Bath & Body Works, Black & Decker, rue 21, J. Crew, and Banana Republic. Also available are all manner of housewares, home furnishings, children's apparel, lingerie, and luggage.

Unfortunately, hungry shoppers don't have the healthiest options from which to choose; the majority of eateries in the food court are of the Dairy Queen and Pretzel Time variety. There is an Eat 'N Park located nearby, however, where you can at least procure a salad.

RESTAURANTS

A Zelie institution since 1810, the **Kaufman House** (105 S. Main St., Zelienople, 724/452-8900, www.kaufmanhouse.com) has a total of four dining rooms, a coffee shop, and a lounge. And although the restaurant has something of an upscale feel, the appetizers and entrées here are pleasingly all-American,

with steaks, chicken, sandwiches, salads, and burgers leading the charge.

A self-described beanery, eatery, brewery, and community center, the **North Country Brewing Company** (141 S. Main St., Slippery Rock, 724/794-2337, www.northcountry brewing.com, Mon.–Thurs. 11 A.M.–11 P.M., Fri.–Sat. 11 A.M.–midnight, Sun. 11 A.M.–10 P.M.) is close to McConnell's Mill State Park. The on-site brewery is phenomenal, the weekly specials often include wild game, and the creatively built sandwiches and burgers are exactly what you'd expect to find in a college town: Mouth-watering and especially large. Check the website for live music schedules.

The first six-pack shop to ever grace the streets of Slippery Rock, **B and J Coney Island** (635 Kelly Blvd., Slippery Rock, 724/794-4899, www.bjconeyisland.com) sells burgers, fries, and, of course, a wide selection of cold beer.

ACCOMMODATIONS

Particularly popular with golfers, **Conley Resort** (740 Pittsburgh Rd., Butler, 800/344-7303, www.conleyresort.com) offers all guests a complimentary breakfast as well as use of the on-site waterpark, which consists of two slides, a pool, a sauna, a hot tub, and a replica of a pirate ship with its own water canon. Guests also receive a discount at the resort's golf course. Rooms here are nothing to shout about, but are certainly clean and comfy enough. And since Conley is such a spacious place, it's also a popular spot for business meetings and conferences. Rooms start at $104 a night.

A four-room bed-and-breakfast located in a historic 1928 brick house, **Copper Penny Manor B&B** (856 Evans City Rd., Renfrew,

724/789-7968, www.copperpennymanor .com) sits on five acres of land, which is also home to a chicken pen, a smokehouse, a carriage house, and a barn. Each room, which has its own balcony, is decorated in a fairly standard country fashion. Rooms are $79 a night.

Family-run and located just five minutes from Beaver's shopping district, **Willows Inn** (1830 Midland Beaver Rd., Industry, 724/643-4500, www.willowsinnpa.com) has 30 recently remodeled rooms, free wireless access, and famously delicious smorgasbords. There's also a banquet hall and a pub on-site. Penn State's Beaver campus is a 10-minute drive away, and both Geneva College and Old Economy Village are 20 minutes away. Rooms start at the very reasonable rate of $65 a night.

PRACTICALITIES
Tourist Offices

The Beaver County Recreation & Tourism Department is located in the Bradys Run Recreation Facility at 526 Bradys Run Road in Beaver Falls; office hours are Monday–Friday 8:30 A.M.–4:30 P.M. Call them at 724/891-7030 or 800/342-8192. The department's website is www.visitbeavercounty.com.

The Butler County Tourism & Convention Bureau (www.visitbutlercounty.com) can be found at 310 East Grandview Avenue in Zelienople or contacted at 724/234-4619 or 866/856-8444. Office hours are Monday–Friday 8:30 A.M.–4:30 P.M.

Media

The *Butler Eagle* (www.butlereagle.com) is a major daily newspaper serving the residents of Butler County, while *Cranberry Magazine* (www.cranberrymagazine.com) documents the suburban communities of Cranberry, Seven Fields, Wexford, Mars, Zelienople, Harmony, and Evans City. While in Beaver County, pick up the daily *Beaver County Times* (www.timesonline.com).

Getting There

Driving to both Beaver and Butler Counties from Downtown Pittsburgh is a breeze: Simply take Route 22 west to Route 30 west to reach Beaver. For Butler, head out of the city on I-279 north, which turns into I-79 north. You'll find that the majority of Pittsburgh's Yellow Cab drivers will be all too happy to shuttle you anywhere within the two counties, although be sure to ask about any extra fees you might accrue by traveling outside Allegheny County.

Getting Around

The Beaver County Transit Authority (724/728-8600, www.bcta.com) is responsible for operating the region's bus service; schedules, maps, and more can be found on the authority's website. For information about travels in and around Butler County, visit the website of The Bus at www.thebus butlerpa.com. Information about various limousine and taxi services in Butler County can be found at www.visitbutlercounty .com. Or, call the National Taxi Directory (www.1800taxicab.com) toll-free at 800/ TAXI-CAB (800/829-4222) for further information. The NTD offers telephone numbers of the nearest taxi companies based on the phone number you're calling from.

BACKGROUND

The Setting

Because of the three rivers which wind and wend their way throughout all stretches of the city, and also because of the small hills and deep valleys that seem to appear out of nowhere in this region, Pittsburgh is well known as an often difficult-to-traverse part of the country. Yet it's also known as a deeply beautiful place. Much of Southwestern Pennsylvania, as well as much of suburban Pittsburgh, is heavily forested; many regions are blanketed with strong trees and wildlife.

Within Pittsburgh's inner-city limits, the story is much different. The majority of the neighborhoods where tourists will find themselves are quite urban, and many of the most interesting East End areas are surrounded by low-income neighborhoods.

GEOGRAPHY AND CLIMATE

Pittsburgh is located in the southwest corner of the state of Pennsylvania, where it sits near the foothills of the Allegheny Mountains. The city sits 696 feet above sea level.

In total, Pittsburgh consists of 58.3 square miles, with 55.6 square miles consisting of landmass and 2.7 square miles consisting of

© DAN ELDRIDGE

water. In other words, approximately 4.75 percent of the City of Pittsburgh is water.

The city sits on a land mass known as the Allegheny Plateau; this is the area where the city's three rivers—the Allegheny, the Monongahela, and the Ohio—come together at the westernmost tip of the Downtown Pittsburgh area, which is also known as the Golden Triangle.

Pittsburgh is a particularly hilly city, and while it has a continental climate with four seasons, it's also a relatively rainy and snowy place, with approximately 37 inches of rain annually and 43 inches of snow annually.

Pittsburgh's temperature varies widely throughout the year, with the winter months of December, January, and February averaging a low temperature of a chilly 22°F, and the summer months of June, July, and August averaging a high temperature of a rather steamy (and often humid) 82.6°F.

ENVIRONMENTAL ISSUES

Because of the many industrial factories and steel-producing mills that dotted the Pittsburgh cityscape for roughly 150 years, it was inevitable that the town would eventually suffer from the effects of environmental pollution. In fact, during much of the 20th century, the entirety of Pittsburgh was so smoke- and soot-covered that visitors nicknamed it "The Smoky City"; still very much a part of Steel City lore are stories of businessmen leaving the confines of their Downtown offices during the lunch break and returning an hour later to find their white shirts turned dark gray. As a result of the pollution, an alarmingly large number of Pittsburghers living within the city limits at the time suffered from respiratory illnesses. But thanks to the steadfast efforts of one of the city's most popular mayors, David Lawrence, things began

David L. Lawrence Convention Center

to change for the better during the 1950s, as smoke control became a leading local issue.

And although Pittsburgh has a good distance to travel before it becomes a leading national light in the area of environmental pollution control (emissions from public buses are still a heated issue, for instance), many changes have been made for the better. The locally based Green Building Alliance (www.gbapgh.com) is a nonprofit organization concerned with integrating environmentally responsible design into new area construction. Pittsburgh can now claim the world's first green convention center and the world's largest green building, The David L. Lawrence Convention Center. And partly due to the efforts of the U.S. Green Building Council's Washington, D.C.–based LEED (Leadership in Energy and Environmental Design) program, Pittsburgh is also home to 40 buildings registered under the council's rating system.

History

It's something of a little-known fact that Pittsburgh's history is very much intertwined with that of our nation's first president, George Washington, who first visited the area in 1753. Then a 21-year-old major, Washington surveyed the land at the junction of the Allegheny and Monongahela Rivers (the current location of Point State Park), and wrote that it was "extremely well suited for a Fort; as it has the absolute Command of both Rivers."

Perhaps not surprisingly, the French were also impressed by the city's strategic location at the fork of the three rivers. In 1754, they managed to drive Washington's Virginia militia away, and then built a fort on the site themselves. It was named Fort Duquesne.

Four years passed, and the British, led by General John Forbes, managed to defeat the French and reclaim the fort, which was first rebuilt and then renamed. (The wily French had burned the fort to the ground before fleeing.) The new site became known as Fort Pitt, after William Pitt, the English prime minister. On the first day of December, General Forbes named the camp at Fort Duquesne "Pittsburgh."

In 1787, roughly a decade after a heated dispute between the states of Virginia and Pennsylvania, both of whom wanted to claim Pittsburgh as their own, the Pittsburgh Academy was founded in a small log cabin; it would eventually become the University of Pittsburgh. Clearly, Pittsburgh was becoming an

PITTSBURGH IN FLAMES: THE GREAT RAILROAD STRIKE OF 1877

As a town with a blue-collar soul, it is perhaps not surprising that Pittsburghers have long stood strong for workers' rights. In 1877, however, one particularly unfortunate incident resulted in riots and massive fires that charred great portions of the city.

As is the case when most workers strike, the situation that started on July 14 in Martinsburg, West Virginia, revolved around money; the Baltimore & Ohio Railroad company had seen fit to reduce its workers' wages for the second time that year. In response, the workers refused to let any of the company's supplies or its building materials pass along the railroad lines.

Along with Martinsburg, towns as far away as Baltimore and Chicago saw violence when state militias engaged in battle with their own strikers. But the worst violence of all occurred right here in Pittsburgh, when members of the Pennsylvania state militia killed and wounded nearly 50 workers. Instead of ending the episode, however, all hell broke loose within the city. After the violence had settled and cleared, 39 buildings in the areas surrounding the Strip District had been burned to the ground. More than 100 locomotives had been beaten senseless and more than 1,200 train cars had been destroyed. Clearly, Pittsburgh wasn't interested in giving up without a fight. The madness, insanity, and killings continued for nearly a month, until President Hayes sent in federal reinforcements who finally managed to quell the strikers.

the Kaufmann's clock, Downtown

outpost to reckon with; the weekly *Pittsburgh Gazette,* the first newspaper to exist west of the Alleghenies, had seen its first issue the year prior. In 1816, Pittsburgh was finally incorporated as a city. By 1820, Pittsburgh's population was just more than 7,000. A decade later, it had grown to more than 12,500.

Pittsburgh had its first experience with major tragedy in 1845, when a fire destroyed roughly a third of the city and left about 12,000 people homeless. Less than a decade later, Pittsburgh's reputation as the "Smoky City" began to grow: The Jones & Laughlin Steel Corporation was founded in 1853. The Clinton iron furnace opened in 1859. And then in 1864, at the age of 29, Andrew Carnegie decided to join the iron business. A Scotsman, he soon became known as the richest man in America. In 1889 he dedicated the region's first Carn-

egie Library, which still operates in Braddock, and in 1900 he founded the Carnegie Technical School, now known as Carnegie Mellon University.

A true city of industry, Pittsburgh continued cranking through a series of milestones for the next 50 years: The first World Series was played here in 1903; the first motion picture house opened here in 1905; the country's first commercial radio station broadcast from here in 1920. For all its successes, however, Pittsburgh's reputation as an unpleasant place to visit managed to precede it. At the time, the town was known as one of the most polluted cities in America; streetlights were often kept on throughout the day. That all began to change in 1946, though, when Mayor David Lawrence kicked off the city's first official Renaissance, an urban renewal plan that eventually stripped Pittsburgh of its Smoky City image and managed to transform it into the epicenter of medicine, education, and technology that it is today. One of the city's biggest triumphs came in 1953, when Dr. Jonas Salk discovered the polio vaccine at the University of Pittsburgh.

Although its population has been in steady decline for decades, Pittsburgh continues to march on as a top-ranked metropolis, and in 1985 it was named "America's Most Livable City" by Rand-McNally's *Places Rated Almanac.* In 1989, the city elected its first female mayor, the much-loved Sophie Masloff. And then in 2006, another victory: The Pittsburgh Steelers, whose successful 1970s franchise resulted in the town becoming known as the City of Champions, managed to regain a touch of their former glory by winning a fifth career Super Bowl.

PITTSBURGH TODAY

No one can deny that Pittsburgh made giant leaps in its effort to become a world-class city during the urban redevelopment process known as Renaissance II: Officially begun in 1980, this was when the city saw construction of Three Rivers Stadium and a bevy of Downtown skyscrapers and shopping centers, including USX Tower, Mellon Bank Tower, Oxford Centre, and PPG Place. Pittsburgh's intention was to transform itself from a city of industry into a tech, medicine, and education hub. This was all well and good, until along came the disaster known as Renaissance III.

Led by then-Mayor Tom Murphy, R3 was centered on redeveloping and revitalizing the city's Downtown core, especially the area around Market Square. Pittsburghers weren't fond of Murphy's plan—to drive out decades-old retailers and bring in big-box chains—and ultimately the scheme failed. Today, the abandoned 5th and Forbes Corridor, as the area is known, is filled with empty storefronts.

As if that weren't enough, Pittsburgh in the early part of the 21st century has been feeling the burn of a serious image crisis, during which many of the town's young and creative types have left in search of brighter opportunity and better jobs elsewhere. Attempting to halt this flow, a group of corporate and civic leaders in 2002 and 2003 created the Image Gap Committee. Soon, the city had burned through roughly $200,000 in grant money to acquire a new motto, a Pittsburgh font, and even a city-specific color scheme. The so-called Pittsburgh Regional Branding Initiative was widely mocked. The city's image doesn't seem to have improved much in the interim.

Until very recently, all eyes were on the newly elected Mayor Bob O'Connor, who won the spot in a November 2005 landslide election. Although O'Connor was a Democrat, few of Pittsburgh's progressive types were holding much hope for change. With Pittsburgh's infamous "old boy" network still firmly in place throughout city government, the prevailing attitude seemed to be one of simply waiting it out. The big question at the time of O'Connor's election was whether the city could continue to move forward before those in power began to retire or otherwise fade away. And then coincidentally, mere weeks after O'Connor took office, he was diagnosed with brain tumors and a rare form of cancer. On September 1, 2006, O'Connor passed away at UPMC Shadyside Hospital. He was 61 and had only served as mayor for a mere six months. His replacement? The 26-year-old Luke Ravenstahl, who at the time

a gargoyle protects a decades-old brick building, Downtown

was serving as City Council President. To much of Pittsburgh's progressive community, the entire drama was an almost unbelievable case of "be careful what you wish for."

Of course, it remains to be seen whether or not someone as young as Ravenstahl can suc-cessfully run a major metropolitan city, and no one yet knows whether he'll throw his hat in the ring or not come reelection time. But as usual, the future of the City of Pittsburgh can probably best be expressed with one lone punctuation symbol: a question mark.

Economy

Pittsburgh first became an economic power-house in the mid-1800s, thanks to the efforts of Scottish immigrant Andrew Carnegie and others involved in the city's iron, steel, and glass industries. The American steel industry suffered a massive collapse in the early 1980s, however, as production began moving to more affordable plants overseas. Displaying the most admirable side of its entrepreneurial and hardworking nature, Pittsburgh stead-fastly refused to wither away and took im-mediate and massive strides to reinvent itself. The city today owes its economic strength to a diverse mixture of healthcare, education, technology, and biotechnology. Finance and tourism also play important roles.

The University of Pittsburgh Medical Center (UPMC) is by far the region's larg-est employer, with nearly 27,000 employ-ees in Allegheny County alone. West Penn Allegheny Health System and the University of Pittsburgh both employ approximately 10,000 area residents each. Nonetheless, Pittsburgh continues to lead the country in population decline. Although the city claimed 677,000 residents in 1950, today less than 317,000 remain. This likely has much to do with Allegheny County's current per capita income, which rests at $22,491.

A number of Fortune 500 and Fortune 1000 companies continue to be headquar-tered in Pittsburgh, including Alcoa, H. J. Heinz, and PPG Industries.

HEALTHCARE

It simply isn't possible to overstate the contri-bution of the University of Pittsburgh Medi-cal Center to the local economy. Easily the largest employer in Western Pennsylvania, UPMC is also responsible for much of the area's construction boom; the organization spends roughly $250 million annually on construction activity. And because of the pa-tients, families of patients, and investment dollars it attracts from around the county, UPMC estimates that every dollar it spends generates $1.25 for the region itself. Consid-ering that UPMC's annual budget stretches just past $5 billion, it goes without saying that the center's contribution is invaluable for the Southwestern Pennsylvania region.

West Penn Allegheny Health System, the region's second-most important economic leader in the healthcare industry, consists of Allegheny General Hospital, West Penn Hos-pital, Canonsburg General Hospital, as well as a number of other regional hospitals.

EDUCATION

Referred to by some civic boosters as The College City, the greater Pittsburgh area is home to 33 colleges and universities, the most

the headquarters of Pittsburgh-based General Nutrition Centers, Inc.

prominent being the University of Pittsburgh, Carnegie Mellon University, and Duquesne University. Economically, Pitt is the area's powerhouse; the school pours more than $350 million annually into area businesses whose goods and services keep the behemoth afloat. The university's annual payroll exceeds $530 million, and Pitt is responsible for roughly $200 million in government revenues, such as real estate and sales taxes, each year.

More than 130,000 college and university students matriculate at a Pittsburgh area school each year. Some schools, such as Carlow College, Chatham College, the Art Institute of Pittsburgh, Point Park University, and Robert Morris University, sit right within the city limits. Other schools, such as Seton Hill University, Slippery Rock University, Indiana University of Pennsylvania, and Washington & Jefferson College, are spread throughout the southwestern region of the state.

TECHNOLOGY AND BIOTECHNOLOGY

Pittsburgh's tech and biotech industries are much larger and more developed than even most locals realize. Carnegie Mellon University continues to take giant strides in the fields of robotics and software engineering; the school's Federally Funded Research and Development Center spent upward of $43 million in 2003.

Organizations such as the Pittsburgh Lifesciences Greenhouses (a joint venture between Pitt and CMU) have been instrumental in positioning Southwestern Pennsylvania as a bioscience, nanobiotechnology, and robotics leader. Researchers here study neurological disorders, tissue engineering, and drug discovery, among other biotechnology developments.

To stay abreast of local tech news and information, pick up a copy of *Pittsburgh TEQ* (news.pghtech.org/teq).

The People

In 2003, the U.S. Census Bureau estimated the population of Pittsburgh at 325,337. That figure equals a 2.8 percent population decline from 2000, and a 9.6 percent population decline from 1990. Women and senior citizens are well represented in Pittsburgh; the population is slightly more than 52 percent female, and 16.4 percent of the population are persons over the age of 65. Twenty-seven percent of Pittsburgh's population is black or African American, while the local population of Hawaiians and other Pacific Islanders is so small that the group failed to rate on the census report. Nearly 68 percent of all Pittsburghers are white or Caucasian.

Historically, Pittsburgh has welcomed immigrants since the mid-1700s, the majority being from Southern and Eastern European countries such as Italy and Poland. Pittsburgh saw its largest influx of European immigration during the end of the 19th century and the beginning of the 20th. The majority came in search of work, having heard of Pittsburgh's reputation as an industrial powerhouse. Many of the smaller row houses (or "mill houses") that still stand today in Lawrenceville, the South Side Slopes, and other riverside neighborhoods were first occupied by these Eastern European laborers.

A good number of early immigrants also came to Pittsburgh from Germany and Ireland. The North Side of Pittsburgh, originally a separate city known as Allegheny, is the region where the majority of the city's German immigrants settled, and in the East End neighborhood of Squirrel Hill, Hebrew and Yiddish is still widely spoken on the streets today.

PITTSBURGH'S FAMOUS FACES

Regardless of its plain and simple "jus' folks" facade, the Steel City has cranked out an impressive roster of iconic celebrities in fields as wide ranging as music, literature, the visual arts, and theater. The following is a list of superstars who were either born in the Pittsburgh area, or lived and worked here for a significant length of time.

Actors and Hollywood players: F. Murray Abraham, Steven Bochco, Dan Cortese, Ann B. Davis, Jeff Goldblum, Michael Keaton, Gene Kelly, Dennis Miller, Fred Rogers, George Romero, Tom Savini, Jimmy Stewart, Sharon Stone

Artists and writers: Nellie Bly, Rachel Carson, Mary Cassatt, Willa Cather, Michael Chabon, Annie Dillard, Teeny Harris, Philip Pearlstein, Gertrude Stein, Bunny Yeager, Andy Warhol, August Wilson

Singers and musicians: Christina Aguilera, Perry Como, Billy Eckstine, Stephen Foster, Erroll Garner, Henry Mancini, Trent Reznor

Arts and Culture

Probably because Pittsburgh has for so long been an industrial town with a deeply woven blue-collar temperament, many of the fine arts, performing arts, and visual arts haven't caught on here as quickly or successfully as in other metropolitan cities of equivalent size. And although Pittsburghers tend to vote Democratic, ours is something of a rural-influenced backwoods culture. Professional sports are hugely popular; a citywide passion for the Pittsburgh Steelers in particular seems to be the one cultural quirk that unites all Pittsburghers.

For the most part, Pittsburghers are a very proud people; regional pride is something you're likely to encounter over and over again during your stay. Unlike on the more recently developed West Coast, a large number of Pittsburgh residents have lived in the area their entire lives. In many cases, their parents have as well; grandparents of Pittsburghers in their late 20s and early 30s were quite often European immigrants. Many of those life-long Pittsburghers, especially those who grew up within the city limits and speak with an accent known as "Pittsburghese" (technically North Midland U.S. English) are referred to as "yinzers." This is generally considered a derogatory term, and shouldn't be used outside of familiar company. To learn about the unique Southwestern Pennsylvania accent, visit english.cmu.edu/pittsburghspeech/index.html and www.pittsburghese.com.

© PITTSBURGH GLASS CENTER

Glass Birthday Suit exhibition at Pittsburgh Glass Center

Today, Pittsburgh's arts scene is slowly gaining both traction and national attention. The Pittsburgh Symphony Orchestra has long been noted as being one of the nation's best. And due in large part to the city's extremely low cost of living, young artists and other creative types have been relocating to Pittsburgh—generally in the neighborhoods of the East End—from bigger and more expensive urban areas.

ARTS, CRAFTS, AND FOLK TRADITIONS

At the Smithsonian-affiliated **Senator John Heinz Pittsburgh Regional History Center** (www.pghhistory.org), scads of interesting facts about Western Pennsylvania's history and heritage can be investigated. The 200,000-square-foot museum includes exhibits about Pittsburgh's glass-making and wood-making history; examples of decorative metalwork from a locally based company are also displayed.

At the **Pittsburgh Glass Center** (www.pittsburghglasscenter.org), tours and demonstrations are given in the flame-working and glass-blowing rooms. Classes, private lessons, and studio rentals are available for further study.

At the Strip District's **Society for Contemporary Craft** (www.contemporarycraft.org), works of metal, wood, glass, clay, and fiber can be viewed. Pittsburgh artists are occasionally featured, although the majority of the works are created by nonmainstream artists from around the world.

Pittsburgh Center for the Arts (www.pittsburgharts.org) has frequently changing gallery rooms, a popular schedule of classes for both children and adults in ceramics, jewelry making, printmaking, bookbinding, creative writing, and more.

At **Artists Image Resource** (www.artistsimageresource.org) on the North Side, where silkscreens and other print work are displayed, anyone is welcome to use the studio's paints and supplies to silkscreen his or her own T-shirts, tote bags, or posters for a small fee. Open Studio nights and times change occasionally; contact 412/321-8664 or info@artistsimageresorce.org for more information.

Particularly worthwhile is a day trip to the National Historic Landmark site of **Old Economy Village** (www.oldeconomyvillage.org), the former home of the 19th-century Harmony Society. Here you can tour the site and experience the Harmonists' lifestyle by participating in candle making, bookbinding, and more.

LITERATURE

Pittsburgh has long had a strong literary history, and, in fact, the University of Pittsburgh was the first institution of higher learning in the United States to offer a Master of Fine Arts degree in Creative Nonfiction. Pittsburgh author Lee Gutkind spearheads the program; he's also the founding editor of the literary journal *Creative Nonfiction,* which recently celebrated its 10th anniversary and is headquartered in Shadyside.

Pitt's nationally regarded writing program has seen scores of well-known and widely published instructors; writers of note who are currently on staff include the hard-living fiction writer Chuck Kinder, who was one of Raymond Carver's best friends and, according to rumor, was the Pitt professor that the character in Michael Chabon's *Wonder Boys* is based on. (The street that Kinder's character lives on in the *Wonder Boys* film is S. Atlantic Street in Friendship.) The poet Toi Derricott is also a Pitt instructor, as is Faith

Adiele, a nonfiction writer and the author of *Meeting Faith: The Forest Journals of a Black Buddhist Nun.*

Renowned poet Jack Gilbert (*Views of Jeopardy, Monolithos*) was born in Pittsburgh in 1925. Author David McCullough, who won the Pulitzer Prize for the masterful biography *John Adams,* is also a Pittsburgh native. And although he has since left town, author John Edgar Wideman (*Brothers and Keepers*) wrote a number of highly-regarded novels about African American life in the Pittsburgh neighborhood of Homewood. Pittsburgher Stewart O'Nan's novel *Everyday People* explored the hardscrabble life of African Americans living in the East End neighborhood of East Liberty.

Possibly better known than all of the above combined are Pittsburghers Annie Dillard and Gertrude Stein. Dillard's *An American Childhood* examines the events of her childhood in 1950s Pittsburgh. Stein (*The Autobiography of Alice B. Toklas*) was a legendary feminist novelist and playwright who grew up on the city's North Side and eventually settled in Paris.

MUSIC

Possibly Pittsburgh's most famous musician, historically speaking, was Stephen Collins Foster, who lived in Lawrenceville and is buried in Allegheny Cemetery. Foster was a singer, a song leader, and a composer whose first major success was "Oh! Susanna."

Pittsburgh has also produced its share of jazz legends. Although a native of Dayton, Ohio, Billy Strayhorn's music career officially began in Pittsburgh; today he's best known for composing the jazz staple "Take the A Train." The jazz pianist and composer Erroll Garner was born here in 1921; he went on to play with Charlie Parker, among others. Like Gertrude Stein, jazz drummer Kenny Clarke was born here but chose to settle in Paris. He's known as an important innovator of the bebop drumming style. Earl Hines was another well-known jazz pianist also born in Pittsburgh, as was Mary Lou Williams, who worked with Duke Ellington and Thelonious Monk.

Pittsburgh's most legendary jazz venue was the Hill District's Crawford Grill, which still stands today at 2141 Wylie Avenue. Throughout the 1930s, '40s, and '50s, Pittsburgh's Hill District (then known as "Little Harlem") and the Crawford Grill were both well known and respected in prominent African American social circles.

Since the late 1970s, rock 'n' roll—especially the brand of rock now known as "classic rock"—has been favored in Pittsburgh. One of the area's most famous rockers is Joe Grushecky. As a longtime friend of Bruce Springsteen's, Grushecky has been known to bring the Boss to town—unannounced—to perform secret concerts at small clubs. Local musician Donny Iris was a pop and R&B superstar in his own right throughout the 1970s, and the Clarks, a rock group who still perform and record today, have managed to achieve national and even international success.

Of the city's more recent musical talent, the jam band Rusted Root and the political punk group Anti-Flag have seen the widest recognition outside of the Steel City.

TELEVISION AND FILM

For a short while in the 1990s, thanks largely to the efforts of the Pittsburgh Film Office, it seemed as if Southwestern Pennsylvania was on its way to becoming a budget alternative to Hollywood. Vancouver, British Columbia, seems to be claiming that honor for the time being, but movies and the occasional TV show continue to be filmed here with some regularity.

Certainly the city's proudest television accomplishment was the airing of *Mister Rogers' Neighborhood*, a genuine broadcasting treasure hosted by a true American icon, Fred Rogers, who passed away in February 2003. Produced for 33 years, it was the longest running program ever aired by PBS.

A number of television shows have been set in Pittsburgh but filmed elsewhere, including *Mr. Belvedere*, which followed the trials and tribulations of an upper middle class Beaver Falls family; *My So Called Life*, a hugely popular teen drama that launched the careers of Claire Danes and Jared Leto; *Queer as Folk*, a Showtime series that followed the lives of a group of gay and lesbian friends who partied in the bars on Liberty Avenue; and *The Guardian*, a legal drama which alternated between real shots of Pittsburgh and fake shots filmed on a Culver City lot.

Pittsburgh's film history has been long and varied. Aside with the 1980s classic *Flashdance*, probably the most important movie filmed in the city remains George Romero's *Night of the Living Dead*. Much of the film, which Romero cowrote with fellow Pittsburgher John Russo, was filmed in Evans City, which sits about 30 miles north of the city in Butler County. Romero and Russo continue to live in Pittsburgh, as does famed makeup artist Tom Savini, who worked on Romero's *Dawn of the Dead*, a *Night of the Living Dead* sequel that was filmed in the Monroeville Mall. The follow-up film *Day of the Dead* was also filmed in Pittsburgh, although Romero chose to shoot in (gasp!) Canada during the filming of *Land of the Dead* (2005).

Pittsburgh seems to be a popular setting for frightening films; quite a few scenes from *The Silence of the Lambs* were shot in the Carnegie Museum of Natural History. *Stigmata* (1999) was based here and *The Mothman Prophecies* (2002) was filmed here.

Other popular movies filmed in and around Pittsburgh include *The Deer Hunter*, *Wonder Boys*, and *Dogma*.

ESSENTIALS

Getting There

Thanks to its easy-to-navigate Pittsburgh International Airport, its bus and train depots, and its convenient location on I-76 between Chicago and Philadelphia, you shouldn't expect any problems getting into or out of the Greater Pittsburgh area.

BY AIR

More than 14 million travelers each year land at **Pittsburgh International Airport** (412/472-5510 or 412/472-3525, www.flypittsburgh.com), which currently holds the distinction of being the fourth-largest airport in the United States. (Denver International currently holds the title.) Located 16 miles northwest of Downtown, PIT was one of the first American airports to construct a mammoth, mall-like shopping center on its premises. Along with a collection of more than 100 stores and restaurants, the airport boasts a full-service U.S. Post Office, a nondenominational chapel featuring a daily Roman Catholic mass, and six international gates. Be sure to look out for the gorgeous and appropriately titled Alexander Calder mobile, *Pittsburgh.*

A total of 12 airlines serve Pittsburgh International, including Jet Blue (www.jet blue.com), which flies to New York's JFK and Boston's Logan International Airport. Other budget airlines serving PIT include AirTran (www.airtran.com), Southwest (www.south west.com), and USA 3000 (www.usa3000 .com), which offers cheap flights to Cancun, Aruba, and the Dominican Republic.

Cheap public transport to and from the airport begins and ends with the **28-X Airport Flyer** bus, a bargain at $2.25. The route begins at Carnegie Mellon University before making its way past the University of Pittsburgh, down 5th Avenue in Oakland and into Downtown. Allow 45 minutes if traveling from Oakland, or 30 minutes if traveling from Downtown. Contact **Port Authority** (412/442-2000, www.ride gold.com) for scheduling information. Beware that the first 28-X of the day doesn't arrive at the airport until 5:47 A.M., however, so the bus isn't a reliable option if you have an early morning flight. (For domestic flights, allow a minimum of one hour to check in and get through security; allow two hours if you're flying internationally.) The final 28-X of the day, which departs from the lower level ground transportation area outside the baggage claim, leaves just past midnight at 12:08 A.M.

A **Yellow Cab taxi** (412/321-8100) will take you to Pittsburgh International at any time of the day or night, but expect to pay around $45 from Downtown, not including a gratuity. Calling Yellow Cab well in advance and booking a taxi is highly recommended, as is booking much earlier than you actually need to: Yellow Cabs in Pittsburgh have a nasty habit of not showing up when they say they will. Should your cab fail to arrive, you'll find a taxi rank outside most Downtown hotels at just about any hour of the day or night.

Your only other transport option to the airport, aside from booking a private car (look in the telephone book under "Airport Transportation" to explore that option), are the customer courtesy shuttles that run regularly from most Downtown hotels. Inquire at your hotel about this service.

PIT offers a long-term parking lot for travelers who need to leave their vehicles at the airport for days or weeks at a time, although two private companies offer much cheaper rates. **Charlie Brown's Airport Parking** (412/262-4931, www.charliebrowns parking.com) charges $6.25 per day or $39.99 per week; the rates at **Globe Transportation** (412/264-4373, www.globeparking.com) are slightly higher at $6.50 per day and $41.50 per week. Coupons offering substantial discounts can be found at both companies' websites, and both companies are open around the clock.

BY TRAIN

Pittsburgh's **Amtrak station** (412/471-6170, www.amtrak.com) is located Downtown at 1100 Liberty Avenue, directly across the street from the building that formerly housed the Greyhound bus station and directly on the border of the Strip District. Trains depart daily for destinations throughout the United States and Canada, although fares on nondirect routes are generally higher than those offered by Greyhound. Trips on Amtrak also tend to take substantially longer than those on the bus—not necessarily a bad thing, as most American train routes pass through surroundings that highway travelers never get a chance to witness.

Popular destinations include Washington, D.C. ($39, 7.5 hours), Philadelphia ($42, 7.5 hours), and New York City ($56, 9 hours).

BY BUS

Formerly located across from the Amtrak station at Liberty Avenue and 11th Street, the **Greyhound depot** (990 2nd Ave., 412/392-6513 or 800/231-2222, www.greyhound.com) has temporarily relocated to a rather inconvenient spot next to Allegheny County Jail, Downtown. The easiest way to reach the depot by foot is to walk along the Eliza Furnace Trail (a.k.a. the Jail Trail), which begins where Grant Street meets the Monongahela River. The trail runs along the Monongahela; a walk to the bus station, which you'll find just past the jail on your left, should take about 10 minutes. The station's parking lot sits underneath the 10th Street Bridge, which leads to the South Side. A new station is scheduled to open at the original station's location (Liberty Ave. at 11th St.) sometime in February 2008.

Getting Around

PUBLIC TRANSPORTATION

Port Authority Transit (412/422-2000, www.ridegold.com) operates buses, trains, and two inclines within Allegheny County. Bus, train, and incline rides are $1.75. Transfers cost an extra $0.50; they're generally good for three or four hours and can be used for one ride going in any direction.

The train, known locally as the "T," has four stops in Downtown and another at Station Square. The train also travels through the suburbs of the South Hills; the line ends at South Hills Village Mall. Riding within the "Downtowner Zone," which includes any of the four Downtown stops, is free. The city's two inclines travel up and down Mount Washington. The Monongahela Incline begins across the street from Station Square and discharges passengers on Grandview Avenue. The Duquesne Incline also ends on Grandview Avenue but roughly a mile to the west in the Duquesne Heights district. (This is where Mount Washington's most expensive restaurants are located.) Its street-level station is somewhat inconveniently located along a busy road. If you'd like to ride both inclines, your best bet is to take the Monongahela Incline from Station Square up to Mount Washington, and then walk down Grandview Avenue to the Duquesne Incline. Take the Duquesne down to street level, where you can then walk across a pedestrian bridge to a parking lot. Head toward the river, where you'll find a footpath that conveniently leads back to Station Square.

Weekly and monthly transit passes can be purchased at the **Port Authority Downtown Service Center** (534 Smithfield St., 412/255-1356) or at most Giant Eagle grocery stores.

DRIVING

Because Pittsburgh's public transportation system is relatively reliable, getting by without a car can certainly be done. To fully explore the city's outer reaches, however, a car is a necessary accoutrement. Pittsburgh is a notoriously confusing city to navigate, however, so consider investing in a street atlas. Rand McNally's spiral-bound *Pittsburgh: Street Guide*

The biking scene in Pittsburgh is slowly improving. Just make sure you're fully prepared for a ride through the concrete jungle.

is a good choice. Also be aware that most neighborhoods within the city limits require all drivers to display a neighborhood-specific parking sticker in their window. If you park without a sticker, you'll need to move your car within one hour to avoid a ticket.

Rental cars are available at various locations throughout the city. At the Pittsburgh International Airport, you'll find rental counters for nine agencies, including **Budget** (800/527-0700, www.budget.com), **Dollar** (800/800-4000, www.dollarrentacar.com), and **Hertz** (800/654-3131, www.hertz.com), on the same level as baggage claim.

TAXIS

Yellow Cab (412/321-8100, www.pghtrans. com/yellow_cab_pgh.html) is the city's solitary taxi company. Contrary to popular belief, cabs *can* be hailed in Pittsburgh, but only in certain parts of town (Downtown,

the South Side, and Station Square are your best bets). If absolutely no cabs are around, try walking to the closest hotel; empty taxis often wait outside for potential passengers. During late-night hours and especially on the weekends, cabs converge en masse on the South Side and at Station Square.

BICYCLING

In 1990, a poll in *Bicycling* magazine ranked Pittsburgh among the 10 worst U.S. cities for cycling. But the biking landscape has lately seen a series of radical changes, thanks especially to **Bike Pittsburgh** (412/726-5872, www.bike-pgh.org), a nonprofit cycling and advocacy group committed to making the city safer and more accessible for cyclists. With very few exceptions, Pittsburgh's roadways lack bicycle lanes, so take special care to travel safely on busy or crowded roads. To explore further reaches of the city without the added stress of traffic, download a map of the **Three Rivers Heritage Trail** at www.friendsoftheriverfront.org (see *Bicycling* in the *Recreation* chapter for more information).

DISABLED ACCESS

Yellow Cab operates a special service for people in wheelchairs and the otherwise mobility impaired. The company's specially equipped Ford Windstar minivans have a fold-down ramp and rear-entry access, a universal wheelchair tie-down system, and air conditioning with separate backseat controls. Curb-to-curb service is offered; passengers pay no extra rates or special fees. For more information call 412/321-8100 or visit www.pghtrans.com/wheelchair_cab_pgh.html.

Tips for Travelers

WEATHER

Depending on whom you ask, the average annual rainfall in Pittsburgh is somewhere between 37 and 40 inches a year, which may or may not mean that the Steel City sees more precipitation than Seattle, an unfounded factoid that you'll likely hear over and over during your stay. But one thing's for sure: Thanks to the hilly topography of the immediate area and the effect of Lake Erie, which sits about 125 miles to the north, Southwestern Pennsylvania is well known as a region with 12 months of wildly unpredictable weather. And what's more, Pittsburgh is not a particularly good place for the depressed: Roughly 200 days of cloud cover are clocked here annually, which means the town once known as "Smoky City" remains one of the cloudiest places in America. (Juneau, Alaska tops the list.)

Happily, however, we do experience four complete seasons in Western Pennsylvania. Summers get good and hot, with the temperature generally hanging between 70 and 80°F (although much hotter days are not uncommon). Winter temperatures settle in somewhere between 20 and 30°F. For detailed day-to-day weather system tracking, log on to the **Weather Channel** online (www.theweather channel.com), or take a look at **KDKA**'s local online forecast (weather.kdka.com).

HOURS

Generally speaking, Pittsburgh is a town that rolls up its sidewalks fairly early. Bars here close at 2 A.M., and if business is slow during the week, they may close earlier than that. (Thankfully, business is *never* slow in a Pittsburgh bar on the weekend.) If you're staying on the East End, or anywhere on the South Side, expect the streets to get particularly rowdy around 15 minutes before the bars close on weekend nights. The South Side's East Carson Street in particular can be a frightening place at 2 A.M.; fistfights and police cruisers are a not uncommon sight.

Restaurants, too, tend to call it a day fairly early in the evening here. Unlike the fine-dining scenes in cities like Philadelphia, Chicago, or San Francisco, you may be surprised to find that a popular eatery has stopped serving as early as 10 or 10:30 P.M., even on weekends. Always call ahead if your evening has gotten off to a late start.

And as is the situation in most financial districts, downtown Pittsburgh becomes something of a ghost town on weekends, and by about 6 P.M. on weekdays, assuming there are no parades, festivals, or art crawls taking place.

TIPPING

At restaurants, servers should be tipped 15 percent of the check for average service, or 20 percent for exceptional service. At coffee shops, leave the barista a few coins for a simple drink, such as house coffee. (Or simply drop your change into the barista's tip jar.) If you're ordering a more complicated espresso-based drink, it's not uncommon to leave a dollar. A 15–20 percent tip is also appropriate for taxi drivers, as well as anyone else performing a service for you, such a massage therapist, a hairdresser, or an attendant or manicurist at a spa or salon.

In hotel rooms, you'll often find an envelope with the name of your room's attendant written on the front. If exceptional service is important to you, be sure to leave anywhere from $2–10 a day, depending on the quality of the hotel itself. (Attendants at more expensive hotels expect larger tips, while attendants at budget hotels usually aren't tipped at all.) A hotel concierge should be tipped anywhere between $5–10. If a particularly complicated or time-sensitive service was performed, tip accordingly.

At bars, a minimum tip of a dollar per drink is expected, unless you're ordering a round, in which case you could probably get away with a bit less. Bartenders in Pittsburgh's dive bars don't necessarily expect a dollar a drink, even if the bar in question is particularly popular. Tip well in these busy places, however, and you'll often find that your service improves.

SMOKING

The city council has long discussed banning the practice of smoking in workplaces, restaurants, and bars, but for the time being, those planning a night out in the Steel City would be well advised to stock up on Febreze. (See sidebar *Smoking Ban* in the *Restaurants* chapter for more details.) As Pittsburgh isn't a particularly health-conscious city, you can expect to encounter smokers just about anywhere you wander, although some exceptions apply: There are currently more than three dozen smoke-free restaurants and bars in the city. To access an updated list, visit www .nosmokedining.org/pittsburgh.htm.

Health and Safety

As North American urban areas go, Pittsburgh is a relatively safe place, and locals are almost always more than happy to help a lost, confused, or otherwise disoriented outsider. And while the city does claim a rather high number of dangerous, no-go areas, the majority of these neighborhoods are safe during the day, and most are in obscure enough locales that the average tourist has little chance of stumbling into them.

Neighborhoods in which you'd be wise to keep your wits about you include the North Side, assuming you're north of the Andy Warhol Museum or in the area surrounding the Mattress Factory. (The area known as the North Shore, where PNC Park, Heinz Field, and the Carnegie Science Center are located, is quite safe.) Also take care in the East End. While East Liberty is newly gentrifying and has much to offer visitors, it's still something of a downtrodden locale. Parts of deep Lawrenceville (near the Allegheny River) can be a bit rugged, as can parts of Garfield, including the stretch of the Penn Avenue Corridor between the Allegheny Cemetery and the entrance to East Liberty. When exploring the Penn Avenue Corridor, avoid entering the residential streets on the side of Penn Avenue that sits opposite to Bloomfield.

The Hill District and Uptown should also be avoided after dark, so should you find yourself at a Mellon Arena event at night, take care to walk back in the direction of Downtown.

HOSPITALS
AND PHARMACIES

The majority of Pittsburgh's hospitals and healthcare centers are clustered within the university district of Oakland. These include **UPMC Presbyterian** (http://presbyterian .upmc.com), **UPMC Montefiore** (http://monte fiore.upmc.com), **UPMC Cancer Institute** (http://www.upci.upmc.edu), **Children's Hospital of Pittsburgh** (www.chp.edu), **Magee-Womens Hospital** (http://magee .upmc.com), **The Eye & Ear Institute** (eye andear.upmc.com), **Western Psychiatric Institute and Clinic** (http://wpic.upmc .com), and even **The Western PA School for the Blind** (www.wpsbc.org).

Mercy Hospital (www.mercylink.org) is located in between Oakland and Downtown in the Uptown neighborhood, while **Allegheny General Hospital** (www.wpahs .org/agh) is located in North Side, and the **Western Pennsylvania Hospital** (www .wpahs.org/wph) is found on Bloomfield's Liberty Avenue. A comprehensive list of every hospital in Allegheny County, which includes links to each hospital's respective website, can be accessed at www.alleghenycounty.net/ hospital.html. **UPMC Health Plan** is one of the area's most popular and widely used insurance programs. For information, visit www.upmchealthplan.com.

EMERGENCY SERVICES

To call the police, or for fire or medical emergencies, dial 911. For an electrical emergency, dial 412/393-7000. If you have a gas emergency in Pittsburgh, dial 412/442-3095. The Poison Information Center can be contacted at 412/681-6669. For water and sewer emergencies in Pittsburgh, dial 412/255-2429. The toll-free number for PA Crime Stoppers is 800/472-8477.

Information and Services

MEDIA AND COMMUNICATION
Phones and Area Codes

On February 1, 1998, Pittsburgh gained a new area code, 724, for telephone numbers existing outside the city limits. The change affected nearly 1.5 million phone lines. The vast majority of those were outside Allegheny County, although a small number of areas within Allegheny County were affected as well.

Other counties using the 724 area code include Armstrong, Beaver, Butler, Fayette, Greene, Indiana, Lawrence, Mercer, Washington, and Westmoreland Counties, as well as parts of Clarion, Crawford, and Venango Counties. The vast majority of neighborhoods within Allegheny County, which includes the City of Pittsburgh, use the 412 area code. No matter where you're calling to or from, however, you'll always need to dial the appropriate area code before dialing the phone number.

Internet Services

All branches of the **Carnegie Library of Pittsburgh** (412/622-3114, www.clpgh.org) offer free Internet access; a library card is required to get online. Visitors from out of town or abroad can request a temporary library card by showing a state-issued driver's license or a valid passport. The main branch of the Carnegie Library in Oakland conveniently offers free wireless service on its first and second floors. Wireless access is also available at a number of cafés around town, including all seven **Crazy Mocha** locations (www.crazymocha.com) and all **Panera Bread** locations (www.panerabread.com). Most major hotels offer free high-speed wireless as well, as does the Pittsburgh International Airport.

Mail and Messenger Services

The **United States Postal Service** maintains post offices in almost every Pittsburgh neighborhood; visit www.usps.com to search for a specific location or call 800/275-8777. For those who prefer to avoid doing business with the U.S. government, there are three corporate options. Both **UPS** (800/742-5877, www.ups.com) and **FedEx** (800/463-3333, www.fedex.com) are handy for sending overnight packages or international shipping; call or go online to find the nearest location. For post office box rentals, **Mailboxes Etc.** (414 S. Craig St., 412/687-6100 or 800/789-4623, www.mbe.com) and **The UPS Store** (1739 E. Carson St., 412/381-7755,

www.theupsstore.com) are both reliable alternatives to the USPS. Both stores offer 24-hour mailbox access and a slew of other products and services, such as copying, packaging, and shipping.

All three of Pittsburgh's bike messenger companies also deliver by car, should you need something picked up or delivered to a location that isn't within realistic cycling distance. The city's largest service is **Jet Messenger** (412/471-4722). Your other choices are **American Expediting Company** (412/321-4546, www.amexpediting.com) and **Quick Messenger** (412/481-5000).

Magazines and Newspapers

Pittsburgh's two daily newspapers include the left leaning **Pittsburgh Post-Gazette** (www.post-gazette.com) and the conservative **Pittsburgh Tribune-Review** (www.pittsburghlive.com), which also distributes a free evening tabloid, the **Trib PM.** The city's solitary alternative weekly, **Pittsburgh City Paper** (www.pghcitypaper.com), is useful for its arts and entertainment listings, as well as for its well-reported news and feature stories.

Other area newspapers include **Pittsburgh Business Times** (www.bizjournals.com/pittsburgh), which is closely watched by the city's white-collar crowd; **New Pittsburgh Courier** (www.newpittsburghcourier.com), a weekly focusing primarily on African American news and events; **Pittsburgh Catholic** (www.pittsburghcatholic.org), which serves Western Pennsylvania's considerable Catholic population and, tellingly enough, boasts the city's largest circulation; and **Out** (www.outpub.com), a gay and lesbian paper serving the tristate area.

Pittsburgh Magazine (www.wqed.org/mag) is the area's best monthly; it offers feature stories as well as all manner of local arts, food, and travel information. Other area magazines with heavy concentrations of arts and culture coverage include **Pittsburgh Quarterly** (www.pittsburghquarterly.com) and **Whirl** (www.whirlmagazine.com), the latter of which is filled largely with photos of local celebrities flitting about at high-society fundraisers. **The Pittsburgh Metropolitan** (www.pittsburghmetropolitan.com) follows the same general format as *Whirl,* but with substantially more journalistic features.

Pittsburgh has a healthy independent publishing scene. **Creative Nonfiction** (www.cerativenonfiction.org) is a highly respected journal published by Pitt instructor Lee Gutkind, who was instrumental in establishing the literary journalism genre. **The New Yinzer** (www.newyinzer.com) is an online literary journal featuring fiction, poetry, and experimental prose; special print issues are occasionally published. **Paper Street Press** (www.paperstreetpress.org) is a print literary journal published biannually; it features fiction and poetry. **Young Pioneers** (www.youngpioneers.com) is a quarterly publication covering the self-improvement and personal growth industries. It was founded by this book's author, who continues to act as its editor in chief.

Radio and TV
Affiliates of every major network exist in Pittsburgh. The city's **PBS** station, **WQED** (www.wqed.org), holds the distinction of being the first community-owned station in the country. **PCTV21** (www.pctv21.org) is Pittsburgh's public access station.

The city has a multitude of radio stations; check **Gregory's Radio Guide** (www.gregorysradioguide.com/pittsburg.html) for a decent listing of area stations. Slightly more complete is About.com's listing of Pittsburgh stations (www.pittsburgh.about.com/od/radio).

Some of the more popular area stations include **WDUQ 90.5 FM** (jazz and public radio); **WQED 89.3 FM** (classical and public radio); **WYEP 91.3 FM** (community-supported adult alternative); **WDVE 102.5 FM** (hard rock and classic rock); **3WS 94.5 FM** (oldies); **105.9 The X** (alternative rock); **WTAE 1250 AM** (sports); **Y108 FM** (country); **KDKA 1020 AM** (news and talk); **WAMO 106.7 FM** (hip-hop and R&B); and **WRCT 88.3 FM** (free-form independent music from Carnegie Mellon).

PUBLIC LIBRARIES
Enter a public library anywhere in the city of Pittsburgh, and you're entering not only a sacred monument to learning and growth. You're also passing through an important chapter—so to speak—of Pittsburgh's history.

The Scottish industrialist and philanthropist Andrew Carnegie was responsible for the creation of every last library in Pittsburgh, as he was for many other free libraries across the United States and even throughout the world. Without Carnegie's impetus to share the gift of education with the working-class employees of his steel mills, the free library as we know it today likely wouldn't exist. It is worth noting, however, that not all of Carnegie's employees, who saw their wages lowered so that library construction could go forward, saw fit to return the love. Said one such steel worker in Margaret Byington's *Homestead: The Households of a Mill Town:* "We'd rather they hadn't cut our wages and let us spend the money for ourselves. What use has a man who works 12 hours a day for a library, anyway?"

© DAN ELDRIDGE

Carnegie Library of Pittsburgh Main

The **Squirrel Hill** (5801 Forbes Ave., 412/422-9650) branch of the Carnegie Library also experienced renovations recently. The Arthur Lubetz and Associates architecture firm is responsible for the $4.7 million exterior and interior modernist design; ALA currently plans to take part in revitalizing every library in the Carnegie system. The **Downtown** (612 Smithfield St., 412/281-5945) and **Homewood** (7101 Hamilton Ave., 412/731-3080) locations have also been recently renovated. Other library branches can be found in **East Liberty** (130 S. Whitfield St., 412/363-8232), **Mount Washington** (315 Grandview Ave., 412/381-3380), **Lawrenceville** (279 Fisk St., 412/682-3668), and the **South Side** (2205 E. Carson St., 412/431-0505). Visit www.clpgh.org or any city library location to view a map of the entire 18-branch system.

Good point. Nonetheless, the Carnegie Library system today is a thing of wonder, even if some branches have been shuttered recently because of the city's ongoing financial troubles. To find the branch nearest you, visit www.clpgh.org.

Carnegie Library of Pittsburgh Main (4400 Forbes Ave., 412/622-3114) is located in Oakland, directly across from Pitt's Hillman Library; Schenley Plaza separates the two. This main branch recently underwent extensive renovations, and now features free high-speed wireless Internet service on its first and second floors, a magazine room, an outdoor reading deck, and a Crazy Mocha café. The main branch also offers a career services center, an art and music room with an extensive collection of CDs, DVDs, and books on tape, and a superb magazine and newspaper collection.

PLACES OF WORSHIP

Because Pittsburgh is so heavy with Italian and Eastern European immigrants, Catholicism is practically omnipresent. If it's a Catholic Chapel you're after, you won't need to look too terribly hard. In fact, in some neighborhoods (including Bloomfield, where this book was written), the ringing of church bells can still be heard throughout the day. To plug more effectively into the local scene, pick up a copy of the *Pittsburgh Catholic* (800/392-4670, www.pittsburghcatholic.org) at just about any chapel, or take a look at the website of the **Roman Catholic Diocese of Pittsburgh** at www.diopitt.org.

The East End neighborhood of Squirrel Hill is one of the largest Jewish neighborhoods on the East Coast; here you'll find nearly two dozen synagogues. **Beth Shalom** (5915 Beacon St.) is one of the neighbor-

detail of the East End's First United Methodist Church

hood's most popular. Visit the Pittsburgh page at **ShtetLinks** (www.shtetlinks.jewishgen.org) for a fairly comprehensive list of synagogues in Squirrel Hill and beyond.

The **Jewish Community Center** (5738 Forbes Ave., 412/521-8010, www.jccpgh.org) is located at the corner of Forbes and Murray Avenues in Squirrel Hill. Often referred to by locals as the JCC, here you'll find a fitness center, art classes for children and adults, theater and musical performances, and much more, including the **American Jewish Museum,** which is the solitary museum in the western part of Pennsylvania devoted solely to the exploration of Jewish history and culture. And yes, all races, religions, and creeds are welcome at the JCC.

Pittsburgh is also home to the **Sri Venkateswara Temple** (1230 S. McCully Dr., Penn Hills, 412/373-7650, www.svtemple .org), one of the oldest Hindu temples in the country. The Hare Krishna community of **New Vrindaban** (304/843-1600, www .newvrindaban.com) is located about an hour's drive from Pittsburgh in Moundsville, West Virginia. Call or visit the community's website for detailed directions.

Buddhists in the Pittsburgh area congregate at Sewickley's **Zen Center of Pittsburgh** (124 Willow Ridge Rd., 412/741-1262, www .prariewindzen.org), a Soto Zen Temple with a resident priest. **Stillpoint** (137 41st St., 412/366-4268, www.stillpointzen.org) is a Soto Zen practice community that gathers regularly in Lawrenceville. The North Side's **Mattress Factory** (500 Sampsonia Way, 412/231-3169, www.mattressfactory.org) hosts a morning *zazen* (meditation session) every Tuesday 7–8 A.M. The Zen Center's Rev. Kyoki Roberts hosts the session.

Muslims in Pittsburgh are well served by the mosque at the **Islamic Center of**

Pittsburgh (4100 Bigelow Blvd., 412/682-5555, www.icp-pgh.org), conveniently located in North Oakland and within easy walking distance of all Oakland universities.

In Pittsburgh, even the tattooed and pierced set has a church to serve their specific needs. **The Hot Metal Bridge Faith Community** (2000 E. Carson St., 412/481-4010, www.hotmetalbridge.com, Sun. worship 11 A.M.) is something of a nondenominational community geared toward people who tend to find standard church services too *standard*. They meet and share meals at the Goodwill Building on the South Side.

To view a brief listing of city and suburban churches for those with Presbyterian, Baptist, Lutheran, or Unitarian leanings, visit www.greaterpittsburgh.com/html/sgp97.html.

MAJOR BANKS

The Pittsburgh area's two largest financial service organizations are **PNC Bank** (www.pncbank.com) and **Citizens Bank** (www.citizensbank.com); the latter bought out the Pittsburgh-headquartered Mellon Bank back in 2001. Both PNC and Citizens have branch locations and automatic teller machines (ATMs) in all reaches of the city. **Dollar Bank** (www.dollarbank.com) is another area bank with numerous locations; the bank's no-fee and no-minimum checking accounts are a popular draw. Other banks you'll encounter around town include **National City Bank** (www.nationalcity.com), which is headquartered in Cleveland and has branches in five states; **Parkvale Bank** (www.parkvale.com), which claims to offer a personalized banking experience; **Iron and Glass Bank** (www.ironandglass.com), with branches located in the South Hills suburbs; and **Mars National Bank** (www.marsbank.com), with branches located in the North Hills suburbs. Most major banks can handle foreign currency exchanges even for customers without an account, but be prepared to pay a substantial service charge.

Be aware that many Pittsburghers still refer to ATMs as "MAC" machines. This is a stubborn holdover from the days of Mellon Bank, which referred to its ATMs as "money access machines."

RELOCATION

If you're thinking about the possibility of making the Greater Pittsburgh area your permanent home, do yourself a favor and spend some time on the comprehensive and educational website (www.pittsburghchamber.com/public/cfm/homepage_chamber/index.cfm) put together by the Greater Pittsburgh Chamber of Commerce and the Allegheny Conference on Community Development. Here you'll find business resources and demographic information about the area, as well as a cost-of-living calculator, career information, and useful information about life in the region.

Also visit www.xplorion.org, which contains loads of information about living, working, playing and investing in the area. Should you find yourself in Downtown Pittsburgh with a bit of time to kill, wander over to the **Regional Enterprise Tower** at 425 6th Avenue, near the Omni William Penn Hotel. **Xplorion** is located on the ground floor, and the use of computer terminals is free.

Finding a Job

To search the current listings of jobs offered by the City of Pittsburgh, visit the city's site at www.city.pittsburgh.pa.us/employmentcenter. You can also call the job hotline at 412/255-2388; listings are updated weekly.

The Pittsburgh Technology Council provides job seeking info and networking events for those with interest or experience in the tech or biotech fields. Visit http://careers.pghtech.org/resume for more information and regularly updated schedules.

Other useful online search engines include www.careerbuilder.com, www.monster.com, http://pittsburgh.craigslist.org, and www.hotjobs.yahoo.com. All sites allow job seekers to search for positions by specific region.

The University of Pittsburgh Medical Center has long been one of the city's largest employers. To access its online list of regularly updated open positions, visit http://jobs.upmc.com. The Career Web portal located at http://pittsburgh.careerweb.com has a wide range of listings for both skilled and unskilled workers, including positions in the education, entertainment, and service industries.

The *Pittsburgh Post-Gazette,* the *Pittsburgh Tribune-Review,* and the *Pittsburgh City Paper* all carry job listings.

Housing

The University of Pittsburgh provides a wonderful service through its **Housing Resource Center.** Apartment listings, roommate matching services, sublets, and housing guides can be accessed even by nonstudents at www.pitt.edu/~property/city.html. The same site also includes information about purchasing a home in Pittsburgh, how to find the best housing insurance for your needs, and how to pick the perfect neighborhood. There's even information about local hotels and B&Bs, should you find yourself temporarily without a roof over your head.

Many Pittsburghers interested in renting, subletting, or finding a prospective roommate do a brisk business on Craigslist. The local site can be accessed at http://pittsburgh.craigslist.org. You might also scan the bulletin boards and message boards throughout the Pitt and CMU campuses; housing notices are often posted here.

Agencies involved in the renting and selling of homes are located in a number of Pittsburgh neighborhoods, especially Shadyside and Squirrel Hill. One particularly popular agency, **Franklin West** (272 Shady Ave., Shadyside, 412/661-1151, www.franklinwest.com), specializes in contemporary apartments and townhouses.

RESOURCES
Suggested Reading

HISTORY AND GENERAL INFORMATION

Bell, Thomas. *Out of this Furnace*. University of Pittsburgh Press, 1976. An emotionally wrenching story that tells of the trials and tribulations of three generations of a Slovakian family who immigrated to America and ended up working in the Braddock steel mills.

Lorant, Stefan. *Pittsburgh: The Story of an American City*. The Derrydale Press, 1999. Based on decades of tireless research, this heavy, hardcover coffee-table book tells nearly every last facet of the city's story, from the battles of the mid-1750s to the 1990s. If you only buy one book about Pittsburgh, by all means make it this one. Incredibly detailed and packed with dozens and dozens of gorgeous photos, *Pittsburgh* officially reset the standard for historical and cultural books about cities.

Toker, Franklin. *Pittsburgh: An Urban Portrait*. University Park, 1986. Written by a University of Pittsburgh architecture professor, *Pittsburgh: An Urban Portrait* looks at the city through the lens of its many unique buildings and architectural curiosities.

LITERATURE AND FICTION

Beard, Philip. *Dear Zoe*. Viking, 2005. An Aspinwall lawyer turned novelist penned this story about a 15-year-old girl whose stepsister dies in a hit-and-run accident. The owner of Beard's neighborhood bookstore, The Aspinwall Bookshop, played a major role in getting *Dear Zoe* into print.

Chabon, Michael. *The Mysteries of Pittsburgh*. Harper Perennial, 1989. Chabon is a graduate of the University of Pittsburgh and a former employee of Jay's Bookstall; *Mysteries* was his first novel and also the book that was meant to catapult his rising star into the stratosphere. It didn't happen exactly that way, but this is nonetheless an incredible read about the existential and sexual dilemmas of a group of young adults passing their first summer after college.

Dillard, Annie. *An American Childhood*. Harper Perennial, 1988. Dillard ponders her 1950s Pittsburgh childhood in this classic book about growing up, seeing the world anew, and the unavoidable pain of slowly becoming an adult.

Gutkind, Lee. *The People of Penn's Woods West*. University of Pittsburgh Press, 1984. Still an instructor of creative nonfiction at the University of Pittsburgh, this was one of Gutkind's earliest books. A series of essays about backwoods folks he encountered on his many motorcycle journeys, the book was also the basis of the documentary film.

Jakiela, Lori. *Miss New York Has Everything.* 5 Spot, 2006. A writing instructor at Pitt's Greensburg campus, Jakiela's memoir (of sorts) is about her turn as a jet-setting airline attendant and her eventual return to the Steel City.

Laskas, Jeanne Marie. *The Balloon Lady and Other People I Know.* Duquesne University Press, 1996. An uncommonly well-written collection of essays about an uncommonly interesting group of characters by a University of Pittsburgh writing instructor and Washington County resident.

O'Nan, Stewart. *Everyday People.* Grove Press, 2001. A fictional tale about gangs, drugs, and the life of hard knocks in East Liberty, a neighborhood that remains dangerous and exceedingly poor, even while some pockets are quickly becoming gentrified.

Wideman, John Edgar. *Brothers and Keep-* *ers.* Holt, Rinehart and Winston, 1984. One of the most popular books from this formerly Pittsburgh-based writer who long chronicled life in the Homewood ghetto. In *Brothers and Keepers,* Wideman waxes poetic about the differences between his life, heavy with learning and culture, and the life of his brother, who is serving a life sentence in jail.

Wilson, August. *Fences.* Samuel French, Inc., 1986. Probably the most legendary play ever penned by Hill District native August Wilson, the story, for which Wilson was awarded the Pulitzer Prize, concerns the struggle of Troy Maxson, a proud black man who can't quite get a grasp on the quickly changing world of the 1960s.

Various authors. *Pittsburgh Love Stories.* The New Yinzer, 2004. Featuring nonfiction and prose by Pittsburgh writers both well known (Lee Gutkind, Stewart O'Nan) and obscure, this is a fantastic collection of passionate love letters written to one of the most intriguing cities in America. If you can't quite understand why some Pittsburghers love their city as much as they do, pick this one up immediately.

Internet Resources

GENERAL INFORMATION

About.com
www.pittsburgh.about.com

A good destination for keeping abreast of upcoming events and local news, About's Pittsburgh site also boasts info about finding a job, finding a home, and finding something fun to do with the family. Here you'll also find lots of links to local sites.

Carnegie Library of Pittsburgh
www.clpgh.org

The Carnegie Library's website is an absolutely indispensable research site for scholars of all things Pittsburgh. Click the "Research Databases" link on the left-hand side of the homepage, and you'll be directed to a wonderfully detailed collection of Pittsburgh data, be it cultural, historical, or just about anything else. Don't miss Pa Pitt's Master Index.

City of Pittsburgh
www.city.pittsburgh.pa.us

The official City of Pittsburgh site provides information about city parks, tourism, road closures, and city-sponsored events. New residents will appreciate the site's garbage collection schedules, road closure info, and business news.

The College City
www.thecollegecity.com

Particularly useful for its fantastic collection of local links, this site should also be the first stop for any college student interested in area schools. It's also a useful site for new residents and tourists looking to discover the city's youthful and active opportunities.

Global Pittsburgh
www.globalpittsburgh.org

This wonderfully useful site is concerned with connecting Pittsburgh's various international communities. Visitors or new residents from abroad can easily track down job opportunities, new friends and activities, and information about immigration.

Imagine Pittsburgh
www.imaginepittsburgh.com

Launched as part of a three-year, $3 million marketing campaign to increase awareness about the Pittsburgh area's numerous achievements, as well as its nearly unlimited possibility for growth, this site does a wonderful job of explaining why Pittsburgh is such an incredible place. You'll also find links to the helpful tourism sites of 11 surrounding counties.

Pittsburghese
www.pittsburgese.com

This is a hilariously good-natured guide to one of North America's most curious regional dialects, Pittsburghese. It includes a glossary, a translator, an audio quiz—even Pittsburghese calisthenics. (Believe me, yinz are gonna need it.)

Pittsburgh Indymedia
www.pittsburgh.indymedia.org

This community-based media site is filled with regional news, most with a heavily liberal bias. Pittsburgh's activism community is surprisingly large, and this is where many of them congregate. Information about upcoming protests and antiwar marches can be found here.

Pittsburgh Roars
www.pittsburghroars.com

Something of an online celebration of the fun and excitement to be had in Pittsburgh, this site contains info about arts, attractions, and various unique events going on in the city at any given time. You can also purchase a Roars Pass here ($10 adult, $5 child 12 and under), which will save you money at literally dozens of area museums, theaters, shopping centers, and more.

Roboto Board
board.nevertellmetheodds.org

This is a message board maintained by The Mr. Roboto Project, a local DIY and punk community. Many threads lean toward the juvenile or self-righteous, but the regular posters are a collective clearinghouse of obscure Pittsburgh trivia. If you have a question about the city that you can't find an answer to, you might try asking here.

VisitPittsburgh
www.visitpittsburgh.com

The Greater Pittsburgh Convention & Visitors Bureau site is where you'll find all the necessary information to plan a vacation or business trip to the Steel City. Essentially a mini online guidebook, VisitPittsburgh also allows visitors to book hotel and vacation packages. Particularly useful are the suggested itineraries for those interested in taking day trips to the nearby counties and countryside.

EVENT LISTINGS

Pittsburgh Post-Gazette Events Calendar
www.post-gazette.com/events

This is a regularly updated listing of mostly mainstream and family-friendly events, such as theater and symphony performances, art gallery openings, sporting events, fairs, and festivals.

This Is Happening
www.thisishappening.com

Created with the intention of convincing the young and hip that there are, in fact, interesting and unusual things to do in Pittsburgh, the site is searchable by subject but can be confusing to navigate; you're better off subscribing to the site's free weekly events email, which will conveniently appear in your in-box every Thursday.

PITTSBURGH'S BEST BLOGS

Pittsburgh's blogging community is equal parts political, apolitical, pissed off, pleased with itself, deadly serious, and seriously sarcastic. Naturally, there are hundreds (if not thousands) of blogs about life in the Steel City, and half of the fun is discovering new blogs you've never read before. Here are five to get you started.

The Burgh Blog
www.theburghblog.com

This is an amusing and sometimes sarcastic look at local events.

I Heart Pgh
www.iheartpgh.com

This is a quirky, well-edited, and frequently updated listing of events, especially those with a focus on the arts.

Overheard in Pittsburgh
www.overheardinpgh.blogspot.com

This site is a local version of the legendary NYC site.

Pittsblog
www.pittsblog.blogspot.com

Local politics and current events from a University of Pittsburgh law professor are featured here.

Pittsburgh Bloggers
www.pghbloggers.org

A blog about local blogs, it is useful largely because of its incredibly extensive collection of links.

Index

A

accommodations: 202-215; Altoona, State College, and Johnstown 229-230; Beaver County and Butler County 233-234; Downtown 204-206; Greater Pittsburgh 214-215; Laurel Highlands 224; North Side 211-212; Oakland 207-209; Shadyside 212-214; South Side 209-210; see also Accommodations Index
adventure sports: 194
African American culture and heritage: 29, 135, 174
Agnes R. Katz Plaza: 31
Airport Ice Arena: 187
airport shuttles: 248
air travel: 247-248
A. J. Palumbo Center: 134-135
Allegheny Cemetery: 57
Allegheny County Courthouse: 27
Allegheny Observatory: 61
Allegheny West Historic District: 52
Altoona, State College, and Johnstown: 225-231
American Jewish Museum: 56-57
Amtrak: 248-249
amusement parks: Idlewild Park and Soak Zone 221-222; Kennywood 26, 62; Lakemont Park & Island Waterpark 228; Sandcastle 186
Anchors Aweigh: 186
Andy Warhol Bridge: 36
Andy Warhol Museum: 19, 22, 26, 52, 122-123, 124, 136-137
antiques: 166
aquariums: Carnegie Science Center 54; PPG Aquarium 60-61
Arsenal Field: 57-58
Arsenal Park: 58
Artists Image Resource: 244
arts and crafts: 149-151
arts and entertainment: 106-146; see also Nightlife Index
Aspinwall Marina: 185
ATMs: 258

Attack Theatre: 135
Audubon Center for Native Plants: 62
August Wilson Center for African American Culture: 29

B

banks: 258
bars: 114-119
baseball: 173-175
basketball: 175, 178
Bayernhof Music Museum: 124
B-Cubed Skate Park: 199
Bear Run Nature Reserve: 220
Beaver County and Butler County: 231-234
Beechwood Farms Nature Reserve: 61-62
Benedum Center for the Performing Arts: 31, 131
Bessemer converter: 24, 49
bicycling: 21, 171-172, 250-251
Bike Pittsburgh: 250
billiards: 196
Black Sheep Puppet Festival: 144
Bloomfield and Lawrenceville: 15; Map 6 294-295
boating: 185-186
book and music shops: 151-154
botanical gardens: Phipps Conservatory and Botanical Gardens 19, 43-44; Rodef Shalom Biblical Garden 44-45
bowling: 197
Box Heart: 128
Boyce Park: 187-188, 194
Breathe Yoga Studio: 200
Brew House Space 101: 128
Bridge of Sighs: 27
Buhl Planetarium & Observatory: 54
business and entertainment hours: 251-252
bus transportation: 249
Butler County: 231-234
Byham Theater: 31, 132

C

Calvary United Methodist Church: 26, 52, 54

Car and Carriage Museum: 125
Carnegie, Andrew: 41, 238
Carnegie Library of Pittsburgh: 21, 256
Carnegie Mellon University (CMU): 39-41
Carnegie Museum of Art: 19, 22, 41-42
Carnegie Museum of Natural History: 19, 22, 42
Carnegie Music Hall: 135
Carnegie Science Center: 24, 26, 54, 137
car rentals: 250
car travel: 249-250
Cathedral of Learning: 26, 42-43
caves/caverns: 222-223, 228-229
cemetery: 57
Charity Randall Theatre: 132
Chevrolet Amphitheatre: 135-136
Children's Museum of Pittsburgh: 124-125
children's stores: 162-163
churches: see places of worship
cinema: 136-138; Andy Warhol Museum 136-137; Carnegie Science Center Omnimax Theater 24, 137; Harris Theater 22, 31, 137; Manor Theater 137; McConomy Auditorium 137-138; Melwood Screening Room 22, 138; Oaks Theater 22, 107, 138; Regent Square Theater 22, 138; Squirrel Hill Theatre 138
City Theatre: 22, 107, 132-133
Clayton: 125
climate: 235-236, 251
Climbing Wall, The: 168, 194
clothing and accessories: 154-157
Club One: 189
concert venues: 134-136; A. J. Palumbo Center 134-135; Carnegie Music Hall 135; Chevrolet Amphitheatre 135-136; Mellon Arena 136; Pepsi-Cola Roadhouse 136; Post-Gazette Pavilion 136
Critical Mass: 172
Cultural District: 19, 29-31
culture and arts: 243-246

D
dance: 135
Dance Alloy: 135
dance clubs: 113-114

Dasani Blue Bikes Program: 21, 172
day trips: see excursions (from Pittsburgh)
demographics: 242
Digging Pitt Gallery: 129
disabled access: 251
docks and marinas: 184, 185
Doughboy Square: 59
Downtown Pittsburgh: 12; Map 1 284-285
Downtown TriAnglers: 168, 184
driving: 249-250
Duquesne Dukes: 175, 178
Duquesne Incline: 24, 26, 50, 51

EF
economy: 240-241
education: 240-241
E-Fest: 141
Eliza Furnace Trail (Jail Trail): 20, 171
emergency services: 253
employment: 258-259
environmental issues: 236
excursions (from Pittsburgh): 216-234; map 218
Fallingwater: 217, 219-220
Fe Gallery: 129
festivals and events: 139-146; Black Sheep Puppet Festival 144; E-Fest 141; First Night Pittsburgh 139-140; Fourth of July 141; Hothouse 142; Johnstown Folkfest 226; Light Up Night 140; Mexican War Streets House and Garden Tour 144; Oktoberfest 144-145; Pedal Pittsburgh 140; Pennsylvania Microbrewers Fest 142; Pitt Nationality Rooms Holiday Tours 140; Pittsburgh Blues Festival 142-143; Pittsburgh Dragon Boat Festival 145; Pittsburgh Folk Festival 140-141; Pittsburgh International Children's Festival 141; Pittsburgh Irish Festival 145; Pittsburgh New Works Festival 145; Pittsburgh Three Rivers Regatta 143; Pittsburgh Triathlon and Adventure Race 143; Pittsburgh Vintage Grand Prix 143; Richard S. Caliguiri City of Pittsburgh Great Race 145-146; St. Patrick's Day Parade 141; Three Rivers Arts Festival 107, 144; Three Rivers Film Festival 146

film: 245-246
First Night Pittsburgh: 139-140
fishing: 184-185
Fitness Factory: 189
Flagstaff Hill: 45
food: see restaurants
Forbes Field: 20, 40
Forbes, John: 237
Fort Duquesne Bridge: 18
Fort Necessity National Battlefield: 220-221
Fort Pitt Blockhouse: 32
Fort Pitt Museum: 125
Foster, Stephen: 57
Fourth of July Festival: 141
Fox Chapel Yacht Club: 185
Frank & Sylvia Pasquerilla Heritage Discovery Center: 226-227
Free Ride: 172
Frick Art and Historical Center: 125
Frick Art Museum: 125
Frick Park: 56, 125
Friends of the Riverfront: 21, 172
furniture: 158-160
Future Tenant: 128

G
Galleria at Pittsburgh Mills: 128
galleries: 128, 130-131; Box Heart 128; Brew House Space 101, 128; Digging Pitt; Gallery 129; Fe Gallery 129; Future Tenant 128; Garfield Artworks 123; James Gallery 107, 128; Manchester Craftsmen's Guild 130; Mendelson 130; ModernFormations 123; Pittsburgh Center for the Arts 130, 244; Pittsburgh Glass Center 123, 130, 244; Silver Eye Center for Photography 130-131; Society for Contemporary Craft 24, 131, 244; Space 31, 131; Wood Street Galleries 107, 131
Garfield Artworks: 123
Gateway Clipper Fleet: 26, 47-48
gay and lesbian nightlife: 120-121
geography: 235-236
George Westinghouse Museum: 126
gifts: 160-161
Grandview Avenue: 18, 24, 27, 50, 51

Grandview Park: 24
gratuities: 252
greater Pittsburgh: 61-64, 214-215; Map 7 296-297
Great Meadow: 220-221
grocery stores: 97
guided and walking tours: 191-193
gyms and health clubs: 189-190

H
Harmony Historic District: 231-232
Harmony Museum: 231
Harris Theater: 22, 31, 137
Hash House Harriers: 196
health and beauty: 161-162
healthcare: 240
health clubs: 189-190
health and safety: 252-253
Heinz Field: 55
Heinz Hall: 29-30, 133
Henry Denis Ziegler log house: 232
Henry Kaufmann Building: 57
Hidden Valley Four Season Resort: 188
Highland Park: 169
hockey: 181-182
home decor: 158-160
horse racing: 182
Horseshoe Curve National Historic Landmark: 217, 227
hospitals: 253
Hothouse: 142
housing: 259

IJ
Ice Castle Arena: 187
ice skating: 187
Idlewild Park and Soak Zone: 221-222
Imperial Skatepark: 168, 199
inclines: 26, 50, 51, 228
information and services: 253-259
internet services: 254
Iron City Brewery: 59-60
James Gallery: 107, 128
Jewish Community Center (JCC): 56-57
Jimmy Stewart Museum: 221
Johnstown: 225-231
Johnstown Flood Museum: 227-228
Johnstown Folkfest: 226

Johnstown Inclined Plane: 228
Jumonville Glen: 221
Just Ducky Tours: 191

KL

kayaking: 183-184
Kayak Pittsburgh: 21, 168, 183
Kelly-Strayhorn Community Performing
    Arts Center: 133
Kennywood: 26, 62
Kentuck Knob: 220, 222
Keystone Bass Buddies: 184-185
kids' stores: 162-163
Ladbroke at the Meadows: 182
Lakemont Park & Island Waterpark: 228
Laurel Caverns: 222-223
Laurel Highlands: 219-225
lawn bowling: 196-197
Lawrenceville: see Bloomfield and
    Lawrenceville
libraries: 255-256
Light Up Night: 140
literature: 244-245
live music: 108-109, 112-113
lounges: 119-120

M

magazines: 254-255
mail service: 254
Manchester Craftsmen's Guild: 130
Manor Theater: 137
maps: 2-3, 218, 281-299
marinas: 185
Market Square: 31-32
Mattress Factory: 19, 22, 107, 126
McCall Panthers Hall of Champions: 178
McConnell's Mill State Park: 217, 232
McConomy Auditorium: 137-138
McKinley Skatepark: 199
Mellon Arena: 136
Mellon Park: 169-170
Mellon Park Tennis Center: 198
Melwood Screening Room: 22, 138
Mendelson: 130
men's clothing and accessories: 157
messenger services: 254
Mexican War Streets House and Garden
    Tour: 144

Millvale: 102
Millvale Riverfront Park: 55-56
Mr. Small's Skatepark: 199
ModernFormations: 123
Molly's Trolleys: 192
Monongahela Incline: 18, 24, 26, 50, 51
Monroeville Mall: 62-63
mosques: see places of worship
Mount Washington: 14, 18, 24, 50; Map 3
    288-289
museums: 122-128; American Jewish
    Museum 56-57; Andy Warhol Museum
    19, 22, 26, 52, 122-123, 124, 136-137;
    Bayernhof Music Museum 124; Car
    and Carriage Museum 125; Carnegie
    Museum of Art 19, 41-42; Carnegie
    Museum of Natural History 19, 42;
    Carnegie Science Center and UPMC
    SportsWorks 26, 54; Children's
    Museum of Pittsburgh 124-125; Fort
    Pitt Blockhouse 32; Fort Pitt Museum
    125; Frank & Sylvia Pasquerilla Heritage
    Discovery Center 226-227; Frick Art
    and Historical Center 125; Frick Art
    Museum 125; George Westinghouse
    Museum 126; Harmony Museum
    231; Jimmy Stewart Museum 221;
    Johnstown Flood Museum 227-228;
    Mattress Factory 19, 22, 107, 126;
    Pennsylvania Trolley Museum 126-127;
    Photo Antiquities Museum 127;
    Pittsburgh Regional History Center
    123-124; Railroaders Memorial Museum
    229; Senator John Heinz Pittsburgh
    Regional History Center 18, 26, 37-38,
    244; Soldiers and Sailors Memorial
    46-47; Tour-Ed Mine Museum 127-128;
Western Pennsylvania Sports Museum 37;
    Westmoreland Museum of American
    Art 223
music: 245

N

National Aviary: 19, 24, 54-55
Nationality Classrooms: 20, 22, 43, 140
nature reserves/wildlife sanctuaries: Bear
    Run Nature Reserve 220; Beechwood
    Farms Nature Reserve 61-62

Nego Gato: 135
Nemacolin Woodlands Resort: 188
newspapers: 254-255
nightlife: 106-121; *see also* Nightlife Index
North Shore: 19, 55-56
North Side: 14; Map 4 290-291

O

Oakland: 13; Map 2 286-287
Oakmont Yacht Club: 185
Oaks Theater: 22, 107, 138
Ohiopyle State Park: 217, 223
Oktoberfest: 144-145
Old Economy Village: 217, 232-233, 244
Oliver Bath House: 168, 194-195
Omnimax Theater at Carnegie Center: 24, 137
O'Reilly Theater (Pittsburgh Public Theater): 22, 30-31, 134
Original Oyster House: 32
Ormsby Pool: 195

P

parks: 169-170; Arsenal Park 58; Boyce Park 187-188, 194; Frick Park 56, 168, 169; Highland Park 169; McConnell's Mill State Park 217, 232; Mellon Park 169-170, 198; Millvale Riverfront Park 55-56; Ohiopyle State Park 217, 223; Point State Park 32-33; Riverview Park 61; Schenley Park 19, 26, 45, 170, 187, 195, 198; Settler's Cabin Park 194; South Park 194
Pedal Pittsburgh: 140
Penn Avenue Corridor: 19, 21, 123
Penn's Cave: 228-229
Pennsylvania Fish and Boat Commission: 185
Pennsylvania Microbrewers Fest: 142
Pennsylvania National Bank: 59
Pennsylvania Trolley Museum: 126-127
Pepsi-Cola Roadhouse: 136
pet supplies and grooming: 163
pharmacies: 253
Phipps Conservatory and Botanical Gardens: 19, 43-44
phones: 253-254
Photo Antiquities Museum: 127

pinball: 197
Pitt Nationality Rooms Holiday Tours: 140
Pitt Panthers: 178
Pittsburgh Blues Festival: 142-143
Pittsburgh Boat Show: 186
Pittsburgh Center for the Arts: 130, 244
Pittsburgh City Paper: 19, 21, 90, 254
Pittsburgh Dragon Boat Festival: 145
Pittsburgh Folk Festival: 140-141
Pittsburgh Glass Center: 123, 130, 244
Pittsburgh Grotto: 194
Pittsburgh Harlequins Rugby Football Club: 182-183
Pittsburgh History and Landmark Foundation Tours: 192
Pittsburgh International Airport: 247
Pittsburgh International Children's Festival: 141
Pittsburgh Irish Festival: 145
Pittsburgh Neighborhood Tours: 192
Pittsburgh New Works Festival: 145
Pittsburgh Passion: 178-179
Pittsburgh Penguins: 181-182
Pittsburgh Pirates: 173-175
Pittsburgh Playhouse: 22, 134
Pittsburgh Post-Gazette: 21, 254
Pittsburgh Public Theater (O'Reilly Theater): 22, 30-31, 134
Pittsburgh Regional History Center: 123-124
Pittsburgh Steelers: 179-181
Pittsburgh Step Trek: 48
Pittsburgh Three Rivers Regatta: 143
Pittsburgh Triathlon and Adventure Race: 143
Pittsburgh Vintage Grand Prix: 143
Pittsburgh Walking: 192-193
Pittsburgh Xplosion: 178
Pittsburgh Zoo: 60-61
places of worship: 256-258
PNC Park: 55
PNC Park Tours: 193
Point Breeze: *see* Squirrel Hill and Point Breeze
Point State Park: 18, 32-33
Polish Hill Bowl: 200
postal service: 254
Post-Gazette Pavilion: 136

PPG Aquarium: 60-61
PPG Place: 32, 33-35, 168, 187
Primanti Brothers: 32
Prime Outlets: 233
Purnell Center for the Arts: 22, 40

QR

Quantum Theatre: 132
queer nightlife: 120-121
Rachel Carson Bridge: 36, 37
radio: 255
Railroaders Memorial Museum: 229
Railroad Strike of 1877: 237
rail travel: 248-249
Rangos Omnimax Theater: 54
Regent Square Theater: 22, 138
relocating: 258
restaurants: 65-105; Aloona, State
     College, and Johnstown 223-224, 229;
     Beaver County and Butler County 233;
     Bloomfield and Lawrenceville 101-105;
     Downtown 67, 69-71; Laurel Highlands
     223-224; Mount Washington 87-89;
     North Side 89-90; Oakland 75-79;
     Shadyside 90-95; Sharpsburg 77;
     South Side 80-86; Squirrel Hill and
     Point Breeze 96, 98-101; Strip District
     71-74; see also Restaurant Index
Richard S. Caliguiri City of Pittsburgh
     Great Race: 145-146
Rink at PPG Place: 168, 187
Rivers of Steel Heritage Tours: 193
Riverview Park: 61
Roberto Clemente Bridge: 36-37
Robotics Institute: 40
rock & bowl: 197
Rodef Shalom Biblical Garden: 44-45
rowing: 183-184
rugby: 182-183
Ruggers Pub: 183
running club: 196

S

Safe Boating Council: 186
Sandcastle: 186
Schenley Park: 19, 20, 26, 45, 170
Schenley Park Pool: 195
Schenley Park Skating Rink: 187
Schenley Park Tennis Courts: 198
Schenley Plaza: 45-46
Schoolhouse Yoga: 200
Segway in Paradise: 193
Senator John Heinz Pittsburgh Regional
     History Center: 18, 26, 37-38, 244
Settler's Cabin Park: 194
Seven Springs Mountain Resort: 168, 188
Sewickley: 150
Sewickley Valley YMCA: 150
Shadyside: 14; Map 5 292-293
Sharpsburg: 77
shoe stores: 164
shopping: 147-166; see also Shops Index
shopping centers: 164-166
sights: 25-64; Altoona, State College, and
     Johnstown 226-229; Beaver County
     and Butler County 231-233; Bloomfield
     and Lawrenceville 57-61; Downtown
     27, 29-37; Greater Pittsburgh 61-64;
     Laurel Highlands 219-223; Mount
     Washington 14, 18, 24, 50; North Side
     52, 54-56; Oakland 39-47; South Side
     47-49; Squirrel Hill and Point Breeze
     56-57; Strip District 37-39; see also
     specific place; sight
Silver Eye Center for Photography: 130-131
16:62 Design Zone: 129
skateboarding: 199-200
skiing: 187-188
Smithfield Street Bridge: 35
smoking: 73, 252
snowboarding: 187-188
snowmobiling: 187
Snozone: 188
Society for Contemporary Craft: 24, 131,
     244
Soldiers and Sailors Memorial: 46-47
South Park: 194
South Side: 13; Map 3 288-289
South Side Athletic Club: 189
South Side Riverfront Park: 185
South Side Slopes: 26, 48
SPACE: 31, 131
spectator sports: 173-175, 178-183
sports celebrities: 176-177
Squirrel Hill and Point Breeze: 15; Map 5
     292-293

Squirrel Hill Theatre: 138
Squonk Opera: 132
St. Anthony's Chapel: 63-64
State College: 225-231
Station Square: 18, 48-49
Station Square Marina: 185
Still Mountain Tai Chi and Chi Kung: 200-201
St. Michael's Rectory: 48
St. Nicholas Croatian Catholic Church: 64
St. Patrick's Church: 38-39
St. Patrick's Day Parade: 141
St. Paul Cathedral: 47
St. Paul of the Cross Retreat Center: 48
Strip District: 12, 18; Map 1 284-285
Sweetwater Center for the Arts: 150
swimming pools, public: 194-195
synagogues: see places of worship

T
taxis: 248, 250
technology: 241
television: 245-246, 255
temples: see places of worship
tennis: 195, 198-199
theater: 131-134; Benedum Center for the
    Performing Arts 31, 131; Byham Theater
    31, 132; Charity Randall Theatre 132;
    City Theatre 22, 107, 132-133; Heinz
    Hall 133; Kelly-Strayhorn Community
    Performing Arts Center 133; O'Reilly
    Theater (Pittsburgh Public Theater)
    22, 134; Pittsburgh Playhouse 22, 134;
    Purnell Center for the Arts 22, 40;
    Quantum Theatre 132; Squonk Opera
    132; Zany Umbrella Circus 134
This is Happening: 21
Three Rivers Arts Festival: 107, 144
Three Rivers Film Festival: 146
Three Rivers Heritage Trail: 19, 20, 55-56,
    171, 251
Three Rivers Rowing Association: 183-184

Three Sisters: 19, 35-37
tipping: 252
Tour-Ed Mine Museum: 127-128
tours, guided and walking: 191-193
trails: 171
train transportation: 248-249
transportation: 247-251; bus routes
    298-299

UVWXYZ
ultimate frisbee: 197
UMOJA African Arts Company: 135
University Art Gallery: 20
University of Pittsburgh: 42-43
UPMC SportsWorks: 26, 54
vegan restaurants: 81
Venture Outdoors: 183, 184
Vygor Fitness and Nutrition: 189-190
Wagner-Bentel House: 231-232
walking tours: 191-193
Warhol, Andy: 53
Washington's Landing Marina: 185
Washington's Landing Tennis Courts:
    198-199
water activities: 183-186
water park: 186
wave pools: 194
weather: 235-236, 251
Western Pennsylvania Sports Museum: 37
Westmoreland Museum of American Art:
    223
winter recreation: 187-188
women's clothing and accessories: 154-157
Wood Street Galleries: 107, 131
World Pinball Championships: 197
X Shadyside: 190
yachting and boating: 185-186
YMCA: 190
yoga and meditation: 200-201
Zany Umbrella Circus: 134
zoo: 60-61

Restaurants Index

Abay Ethiopian Cuisine: 81, 94
Abruzzi's: 84
Aladdin's Eatery: 100-101
Ali Baba: 79
Aspinwall Grille: 77
Azul Bar y Cantina: 91
Beehive: 21, 23, 82-83
B and J Coney Island: 233
Bloomfield Bridge Tavern: 20, 68, 105
Bona Terra: 77
Bruschetta's: 84-85
Buffalo Blues: 90-91
Cafe Allegro: 83
Cafe du Jour: 83-84
Cafe on Main: 77
Cafe Zao: 19, 70
Cafe Zinho: 94
Cambod-Ican Kitchen: 82
Casablanca Bistro: 70
Casbah: 81, 94-95
CC's: 77
Chaya Japanese Cuisine: 98
Chocolate Celebrations and The
   Milkshake Factory: 85
Chocolate Moose, The: 95
Church Brew Works, The: 23, 110
Cliffside Restaurant: 88
Club Sandwich & Deli: 77
COCA Café: 66, 102-103, 129
Coffee Tree Roasters (Shadyside): 93
Coffee Tree Roasters (Squirrel Hill and
   Point Breeze): 99
Common Plea Restaurant: 67
Cozumel: 95
Crazy Mocha (Bloomfield): 66, 103
Crazy Mocha (Shadyside): 93-94
Dave and Andy's: 79
Del's Bar & Ristorante Delpizzo: 104
DeLuca's Restaurant: 18, 24, 66, 71-72
Dish: 84
D's Six-Pax and Dogs: 66, 96
East End Food Co-op: 81, 96, 97
Eleven: 74
Fat Heads: 18, 23, 80
Franco's Ristorante: 91

Franktuary: 67
Fuel and Fuddle: 20, 75
Georgetowne Inn: 87
Girasole: 94
Gran Canal Caffe: 77
Grand Concourse: 18, 24, 66, 80-81
Grandview Saloon: 24, 66, 87-88
Grasso Roberto: 105
Gullifty's: 96
Gypsy Café: 85
Harris Grill: 91-92
Hemingway's: 75
Hunan Kitchen: 81, 98
Ibiza Tapas and Wine Bar: 86
India Garden: 20, 77-78
Jean-Marc Chatellier: 102
Kaufman House: 233
Kaya: 74, 81
Kazansky's Delicatessen: 96, 98
Kiva Han: 76, 81
Klavon's Ice Cream Parlor: 24, 74
La Feria: 95
La Prima Espresso Company: 24, 73-74
Lemon Grass Café: 69
Lemont Restaurant: 88
Le Pommier: 84
Ligonier Tavern: 223-224
Lucca: 78
Lulu's Noodles: 75-76
Luma: 77
Mad Mex: 20, 78, 81
Madonna's Restaurant: 70
Main Moon Restaurant: 224
Mallorca: 86
Map Room: 98
Mel's Restaurant and Bar: 229
Milky Way: 100
Mineo's: 100
Monterey Bay Fish Grotto: 88-89
Nakama Japanese Steak House: 82
Nine on Nine: 70
North Country Brewing Company: 233
Oishii Bento: 76
Opus: 71
Original Fish Market: 71

Original Hot Dog Shop: 79
Original Oyster House: 67, 69
Outback Steakhouse PNC Park: 19, 89
Paddy Cake Bakery: 105
Pamela's Diner: 18, 66, 72
Penn Brewery: 23, 90
People's Indian Restaurant: 20, 104
Piccolo Forno: 129
Pierogies Plus: 68
Pittsburgh Deli Company: 92
Pizza Italia: 20, 104-105
Pizza Vesuvio: 85
Point Brugge Café: 66, 100
Prantl's Bakery: 95
Pretzel Shop, The: 86
Primanti Brothers: 21, 23, 68, 72
Quiet Storm, The: 81, 103
Ray's Marlin Beach Bar & Grill: 101
River Moon Café: 103-104
Roland's Seafood Grill: 66, 72-73
Rose Tea Café: 101
Ruthie's Diner: 224
Sewickley Cafe: 150
Sewickley Hotel: 150
Six Penn Kitchen: 24, 71
61C Café: 99
Soba: 81, 92
Spice Island Tea House: 66, 76
Square Café, The: 98

Sree's Indian Food: 20, 69
Star of India: 78
Sukhothai: 69
Summit Diner: 229
Sushi Boat: 76
Sushi Kim: 24, 73
Sushi Too: 92
Sweet Basil & La Filipiniana: 99
Taco Loco: 85
Taj Mahal: 20, 91
Tango Café: 99
Tap Room: 69
Taste of India: 104
Tazza D'Oro: 91
Tessaro's: 24, 101
Thai Cuisine: 102
Thai Me Up: 82
Thai Place Café: 92-93
Tin Angel, The: 88
Tram's Kitchen: 102
Typhoon: 93
Umi: 81, 93
Union Grill: 75
Vincent's of Greentree: 91
Wheel Deliver: 90
Wilson's Bar-B-Q: 89
Zarra's: 78
Zenith, The: 66, 81

Nightlife Index

Altar Bar: 111
Bar 11: 114
Bash: 113
Bloomfield Bridge Tavern: 20, 23, 114
Brillobox: 23, 108
Cefalo's Restaurant & Nightclub: 111
Charlie Murdock's: 110-111
Church Brew Works: 110
Club Café: 19, 107, 109
Club Havana: 119
Club Zoo: 109
Dee's Café: 18, 20, 23, 114
Dejavu Lounge: 107, 119-120
Doc's Place: 114-115

Donnie's Place: 120-121
Dowe's on 9th: 109
Firehouse Lounge: 120
5801 Video Lounge & Café: 121
Garfield Artworks: 109
Gooski's: 20, 23, 107, 115
Jack's Bar: 20, 23, 115-116
Kelly's Bar: 23, 116
Lava Lounge: 23, 116
Matrix: 113-114
ModernFormations Gallery: 109, 112
Moondog's: 112
Mr. Roboto Project: 112
Mr. Smalls Theatre: 110, 112-113

Mulaney's Harp & Fiddle: 116
Pegasus: 121
Peter's Pub: 21, 116
Piper's Pub: 20, 23, 116-117
Pittsburgh Eagle: 121
Priory, The: 111
Redbeard's: 117
Red Room: 120
Rex Theatre: 113
Saddle Ridge: 114
Shadow Lounge: 120
Sharp Edge Beer Emporium: 20, 23, 117

Side Kicks: 121
Silky's Sports Bar & Grill: 23, 117-118
Smiling Moose, The: 20, 118
Smokin' Joe's: 23, 118
Sphinx Cafe: 111
Squirrel Hill Café: 23, 118
31st Street Pub: 113
Thunderbird Café: 118
Tiki Lounge: 23, 119
Union Project, The: 111
Z Lounge: 23, 120

Shops Index

Avalon: 166
Babyland: 162-163
Bailey & Bailey: 150, 154-155
B & B Studio: 149
Bead Mine, The: 149
Big Idea Infoshop: 151
Bombshell Boutique: 155
Bow Wow Doggie Daycare: 163
Caesars: 155
Caliban Bookshop: 151
Charles Spiegel for Men/The Garage: 148, 158
Cheryl W: 155
Choices: 155
Cosmetique Destefino's: 161
Culture Shop: 18, 160
Dean of Shadyside: 161-162
East End Food Co-op: 96, 97
eb Pepper: 155-156
E House: 18, 160
Eide's Entertainment: 151-152
Emphatics: 148, 156
Eons: 166
Essensia Day Spa: 162
Exchange, The: 152
Foodland: 97
Footloose: 164
Galleria, The: 164-165
Giant Eagle: 97
Golden Bone Pet Resort: 163
Hot Haute Hote: 24, 158

Irish Design Center: 149
Jay's Bookstall: 152
Jerry's Records: 152
Joseph-Beth Booksellers: 22, 148, 153
Kards Unlimited: 148, 160
Knit One: 149
Littles: 164
Lotus Food Co.: 97
MaxAlto: 148, 156
MCN Salon: 162
Miller's Antique Mall: 165
Moda: 158
Paul's CDs: 153
Pavement Shoes: 129
Pennsylvania Macaroni Company: 97
perfect: 150, 156
Perlora: 159
Pittsburgh Center for the Arts: 150-151
Pittsburgh Jeans Company: 18, 156-157
Pleasant Present, A: 160-161
Pursuits: 157
Record Village: 153
REI: 194
Scavenger's Antiques and Collectibles: 129
720 Records: 148, 153-154
Sewickley Spa: 148, 162
Shop 'n Save: 97
Shur Save: 97
Smiley's: 163
SouthSide Works: 18, 22, 148, 165

Store at the Society for Contemporary Craft, The: 151
Sugar Boutique: 129
Ten Thousand Villages: 161
Ten Toes: 164
Thriftique: 148, 166
Time Bomb: 158
Tots & Tweeds: 163
Trader Jack's: 165

Trader Joe's: 97
University of Pittsburgh Book Center: 154
Waterfront, The: 165-166
Watermelon Blues: 161
Weiss House: 159
Whole Foods Market: 97
Wholley's Market: 97
Who New?: 129, 159-160

Accommodations Index

Allegheny YMCA: 204
Appletree Inn: 212-213
Arbors Bed & Breakfast: 214
Conley Resort: 233
Copper Penny Manor B&B: 233-234
Courtyard Marriott Downtown: 205-206
Courtyard Marriott Shadyside: 213
Doubletree Hotel Pittsburgh City Center: 206
Family House: 208
Forbes Avenue Suites: 208-209
Hampton Inn University Center: 207
Hilton Pittsburgh: 204
Holiday Inn Express Hotel & Suites: 209-210
Holiday Inn Select at University Center: 209
Homestead Retreat and Guesthouse: 230
House of Zen Guest House: 212
Hyatt Regency Pittsburgh International Airport: 215
Inn at Oakmont, The: 215
Inn at 714 Negley, The: 213-214

Inn on the Mexican War Streets: 203, 211
Lodge at Chalk Hill: 224
Majestic World Lodge and Retreat: 229
Marriott Springhill Suites: 211
Morning Glory Inn: 210
Nemacolin Woodlands: 224
Omni William Penn: 203, 204-205
Parador: 203, 211
Pittsburgh Marriott City Center: 205
Priory, The: 212
Quality Inn University Center: 208
Renaissance Pittsburgh Hotel: 203, 206
Residence Inn Marriott: 209
Sewickley Country Inn: 214
Shadyside Inn & Suites: 207
Sheraton Hotel Station Square: 210
Stone House Inn: 224
Stone Ridge Bed & Breakfast: 230
Sunnyledge Boutique Hotel: 203, 214
Westin Convention Center Pittsburgh: 205
Willows Inn: 234
Wyndham Garden Hotel: 209

Acknowledgments

It's difficult for me to know exactly who to thank on this page, especially considering the fact that it took the better part of a year for *Moon Pittsburgh* to finally reach its completion. A large number of talented people participated in bringing this project to life, but I suppose it would only be logical to begin by giving a very sincere thanks to Rebecca Browning, Avalon Travel Publishing's acquisitions manager who brought me on board in the first place. Without her faith in my abilities as both a writer and a reporter, I wouldn't be penning these words now. Thanks also to Avalon editors Grace Fujimoto and Erin Raber, both of whom added considerably to the quality of my often-awkward prose. An especially warm thanks goes out to the woman who is most certainly Avalon's kindest and most empathetic employee, production coordinator Elizabeth Jang. I've truly enjoyed our conversations and I hope they'll continue even when we're no longer working together.

So many of my friends and acquaintances assisted with the creation of this book. Sarah Krier was undoubtedly one of the most pivotal; she was largely responsible for encouraging me to pursue this project in the first place. Sarah also proofed my original proposal with a scholar's eye and even allowed me to temporarily turn her walk-in closet into an office. Thanks to Fabian Bautista,

whose beautiful photos grace many of the pages of this book, and to Michael Walsh of 3 Design Group, a native Pittsburgher who offered priceless assistance on the shopping and restaurants chapters. A very special thanks goes out to Mara Rago, an especially talented photographer whose images are also seen throughout this book, including on its cover. Thanks to the very clever Kathryn Bursick, who gave this guide one of its very first copy edits.

To my parents, whose willingness to assist with this project went well above and beyond the call of duty. I thank you from the bottom of my heart. Your examples of love, patience, and forgiveness will always be an inspiration to me.

My most passionate and ardent thanks, however, go to the most intriguing and stunningly gorgeous Pittsburgher I know, Carrie Ann. Without her constant stream of practical advice, her sense of good humor, her technological know-how, her artistic genius, her near-exhaustive generosity, her car, her computer, and most importantly, her love, my life during the research and writing phases of this project would have undoubtedly amounted to little more than a simple disaster. I consider myself unbelievably lucky that you've entered my life, Carrie. I'm not entirely sure I deserve you, but I love you with all my heart, just the same.

Photo Credits

www.moon.com

For helpful advice on planning a trip, visit www.moon.com for the **TRAVEL PLANNER** and get access to useful travel strategies and valuable information about great places to visit. When you travel with Moon, expect an experience that is uncommon and truly unique.

HANDBOOKS | METRO | OUTDOORS | LIVING ABROAD

CONVERSION TABLES

°C = (°F - 32) / 1.8
°F = (°C x 1.8) + 32
1 inch = 2.54 centimeters (cm)
1 foot = 0.304 meters (m)
1 yard = 0.914 meters
1 mile = 1.6093 kilometers (km)
1 km = 0.6214 miles
1 fathom = 1.8288 m
1 chain = 20.1168 m
1 furlong = 201.168 m
1 acre = 0.4047 hectares
1 sq km = 100 hectares
1 sq mile = 2.59 square km
1 ounce = 28.35 grams
1 pound = 0.4536 kilograms
1 short ton = 0.90718 metric ton
1 short ton = 2,000 pounds
1 long ton = 1.016 metric tons
1 long ton = 2,240 pounds
1 metric ton = 1,000 kilograms
1 quart = 0.94635 liters
1 US gallon = 3.7854 liters
1 Imperial gallon = 4.5459 liters
1 nautical mile = 1.852 km

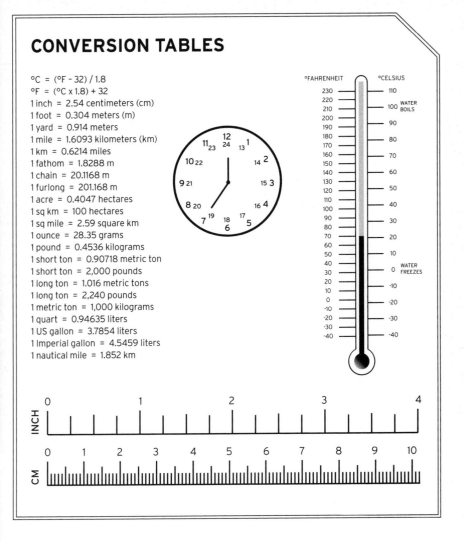

MOON PITTSBURGH

Avalon Travel Publishing
1400 65th Street, Suite 250
Emeryville, CA 94608, USA
www.moon.com

Editors: Grace Fujimoto, Erin Raber
Series Manager: Kathryn Ettinger
Acquisitions Manager: Rebecca K. Browning
Copy Editor: Marisa Solís
Graphics Coordinator: Elizabeth Jang
Cover Designer: Elizabeth Jang
Production Coordinator: Darren Alessi
Map Editor: Kevin Anglin
Cartographer: Suzanne Service
Cartography Director: Mike Morgenfeld
Proofreader: Ellie Behrstock
Indexer: Greg Jewett

ISBN-10: 1-59880-042-6
ISBN-13: 978-1-59880-042-5
ISSN: 1936-4911

Printing History
1st Edition – June 2007
5 4 3 2 1

Front cover photo: *Mr. Dig*, by Glennis McClellan, copyright 2003, Carnegie Museum of Natural History, *DinoMite Days* ®, Pittsburgh, Pennsylvania. *Mr. Dig* is owned by The Hillman Company, and is on display at PPG Place, Pittsburgh, PA. Photo by Mara Rago.

Title page: *The Two Andys* by Tom Mosser and Sarah Zeffiro, a 2005 Sprout Public Art community mural at 628 Smithfield Street in Downtown Pittsburgh. Photo by Tom Mosser.

Printed in the United States by Worzalla

KEEPING CURRENT

If you have a favorite gem you'd like to see included in the next edition, or see anything that needs updating, clarification, or correction, please drop us a line. Send your comments via email to feedback@moon.com, or use the address above.

MAPS

Pittsburgh Map Index 282-283

Map 1: Downtown and Strip District 284-285

Map 2: Oakland 286-287

Map 3: South Side and Mount Washington 288-289

Map 4: North Side 290-291

Map 5: Shadyside, Point Breeze, and Squirrel Hill 292-293

Map 6: Bloomfield and Lawrenceville 294-295

Map 7: Greater Pittsburgh 296-297

Pittsburgh Bus Routes 298-299

=====	Expressway	**(**	Highlight	✈	Airport
=====	Primary Road	○	City/Town	▲	Mountain
=====	Secondary Road	◉	State Capital	✦	Unique Natural Feature
= = = = =	Unpaved Road	✸	National Capital		
- - - - -	Trail	★	Point of Interest	♠	Park
• • • • •	Ferry	•	Accommodation	⌁	Golf Course
⌑-⌑-⌑	Railroad	▼	Restaurant/Bar	**P**	Parking Area
▥▥▥▥▥	Pedestrian Walkway	■	Other Location	⌂	Church

6

MORNINGSIDE

River

BUTLER ST

Highland
Park

STENTON

STANTON
HEIGHTS

WASHINGTON BLVD

Allegheny

Cemetery

8

NEGLEY AVE

LINCOLN AVE

PENN AVE

EAST
LIBERTY

FRIENDSHIP

BLOOMFIELD **2**

5

BAUM BLVD

FRANKSTOWN AVE

SHADYSIDE

POINT
BREEZE

N BRADDOCK AVE

5TH AVE

8

FORBES AVE

WILKINS AVE

DALLAS AVE

CENTRAL
OAKLAND

Schenley

FORBES AVE

SQUIRREL HILL

Frick

Park

HOBART ST

REGENT
SQUARE

Park

376 22 30

S BRADDOCK AVE

HAZELWOOD AVE

WEST
HOMESTEAD

River

Monongahela

E 8TH AVE

837

28

130

◆ SIGHTS

12 ST. PATRICK'S CHURCH
24 THE THREE SISTERS
30 ◉ SENATOR JOHN HEINZ PITTSBURGH REGIONAL HISTORY CENTER
46 AUGUST WILSON CENTER FOR AFRICAN AMERICAN CULTURE
53 POINT STATE PARK
54 FORT PITT MUSEUM
57 PPG PLACE
59 MARKET SQUARE
73 ALLEGHENY COUNTY COURTHOUSE
77 SMITHFIELD STREET BRIDGE

◆ SHOPPING AND RECREATION

2 MOLLY'S TROLLEYS
5 BOW WOW DOGGIE DAYCARE
6 THE POLISH HILL BOWL
8 SCHOOLHOUSE YOGA
11 THE STORE AT THE SOCIETY FOR CONTEMPORARY CRAFT
18 HOT HAUTE HOT
26 MCN SALON
28 EIDE'S ENTERTAINMENT
56 THE RINK AT PPG PLACE
61 DOWNTOWN TRIANGLERS - VENTURE OUTDOORS
68 PITTSBURGH PENGUINS
69 YMCA
72 ◉ EMPHATICS
75 DUQUESNE DUKES
78 ELIZA FURNACE TRAIL

◆ ACCOMMODATIONS

34 ◉ RENAISSANCE PITTSBURGH HOTEL
38 COURTYARD MARRIOTT DOWNTOWN
48 WESTIN CONVENTION CENTER PITTSBURGH
55 HILTON PITTSBURGH
63 ◉ OMNI WILLIAM PENN
65 DOUBLETREE HOTEL PITTSBURGH CITY CENTER
66 PITTSBURGH MARRIOTT CITY CENTER

◆ RESTAURANTS

4 KLAVON'S ICE CREAM PARLOR
13 KAYA
14 ◉ PAMELA'S DINER
15 ◉ DELUCA'S RESTAURANT
16 LA PRIMA ESPRESSO COMPANY
21 PRIMANTI BROTHERS
22 ◉ ROLAND'S SEAFOOD GRILL
27 ELEVEN
29 SUSHI KIM
31 LEMON GRASS CAFÉ
33 OPUS
35 SIX PENN KITCHEN
37 CAFE ZAO
39 CASABLANCA BISTRO
43 NINE ON NINE
47 ORIGINAL FISH MARKET
52 SREE'S INDIAN FOOD
58 PRIMANTI BROTHERS
60 ORIGINAL OYSTER HOUSE
62 FRANKTUARY
64 TAP ROOM
70 MADONNA'S RESTAURANT
71 SUKHOTHAI
74 COMMON PLEA RESTAURANT

◆ ARTS AND ENTERTAINMENT

1 31ST STREET PUB
3 DONNIE'S PLACE
7 ◉ GOOSKI'S
9 MULLANEY'S HARP & FIDDLE
10 SOCIETY FOR CONTEMPORARY CRAFT
17 ◉ DEJAVU LOUNGE
19 FIREHOUSE LOUNGE
20 BASH
23 CLUB ZOO
25 DOWE'S ON 9TH
32 BYHAM THEATER
36 O'REILLY THEATER (PITTSBURGH PUBLIC THEATER)
40 HEINZ HALL
41 BENEDUM CENTER
42 HARRIS THEATER
44 FUTURE TENANT
45 SIDE KICKS
49 ◉ WOOD STREET GALLERIES
50 SPACE
51 PEGASUS
67 MELLON ARENA
76 A J PALUMBO CENTER

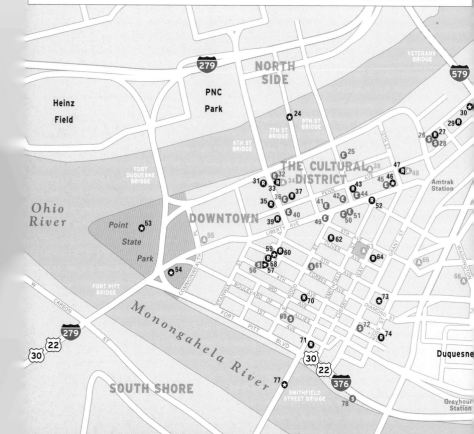

✪ SIGHTS

- **5** ST. PAUL CATHEDRAL
- **15** RODEF SHALOM BIBLICAL BOTANICAL GARDEN
- **18** SOLDIERS AND SAILORS MEMORIAL
- **21** ◖ CATHEDRAL OF LEARNING
- **22** SCHENLEY PLAZA
- **23** CARNEGIE MUSEUM OF ART/ CARNEGIE MUSEUM OF NATURAL HISTORY
- **25** CARNEGIE MELLON UNIVERSITY
- **42** PHIPPS CONSERVATORY AND BOTANICAL GARDENS
- **43** ◖ SCHENLEY PARK AND FLAGSTAFF HILL

◗ RESTAURANTS

- **3** ZARRA'S
- **8** LULU'S NOODLES
- **9** ALI BABA
- **11** STAR OF INDIA
- **12** KIVA HAN (CRAIG STREET)
- **13** LUCCA
- **14** UNION GRILL
- **30** SUSHI BOAT
- **31** OISHII BENTO
- **32** HEMINGWAY'S
- **33** THE ORIGINAL HOT DOG SHOP
- **34** KIVA HAN (FORBES AVENUE)
- **35** DAVE AND ANDY'S
- **36** FUEL AND FUDDLE
- **37** ◖ SPICE ISLAND TEA HOUSE
- **40** INDIA GARDEN
- **41** MAD MEX

◉ ARTS AND ENTERTAINMENT

- **1** MELWOOD SCREENING ROOM
- **16** PETERSEN EVENTS CENTER
- **20** CHARITY RANDALL THEATRE
- **24** CARNEGIE MUSIC HALL
- **26** MCCONOMY AUDITORIUM
- **29** PETER'S PUB
- **45** PITTSBURGH PLAYHOUSE

◎ SHOPPING AND RECREATION

- **6** IRISH DESIGN CENTER
- **7** WATERMELON BLUES
- **10** CALIBAN BOOKSHOP
- **17** PITT PANTHERS/ PITTSBURGH XPLOSION
- **19** UNIVERSITY OF PITTSBURGH BOOK CENTER
- **27** JAY'S BOOKSTALL
- **28** AVALON
- **47** SCHENLEY PARK POOL
- **48** SCHENLEY PARK TENNIS COURTS AND SKATING RINK

◔ ACCOMMODATIONS

- **2** RESIDENCE INN MARRIOTT
- **4** HOLIDAY INN SELECT AT UNIVERSITY CENTER
- **38** FORBES AVENUE SUITES
- **39** WYNDHAM GARDEN HOTEL
- **44** HAMPTON INN UNIVERSITY CENTER
- **46** QUALITY INN UNIVERSITY CENTER

UPPER HILL

NORTH OAKLAND

University

of

Pittsburgh

WEST OAKLAND

CENTRAL OAKLAND

SOUTH OAKLAND

0   0.2 mi

0   0.2 km

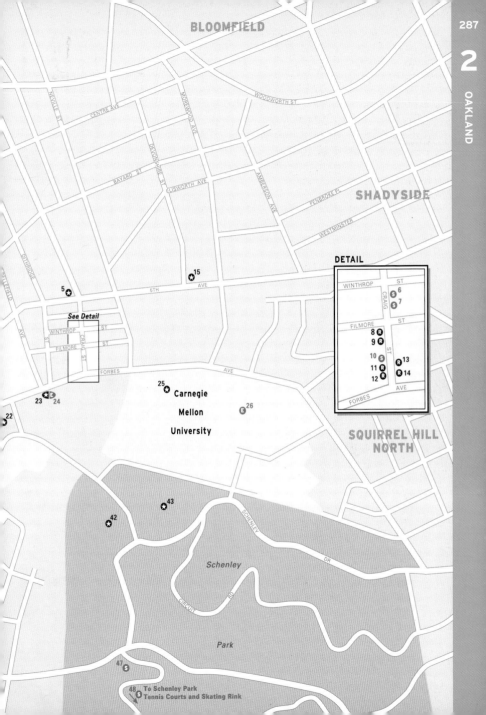

BLOOMFIELD

SHADYSIDE

SQUIRREL HILL
NORTH

WOODWORTH ST

NEVILLE ST

CENTRE AVE

MORENOOD AVE

DEVONSHIRE ST

BAYARD ST

ELLSWORTH AVE

ANDERSON AVE

PENBROKE PL

WESTMINSTER

DITHRIDGE ST

5TH AVE

15

5

See Detail

WINTHROP ST

FILMORE ST

CRAIG ST

FORBES AVE

25 Carnegie

Mellon

University

26

23 24

22

43

42

Schenley

SCHENLEY DR

Park

CHICON RD

47

48 To Schenley Park
Tennis Courts and Skating Rink

DETAIL

WINTHROP ST

CRAIG ST

6

7

FILMORE ST

8

9

10

11

12

13

14

FORBES AVE

◆ SIGHTS

3 THE DUQUESNE INCLINE	**16** THE MONONGAHELA INCLINE
9 GATEWAY CLIPPER FLEET	**68** SOUTH SIDE SLOPES
14 STATION SQUARE	

● RESTAURANTS

1 MONTEREY BAY FISH GROTTO	**40** CAMBOD-ICAN KITCHEN
2 GEORGETOWNE INN	**42** CHOCOLATE CELEBRATIONS AND THE MILKSHAKE FACTORY
4 GRANDVIEW SALOON	
5 CLIFFSIDE RESTAURANT	**44** FAT HEADS
6 THE TIN ANGEL	**46** BRUSCHETTA'S
7 LEMONT RESTAURANT	**47** THAI ME UP
13 GRAND CONCOURSE	**51** LE POMMIER
20 ABRUZZI'S	**57** IBIZA TAPAS AND WINE BAR
25 CAFE DU JOUR	**58** MALLORCA
29 CAFE ALLEGRO	**59** THE PRETZEL SHOP
31 GYPSY CAFÉ	**62** DISH
34 BEEHIVE	**65** THE ZENITH
35 PIZZA VESUVIO	**66** TACO LOCO
39 NAKAMA JAPANESE STEAK HOUSE	

● ARTS AND ENTERTAINMENT

8 CHEVROLET AMPHITHEATRE	**33** DEE'S CAFÉ
15 REDBEARD'S	**38** REX THEATRE
17 SADDLE RIDGE	**45** PIPER'S PUB
18 MATRIX	**49** SMOKIN' JOE'S
24 SILVER EYE CENTER FOR PHOTOGRAPHY	**50** TIKI LOUNGE
27 JACK'S BAR	**52** Z LOUNGE
28 CLUB CAFÉ	**54** LAVA LOUNGE
30 CITY THEATRE	**61** BAR 11
32 THE SMILING MOOSE	**63** BREW HOUSE SPACE 101

● SHOPPING AND RECREATION

11 JUST DUCKY TOURS	**41** THE BEAD MINE
12 PITTSBURGH HISTORY AND LANDMARKS FOUNDATION TOURS	**43** THE EXCHANGE
	48 SOUTH SIDE ATHLETIC CLUB
19 DASANI BLUE BIKES PROGRAM	**53** ORMSBY POOL
22 OLIVER BATH HOUSE	**55** PERLORA
23 PITTSBURGH PASSION	**56** PITTSBURGH JEANS COMPANY
26 BREATHE YOGA STUDIO	**60** RUGGERS PUB
36 E HOUSE	**67** JOSEPH-BETH BOOKSELLERS/ SOUTHSIDE WORKS
37 CULTURE SHOP	

○ ACCOMMODATIONS

10 SHERATON HOTEL STATION SQUARE	**64** MORNING GLORY INN
21 HOLIDAY INN EXPRESS HOTEL & SUITES	

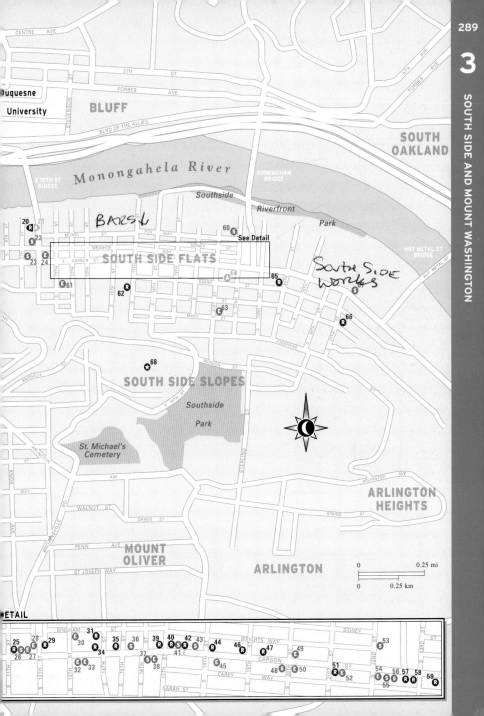

W JEFFERSON ST

ARMANDALE ST

GARFIELD

KATURY WAY

MONTEREY

ALPINE AVE

JACKSONIA ST

SIBERIAN

VETO ST

BUENA VISTA ST

RESACA PL

ARCH ST

HAZLIP

BOYLE

LORAINE

WAY

PARKHURS

SAMPSONIA WAY

2 **E** N TAYLOR AVE

ALTO ST

NORTH SIDE

1 **R**

PENNSYLVANIA AVE

ELOISE ST

ALLEGHENY WEST

4 5 W NORTH AVE

ST

BEHAN

BRIGHTON

MONTGOMERY

COMMONS

NORTH

National

SHERIDAN AVE

BUTTERCUP

4 **4**

GALVESTON

WAY

AVE

ROPE

Aviary

7 **E** 7

BEECH

WAY

6 **6**

DOUNTON

AVE

WAY

W

OHIO

ST

WESTERN

WAY

West

ALLEGHENY

3 **3**

MAOLIS

AVE

LINCOLN

AVE

Park

CENTER

N

AVE

RIDGE

65

I 279

W GENERAL ROBINSON S

15 **S**
PNC Park

11 **S** Heinz Field

NORTH SHORE

STEELER WAY

12 **E**

13 **★**

DR

NORTH   SHORE

14 **14**

Allegheny

0   0.2 mi

FORT
DUQUESNE
BRIDGE

River

0   0.2 km

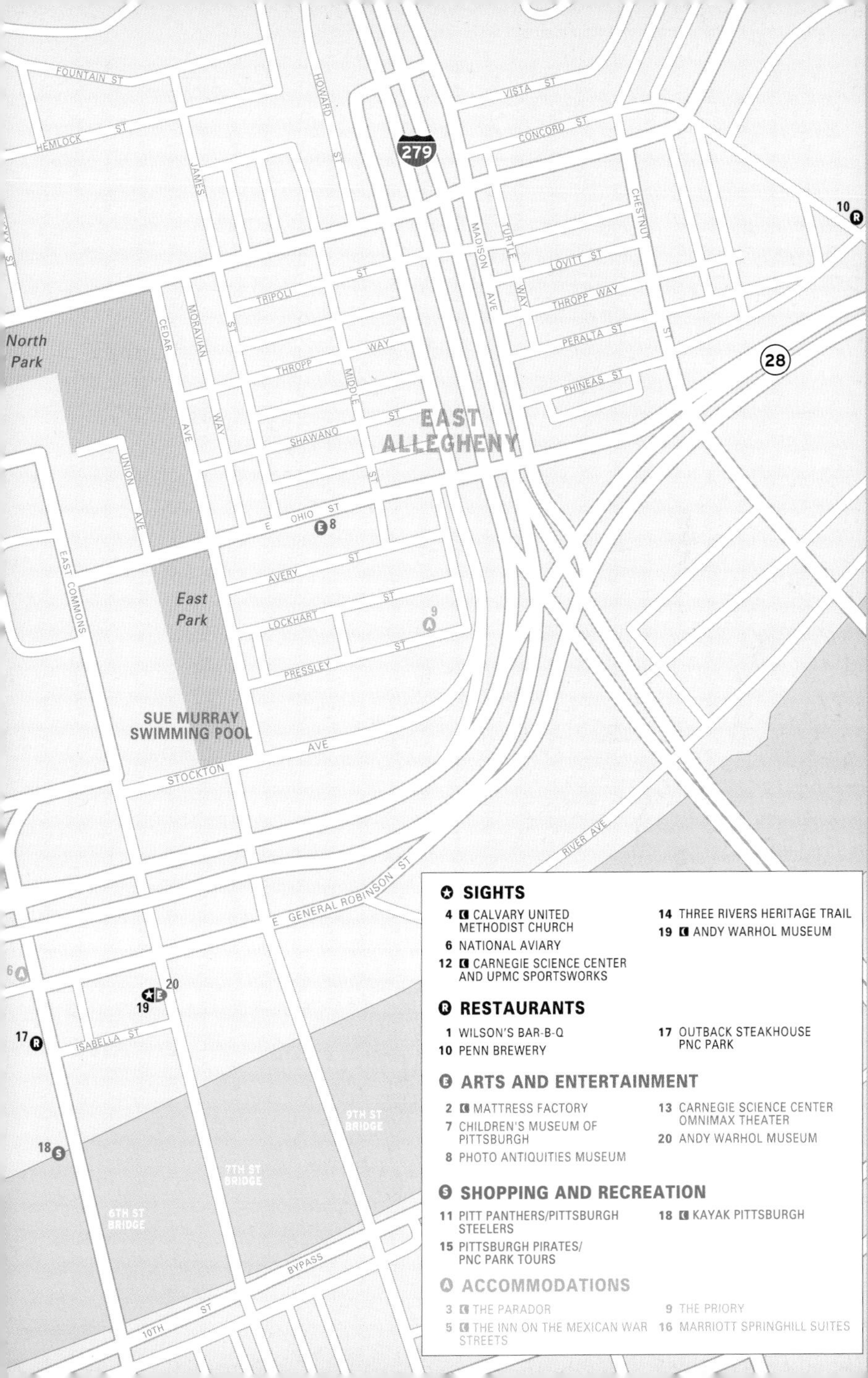

FOUNTAIN ST
HEMLOCK ST
VISTA ST
CONCORD ST
HOWARD
279
JAMES
MADISON AVE
LUTELA WAY
CHESTNUT
LOVITT ST
THROPP WAY
PERALTA ST
PHINEAS ST
TRIPOLI ST
MORAVIAN WAY
CEDAR AVE
THROFF WAY
MIDDLE WAY
SHAWANG
ST
EAST ALLEGHENY

North Park

10 R

28

UNION AVE
E OHIO ST
8
AVERY ST
LOCKHART ST
9
PRESSLEY ST

East Park

EAST COMMONS

SUE MURRAY SWIMMING POOL

AVE
STOCKTON

RIVER AVE

E GENERAL ROBINSON ST

6

20
19

17 R

ISABELLA ST

7TH ST BRIDGE

7TH ST BRIDGE

18 S

6TH ST BRIDGE

10TH ST

BYPASS

✪ SIGHTS

4 ◖ CALVARY UNITED METHODIST CHURCH
6 NATIONAL AVIARY
12 ◖ CARNEGIE SCIENCE CENTER AND UPMC SPORTSWORKS

14 THREE RIVERS HERITAGE TRAIL
19 ◖ ANDY WARHOL MUSEUM

❶ RESTAURANTS

1 WILSON'S BAR-B-Q
10 PENN BREWERY

17 OUTBACK STEAKHOUSE PNC PARK

🎭 ARTS AND ENTERTAINMENT

2 ◖ MATTRESS FACTORY
7 CHILDREN'S MUSEUM OF PITTSBURGH
8 PHOTO ANTIQUITIES MUSEUM

13 CARNEGIE SCIENCE CENTER OMNIMAX THEATER
20 ANDY WARHOL MUSEUM

🛍 SHOPPING AND RECREATION

11 PITT PANTHERS/PITTSBURGH STEELERS
15 PITTSBURGH PIRATES/ PNC PARK TOURS

18 ◖ KAYAK PITTSBURGH

⌂ ACCOMMODATIONS

3 ◖ THE PARADOR
5 ◖ THE INN ON THE MEXICAN WAR STREETS

9 THE PRIORY
16 MARRIOTT SPRINGHILL SUITES

✪ SIGHTS

59 JEWISH COMMUNITY CENTER AND THE AMERICAN JEWISH MUSEUM
81 FRICK PARK

🔴 RESTAURANTS

4 HARRIS GRILL
6 SOBA
7 UMI
9 CRAZY MOCHA
12 CAFE ZINHO
13 ABAY ETHIOPIAN CUISINE
19 CASBAH
20 TYPHOON
26 PITTSBURGH DELI COMPANY
28 GIRASOLE
30 SUSHI TOO
34 COZUMEL
37 THE CHOCOLATE MOOSE
39 COFFEE TREE ROASTERS
40 PRANTL'S BAKERY
41 LA FERIA

42 THAI PLACE CAFÉ
53 ◖ POINT BRUGGE CAFÉ
62 COFFEE TREE ROASTERS
64 ROSE TEA CAFÉ
65 ALADDIN'S EATERY
66 HUNAN KITCHEN
69 61C CAFÉ
70 GULLIFTY'S
71 SWEET BASIL & LA FILIPINIANA
72 CHAYA JAPANESE CUISINE
73 MILKY WAY
74 MINEO'S
76 KAZANSKY'S DELICATESSEN
79 TANGO CAFÉ
82 THE SQUARE CAFÉ
83 D'S SIX-PAX AND DOGS
84 THE MAP ROOM

🎭 ARTS AND ENTERTAINMENT

3 CLUB HAVANA
5 5801 VIDEO LOUNGE & CAFÉ
10 MENDELSON
32 DOC'S PLACE
49 PITTSBURGH CENTER FOR THE ARTS

54 FRICK ART AND HISTORICAL CENTER
60 SQUIRREL HILL CAFÉ
67 MANOR THEATER
68 SILKY'S SPORTS BAR & GRILL
80 SQUIRREL HILL THEATRE

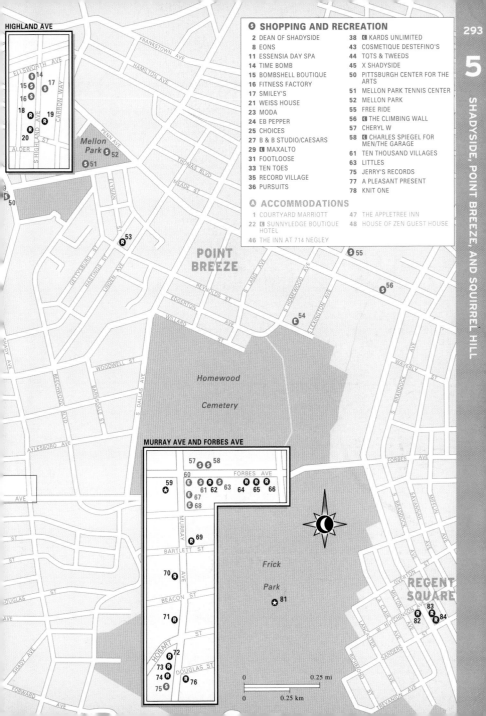

HIGHLAND AVE

§ SHOPPING AND RECREATION

- 2 DEAN OF SHADYSIDE
- 8 EONS
- 11 ESSENSIA DAY SPA
- 14 TIME BOMB
- 15 BOMBSHELL BOUTIQUE
- 16 FITNESS FACTORY
- 17 SMILEY'S
- 21 WEISS HOUSE
- 23 MODA
- 24 EB PEPPER
- 25 CHOICES
- 27 B & B STUDIO/CAESARS
- 29 ⓒ MAXALTO
- 31 FOOTLOOSE
- 33 TEN TOES
- 35 RECORD VILLAGE
- 36 PURSUITS
- 38 ⓒ KARDS UNLIMITED
- 43 COSMETIQUE DESTEFINO'S
- 44 TOTS & TWEEDS
- 45 X SHADYSIDE
- 50 PITTSBURGH CENTER FOR THE ARTS
- 51 MELLON PARK TENNIS CENTER
- 52 MELLON PARK
- 55 FREE RIDE
- 56 ⓒ THE CLIMBING WALL
- 57 CHERYL W
- 58 ⓒ CHARLES SPIEGEL FOR MEN/THE GARAGE
- 61 TEN THOUSAND VILLAGES
- 63 LITTLES
- 75 JERRY'S RECORDS
- 77 A PLEASANT PRESENT
- 78 KNIT ONE

Ⓐ ACCOMMODATIONS

- 1 COURTYARD MARRIOTT
- 22 ⓒ SUNNYLEDGE BOUTIQUE HOTEL
- 46 THE INN AT 714 NEGLEY
- 47 THE APPLETREE INN
- 48 HOUSE OF ZEN GUEST HOUSE

POINT BREEZE

MURRAY AVE AND FORBES AVE

Homewood Cemetery

Frick

Park

REGENT SQUARE

0   0.25 mi

0   0.25 km

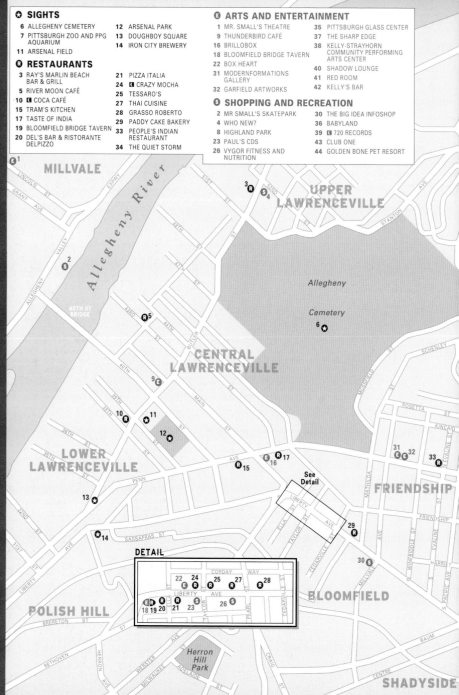

✪ SIGHTS

- 6 ALLEGHENY CEMETERY
- 7 PITTSBURGH ZOO AND PPG AQUARIUM
- 11 ARSENAL FIELD
- 12 ARSENAL PARK
- 13 DOUGHBOY SQUARE
- 14 IRON CITY BREWERY

🍴 RESTAURANTS

- 3 RAY'S MARLIN BEACH BAR & GRILL
- 5 RIVER MOON CAFÉ
- 10 ◖ COCA CAFÉ
- 15 TRAM'S KITCHEN
- 17 TASTE OF INDIA
- 19 BLOOMFIELD BRIDGE TAVERN
- 20 DEL'S BAR & RISTORANTE DELPIZZO
- 21 PIZZA ITALIA
- 24 ◖ CRAZY MOCHA
- 25 TESSARO'S
- 27 THAI CUISINE
- 28 GRASSO ROBERTO
- 29 PADDY CAKE BAKERY
- 33 PEOPLE'S INDIAN RESTAURANT
- 34 THE QUIET STORM

🅔 ARTS AND ENTERTAINMENT

- 1 MR. SMALL'S THEATRE
- 9 THUNDERBIRD CAFÉ
- 16 BRILLOBOX
- 18 BLOOMFIELD BRIDGE TAVERN
- 22 BOX HEART
- 31 MODERNFORMATIONS GALLERY
- 32 GARFIELD ARTWORKS
- 35 PITTSBURGH GLASS CENTER
- 37 THE SHARP EDGE
- 38 KELLY-STRAYHORN COMMUNITY PERFORMING ARTS CENTER
- 40 SHADOW LOUNGE
- 41 RED ROOM
- 42 KELLY'S BAR

🛍 SHOPPING AND RECREATION

- 2 MR SMALL'S SKATEPARK
- 4 WHO NEW?
- 23 HIGHLAND PARK
- 23 PAUL'S CDS
- 26 VYGOR FITNESS AND NUTRITION
- 30 THE BIG IDEA INFOSHOP
- 36 BABYLAND
- 39 ◖ 720 RECORDS
- 43 CLUB ONE
- 44 GOLDEN BONE PET RESORT

MILLVALE

Allegheny River

UPPER LAWRENCEVILLE

Allegheny Cemetery

CENTRAL LAWRENCEVILLE

LOWER LAWRENCEVILLE

FRIENDSHIP

See Detail

BLOOMFIELD

POLISH HILL

DETAIL

CORDAY WAY

LIBERTY AVE

SHADYSIDE

Herron Hill Park

MORNINGSIDE

BAKER
BUTLER

HIGHLAND
PARK BRIDGE

ST

Pittsburgh Zoo and
PPG Aquarium ✪7

*Highland
Park*
Ⓢ8

BUNKERHILL ST

STANTON
HEIGHTS

MORNINGSIDE AVE

CHISLETT ST

STANTON AVE

HAMPTON

BRYAN ST

HIGHLAND
PARK

ST

WELLESLEY

AVE

AVE

STANTON

ST

HERBERTON ST

JACKSON

AVE

WASHINGTON BLVD

GARFIELD

N ATLANTIC ST

N NEGLEY AVE

HIGHLAND ST

AVE

EAST
LIBERTY

LIBERTY

34Ⓡ

35Ⓔ

36Ⓢ

PENN CIRCLE N

PENN CIRCLE W

PENN CIRCLE E

38Ⓔ 39
Ⓢ

40Ⓔ Ⓔ
41

Ⓔ42

Ⓔ43

37Ⓔ

S NEGLEY AVE

PENN CIRCLE

BROAD ST

LIBERTY BLVD

FRANKSTOWN AVE

LINCOLN AVE

WASHINGTON BLVD

5TH

FAIRMOUNT

ST

AVE

S AIKEN

BLVD

AVE

S NEGLEY AVE

COLLEGE ST

HIGHLAND AVE

WALNUT ST

SHADY AVE

ELLSWORTH AVE

Ⓢ44

0   0.25 mi

0   0.25 km

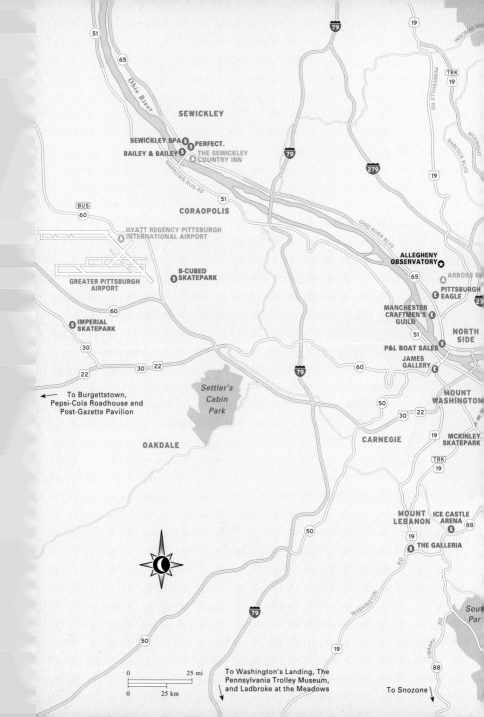

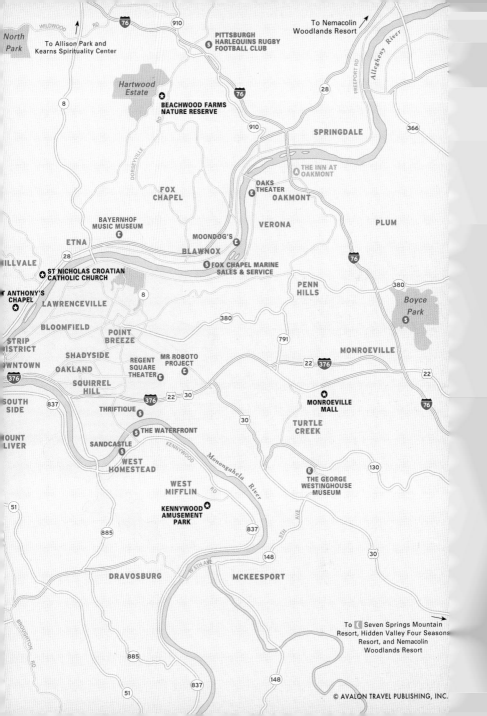

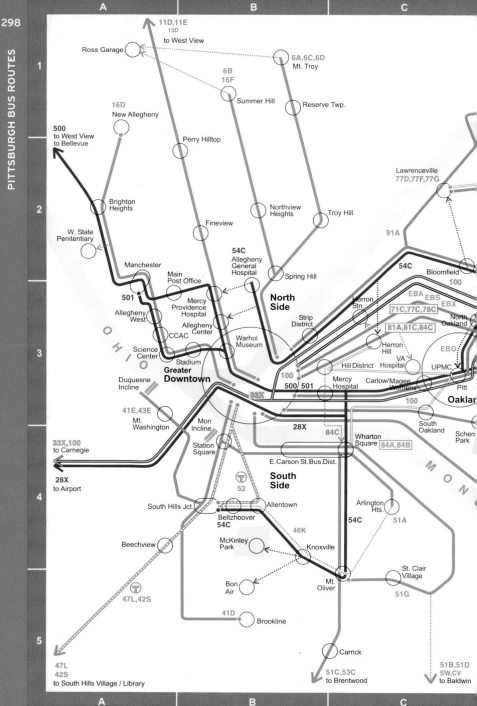

11D,11E
13D
to West View

Ross Garage

6A,6C,6D
Mt. Troy

6B
16F

Summer Hill

Reserve Twp.

16D
New Allegheny

Perry Hilltop

Northview
Heights

Troy Hill

Lawrenceville
77D,77F,77G

91A

Brighton
Heights

Fineview

500
to West View
to Bellevue

W. State
Penitentiary

54C
Allegheny
General
Hospital

Spring Hill

North
Side

54C

Bloomfield

100

Manchester

501

Allegheny
West

Main
Post Office

Mercy
Providence
Hospital

Allegheny
Center

CCAC

Science
Center

Stadium

Warhol
Museum

Strip
District

Herron
Stn.

EBA EBS
EBX

71C,77C,78C

81A,81C,84C

North
Oakland

Herron
Hill

VA
Hospital

EBO

OHIO

Greater
Downtown

Hill District

100

500/501

Mercy
Hospital

UPMC

Pitt

Oaklar

Carlow/Magee
Womens

100

Duquesne
Incline

41E,43E

Mt.
Washington

Mon Incline

33X

28X

84C

Wharton
Square

84A,84B

South
Oakland

Schen
Park

33X,100
to Carnegie

Station
Square

E. Carson St. Bus. Dist.

MON

28X
to Airport

52

South
Side

South Hills Jct.

Allentown

Arlington
Hts.

51A

Beltzhoover
54C

46K

54C

Beechview

McKinley
Park

Knoxville

St. Clair
Village

47L,42S

Bon
Air

Mt.
Oliver

51G

41D

Brookline

Carrick

47L
42S
to South Hills Village / Library

51C,53C
to Brentwood

51B,51D
SW,CV
to Baldwin

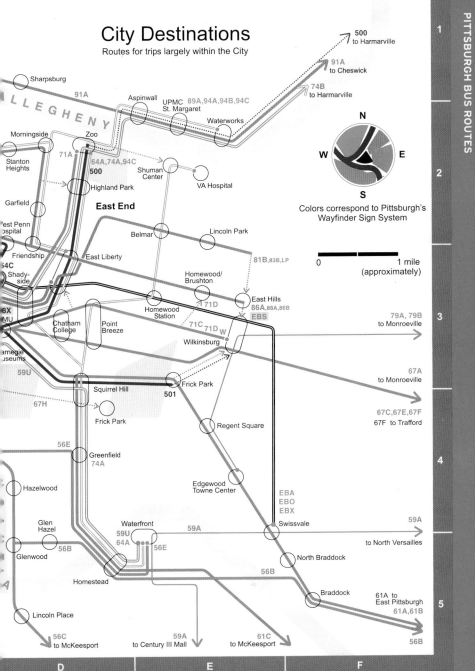

City Destinations

Routes for trips largely within the City

500 to Harmarville

91A to Cheswick

74B to Harmarville

Sharpsburg

ALLEGHENY

91A

Aspinwall

UPMC St. Margaret

89A,94A,94B,94C

Waterworks

Morningside

Zoo

N

W   E

S

Stanton Heights

71A

64A,74A,94C

500

Shuman Center

VA Hospital

Highland Park

Colors correspond to Pittsburgh's Wayfinder Sign System

Garfield

East End

est Penn ospital

Belmar

Lincoln Park

Friendship

East Liberty

64C

Shady-side

Homewood/ Brushton

81B,83B,LP

8X MU

171D

East Hills **86A,88A,86B**

EBS

79A, 79B to Monroeville

Chatham College

Point Breeze

Homewood Station

71C 71D W

Wilkinsburg

arnegie useums

59U

67A to Monroeville

Squirrel Hill

501

Frick Park

67C,67E,67F 67F to Trafford

67H

Frick Park

Regent Square

56E

Greenfield **74A**

Edgewood Towne Center

EBA EBO EBX

Hazelwood

Glen Hazel

Waterfront

59U

64A

56B

Glenwood

59A

56E

Swissvale

59A

to North Versailles

Homestead

North Braddock

56B

Lincoln Place

Braddock

61A to East Pittsburgh

61A,61B

56C to McKeesport

59A to Century III Mall

61C to McKeesport

56B

0   1 mile (approximately)